BEYOND EMPIRE

Beyond Empire

by

ESMÉ WINGFIELD-STRATFORD, D.SC.

Empire is no more! and now the lion and wolf
shall cease.

BLAKE

Nought shall make us rue
If England to itself do rest but true.

SHAKESPEARE

PHOENIX HOUSE
LONDON

Made in Great Britain
at the
Aldine Press · Letchworth · Herts
for
J. M. DENT & SONS LTD
Aldine House · Bedford Street · London
A Phoenix House publication
First published 1964

76775

CONTENTS

v

BOOK IV

BOOK V

INTRODUCTION

I CAN BEST explain the theme and purpose of this book by indicating the almost universally accepted historical and political dogma that it sets out to challenge. This is based on the assumption that British civilization in no way differs in kind from that of any other member of a European family of nations, of which Britain is assumed to be a by no means especially distinguished member. In such imposing treatises as, for instance, Mr Toynbee's *Study of History*, this standpoint is simply taken for granted. Britain is lumped into some category of Western, or European, or capitalist, or colonializing Powers according to taste.

With this goes the kindred assumption that the British Empire is, or was, just one among a number of competing members of the same imperial species—French, German, Spanish and so forth; and by way of jumping this claim it is assumed that every British colony or alleged 'possession' becomes automatically part of such an Empire.

This dogma, I submit, is so muddled in point of thinking, and false in point of fact, as to reduce any writing, historical or otherwise, based on it to the level of 'a tale told by an idiot ... signifying nothing'.

What I have tried to show is that British or British-born civilization is unique, and the direct negation of the imperial conception. The more empire the less British.

Empires, properly so called, are a species as old as, and perhaps older than, history, and have swelled and burst like gigantic bubbles on the stream of time. They are the organized embodiment of the will to power—*regere imperio populos*. As such, they tend to become to an ever increasing degree centralized and autocratic; the quintessence of the imperial principle is the modern totalitarian state. In that form it is already passively submitted to by something approaching half of the world's population. Unless effectively challenged it will inevitably become embodied in a world-wide empire of slavery and stagnation—culminating, not inconceivably, in death and the extinction of our species.

That challenge can come only from an order of world civilization embodying a different and superior principle, in the sense that life is superior to death; a principle of freedom as opposed to one of power or, to translate it into the most up-to-date terms, of Commonwealth as opposed to Empire. That order, though far from consummated, is sufficiently in being to look the other in the face across the barrier of the Iron Curtain, and it is not too much to say that whatever hopes there may be for the continued upward evolution and not inconceivably the survival of humanity rest with it.

It has already grown beyond the stage when it could be comprehended in the epithet 'British'. But it has evolved out of what was in the fullest sense a British and British-born order of civilization, and one that, unlike that of Empire, was not a recurrent but a new and unique phenomenon.

I hasten to add that this affords no excuse for patriotic boasting. It is in no sense due to any inherent virtue in the British people, but to an almost miraculously lucky or providential conjunction of circumstances, largely geographical, which I have tried to elucidate in the early stages of the book.

I shall not attempt to anticipate or summarize a theme whose unfolding development I have sought to record with the least possible intrusion of my own personality. I am not holding a brief for any thesis or seeking to accommodate the facts to a prefabricated framework of dogma. As far as I have been capable of doing so I have allowed them to be their own interpreters, and let the argument develop itself along its own lines by the free impulsion of its own creative immanence.

But try as I might to prune it of everything not absolutely vital to its exposition,[1] I have found it impossible to enlarge the scope of the present volume to include the still unfolding phase in the present century. This, if time and opportunity are granted me, I shall hope to cover in a successor, dealing with the liquidation of anything capable either of being stigmatized as a British Empire or of conflicting with the new world order of free civilization, that can at least claim to be British in origin and to embody a spirit authentically British in trend and principle.

Esto perpetua!

---

[1] Limitation of space has forced me to cut not only to the bone but into it, by eliminating all reference to the triumph of the Commonwealth principle in the union of the larger of the two main British islands, and to the tragic event of the repeated attempt to apply the imperial principle, in however modified a form, to the subjugation of the smaller. For that, I can only enter a plea of cruel necessity.

BOOK ONE

1

EVERYMAN'S ISLAND

TIME WAS, after the dawn of human but before that of written history, when this island that we call Britain was not an island at all, but part of the European mainland less distinguishable than Spain or Italy. That in course of time it should have gained not only insulation from, but unqualified independence of, the continental mainland, and become the begetter of its own—and that a world-wide—order of civilization, is an event so improbable on the face of it, and demanding such a unique combination of circumstances, as to give cause for thankfulness rather than self-congratulation. And yet the plain fact is that it actually happened.

Clearly what was needed in the first instance was for Britain to become not only an island but exactly the right kind of island for the purpose indicated. The decisive event therefore of her history is that from which it starts, when at some prehistoric but not pre-human date the North Sea, bursting into the Channel, or *vice versa*, insulated her in the formal, geographical sense, though unnumbered generations were to pass before in the human and historical sense she could be said to have attained full insular status by the control of her sea approaches. Pending that, she was in effect Everyman's Island. Every barbaric chieftain, that is to say, who on trade or settlement bent was capable of making the Channel crossing or braving the mists and storms of the North Sea, was free to step ashore and carve for himself and his ship-mates in his own way, which resulted in a cumulative mix-up of stocks and traditions, and a mongrelization by petty increments of the insular population. If we consider the limits set by the exiguous dimensions of contemporary shipping and the lack of any organized civilization in Nordic Europe, we shall realize how niggling and gradual this process of chronic infiltration must necessarily have been.

It was halted—and suspended indefinitely—by an event that seemed in the human sense to have reversed the process of nature and deprived Britain of her insular status as effectively as if the chalk isthmus had never been broken through, and the Channel had become no longer a sea, but a river whose basin took in the English lowlands up to their western and northern foothills. The Empire of the Mediterranean hinterland, that had grown out of the Roman city state, had bulged out its circumference to the utmost limit of a capacity for expansion that enabled it to take this most accessible and fertile part of Britain into the orbit of an imperial sway by which, as its laureate bard proclaimed, it was its divinely commissioned task to rule the nations—*regere imperio populos.*

Thus for the first and only time England was integrated into the fabric of a continental civilization, and became in the fullest sense European. After the process of her conquest had been got through, she settled down to the never-to-be-repeated experience of a reign of peace and law substantially unbroken for a matter of some three centuries. But it was a peace of perfect stagnation, and the time must surely be accounted as the dullest and most uncreative in the whole of her history. How nearly Roman civilization in England came to perishing by the dry rot of its own boredom we can never know by the written record, for there is none; but it is at least significant that the latest research points to the fact that the neatly planned Roman cities had begun to crumble patchily to rubble before any barbarian conqueror had set foot within their walls.[1] The account in old-fashioned textbooks of a withdrawal of the legions[2] and an Anglo-Saxon conquest, at dates neatly specified, is one that no longer holds water. Some sort of machinery of imperial administration would appear to have gone on ticking over till it petered out of its own accord—and when exactly that was, probably no one even at the time could have said.

But this at least we can say for certain, that ever since—whether or not we are to account for it by some deep-seated instinct or memory— the inhabitants of what was once the Province Britannia have been ready to go to all lengths rather than suffer themselves to be integrated for a second time into the temporal fabric of any European empire or super-state. To that extent, at least, England may be said to have reverted, and for good, from a continental to an insular status, during the time of troubles that used to be spoken of as the Anglo-Saxon conquest, but is now seen to have been much more of a chaotic imbroglio of native chieftains and adventurers from overseas, each playing for his own hand, and only in the course of generations sorting themselves out into something like an intelligible pattern.

But words, particularly when they are supercharged with reaction stimulus, are not to be taken for granted without scrutiny of their

[1] See especially *Roman Britain*, by R. G. Collingwood and J. N. L. Myres, Ch. XII.

[2] Like the old soldiers they were, they did not so much depart as simply fade away.

factual backing, and this word 'insular' is a case in point. From its literal significance of living on, or appertaining to, an island, it may be extended to cover a state of mind that is arbitrarily assumed to be the effect of an insular domicile. Thus it is the pose of a certain sort of Englishman to talk of a native insularity—in which he himself explicitly disclaims participation—as if it consisted in a diehard determination to enclose the mind in a hermetically sealed chamber, proof against all foreign ideas and influences. And no doubt there are many Englishmen, as there are many (and perhaps even more) Frenchmen, and an incomparably greater proportion of the inhabitants of totalitarian countries, whose minds do indeed answer to this description. But as these latter do not happen to live on islands, nobody dreams of stigmatizing them by the epithet 'insular'.

But there is another sort of insularity that may be spoken of with greater accordance with historic truth as English, which aims at accepting every civilizing influence from overseas, in the spirit of the Pauline injunction to prove all things and hold fast to that which is good. That Englishmen never shall be slaves is no bar to their becoming pupils to the best teachers that love or money can procure.

And that, in spite of the recurrent havoc and destruction wrought by invasion from overseas and strife among the different sections of an as yet disunited population, was most conspicuously the attitude of the English themselves in the epoch usually spoken of as Anglo-Saxon—so much more dynamic and fruitful than that of the full-blown Roman domination. Perhaps it was the most explicit contribution that these latest Teutonic arrivals had to make to the evolving personality of British civilization.

We cannot fail to remark the eagerness of the barbarian sovereigns, who parcelled out the former Roman province between them, to get themselves included within the orbit of a new Roman *imperium*, only this time a spiritual one. King Ethelbert of Kent did not need to abate one jot of his rather shadowy overlordship of a large part of England when he allowed his Frankish consort to persuade him to apply for a mission from Pope Gregory the Great to convert him and his subjects from their ancestral heathendom. And, indeed, far from any diminution of sovereignty, he may have felt his social status to have been not a little enhanced by his submission to the rite of baptism, and consequent admission to the Catholic and civilized society that Queen Bertha already adorned.

Rome had come back to her lost province, but in how different a guise! It was now no longer a question of the legions sweeping irresistibly over the land with fire and sword—'making a desert and calling it peace'. If we are to talk of a second Roman conquest it is only in the sense that we do of a reigning beauty making a conquest of her lovers.

In the case of Ethelbert, at least, it would appear that he was keener on expediting the arrival of the mission from Rome than its own leader, who developed cold feet in Gaul and had to be kept up to the mark by pontifical gingering, only to find himself, on arrival, pushing at an open door. And apart from the reactions of a few incurably last-ditch heathen diehards like the Mercian Penda, the spiritual conquest encountered even less serious opposition than the former physical one.

And yet in spite of an entire absence of any but moral compulsion— or perhaps because of it—this second Roman conquest proved, by almost every test that can be applied, more effective than the first. It lasted not for a mere three or four centuries, but getting on for a millennium. It set up its organization in every town and remote parish over a wider area than that which the Caesars had ever attempted to cover. It reinforced it by planting communities of dedicated specialists, largely at the expense of the lay section of the community, at selected points all over the country. It met the day-to-day needs of its parochial staff by an effective fiscal system on a ten per cent footing of lay contribution, the principle of which, at least, was not disputed. It got beneath the skin of the national life in a way that the imperial set-up had signally failed to do. It had its historians, its poets, its masterpieces of architecture and sculpture, and at least up to the time of the Norman Conquest it had a practical monopoly in works of creative genius.[1] What English civilization had become, at any rate in those first troubled centuries before the closing of the sea gates, was the product of Roman tutelage. No Pontiff could have been so desirous of imposing the yoke of his spiritual *imperium* on English shoulders as the leading spirits in England were to get it imposed.

And this particularly applies to the greatest Englishman—certainly of that and perhaps of all time. For when King Alfred, after his victorious counter-offensive against King Guthrum's Viking host, resumed control of his scorched and devastated realm, his first care was to build up the shattered fabric of its civilization from the foundations on the only model available to him, that which he had had impressed on his mind when he had been taken to Rome by an almost fanatically Catholic father in his impressionable infancy. To bring back the Latin language, to refound the monasteries, to re-educate the native clerisy (to adopt Coleridge's much needed expression) up to pre-invasion standards—even if the King himself had to translate the key classics for them—in short to bring back Rome to England in full spiritual power, was the task to which this combination of hero, saint and statesman set his hand, and in which he enjoyed a measure of success which no other man of that time could conceivably have approached.

[1] From the time it got fairly planted. I am not counting pre-Christian works such as *Beowulf*.

And in all this, from first to last, there was not the least element of any save moral compulsion.

Thus this least insular-minded of Englishmen set a pattern and example for all subsequent generations of what I shall dare to define as insulation without insularity—by which is implied an openness to all civilizing influences from overseas, coupled with an uncompromising refusal to have anything whatever imposed on England from without, except of her own free choice and on her own terms.

But to envisage the end without devising the necessary means was not the way of this most realistic of idealists. Insulation, as he was the first of all his countrymen to perceive, can be made effective only by sea power. An invader who has set foot on your shores has won more than half the battle in advance. For an island people there can be neither security nor freedom without the control of its sea approaches, though to deny these to the hitherto almost unchallenged rulers of the waves was a thing easier said than done. But it had got to be done; Alfred and his successors set themselves to do it and, for not far short of a century, they did. With the means, or lack of means, at their disposal, it was a *tour de force* of astonishing brilliance. But it was too brilliant to last. The foundations were lacking. The mixed Celtic, Teutonic, Danish populace was not sufficiently welded together or united behind its West Saxon kings to hold the course. A weak or immature hand on the controls was all that was needed to bring about the lapse or collapse of the newly acquired sea power, the reopening of the invasion routes, and another Danish conquest followed by the renewed de-insulation of an England that was temporarily forced into the pale of a Nordic federation too loose to be called an empire. Anglo-Saxon civilization had shot its bolt. Its creative potentiality, its *élan vital*, was like an exhausted battery.

As was to happen time and again in the course of the coming centuries to continental countries with open land frontiers, it had overstrained its resources. Something more was needed to pull the nation together and put power behind the punch of its rulers before the insular status, that was the *sine qua non* of its free civilized development, could be not only attained but guaranteed to last.

2

INSULATION THROUGH
CONQUEST

NO EVENT HAS ever been explained by so many different authorities to so many different effects as that recorded in the couplet that to many of us formed our first introduction to history:

> William the Conqueror on England did fix
> In ten hundred and sixty six—

the dominant tendency being to explain it as the submergence of an insular and predominantly Teutonic civilization—regrettably or otherwise according to choice—by a continental and Latin-inspired one. But the supremely decisive significance of what happened when Duke William fell down on Pevensey beach and grasped the realm of England with both his hands is one of those things that are so overwhelmingly obvious as to have escaped notice altogether.

Put it this way—that for the six centuries between the arrival of Hengist the Jute and that of William the Norman, England (except for the precarious interlude of sea power under the House of Alfred) was the island of everyman who could in sufficient force make the landing. Time and again the invaders had made their landfall according to plan without any attempt to stop them; and the last failure was the worst, when King Harold Godwinson, a commander not inferior to William himself, was forced to rush northward to defeat a Viking host that had been suffered to make an unopposed landing in Yorkshire, and leave to his fleet, for the bare fortnight he required to do the business, the task of holding the Channel against the expeditionary force that William was known to have mobilized on the opposite shore. But the scratch collection of ships that did duty for a fleet had already quitted station and gone home. The overloaded Norman troopships were allowed to plod their way northward without the least interference, and even when the Duke's flagship got parted in the night from the

6

convoy, not an English ship hove in sight to take advantage of the matchless opportunity for ending the war and him there and then. When he fetched up on the beach, in however undignified a posture, he must have realized that it was checkmate for Harold in one.[1] The decision had gone against England by default—default of sea power. And, once he had fixed on England, Duke William was not the man to let it go that way again.

Nor did he. The burden that had broken the backs of so many English fighting kings had dropped, like that of Christian in *The Pilgrim's Progress*, from his shoulders, for all the world as if it had fallen into the sea on his landing. And yet William's mind had none of the sweep and vision of Alfred's. His ideas of defence were essentially those of a landsman, and relied on a system of garrisoned castles, sited at key points, to hold up an invader, *after landing*, for long enough for his own field army to be rushed to the support of the local defenders. This was not Alfred's solution of the problem, nor the one eventually adopted, but as a provisional expedient it worked. The Vikings, the scourge of so many generations, were soon back at their old game, and eager to join hands with the native resistance. They hovered about the coast and even contrived to get ashore at one point, but experience of the Conqueror's reactions soon convinced them that the game had ceased to be worth the candle, and like the realists they were, they faded out of the picture, leaving the unhappy English to bear the full brunt of his vengeance. A last project of invasion petered out ignominiously before it ever got launched on the High Seas.

And that really was the end. Henceforth England—and in due course Britain—was to enter into the full and unbroken control of her own sea approaches. It was to be challenged time and again, but never successfully.[2] And it is a fact as certain as that of the Conquest itself that whereas for six centuries before this last of her conquerors set foot on her shores, she had been, in the sense I have indicated, Everyman's Island, subject to the perpetual threat and the chronic reality of invasion and conquest from overseas, so for nine centuries at least, dating from that event, she has been a perfectly self-contained sovereign entity, sealed off from any outside interference or coercion whatever and free behind the invisible barrier of her sea power to develop her own collective personality in inviolate security on her own lines. It is as if the Conquest had had the immediate and permanent effect of

---

[1] I have not the least doubt that what made Hastings a foregone conclusion was the exhaustion of Harold's mobile arm, his essential cavalry, in piercing the Viking shield wall in his amazing victory up north. But it left him with no choice but that of a static defence against William's highly mobile command.

[2] I do not count as invaders those who like Louis of France in 1216, and William of Orange in 1688, arrived by invitation.

transforming the invasion routes that had converged during all these centuries on her coasts into one-way tracks radiating outwards to the Continent and transforming her from the likeness of anvil to that of hammer.

The next Norman conquest was when, a bare forty years after the first, the Conqueror's youngest son crossed the Channel in the reverse direction, and with a force largely English in composition and tactics conquered Normandy itself from his eldest brother; and this was merely the first of a long series of unreciprocated insular eruptions on to the mainland, a phenomenon undreamed of in pre-Conquest days.

In effect, therefore, if not in intention, and on the longest reckoning, William the Conqueror might with hardly less appropriateness be styled William the Liberator.

This is not to deny that the immediate and ostensible effect of the Conquest was, in the harshest sense, what the word implies, the ruthless subjection of the native stock, or stocks, to the yoke of an imposed master breed that it took generations to weave into the texture of national life; though it may be doubted whether any less drastic means would have sufficed than this compounding, as in a mortar, of its divergent elements to have given England the unity that was the essential prerequisite of the effective and permanent insulation that she did, in fact, achieve.

But what to some may seem the most grievous of all effects of the Conquest was on the spiritual side, for it did indeed involve the axeing to root level of the once gracious and promising, though now over-strained and moribund, insular culture, and the compulsive injection of as much of the Romanizing leaven into the stolid lump of England's inertia and indiscipline as might be required to bring about her unquali-fied submission to the pontifical *imperium*—to debarbarize her, in short, by re-Latinizing her. This, it might be said, was de-insulation with a vengeance. The Norman Duke, who had come to England with what amounted to a crusading mandate from the Holy See, might be thought to have fulfilled it by bringing her back to Europe, as it were, by the scruff.

But to think thus is to ignore the distinction between insulation, by which is implied insular status, and insularity, which is a state or attitude of mind that may, or may not, be associated with it. I have spoken of insulation without insularity, and the overall effect of the Conquest might be summed up sufficiently in that formula. Neither England, nor that devout son of the Church who, by grasping her with both his hands, had come to stand for England in the eyes of Europe, was in any position to dispense with what Rome had yet to impart in the way of civilizing discipline; and by subjecting her to a course of compulsory Romanization under the tutelage of so renowned a European master as his chosen Primate, the Italian Lanfranc, he had signified as much. Nearly half a millennium had yet to pass before there could be any question of her budding civilization being sufficiently mature for England to cut loose from Rome and Europe altogether, and take the shaping of its own destinies into its own hands. Until then the vital question at stake was whether England should bargain for Rome's services on an implied footing of insular independence, or whether she should, in fact as well as fiction, become subject to her imperial dictates in matters spiritual and even temporal. It was the former choice that she eventually made.

It was not in the Conqueror's nature to take his own or his kingdom's orders from anybody, even from God's Vicar on Earth in the person of the awful Hildebrand, who, as Pope Gregory VII, had raised pontifical pretensions to the highest pitch ever envisaged, and in pursuit of them had forced the temporal Head of Christendom to eat dirt at Canossa. But in William he had come up against a will as strong as his own and one who, in reply to a papal demand for his fealty, was capable of intimating to His Holiness, with the most profound respect, that he, for his part, was not prepared to go to Canossa, and unlike Bismarck at a later date, capable of making his words good. For even the most arrogant of Pontiffs had the sense, after that implied warning of 'hands off England', to refrain from pressing the point.

And that indeed might have substantially defined the insular reaction to the long series of attempts by the spiritual Caesar to make his formally acknowledged sovereignty a practical reality, and to force the island civilization into the framework of a wider Catholic or European unity, were it not for a complicating factor—at least in the earlier stages—that tended to confuse the issue. For in the heyday of the Norman-French ascendancy the spiritual Power tended to be regarded by the subjected populace less in the light of a foreign suzerain than as the champion, in however qualified a sense, of the English bottom dog. This accounts for the spontaneous devotion with which the common people embraced the cause of the exiled Primate, Thomas à Becket, whom they greeted on his tragic return with cries of 'Blessed be he that cometh in the name of the Lord!' and whom, after he had been brutally liquidated by some of their still more than half alien bosses, they exalted to the status of a national saint, nearly all of whose miracles, as depicted in the stained glass of his cathedral choir, proclaim him the poor man's—which was as good as to say the Englishman's—friend.

As long therefore as Rome was capable of standing for the principle of 'Hands off the English' there was some qualification at least of popular support for their sovereigns in maintaining that principle of 'Hands off England', and it needed the reduction of the alien master breed to the proportions of an insular aristocracy to unite all classes in a common if unformulated determination to achieve the substance if not the form of insular independence.

I have spoken of insulation without insularity, and this eminently applied to the ordinary Englishman's attitude to the Roman spiritual power as it took shape in the Middle Ages. It was one of strict formal correctness. He was too conscious of his debt to the Church to want to quarrel with her, except in the last resort. But the obedience he was prepared to render to the undoubted Head of Christendom was on a strictly rationed basis, and with the tacit proviso that for most practical purposes the principle afterwards formulated at the Reformation already held good, in the preamended form of 'The Bishop of Rome hath no temporal authority in the *Realm* of England'—though it was the last thing he would have dreamed of saying in plain English. He far preferred to adopt the technique of the son who said, 'I go, Sir', and went not. He was ready and eager to take from the Church all she had in the way of civilizing influence, and made no bones about rendering what immemorial custom recognized as the due fee for her services. But there were limits beyond which he was not prepared to go or allow himself to be imposed on, and these, after a few preliminary demonstrations, came to be well enough understood and respected on both sides to produce a *modus vivendi* according to the rules of a recognized game, for as long as—but no longer than—the rules continued to be informally binding on both parties. But once let them be deliberately flouted on a major issue by either, and there might be no limit at all to the reaction of the other.

It is only on a short-term or superficial view that the Conquest can be thought to have recovered England for full membership of a European or Catholic order of civilization, on the same footing as any other of the budding nations of the mainland. Its effect was precisely the reverse. When at last she emerged in her own proper person from the long ordeal of her suppression by the foreigner, it was in enjoyment of a fully fledged insular security that, except for the minor nuisance of her northern Border and western Marches, put her in the unique position, among European communities, of having no invadable frontiers to bother about. She had the power to be mistress in her own house such as none of her neighbours could aspire to; and the will to use it might not be lacking. Even in the Conqueror's day an observer of superhuman penetration might have divined the first stirrings in her womb of an order of civilization quite different from the European. Certainly the conditions out of which such an order might develop were ideally conjoined.

3

THE LAW OF
CONCRETE LIBERTIES

EVEN THUS early, we see that England has come to stand on a footing of what we might describe as associate membership of the European family, or as much of it as was comprised in the pale of Catholic Christendom. Ostensibly she was as fully integrated with it as any other of its constituent realms or provinces, but in reality the emphasis had shifted from a continental to an insular status. There is a subtle but profound difference between a barely detached fragment of the European mainland and an island standing over against it in complete insular self-containment, not to say self-assertion. For the tide of invasion and conquest had now reversed its direction, and far from there being any question of the Continent again reaching out to draw the island into its orbit, the islanders again and again left their own shores to carve out a dominion for their sovereigns on the mainland. That this always proved beyond their strength, in the long run, to maintain, even after the most sensational victories, was the inevitable but salutary fate of such essays in empire. It is perhaps the one positive advantage that England derived from her concertina-like expansion and retraction, that it helped to sweat any incipient infection by the imperial virus out of her system; though it must be acknowledged that the damage she sustained, safe as she was behind her invasion-proof moat, was a mere fleabite compared to that which she inflicted on her neighbour France, whose soil she converted into a bloody shambles, and to whose régime she imparted a fatal twist in the direction of armed autocracy.

All of which there would be no point in mentioning if it were merely a question of England's taking a hand, though an unprofitable one, in the perennial game of European power politics—which would after all only have confirmed her membership of a chronically quarrelling family. But it goes a great deal further than this; for what England was really doing, though in this most wasteful of all ways and entirely

without realizing it, was to maintain peace within her own borders—
except for such civil strife as might be engendered within them—for
the development of her own liberties in perfect freedom from external
pressure. And perhaps—dubious as the moral may be—there may
have been no way in which she could have done it so effectively as by
violating those of her neighbours.

Not liberty in the abstract, but liberties in the concrete. The difference made by that plural termination is fundamental. Only by
grasping it can we hope to get the gist of all those later developments
that distinguish the British from all other histories, and are the successive stages in the ascent first to a distinctive, and finally to a world,
order of civilization.

Your Englishman has never had much enthusiasm for liberty in the
abstract—or for anything else in the abstract, if it comes to that. Even
today it is notoriously hard to work up his enthusiasm for the most
specious patterns or programmes of what he is most likely to designate
as 'pie in the sky'. Pie on his plate is what he cares about—something
tangible that he claims as his own, or his due, and that he means to
get, or to keep, for that precise reason. He was even more emphatically
of that way of thinking in the Middle Ages.

He did not think of right or liberty as ideals to be striven after, but
of *his* rights and *his* liberties as concrete and definite matters of fact
that—to adapt a song of the First World War—were there because
they were there, because they were there, and for no other reason. Not
even the law had created them: it merely defined and maintained them.

That, at any rate, was the way the English mind worked, and it was
thus that the Englishman thought of the law, his own native law whose
origins were lost in antiquity. That too was there because it was there
and always had been. He no more thought of it as a man-made con-
trivance than he did of some forest oak. The kings who from time to
time had codified it in their dooms were not what we should call
legislators so much as recorders. They were stating a law that was
there already, much as a judge does in his summing up; they were not
making it. That law was no more than the sum total of the various
customary rules and expedients whereby each man's rights and
liberties were guaranteed to him. However crude and complicated they
might be, and however unfairly they might work out in individual
cases, they *were* the law and there was an end of it, except in so far as
they might be modified and developed by the creation of new writs by
the monarch, or by judicial interpretation. For there was nothing fixed
and static about this growing organism, that derived its vitality from
the life of the community and was in no sense a planned and logical
system.

But there actually was such a system in being, with a prestige that made any other law seem barbarous by comparison. This was of course the Law of Rome, which had been so submerged and depraved by the barbarian conquest of the West as to have become almost barbarized itself, but whose rediscovery and exposition by a galaxy of brilliant scholars, one of whom, Lanfranc, was to become Primate of England after the Conquest, was the first manifestation, in Italy, of the awakening Renaissance.

Once having obtained this publicity, as the most consummate achievement of the Roman power that was already regarded as the fountain head of civilization, it was only to be expected that its manifest superiority to all these various equivalents on the Continent of the English Common Law should have caused these latter to be sooner or later discarded in favour of this majestically uniform system, not only in the Latin but even the Teutonic parts of Western Christendom. The only wonder is that the process took so long as it did to consummate, particularly in Germany—partly owing to the fact that the Church, having its own version of Roman Law in the Canon Law, adapted to the requirements of the spiritual Caesar, was anything but co-operative to the idea of his being thus outbid by his temporal rival. But by the end of the Middle Ages the Roman Law might fairly be said to have become *the* law for all that mattered of Catholic Christendom on the continent of Europe, though modified to suit the requirements of a number of petty Caesars, and with little enough regard to the theoretical supremacy of the official holder of the title at Vienna.

It might have been expected as a matter of course, at least by those who persist in regarding her as an undistinguished unit in the European family, that England would have gone the same way—the more so as her Northern British neighbour duly received the principles of Roman Law—a fact that led to dire consequences when a Scottish monarch, nurtured in those same principles, came in course of time to find himself pitchforked on to the throne of England.

But the fact is—and it is one of those dominating facts of history that receive less attention than the innumerable petty ones that clutter up the pages of histories—that the Englishman politely but firmly declined to Romanize himself, or to leave the winding and overgrown tracks of his own Common Law for the straight and scientifically engineered roads that radiated from, and led to, the Eternal City.

To say that it was as momentous a decision as any on record is not to imply that anyone at the time had the least consciousness of the issues at stake, or indeed that there was anything particular to decide, except what the magnates of the realm assembled in conclave in 1236 at Merton decided, when the spiritual power proposed to override the existing law of the land on the minor issue of legitimizing bastards—

substituting its own canonical principles and jurisdiction. The answer was as brief as it was decisive: '*Nolumus leges Angliae mutari*', which is as good as to say: 'We won't stand for changing the laws of England.'

This again might be alleged by an unsympathetic critic to amount to no more than an ebullition of the perennial Englishman's John-Bullishness, that insular unresponsiveness to ideas with which foreigners are never tired of taxing him.

But this will not hold water. Apart from the fact that perhaps a majority of those who made this declaration might have found some difficulty in expressing themselves in English, the record shows that the native reaction to both the Roman and Canon Law was the reverse of insular. Such of the islanders whose business it was to concern themselves with legal matters were as sensible as anyone in Europe of the wisdom and majesty of these supreme products of the Latin genius, and of the advantages to be derived from borrowing from them, of all of which they were determined to avail themselves to the full. And indeed the unfolding development of the English Common Law was notably enriched and fertilized from both of these sources. It was a perfect example of what is implied by the principle of insulation without insularity which, as I have tried to show, has determined England's attitude, in proportion as she has rested true to herself, towards influences from overseas.

She was, in effect, ready to take every advantage of the Roman system except to adopt it. On that point her mind was perfectly and consistently made up and summed up in the sentence already quoted, '*Nolumus leges Angliae mutari*', which was more in the nature of a spontaneous eruption than of a considered decision. The men of that time had no particular consciousness of being at any parting of the ways; they acted as they did because, being what they were, they could not do otherwise. The Englishman, to judge by his own account of himself, was the most uncompromising of conservatives. He was always taking his stand upon the things that he had inherited from his fathers—the old law, the established rights, the immemorial customs. The words 'progress' and 'reform' had no equivalent in his vocabulary. Even the Conqueror had the tact to promise the English that they should have the laws that they had enjoyed under their late English King Edward, which might to some extent sweeten the bitter pill of Norman domination. And the Great Charter itself merely set out to have the law on King John, by confirming and defining the charter of liberties that had been promulgated more than a century before by his great-grandfather Henry I.

It will be obvious from this instance that the insular brand of conservatism was not nearly so static in practice as it might have seemed on a literal interpretation. It proved indeed a way of achieving both progress and reform more fruitful in its results than any other. It was—to use another word far beyond the comprehension of the time—the way of evolution, of organic growth. It was the antithesis of 'radical', in that it did not seek to pluck up institutions by the roots in order to replace them by the most beautifully planned human contrivances, but studied above all things to preserve the thread of vital continuity, and to encourage and foster the spirit of growth—the gardener's, not the mechanic's, way. There is, indeed, another kind of conservatism that aims at petrifying the *status quo* instead of fructifying it, but at the time we are speaking of it was not in evidence. There were few diehards in the thirteenth century, certainly not in the growth of the English Law.

The men who set their faces like a flint against the laws of England being changed—that is to say torn up by the roots to make room for others of a more scientifically contrived origin—were by that very refusal giving them scope to spring up and thrive like healthy plants on their own native soil. By the time it had come to its vigorous maturity, in the reign of Henry III, and had found an expositor of genius, in the person of Justice Henry Bracton (whose book Pollock and Maitland, in their hardly less classic *History of English Law*, describe as 'the crown and flower of English medieval jurisprudence'[1]), the main outlines of English medieval law, according to the same high authority, had been drawn for good and all.[2] 'English Law', they say, 'was by this time recognized as distinctively English and Englishmen were proud of it.'[3] As well they might be, to be able to look Rome in the face in her most impressive aspect.

Not that even now, from the standpoint of a professional lawyer, there would appear to be any comparison between Rome's supreme masterpiece of man-made co-ordination and this proliferation on English soil of a barbaric jungle of inconsistencies and illogicalities, propagating their kind, by dint of precedent, like uncontrollable weeds. How different from a mechanism so marvellously adjusted as to respond to the lightest touch of the controlling hand. Yes indeed—that was just the difference, and the vital difference between the two systems, when the controlling hand happens to be that of Caesar, or a would-be Caesar! You cannot impose your will in the same way on a growing organism. The jungle that is the despair of litigants may also be the headache of despots.

Roman imperial law is, of necessity, wholly adapted to imperial requirements. It was just such a law as might have been expected from a Power operating from a central position in a great inland sea, and expanding its sway over as wide an area of the hinterland in every

[1] Vol. I, p. 206.   [2] Vol. I, p. 206.   [3] Ibid., p. 188.

direction as it was capable of controlling and defending, though with every enlargement of its circumference the strain on its resources increases in geometrical proportion. Consequently it became a life and death matter for such a Power to insulate itself as far as possible behind a perimeter that would serve it in the capacity of an encircling sea. Unfortunately only on her western and to a limited extent on her northern seaboard had Rome been able to achieve this. Otherwise she was doomed to give herself such elbow room as she could by bulging her frontiers farther and farther out into barbarian outlands that she could never hope to master, and into which even the most successful advance (and what came to Varus and his legions, and more than one Caesar, shows what was liable to be the fate of these sallies) only strained her resources nearer to breaking point.

Under these circumstances there was only one thing to do, and Rome did it, at first by necessity, and finally of conscious purpose under the auspices of that most competent of emperors, Hadrian. It was simply to dig herself in behind such frontiers as she had got, to convert them into the classical equivalent of the Maginot line, and to stand perpetual siege behind it, giving up all thought of further expansion. It was literally a last-ditch expedient. Such a line is bound to cave in sooner or later at some point or other. It is to the eternal glory of Rome that she held her lines as long as she did, and that even when in the third century they were repeatedly breached and overrun, and the whole imperial structures eemed to be on the point of collapsing, she staged one of the most astonishing recoveries in history, even though this involved her shifting her centre of gravity from the Tiber to the Bosphorus. But she had held out long enough to maintain an area of peaceful security, like the enclosure within the bailey walls of a castle, within which not only traders and scholars, but missionaries like Paul, could freely circulate, planting seeds of a new faith that, given three centuries of the same conditions, nothing could stop from permeating the area to its uttermost limits.

This was far more than could be put to the score of any other of the world's imperial expansions, but it was not to be had except at the price of all freedom within its borders. You can only organize life under siege conditions—especially within the compass of such a vast perimeter and under conditions of such prolonged and cumulative strain— by subordinating everything and everybody to the behest of one single controller, or as in Rome they called him, *Imperator*. This is the necessity forced on all empires, sooner or later. You cannot run *imperium* and *libertas* in double harness; and though it took centuries finally to convince a most unwilling Rome that it was necessary to jettison the last vestige or pretence of her republican liberties, the logic of facts was too strong for her, and her last desperate rally was achieved only by going all out, and turning Caesar into as uncompromising and uninhibited a despot as any oriental sultan or Grecian tyrant—an autocrat whose will was his law, and the law his will. And it was under such auspices that the Roman Law was being shaped and moulded into the form in which it reached its *ne plus ultra* under the Byzantine auspices of Justinian in the sixth century, to be resurrected by the great jurists of the eleventh.

And no wonder that it should have found willing converts in monarchs and princes, who would find it so ideally adapted to their own requirements, apart from its manifest superiority on its own merits to codes that were mere hotchpotches of barbaric custom and tradition. But in what did this superiority consist, except of its being the most consummate and scientifically forged instrument ever invented for implementing the will of the one individual who controlled it—the officiating Caesar? The whole principle on which it was constructed was one of absolute centricity, and not only absolute power but of power transmitted with frictionless smoothness to every minute part of the human mechanism. What pleases the prince has the force of law—all power descends from the top downwards and radiates from the centre outwards—such is the fiat of Roman Law.

That law was also a product of a state of civilization founded on the principle of slavery, and in which the rights, if any, of the individual tended to be dependent on his status in the social heirarchy. It therefore, saturated as it was by these kindred principles of despotism and slavery, tended to resemble a cone or pyramid, in which all authority tended to radiate and percolate from the apex downwards. And if this should be thought a biased description, it can be replied that in point of fact, wherever the principles of Roman Law have been allowed to prevail, it has worked out precisely in this way—the way of *imperium* without *libertas*, the way of the Bourbons and Hohenzollerns and Hapsburgs and innumerable lesser autocrats; the Caesarian way that in modern times has broadened out into the super-Roman *autobahnen* of the totalitarian super-Caesars.

Britain was already beginning to grope, though blindly and tentatively, after its alternative.

4

THE ODD LAND OUT

THERE IS nothing of planned and scientific Roman directness about what Chesterton so happily described as the rolling English road, the road that—with all the accompanying inconveniences —has grown up in the course of generations and whose form is as much determined by its past as is that of any other growing product. And the growth of the English Law, and consequently of the British constitution and way of civilization, is from the roots upwards, these roots being the rights and liberties of each and every individual cell of which the social body is made up, and it is the principle and spirit of that law that against such rights and liberties, once they have been ascertained, no will of prince nor reason of state—not even the voice of reason—shall prevail.

In the language of the medieval lawyers, the names of two fictitious litigants are continually cropping up—John Doe and Richard Roe— and one would gather that the business of the courts and judges boiled down to ascertaining the lawful rights of these two individuals, and balancing them against each other. The process waxed more and more complicated and encumbered with technicalities unintelligible to any-one but the men of law, who had a direct interest in intensifying and prolonging its complexities, thus giving rise to the proverb, which is the title of the original John Bull story, 'The Law is a Bottomless Pit'. Maybe—but bottomless pits and impenetrable jungles are even more baffling for autocrats than they are for laymen. No Caesar could work his will with the necessary smoothness and efficiency, with John Doe and Richard Roe and all their intractable rights tripping him up and bogging him down at every turn.

And what was worst of all from the point of view of the Sovereign who had hankerings after being a divine Caesar was that he himself was part of the system. Instead of being the all-powerful controller of the state machine, he was, in the eye of the law, only one John Doe amongst others—the biggest of all the Johns, but with his royal rights and liberties, however extensive, as strictly defined as those of

any other John or Richard—which was what Magna Charta was
intended to bring home to the John whose surname happened to be
not Doe but Plantagenet. It naturally took time to impress this view
of the matter on sovereigns who, being only human, would have much
preferred to lord it in their own realms on the same imperial lines as
rival dynasties on the Continent. But the kings of England were either
practical men, who learnt in the hard way to accommodate themselves
to the rules of the game and get what they could within the limits set
for them by the law, or men who, when they did not, and tried, like
the unfortunate Richard II, to Caesarize in good earnest, were unlikely
to survive in the most mortality-prone of all occupations.

The Sovereign had his rights and liberties defined by law like those of
any other John or Richard, and on what was supposed to be a sufficiently
royal scale to enable him to carry on with his job or, as it was said, 'to
live of his own', in normal circumstances; but when income ceased to
balance expenses—as it was sure to do when there was a war on—he
was forced to come to his subjects hat in hand for whatever extra they
could be persuaded to dole out to him, on terms that often amounted
to those of sheer blackmail, and always by dint of hard bargaining, the
record of which is set forth in constitutional histories.

Here we are concerned merely with the question of why things
should have taken this turn in England, and nowhere else of any major
importance [1] on the European mainland. Let it be granted that parliamentary and representative institutions were no English speciality, or
even invention, but sprang up and flourished vigorously under different
names all over the West. Doubtless—but the point is that practically
all of these medieval constitutions turned out to resemble the seed
sown on the rock, and after springing up with every appearance of
vigour, withered away in the course of a few generations because they
lacked moisture. And it might have been thought that parliamentary
institutions in England were likewise destined not to outlast the
coming of the modern age, and that the brief ascendancy of Parliament
and its power to blackmail the Crown under the weak and shaky
Lancastrian dynasty was utterly incapable of maintaining itself against
the strong sovereigns of the House of Tudor. But though in the event
the pace of growth was for a season somewhat retarded, the roots
proved to have struck deeper than ever on the rich island soil, and by
the time all these continental growths had either ceased to cumber
the ground, or remained above it like dead stumps, this English plant,
from a healthy sapling, proved to have grown into a flourishing tree,
with every prospect of becoming, in time, a king of the forest.

[1] Perhaps the most conspicuous apparent exception is the special case of
Switzerland, whose mountainous contours conferred on it something of the
status of an inland island.

Patriotic propaganda will no doubt attribute this to some special virtue or political genius innate in the English mentality. But I do not think so flattering an explanation need be taken seriously. Why on earth should the people on one side of the Channel differ so fundamentally from their opposite numbers on the other? Is it not far more probable that the cards have been dealt by fate so as to put a winning hand into the possession of the islanders, who are entitled to as much credit as and no more than may accrue from their having actualized its potentialities?—a fact that no amount of skill or genius would have put within the scope of practical possibility for those others.

Why? The explanation lies simply in the fact of Britain being not only an island but, from the English point of view, the ideally right sort of island. I am not forgetting that only as late as the eighteenth century could her insulation have been pronounced formally complete; but even though she might at times have had to concede too wide a licence to Marcher and Border lords to set themselves up as armed anarchs and potential rebels, she never felt herself under the necessity of giving her monarchs a free hand, with the appertaining cash, to maintain standing armies capable of enabling them, in the last resort, to set their will above the law, or to make the law the instrument of their will—to function, that is to say, imperially.

Now that was just where England differed from the sovereignties of the Continent, whose open land frontiers made it a vital necessity for them to be armed to the teeth in what was really a perpetual struggle for survival. No Frenchman who had seen what had come to his country by dint of English aggression over more than a century could have wanted to stint his sovereign of the forces or sinews of war lest he should turn them against the liberties of his own subjects. A still stronger instance is that of Machiavelli, a sincere patriot of naturally liberal inclinations, who was so stricken to the heart by the doom that had fallen upon his beloved Italy at the hands of her foreign invaders that he was ready to subordinate every other consideration to the concentrating of all power in the hands of a prince, who was to be a specialist in the arts of war and politics, entirely free from scruples or inhibitions of any description. But 'Old Nick' would have been the last person to harbour illusions about the sort of total tyranny such a deliverer, once he had accomplished his great task of driving out the foreigner, would have imposed on his fellow countryman. In the circumstances it was a price he would have been prepared to pay.

But England could afford, as no continental state could, to let military efficiency take its chance when it was a question of maintaining her civil liberties. She was too secure behind her moat to entertain serious qualms about the threat of seaborne invasion. She was proud enough of her Crécys and Agincourts, of her Black Prince and King

Harry, but these symbols of her fighting prowess were after all in the nature of luxuries. It is to the last degree unlikely that any one of those tens of thousands of able-bodied non-combatants whom Lord Westmorland wished he could have had at Agincourt, would have lost a night's sleep if the news had come that King Harry and all his host had been destroyed. It would not have affected him in the same way as the destruction of their own royal army affected so much of the French civilian population, though no doubt it would have acted on him as a challenge to go out and even up the score on French soil. But not to the extent of inducing John Doe or Richard Roe to trust any crowned Harry or Edward, in time of peace, with more than the bare minimum of armed retainers needed for ceremonial purposes. No danger from abroad was fit to be weighed in the scales against that of the head of the island state developing into an *imperator*, as in point of fact, if not always of form, he was practically bound to do on the European mainland, with its anarchy of armed sovereignties and open land frontiers, sooner or later.

There was another advantage that England derived from being, for practical purposes, what the song has hit off with the epithet of 'right little, tight little island'—though at first blush it might have been supposed to play straight into the hands of despotism. I have already tried to show how the Norman Conquest transformed the status and prospects of England by giving her control of her sea approaches. But it had had another effect of hardly less importance in providing her strong Norman and early Plantagenet sovereigns with a self-contained, controllable administrative area, defined by its encircling seas, of a size almost ideally calculated to relieve the central authority from the necessity or temptation of perpetually reaching out—as Rome had had to do—to the extreme limits of its expansive capacity and consequently of its internal resources.[1] And this insular self-containment vetoed the tendency to sprawl that in one way or another retarded the coalescence of the petty lordships of the Continent into fully integrated national organisms. It was only by dint of superior force continuously applied by the central power on imperial principles that nations like France and Spain were forced into despotic unity, while others, like Germany and Italy, never, until the nineteenth century, succeeded in coalescing at all.

The strongest administrative machine in western Europe operating in an insulated and invasion-proof area produced consequences that no one at the time could have foreseen, and that are very imperfectly,

---

[1] A partial exception is constituted by Edward I's wanton and foredoomed attempt to impose his English yoke on Scotland; but an antagonized Scotland, though a chronic nuisance, was never capable of becoming a mortal menace to England.

if at all, realized, even today. To grasp their significance is to understand why constitutional development in England followed such a fundamenally different course from that of continental nations. It drove the nation into an effective unity as nothing else could. The trouble with the parliaments abroad was that they represented different classes or estates that were independent and closed bodies that a capable monarch could play off against each other, without any fear of having to confront a united or national opposition. And a monarchy, with a competent military force constantly at its disposal, had such an overwhelming advantage over these only sectionally representative bodies, that it was practically bound, sooner or later, to make its will the sole effective power in the state—'L'État, c'est moi'.

But in England nothing of this sort happened, nor—given the special conditions of her insular polity—was it in the least likely to happen. In the first place, no mere class or estate of the realm had any real chance of standing up by itself against the administrative powers at the disposal of the monarchy. There were no English equivalents of the continental feudatories who reigned as little kings over their own provinces, to form the backbone of a noble caste or estate. In an invasion-proof island the lord on the spot, with his impregnable fortress and his mailed chivalry, was no longer a necessity but a plain nuisance, which the Conqueror and his successors did on the whole contrive to keep within manageable limits, by breaking up lordships into scattered units up and down the country and drastically rationing their fortifications.

It came to this, that when early in the thirteenth century England ceased to be part of what might have become a West European Empire and found herself insulated within her own proper limits, with a central power capable of crushing any merely sectional opposition, the various classes which under continental conditions would have elected to stand on their own feet and 'go it alone' as estates of the realm were soon forced to realize what was to be implied in Benjamin Franklin's *dictum*: 'We must all hang together, or most assuredly we shall all hang separately.' This was indeed sufficiently adumbrated in Archbishop Langton's [1] drafting of Magna Charta.

It was a lesson that took a long time to permeate the depths of the common subconsciousness, and indeed seemed at times as if it had struck no deeper roots than it had over the water. For to imagine that the medieval Englishman had any greater aptitude for the principles of parliamentary government than his French or Spanish or German counterpart is to read history backward. Parliaments were a necessity

---

[1] Or if it was not that great patriot prelate who drafted at least the vital and enduring clauses, who could it have been? Certainly not the illiterate ruffians who were operating the baronial racket.

that everybody concerned would have preferred to dispense with, and membership of the faithful Commons, far from being esteemed an honour, was as little sought after and as gladly evaded as jury-service is nowadays. Things worked out in the way they did, without anybody in particular foreseeing or intending it, usually by dint of hard bargaining without any more backing of disinterested idealism than is common among horse-traders or card-sharpers, just because the conditions did happen to be set that way in England and nowhere else in Europe. And even there it might frequently have seemed, by all standards of human probability, to be touch and go.

The lesson to be learned was twofold. The head of the state had got to stand in the eyes of his people as their supremely representative man: no divine Caesar, but a sublimated John Doe with his rights and liberties under the law lawfully defined, like those of any other John or Richard, and without the power to overstep them to any significant extent, because, except for such forces as it might from time to time allow to be improvised for defined tasks overseas, the English, alone of European nations, could and did—pending its brief but unforgettable experience of military rule under the Protectorate—afford to keep its rulers effectively disarmed.

At this point I fear I shall be met with the inevitable objection that the idea of an English nation was so plainly contrary to medieval notions as to ante-date itself. I reply that even if there had not been an English nation in the fullest sense—as most palpably from the time of Magna Charta there was—it would have been necessary not only to invent one but also to supply it with an organ capable of making its voice heard and its will known.

One cannot—least of all with so realistic a people, and one so fertile in expedients as the English—expect to have it both ways. If it was decided that the head of the state was to be under the law, and such a law as the Common Law of England, then obviously in default of imposing his imperial will upon his people, he had got to come to some sort of working arrangement with them—and one does not come to working arrangements with abstractions. As it was not practicable to bargain with each of them individually or even with all of them assembled together in one place, some body had to be formed sufficiently compact and representative of the nation for the Sovereign to do business with. That was how Parliament, by a series of experiments and compromises, came to be evolved out of the assemblies of feudal magnates with whose co-operation the post-Conquest Kings had been able to make do, so long as these chiefs of what amounted to a foreign occupation monopolized the power of the sword and the purse. But this ceased to be the case after the loss of the French provinces had thrown England back to herself, and it became a matter of positive and

practical necessity to enlarge the basic representation so as to confront
the monarchy with an assembly capable of speaking for the nation,
and not, as happened practically everywhere on the Continent, with a
number of closed corporations representing different classes or sections
of it.

Parliament thus developed into the representative body, as the King
into the representative man, of the English nation; and it turned out
that way, not because anybody envisaged either King or Parliament in
such capacities, but because the conditions imposed on Britain by her
unique form of insular status made it inevitable that things should work
out—or, if you like to use that peculiarly British turn of phrase,
muddle through—on these or roughly similar lines. The powerlessness
of any class in the state to stand up on its own feet against an administrative machine applying its pressure in a strictly limited area forced
them together in organic combination in ways that form the commonplaces of constitutional history—a Lower House in which the country
gentry sat cheek by jowl with city burgesses, many of whom looked
forward to purchasing estates and becoming country gentlemen
themselves, and an upper chamber that only centuries later degenerated
into one based on the hereditary principle, but in its original idea (as
Pollard was the first to indicate) was much more based on function,
in a rough attempt to get together those very important people
who did in fact wield enough power in their several capacities, lay or
spiritual, to make their advice and consent essential in any important
undertaking.

Even so, the most important factor of all in ensuring that the seed
thus planted should flourish and develop on English soil alone, not
only through but beyond the Middle Ages, is that the goodness of that
soil was so largely the result of its impregnation by the principles of
the English Common Law. If any monarch or high legal authority had
been able or willing to take the decisive step of substituting the
universally admired principles of the Roman Law, it is difficult to see
how, being once committed herself, like the continental nations, to the
broad road that led to Rome, England could have failed to end up, like
them, under the *imperium* of a divine, even if a national or provincial,
Caesar.

And we can look further ahead and say that if England had not thus
contrived to make and keep herself the odd country out, nothing
could have prevented the swallowing up of all these national *imperia*,
in due course, by that of a divine emperor, in the full Roman sense, at
least of western Europe—and who can say of how much more of the
world's surface?

I am not begging the question of whether this is to be accounted a
bad or a good thing. All I am at this point concerned to establish is

that even thus early England had struck out on a path of her own that put her in a category apart from the other European nations. She may not have been better (there are those who will still maintain that she differed from them as Judas did from his colleagues in the apostolate), but beyond all doubt or question she was different—fundamentally and pregnantly different.

BOOK TWO

1

TUDOR ISOLATIONISM

PARLIAMENTARY government might have plainly seemed, by the last half of the fifteenth century, to have shot its bolt. Such blackmailing claims as Parliament had got conceded by monarchs shaky on their thrones or in their finances, they seemed unlikely to perpetuate after a generation of civil war and aristocratic anarchy that had left the whole country possessed of one overmastering desire for a strong monarchy—and the stronger the better—capable of maintaining its peace and striking down, without too much regard to pedantic notions of justice, anyone who showed the least sign of becoming a potential danger to its authority. And this, as it finally emerged from the long blood-bath called the Wars of the Roses, it flattered itself it had got at last in the adventurer who, with scarcely the decent pretence of a lawful title except that of being exactly the right man for the task, founded the short-lived but incomparably capable Dynasty of Tudor.

Henry VII, whom Bacon—though without penetrating to the ultimate sources of his success—exhibited as the ideal practitioner of the kingly technique, succeeded precisely because he grasped, by intuition, so much more firmly than Bacon himself, or anyone else who has sat in judgment on him, just in what way his position as ruler of England differed from that of continental monarchs, who had armed force to give effect to their will, and consequently thought of themselves primarily as war-lords and—saturated as they were in the principles of the Roman Law—as at least potential Caesars.

Such sovereigns, great and petty, could hardly fail to conform to one overall pattern of behaviour. The impelling motive in all their proceedings was the will to power. They were imperialists to the limit of their capacity, seeking to rule the people with their sway as absolutely as possible within their existing frontiers, and as widely as possible beyond them. Western Europe was thus the arena for a knock-out competition whose only logical conclusion would be the achievement of one all-embracing empire under a single Caesar.

It was the decisive significance of the Tudors to have realized from

26

the first—or acted as if they realized—that a pattern of behaviour imposed by conditions on the Continent was flatly against the whole trend and spirit of English development. England had tasted enough of the bitter fruits of involvement in European power politics to have learnt the lesson—even if she was incapable of formulating it—that the Roman way was not her way, and that by the pursuit of military glory and imperial expansion overseas she would be wantonly throwing away all the advantages of her insular status, and playing a game in which the scales were weighted so hopelessly against her that it amounted to gambling against a certainty. And what was even more important to realize was that for her alone was a policy of complete detachment from continental adventure not only desirable, but feasible. She could sit peacefully behind her moat and devote the whole of her energies to the cultivation of her own way of life, and exploitation of the advantages of her unique situation.

The first of the Tudor sovereigns, who had picked up his wisdom in the hard school of experience and who, as far as we know, had neither the time nor the inclination to indulge in political theorizing, acted as if he had worked out all this in advance, and put it into practice with the accuracy of an expert technician and an appertaining lack of either sentiment or scruple.

Henry VII may not have had more, though he had certainly no fewer, moral inhibitions than other Renaissance princes, and had not the least spark of the glamour that was—and still is for that matter—considered essential to the kingly office; but like the practical business man he was, he knew exactly what his clients expected of him and delivered the goods, without fuss and without fail—as a company director who knows that he is dependent on the support of his share-holders goes all out to give them satisfaction, and is not such a fool as to court dismissal by riding his will roughshod over them.

But provided only that he acted as agent of their will—which was a will to peace at almost any price within his, and their, borders—and that he observed the very elastic limits set by the law, they were a hundred per cent behind him in the most ruthless or arbitrary preventive action he might choose to take against anyone deemed remotely capable of setting himself above the law. Such drastic expedients as Acts of Attainder, the Court of Star Chamber, and a murderous Treason law, were both popular and democratic, and this being known, Henry Tudor, who was as economical of blood as he was of cash, was only once or twice under the necessity of spilling it out of order.

Not only within his borders did he seek peace and ensue it. Wars meant taxes, and it was hardly possible to levy a tax, even with the consent of Parliament, without sparking off a rebellion. Henry VII owed his throne to Parliament and he never forgot it; but he knew that the longer he could make ends meet without its assistance the better both members and their constituents would be pleased, provided only that he did not try to bypass it by raising the wind in illegal ways. To summon it a bare seven times during his reign to co-operate with the Crown in objects of common interest was just about the ideal arrangement for everyone concerned.

People who write about the Tudor 'despotism', as if it were on the same footing with the real despotisms that were being built up overseas, miss the decisive point of difference between them. The continental dynasts aimed at making their will their law, and in the main, and in the long run, succeeded in riding it roughshod over such of their subjects as did not succeed, like the inhabitants of the Dutch Netherlands, in effectively matching force with counter-force. It has been frequently pointed out that the two Tudor Henrys did, at any rate, get their way as signally and sensationally as any Louis or Francis, Charles or Philip. Yes, but with this difference—that unless they could make their way coincide with that predetermined for them by the nation whose agents they were, their tenure of office, and even of life, was not likely to be prolonged. It needed no more than a determined riot to consign an actively unpopular monarch to the scrap heap. They had to keep the right side of their subjects—and consequently it would have been suicidal lunacy for a monarch so wholly at the mercy of his own subjects as the first of the Tudors to have attempted to set up as a despot on the Roman or continental model. The pomp of power, the grace and might of chivalry, the divinity with which Caesars are accustomed to hedge themselves, might be well enough suited to the sort of conditions that prevailed on the Continent, where every prince's hand was against every prince in a non-stop struggle for survival; but in sea-sheltered England this sort of thing was not wanted and, by a ruler who knew his business, was not done. A policy that was in fact, though not yet in name, one of uncompromising Little-Englandism, that reckoned as cheaply of honour as Falstaff and as dearly of money as Shylock, is not one to commend itself to any imagination less worldly wise than that of Francis Bacon. Henry VII is likely to remain as much of a biographical bromide as Sir Robert Walpole or Lord John Russell.

But the tight-lipped monarch of business, though he may have been impelled by no more exalted motive than that of sitting tight and pretty on the *Siege Perilous* to which he had climbed, not only delivered the goods to his people's, and incidentally to his own, order, in fullest measure, but set a pattern of statesmanship not only for his own dynasty but—in so far as she was to make good her breakaway from the unity of Western civilization—for England herself, during the coming centuries.

2

DIVORCE FROM EUROPE

IN THE EARLY years of the sixteenth century nothing might have appeared less on the cards than that England should openly repudiate membership of the spiritual communion that was the binding element of Western civilization. She was little given to those all-out sectarian enthusiasms that were endemic on the Continent and were destined to plunge it into such devastating international and civil conflicts. The Lollard revivalism, that had fluttered the dovecotes of orthodoxy in the age of Chaucer, had never been capable of gathering enough force to make it a serious threat to the Establishment and, though never entirely suppressed, had been burnt out or driven beneath the surface in the course of the fifteenth century. And England, with nine centuries of ostensibly unbroken loyalty to the Holy See to look back upon, might have been supposed to be set fair for as many more. It would have taken a superhumanly penetrating observer to have divined that the bond, though unbroken, was so frayed and rotten that the least strain put upon it would cause it to snap.

As unfortunately the sectarian animosities aroused by that event are still as much alive as ever, the issue at stake is nearly always treated as if it were one primarily of religion; as indeed it might be, if looked at in a European perspective. The great anti-Roman revolt or schism that was comprehended, in its various forms, under the designation of Protestant, did indeed plunge the Continent into a religious or ideological conflict that, after turning a great part of it into a shambles, ended after more than a century in exhausted stalemate.

It would therefore be natural to say that if England was ripe for anything she was ripe for Protestantism—natural, but also misleading. For to Henry VIII, and most of his subjects, the religious issue was really a side-line. What England was ripe for was independence, religious and secular, in the most unqualified sense. And that is what, in the event, and after many vicissitudes, she attained.

But the common, and—if it may be said so without offence— vulgar presentation does not envisage anything so significant as the

Protestant-Catholic dialectic. It is simply treated as if it stemmed from the personal caprice of a crowned villain of melodrama, a lustful tyrant determined to stick at nothing in order to get rid of his innocent consort, and legalize his bigamy with the woman whose head, according to his genial custom, he proceeded to have cut off the moment his passion for her had cooled. The name of Henry VIII in fact has become an even more violent reaction-stimulus than even those of Charles I and George III, and to such an extent that by his Protestant supporters and still more his Catholic detractors he has ceased to be anything recognizably human and—which is saying a great deal—to have become the licensed depository of a greater amount of tendentious balderdash than any other character in British, or perhaps any, history.

And this is not only the case with the professional muckrakers of the screen and biographical drug pedlars of the post-Stracheyan school, but even with grave and revered authorities such as James Gairdner, who opens the concluding and summarizing chapter of his monumental *Lollardy and the Reformation* by remarking that scarcely anyone has denied that Henry VIII was a tyrant—a thing which, in the sense of an arbitrary despot, he neither was, nor, with the worst will in the world, could possibly have been, wholly dependent as he was on the goodwill of his people, without whose positive co-operation he could never have hoped to get away with his flaming defiance of what had hitherto been the unquestioned dictates and taboos of the Western order of civilization.

Tyrants are not as a rule exuberantly popular with their victims, but this was what bluff Hal notoriously contrived to be with the overwhelming majority of his subjects to the day of his death, and few of them were disposed to make heavy weather of his way of hacking through his matrimonial and other entanglements, or failed to give him the support he needed in annihilating potential opposition. So long as the legal formalities were observed—and no Tudor would have dreamed of offing a single head by arbitrary fiat—public opinion was not disposed to be either squeamish or critical. 'Safety first' was a rule that they were more than ready to condone in their sovereigns.

In any case we may leave the censorship of Henry's private conduct to those whose business or pleasure it may be to assume the office. Our sole concern with him is the part that destiny or his own volition caused him to play in consummating the emancipation of the English order of civilization from that of the Continent, an event that, however we may choose to react to it, constitutes one of the decisive turning points of history. And, if the break had got to be made, one can hardly imagine a personality more exactly conditioned by temperament and upbringing to make it effective.

Henry did not burst on to the scene like Athene, fully armed and mature from the forehead of Zeus. He was no more than a lusty young giant of seventeen when the luck of hereditary succession pitchforked him on to the throne. Is it any wonder that the secret of the Tudor technique needed a period of incubation, lasting to the verge of middle age, before it can be said to have become a second nature with him? During that time of supercharged energy that he was burning to discharge in action he was drawn into the orbit of an equally forceful but far more mature personality, that of Thomas Wolsey. He soon was able to convince himself that fate had thrown in his way a minister whom he could safely entrust with the direction of his policy, and who would take off his hands the day-to-day drudgery of administrative spade-work, leaving him free to enjoy the more spectacular functions of kingship.

And beyond question he had picked on the ablest man in his realm, and probably in Europe, for such a post, one whose mastery of the art and science of statecraft may conceivably have been equalled, but certainly not surpassed in the modern age, by that of Richelieu, Bismarck and Talleyrand—a mastery that reached to every level except the highest of all.

For it is essential that we should understand just how it was that this consummate pilot, to whom the helm of state was entrusted at so critical a phase of the voyage, came so near to running the vessel on to the rocks before the skipper woke up to the necessity of dropping him, and himself assumed responsibility for navigating the vessel into open waters.

The secret of Wolsey's brilliance and failure is contained in a single sentence of Bishop Creighton's life of him: 'He was the last English statesman of the old school, which regarded England not as a separate nation, but as an integral part of Western Christendom.' [1]

Just so: the old school—the pre-Tudor school. For though the erudite Prelate may not have appreciated the significance of his admission he let the cat out of the bag about the hero of his biography. What Wolsey had in fact done on taking over the controls of state was to switch them violently into reverse. He had no use for the cheese-paring isolationism of Henry VII. His outlook was essentially that of a good European and a good Catholic; and as such it was his object not only to re-involve England in the imbroglio of continental power politics, but to make her influence dominant by shifting her weight, with precision and finesse, from one side to another of a perpetually fluctuating balance of power. In this he did succeed to the extent of concentring the full blaze of the European limelight on the towering figure of his sovereign, and on the scarlet robe with which his

[1] *Life of Wolsey*, p. 218.

chief minister had succeeded in getting himself invested as a Prince of the Church Universal. As a success story it was enough to capture the imagination of his own and all subsequent ages, so that today his incarnadination on hoardings is reckoned to be a powerful enough stimulus to promote the sale of underwear. But the net result of his activities was to put his sovereign and country into a rather different sort of red.

This is not to blame Wolsey, unless by standards of a purely unworldly Christianity that he would have been the last man to have dreamed of adopting in practice, and would have cut the success story short in its opening paragraph. For there is no sort of success that has not its price, and what man of the world, and above all what churchman of the Renaissance world, would be so unrealistic as to grudge it?

It was a price that had to be paid by the sacrifice not only of soul, but also of freedom. There is no freedom of choice for climbers on those summit reaches where the least false step is likely to be fatal. Wolsey, for all his hubristic megalomania, was too clear-sighted not to realize that he had got to accommodate conscience and policy to the double necessity of keeping in with the Church in which he had risen to the highest rank short of the supreme headship which he coveted, and of the monarch to whose favour he owed every step of his advancement, and who had only to withdraw it to send him toppling headlong to the depths from which he had risen. And so long as Wolsey had all the controls of state committed to him, this imposed a corresponding necessity upon England herself of a spectacular foreign policy that would cause her to stand forth in the eyes of the world as *prima inter pares* of European and Catholic Powers, with her young sovereign as its most spectacular figure. It was power politics, and, to the limit of its capacity, imperial politics—the direct repudiation of everything that the first Tudor had stood for.

But so long as the full blaze of the European limelight continued to be focused on the ample form of the monarch, framed against a background of cardinal red, Henry showed not the least sign of being his father's son, or of having acquired the Tudor secret. What Wolsey must have recognized as the danger of all others to be avoided—of a national policy coming into collision with a super-national one—seemed the last thing to be feared, when the Sovereign himself burst into print with such an uncompromising vindication of the undiluted Catholic doctrine against the newfangled heresy called Protestant, as to earn him from a delighted Pontiff the explicit and unprecedented title of Defender of the Faith. That he, of all people, should turn from defence to attack—while incidentally sticking to the title that he thus stultified—might have seemed as unthinkable a contingency as that of the Cardinal himself turning Protestant. But in Henry's case, little as he or anyone else realized it, that would merely mean turning Tudor: and if that were to come about it would mean the end of Wolsey and a great deal else beside. For to turn Tudor would in effect mean turning insular—and a hundred-per-cent English.

Nearly twenty years is a good innings, and no one but Wolsey could have kept up his end so long. With a thoroughness that Strafford might have envied, he went all out, as if with conscious intention to turn England into a Power, and her Soverign into a despot, on the continental model. For the English way of government and the English Common Law he had an arrogant contempt, and regarded the Commons as serving no other purpose than that of acting as a sort of suction pipe for the extraction of whatever sums he might need to finance the continually mounting cost of a foreign policy that, apart from the glamour of such publicity stunts as that enshrined in nursery legend as the Field of the Cloth of Gold, achieved no results whatever except to empty those bulging coffers that the first Tudor had bequeathed, and to leave no other way of balancing the state accounts than by squeezing the fiscal orange until the pips squeaked—a phrase that would have had no terrors for Wolsey, who was the last person to stand on fine points of constitutional law, but trusted in his ability to carry matters with a high hand with Parliament and its constituents, to the limit of his own and his Sovereign's demands.

And by the sheer drive of his tempestuous will he did indeed succeed in carrying his point, more or less, with Parliament: but only by straining the patience of the country to the verge of the revolutionary breaking point. To this pass had the Cardinal's policy of European involvement, pursued, as it had been, with consummate adroitness, brought the English monarch and nation.

It was at this juncture that the one thing happened that could have saved the situation for the Crown, and much more than the Crown. The now almost middle-aged Sovereign, by some process of subconscious unfolding, as hard to account for as the transformation of chrysalis into butterfly, broke the hypnotic spell that had made him as wax in the hands of his minister and came out in his true and formidable colours as his father's son, with the mystery of the Tudor kingcraft at long last mastered, and harnessed to an energy of will power such as even his father had never possessed. As if to the manner born he gathered up all the controls of policy into his muscular hands, and proceeded henceforth to switch it back to the lines from which Wolsey had diverted it.

This meant the pulling of England as much as possible out of Europe; and, as a necessary consequence, a policy that was uncompromisingly national and insular in principle, though tempered by a characteristically national unwillingness to push the logic of principle to its extreme practical consequences. Sleeping dogs might lie and claims of alien sovereignty go unchallenged so long as they were suffered to remain dead letters. Henry would have been well enough content to rest upon his laurels as Defender of the Faith, if the Faith, or rather the petty Italian despot who functioned as its official plenipotentiary on earth, had only been able and willing to leave England and her Sovereign as free as they had been, in practice, for centuries, to manage at least their major affairs in their own way.

Which was not to be. For as everyone knows, the avalanche that, having swept Wolsey off his feet, gathered momentum enough to overwhelm the whole established spiritual order in England, had started from the King's resolve to get his marriage, that had all along been of doubtful legality, and was now past hope of producing a male heir to the throne, dissolved by the Pope, in order that he might get a younger sister of a former mistress of his to supply the deficiency within the bonds of lawful wedlock. Regarded as a purely personal matter, this might have shown up Henry in almost as unpleasant a marital light as has recently been thrown on the most scurrilous of all his many denouncers, Charles Dickens.[1] But with him it was not primarily—as it *was* with that pillar of Victorian morality—a personal matter, but one of high policy on an issue of vital importance to the nation.

To put it briefly, there was every reason to believe that the King's death, with only a weakly princess to succeed him, would have the effect of plunging the nation back into the chaos and anarchy of civil war, of which the bitter experience of the preceding century had given it an obsessive dread, and from which it had been the special mission of the House of Tudor to deliver it. Whether or not this danger may in the light of subsequent events be judged to have been exaggerated is neither here nor there. The point is that the fear was genuine, that it was rather more than plausible and that it was shared by the King with the overwhelming majority of his subjects—hence the practically free hand they were ready to accord him. It might be hard that a worthy woman should lose her ring, and a far from worthy adventuress her head; but certainly, by the Renaissance way of thinking, interests of state, involving the lives and welfare of millions, were entitled to unconditional priority over those of the highest placed individuals. Certainly no Tudor had either doubts or qualms on the subject.

Nothing therefore can be more futile, or less to the real point, than the various arguments that have been adduced by rival propagandists

---

[1] 'A most intolerable ruffian, a disgrace to human nature'—strong words, even for a Victorian moralist—and when one remembers that Dickens as well as Henry had his Catherine, one rather wonders at his audacity in using them.

to prove that the marriage of Henry to Queen Katherine was, or was not, canonically valid. It ought to be self-evident to anyone, not wilfully blind, that the unhappy Pontiff was governed by motives of pure expediency, in which fear predominated, and that though he was only too ready to connive at far less reputable expedients than mere divorce, including bigamy [1] and incest,[2] to pacify the Defender of his Faith, he was even more afraid of offending the respondent's nephew, the Emperor, Charles V, than he was of offending the petitioner—so long, that is, as the imperial armies, which had already sacked Rome, hovered around poised to finish off what was left—including the Pope himself. When it appeared likely that the balance of military power in Italy was about to swing to the side of the Emperor's rival, the King of France, the way was open for the divorce to go through according to plan, and this was what Wolsey, in his desperate effort to ride two horses at once, was forced to gamble on; but when the balance swung decisively back in the imperial direction, it became evident that there was nothing doing at Rome, and that not Wolsey himself, with all his wizardry, was capable of getting the knot untied short of Doomsday.

Stripped of all pious and legalistic overlay, the plain fact of the matter is that England, as represented by her lawful Sovereign, was debarred from adopting her own solution of a problem of vital urgency, and that for no other reason than that when the course she proposed to adopt did not happen to suit the book of Vatican politics she was expected to knuckle under and make the best she could of the situation. This was a dangerous proposition to put before the England of Henry VIII—or Henry VIII himself, who from the moment that it became apparent to him that the challenge to his own and his country's sovereignty was no longer to be evaded, stepped forth in his proper person to meet it in the spirit of an English—and what is more—of a full blown Tudor Sovereign.

No doubt he was temperamentally of that extreme volitional type that when it is crossed—and still more when it feels itself to be doublecrossed—is ready to go to all lengths and stick at nothing to carry its point. But to carry this point more was needed than a mere combination of self-will and obstinacy. Henry was no Quixote. Nobody was better capable of realizing what it meant for an island—and not even the whole of an island—on the fringe of the Continent to assert its unconditional independence of any authority but its own, and to do this in the way most calculated to affront and outrage the conscience of a Catholic Christendom that had only to unite its forces to crush the rebellion and its author by dint of overwhelming odds. But Henry,

[1] By Henry marrying the new love before being off with the old.
[2] Of Henry's natural son marrying his legitimate daughter.

having once chosen his course, never drew back nor hesitated for a moment. By calculated audacity and a precise adjustment of means to ends, he succeeded in making good his defiance without the odds against him ever materializing. It was an undertaking in which the least mistake or even hesitation would have been fatal. But Henry brought it off and, what matters more than any personal success, vindicated his country's independence of any order of civilization but its own.

This presents a very different picture of him from that of the lecherous villain of propagandist or merely prurient melodrama, though there is no need to go to the other extreme of moral white-washing. A latter-day Dante might conceivably have damned him to as lurid an immortality among the Princes of Hell as Ulysses, though his claim to such infernal pre-eminence among the princes of his time would have been, to say the least, challengeable. But he does indisput-ably rank among the greatest of English Sovereigns, and it is solely with his part in shaping the destinies of his country at the decisive parting of the ways that we need concern ourselves here.

Even so it would be outside the scope of this book to vie with the textbooks in recording the steps by which Henry, once he had fairly assumed the control of his own policy, carried through what would be more appropriately described as a revolution than a reformation, except to bring out one essential feature of the story on which the current voice—or rather the two rival voices of history—is silent or misleading. The idea of a sadistic tyrant, charging blindly ahead like a frustrated bull in the rutting season, is too crude to pass muster. Henry had at least as great a need for restraint as he had for audacity—and for the almost impeccable timing and adjustment of means to ends that in fact characterized his proceedings, after he had reluctantly yielded to the necessity of discarding the minister whose endeavour to combine the now plainly divergent loyalties to his Church and to his Sovereign had so signally broken down. It was a cruel necessity, and even Henry, who on no other occasion displayed the least com-punction about the scrapping of his discarded instruments, would have been content to allow Wolsey to fall soft and holy on to the plump cushions of an archbishopric, had not that incurable intriguer endeavoured to stage a come-back through the good offices of a foreign power.

Whether after that the Cardinal should get what was coming to him, or anticipate it by dying of fright, need concern us no more than it did Henry. The important thing to realize is what his fall, and the King's consequent determination to run his own policy in future on his own lines, implied on the top level of statesmanship. To put it as Henry himself might have, had he been capable of rendering an articulate account of what was so largely with him the result of intuition, he had at last come to realize that a policy of European or Catholic involvement, with its logical consequence of substituting Roman for English principles of government and law, had brought the throne and country to the brink of ruin. But it was still not too late to apply the unformulated technique whose secret was part of the Tudor heritage, though it had taken the second Tudor all these years of eclipse to grow up into its practical mastery.

What was the heart of that Tudor secret of which Henry had at last become an initiate? No more than this: he was henceforth to make his subjects his partners. He was to make them feel that it was not *his* will—still less the will of any minister of his—that was being imposed on *them*, but that he himself had become the vehicle of *their* will. No longer, as in the Wolsey interlude, was he to go against the grain of their inclination, but to study and follow it ostensibly on all occasions —to lead by seeming to follow.

There is no reason to assume that the nation was any more governed by moral considerations than Henry himself. Indeed it may be argued that he deliberately played up to the lowest instincts of its mass consciousness, and in particular to the itch to get something for nothing at the expense of any pockets but those of the lawful taxpayer. But there was also the overriding determination to submit to no outside interference whatever, temporal or spiritual, and to allow England from henceforth to build up her own way of civilization on the foundation of her ancient law and liberties.

Such a determination, so long as it remained dominant, automatically ruled out any question of despotism, Tudor or otherwise, and by an equally inevitable, if unforeseen, long-term logic of events, the emergence of anything fit to be called a British empire. For liberty, in the British sense, is too flatly incompatible with *imperium* in the Roman, to co-exist with it in one and the same polity. That, however, it would take the experience of many generations to bring to light.

King Henry had only the score of the existing game to play to, and only his instinct to play by; but on the vital issue of national liberty— or rather liberties—it was a sound instinct. However ruthless he might be in crushing opposition, as long as he had the support of public opinion he never, once he had got into the saddle, perpetrated Wolsey's mistake of trying to play the Caesar with either his Parliaments or their constituents. In this second half of his reign, he was the first English sovereign who could fairly have been described as a great Parliament man. Nothing could have exceeded the tact and patience with which he handled and humoured his Parliament, no doubt in the full realization that to get it on his side was the *sine qua non* of success in the perilous course to which he was committed. And, as a necessary consequence, he took the most scrupulous care always to be on the

right side of the law in his otherwise most outrageous proceedings—
no such difficult matter once he had contrived to get himself on the
right side of the legislature.

And to get on the right side of Parliament the sovereign recipe was
so to contrive things as never to come to it with his hat in his hand.
He must at all costs find means of 'living of his own', in the medieval
sense, without resource to the tax collector—an almost unimaginably
tough proposition when we consider that the effective resources of the
Crown were shrinking every year owing to the influx of precious
metals from the New World, that had the effect of a vast and cumulative
inflation on an income that was almost entirely non-expansive. Add
to this that he was now committed to go through to the end with his
defiance of a Catholic Christendom that was just beginning to rally its
spiritual and material forces for a supreme counter-offensive against
the revolting elements with which England would, however unwillingly, be forced to align herself; and that even if by some miracle he
managed to avoid the strain and expense of a major war, it would only
be on condition of his insuring himself by the maintenance of an
invasion-proof sea power, which itself involved a heavy additional
burden of expense.

And yet, in the teeth of all apparent probability, he did succeed in
getting the ships and the money in sufficient quantity to carry his
defiance of Catholic Christendom to a successful conclusion. But the
money had to be raised somehow, though it was more than doubtful
whether Parliament itself could have got the taxpayer to foot the bill.
There was only one thing for it. If the Head of the Church were
determined to ride his own, or a temporal Caesar's, will roughshod
over that of the British Sovereign and nation, the Church itself, in so
far as it submitted to his authority, became the vehicle of an anti-
national conspiracy, an imperial fifth column. It might therefore be
argued that the only effective counter was to nationalize the Church,
and to do so at the Church's expense. There had from time immemorial
been a continuous drain of money out of the country into the coffers
of the Vatican—presumably for services rendered. It had been Henry's
first instinct to put pressure on the Pope by freezing these funds until
he proved ready to oblige in the matter of the divorce. Unfortunately,
so long as obliging the King over the water meant disobliging the
Emperor on the spot, this was just what His Holiness, for the life of
him, dared not do. And so, with tempers hardening on both sides,
as one act of hitherto unimaginable defiance followed another, the
Defender of the Faith, with the enthusiastic backing or collusion of at
least the most dynamic section of his subjects, went on to drive through
the full programme of nationalization.

It is not a pretty or an edifying story. Acts of sacrilege, of wholesale plunder, and of calculated, even though rationed, frighfulness, are evil things in themselves, even when done by due process of law and with at least the passive acquiescence of Parliament and the nation.[1]

But in the amoral atmosphere of sixteenth-century politics, it stood to reason that the least weakness or hesitation in the application of the necessary means to so desirable an end as that of national emancipation would have been considerably worse in its effect than any crime in the calendar. For the elimination of a hundred or a thousand common cards in the human pack might well be avoided by the timely sacrifice of one court card. And even the wholesale share-out of the monasteries and their wealth went through with a surprising lack of fuss and hardship. The one or two prominent examples of state terrorism at least accomplished their purpose. There were no more candidates for martyrdom. The inmates and even heads of these mostly depleted and almost bankrupt foundations submitted quietly enough to the inevitable, and not a few of them were pensioned off, or found comfortable billets waiting for them in the now depapalized national Church.

As for Henry, it is improbable that his conscience troubled him about it in the least degree. To the day of his death he was firmly convinced that he was as much the Defender of the Faith as ever, even though he was forced to constitute himself Supreme Pontiff within the limits of his own temporal jurisdiction. The logical absurdity involved in the idea of an insular Catholicism was no bar to its practical efficacy in getting what King and country wanted with the least possible expenditure of blood and treasure.

It all arose out of a divorce—but the divorce that really mattered was that of England herself and of all that England stood, and had it in her to stand for, from the civilization of the Continent. Henceforth there was to be a spiritual gulf deeper than the Channel fixed between continental *imperium* and insular *libertas*, between an ancient empire that was always seeking to re-universalize itself, and a commonwealth in embryo that had not yet awakened to consciousness of its own even potential existence.

[1] Except for one revolt of its most chronically turbulent and backward elements, with which Henry, with no standing army, but a good deal of Machiavellian finesse, was able to deal.

3

HERSELF ALONE

TO TALK OF the Reformation in England as if it were a
religious conflict on anything like the continental footing would
be to misconceive its nature. Naturally it involved, as in other countries,
revolutionary changes in the structure of organized religion. It needed
the breaking of a great many sanctified eggs to make the curious
omelette of Anglicanism. But the breaking of the eggs was only by the
way. The proof of the omelette was in the eating, and provided it
proved reasonably agreeable to English palates its designation on the
menu card was a matter of comparative indifference. To put it plainly,
the religious or sectarian aspect of the conflict was not one with which
the average Englishman was chiefly concerned. Provided he was
allowed a free hand in the conduct of his own business according to
his own lights, he had no particular desire to exchange the Catholic
Mumpsimus for the Protestant *Sumpsimus*. But if, on the other hand,
he found his freedom of choice in secular matters intolerably restricted,
then he was prepared, like his Sovereign, to go to all lengths—or even
in the last resort to go Protestant—to secure it. And once he had taken
the plunge he would not have been English had he been incapable of
persuading himself that he had acted from the first from the purest
religious motives.

During the quarter of a century or so of what is usually spoken of
as the English Reformation public opinion showed itself equally ready
to swing to the Protestant left or Catholic right in pursuit of its own
main chance. Interest and not faith was the prime consideration. It was
nothing loath to connive at Henry VIII's plunder of the monasteries,
because while it lasted it enabled that 'majestic lord' to 'break the
bonds of Rome' without calling upon his subjects to foot the bill. But
when the strong King had given place to a consumptive minor, and
the consummation of the Protestant drive provided a camouflage
behind which the plutocratic clique, that had grown fat by the share
out of Church property, staged a second and uncontrolled racket at the

expense of the nation, the nation took the first opportunity of repudiat-
ing Protestantism and all its works and putting back the religious
clock to where it had been before the Reformation started. And no
doubt if it had been merely a question of religion, and the now de-
reformed Church had been capable of learning its lesson and keeping
out of secular politics, some sort of an enduring *modus vivendi* might
have been patched up.

But in historical time the putting back of clocks is seldom feasible.
It was an utterly different Europe that had come into being from that
of the God-forsaking Renaissance heyday, a Europe in which the
religious, or sectarian, issue had come to dominate all others. There
was no path of return to the profitable isolationism of Henry VII's
golden days. Once a half-Spanish and wholly fanatical queen had got
seated on the throne, England found herself plunged back into the
imbroglio of continental power politics—but no longer, as in Wolsey's
time, as the holder of the balance, but in the humiliating capacity of
a satellite of the great Hapsburg Spanish-Austrian combination that,
with the manpower of half Europe and all the riches of the New World
to command, seriously threatened to start a new empire of the West,
which, though Catholic, would have its temporal Caesar not at Rome
but Madrid in the person of the Spanish Sovereign, who by marrying
the Queen of England thereby constituted himself its effective
suzerain.

Philip II was as single hearted a religious enthusiast as even the
Spain of St Theresa and St John of the Cross could produce, but
imaginative tact was never a Spanish or a Hapsburg trait, and this
dedicated couple vied with each other in rubbing in the humiliation of
their English subjects. Henry VIII had gone to all necessary lengths of
frightfulness without intolerably alienating public opinion, because it
had been done, in the way of state policy, according to the accepted
rules of the game. But the reign of terror set up by his elder daughter
was inspired by a single-hearted crusading zeal that was authentically
Spanish. It was not a matter of policy, but of conscience, to burn heresy
out of the land. And in this faith she proceeded from one blunder to
another. Up to that time Protestantism in England had been less of an
end in itself than a convenient means towards national self-assertion or
individual self-enrichment. There is no evidence that it had made any
significant emotional or subconscious penetration on a national scale.
Indeed, after the experience of the Edwardian racket, public opinion
showed itself more than ready for a swing back to what was capable of
being restored of the former orthodoxy.

But nothing would suffice Philip and Mary but to stage a publicity
campaign for Protestantism such as it would have been utterly incapable of staging for itself. They invested it not only with a religious but

a patriotic halo. The pick of its hitherto rather sombre and uninspiring evangelists—those who stopped behind to face the music instead of fleeing the country while the going was good—were provided with a literally flaming platform. Hugh Latimer, by far the most sympathetic personality among them, spoke no more than the truth when he talked of lighting a candle that the fires of Rome would never put out. But his martyrdom was nothing to the openly vindictive torturing to death of poor, grovelling Archbishop Cranmer, who alive would have served more to discredit the cause he had betrayed than any propaganda, but who had thrust upon him the opportunity of turning the tables on his torturers, by making a candle of his own right arm, surely the most inspired publicity coup on record.

The other victims of the persecution, even if their numbers were not so large as Protestant legend put them, were selected as if with the deliberate intention of shocking and humiliating public opinion to the maximum degree. These mostly poor and humble folk were by no conceivable stretch of imagination a danger to the state. This was not the sort of frightfulness that bluff Harry had practised and got away with; and when it was notoriously perpetrated under the auspices of a foreign power, pity and disgust were intensified by humiliation. It would be generations before Spain and Rome ceased to be national bogeys.

And if anything could have been lacking to put the seal on this humiliation, it was provided when England was dragged into a war on the Continent, no longer as in the conquering days of Crécy and Agincourt, but as a humble auxiliary whose contingent trailed in the wake of the Spanish grand army and helped to pull the chestnuts out of the fire for King Philip at the decisive battle of St Quentin, after which a peace was concluded with France in which English interests were contemptuously disregarded. But this was only the prelude to the most shattering blow to England's prestige that she had sustained for centuries, since by way of evening up the score with Spain the Duc de Guise suddenly swooped down upon England's *pied à terre* on French soil at Calais, and before Mary's corrupt and almost bankrupt administration could or would take the least step to reinforce its undermanned garrison or strengthen its crumbling defences, had snapped it up by a sort of fool's mate.

Realistically regarded, no better thing could have happened for England than to be relieved of the burden of maintaining this sally port on to the Continent, which had ceased to be a paying proposition economically, and provided a standing temptation to involvement in military adventure of a kind bound to be disastrous to an island Power. But the *amour propre* of all English folk, from the Queen down to her humblest subject, had been touched to the quick. The feelings of later generations about the Rock of Gibraltar can give but a faint idea of what Tudor England felt about Calais. The meaning of being a satellite of Spain, and of submission to the Holy See under Spanish auspices, was brought home with a vengeance. The fires of Smithfield and the loss of Calais had penetrated the lowest depths of the national subconsciousness, and engendered an anti-Spanish and an anti-Roman complex that lasted for centuries, and even when in seeming abeyance were ready at any time to erupt with unreasoning violence. The Queen, whose holy zeal had so signally defeated its own purpose, could not have chosen a more dramatically appropriate moment for making her exit from the stage on which she had played her brief part with a sombre pathos that at least had no counterpart in the repertoire of her successor. The curtain had rung down on the tragic prelude to the high comedy of the Elizabethan age, which demanded a more subtle and perhaps a unique artistry in its leading lady.

But when that hitherto almost unknown performer stepped out of the wings to hold the stage for the remainder of the century, no one in the audience, or for that matter in the cast, had the least notion of what the change-over was destined to signify, and how the whole spirit and plot of the drama were fated under her auspices to develop on new and hitherto undreamed-of lines. To all appearances it seemed merely as if one half-sister had taken the place of another on a throne already undermined, and on which she would be lucky to last out for more than a year or two.

However fiercely the contending faiths might be opposed to each other, all their respective adherents were agreed in thinking of the new turn of events as just one more episode in the all-dominating religious conflict. It seemed as plain a choice between Reformation and Counter-Reformation as that posed by Elijah between the cult of Jehovah and that of Baal, whereas of all leading characters of that time, Elizabeth was probably the one least swayed by sectarian zeal of the kind pandemic on the Continent. To steer on a fixed compass bearing of faith would for her have been navigational suicide. She was not of the stuff of which martyrs or crusaders are made, and her religious policy was one of many means to an end both self-regarding and patriotic.

For from the first it was her cue to put herself across the footlights as the living embodiment of her country's idealized personality. A virgin queen was to dramatize herself in much the same part as the virgin goddess had played to the citizens of Athens. And in as far as she could succeed in getting herself accepted in that capacity by her subjects of all denominations, so far she would be pulling her country out of the ideological conflict that was turning Europe into a shambles, and putting it into the way of freedom to follow its own destiny in its own way, without submitting to be drawn back into the orbit of the old faith or crusading on behalf of the new.

Video et taceo—'I see, and am silent'—was the young queen's motto, learnt in how hard a school! We have no record of the motives that must have inspired the first and most difficult decision of the many she would be called on to take in the course of her reign—whether to throw herself into the arms of Spain and of Philip, that were wide open to receive her, or to stake everything on what appeared a fore-doomed attempt to cash in on the Protestant reaction against the rigours of the last reign. Elizabeth had no bias in favour of Pro-testantism. As far as her personal feelings were concerned she would almost certainly have preferred the colour and pageantry of the Catholic ritual. But she must have realized that, unlike her father, she lacked the ships, the men and the money to safeguard her realm against invasion, and that even after the disillusioning experience of the Catholic restoration, Protestantism had not had time to get beneath the skin of a sufficient number of her subjects to form an effective rallying cry. But there was something in her Tudor soul that caused her to divine, with intuitive certainty, that her only chance was to gain time by every device of masculine subtlety and feminine super-subtlety, to unite the country in its own cause, on a basis as far as possible of ideological disinterestedness.

It was Elizabeth's genius—for surely no less emphatic word will meet the case—that apprised her from the first that her best, or only chance, of doing this was to offer herself, in her own proper person, as the symbol of that unity she sought to create, the goddess raised in the public eye above all contending sects and causes, in whose cult all her subjects could pool their differences. She was not going to be the leading lady of the nation for nothing. She had a part to play, and for forty-five years she continued to play it with consummate art, and a success of which no one, when she took the boards, would have dared to dream. It might seem almost incredible that anyone should have the obtuseness to denigrate or ridicule her for the necessary shifts she had to adopt to keep up the part, long after the time that the greatest actresses are suffered to rest on their laurels or adopt elderly roles. This lady, with her wigs and her make-up and the juvenile leads to which she had to conform, dared not let down the company of which she was not only leading lady but acting manageress. However tired she was, whatever strain it put on her failing resources, she had to drive herself on to the end. Her retirement, at almost any time before death came to relieve her, would have been a national disaster of the first magnitude.

And indeed the one besetting element of weakness in her choice of this drama of England's *Gloriana* or *The Virgin Queen*, was that the staging of it involved the acceptance of a life-and-death gamble, and one, by all human reckoning, against crushing odds. Once put on there could be no question of taking it off until Gloriana's England had become sufficiently the fact of real life to be sure of its own continuance without the need for any further stimulus of make-believe. Before that consummation could be guaranteed the show would have to prolong its run for a matter of nearly half a century. And nothing could be more certain than that if the leading lady, on whose triumphant rendering of her part everything depended, were for any cause to be eliminated, there would be no possibility of keeping it on the boards for a day longer. Complete and catastrophic collapse would be the sequel. It was only too well known to the spiritual and temporal chiefs of the Counter-Reformation, who had no more scruples than the underworld bosses in Chicago in settling the accounts of troublesome rivals, that by snipping the thin thread of Elizabeth's life they would be doing more to ensure the triumph of the true faith than by liquidating even a Valois or an Orange.

That Elizabeth could be guaranteed to keep up the part for all these necessary years was thus more than even her most faithful counsellors and loving subjects could believe. They put every conceivable form of pressure, short of actual physical compulsion, on her, to follow her father's example and insure against her own demise by providing the throne with a legitimate successor. But this extraordinary woman kept her nerve and her counsel, and refused to be diverted a hair's breadth from the course of action that, masked by innumerable subterfuges and evasions, she had pursued from the first with underlying consistency. She did not scruple to derive every advantage she could from chaffering with her own person in the royal marriage market, and always with an unspoken resolve to go to all lengths short of clinching the bargain. A woman who pursued this course in common life would be damned for a coquette, and it is the vulgar fashion to speak in this way of Elizabeth. But neither the state problems of a governing sovereign, nor the sex problems incidental to the part of a leading lady on the stage—and Elizabeth was both—are to be judged by the standards of private life. And it could be said with at least as much truth of Elizabeth as of any other leading lady, that whatever her private feelings, she never allowed them to deflect her from the spirit of her part in the slightest degree. The play was with her—as in common decency it ought to be with us—the thing.

This need not be taken to imply that she was without heart or soul beneath the make-up. Leading ladies are the last people likely to wear either on their sleeves. Who knows—or whose business is it to inquire —how much they impart the spirit of their parts into their private lives?

We can never be quite sure, with so consummate a performer, whether she was not acting a part even to herself. But to assume that she was, would be guesswork as wishfully vulgar as the innumerable reconstructions of her alleged sex life.[1] It is by the part she played on the public stage that her importance in the development of her country's civilization is to be measured, and here at least we are on solid ground. The impact she made on her age we can record as factually as we do that of a cannon-ball, without speculating about the feelings or intentions of the gunner.

[1] Or her religious life, for that matter. There have come to light prayers of her own composition and intended for no eye but her own that would, on the face of it, argue her to have been quite as devout a Christian as the next woman, even if she lacked the burning zeal of her half-sister.

4

GLORIANA'S
LITTLE ENGLAND

ALL THIS ABOUT Elizabeth I in a book that sets forth to deal with a situation so different from any that she or her contemporaries were capable of imagining! What is Elizabeth I to the subjects of Elizabeth II?

What indeed, if it be conceded that the past is over and done with, and history therefore incapable of coming alive! But to those of us who cling to the faith that the past never dies, but that the present is its cumulative sum and continuing development, it is possible to return a flat negative to the statement that Elizabeth I is dead[1] except in the purely bodily sense. It is far more to the point to say about her than of the highly dubious character to whom the words were originally applied, that her soul goes marching on. The England that we know, and all that the name has come to signify, might be unimaginably different if it had not grown out of what Elizabeth made it, as the oak from the acorn.

But first let us be clear what this implies; what it is about Elizabeth I that constitutes her enduring significance for posterity. For almost everyone who has thought about the subject at all has his own fully formed notion of it, and these differ one from another within the widest or no limits. And even when the innumerable vulgarizations of 'Elizabeth the Woman', and piously concocted libels about 'Bad Queen Bess the Heretic', have been swept into the rubbish bin, there remain two of those fundamental fallacies that are basic to the current fashion, or voice, of history, and as such are taken for granted by the officiating pundits.

The first of these, which is becoming a little outdated, is that which frames everything in the European setting of a great religious or ideological conflict—Reformation against Counter-Reformation—

---

[1] 'Queen Elizabeth is dead', as we know from Swift, was the fashionable *cliché* when Queen Anne was alive.

into which England is, by choice or necessity, drawn. Elizabeth, by this showing, becomes as essentially the Protestant Queen as her rival Philip is the Catholic King. And no doubt she was, from the moment she cut the bond with Rome by assuming the supreme governorship of her own Church, *a* Protestant Queen, and as such irreconcilably obnoxious to the crusading ardour of the Counter-Reformation. But however much from time to time she might ally herself with the Protestant forces in Europe, it was as a matter of pure national convenience, and in no sense one of religious principle.

Necessarily so, if she were to stand in the eyes of her people for a spirit of national self-sufficiency that is all too loosely described by the word 'patriotism'. For the patriotism signified by the cult of the Virgin Goddess was something peculiar to the English spirit and tradition, that had little in common with the collective will to power that the continental sovereigns sought to embody in their own persons and engender in their subjects. In this insular patriotism that Elizabeth aimed at embodying, the emphasis was less on power than on freedom —or in so far as it could be spoken of as a will to power, it was almost entirely in the sense of power to achieve freedom. And by freedom is signified the uninhibited liberty to evolve a way of life not of insular seclusion, but of self-determination unhampered by allegiance to, or membership of, any wider unity, temporal or spiritual.

It is obvious—or ought to be in the light of recent experience—that no people can be its own master and at the same time enlist itself in the service of any form of militant ideology, except when, as in sixteenth-century Spain and twentieth-century Russia, the national will to power can become so closely identified with ideological fanaticism as to be practically indistinguishable from it. It was fully appropriate that the King of Spain should have been styled His Most Catholic Majesty, since the triumph of the Counter-Reformation under Spanish auspices would have inevitably signified the union of the West under the *imperium* of a Spanish Caesar or Commander of the Faithful, just as the triumph of communism envisaged at the Kremlin would be in effect that of a world-wide tsardom. But though it would have been a tempting lead for Elizabeth to seek to combine all the scattered forces of European Protestantism under her leadership in a counter-crusade against the Counter-Reformation, it was a temptation to which her deepest instincts debarred her from yielding. For even to embark on such a venture would have had the effect of committing England to total participation in the ideological conflict that was draining the lifeblood of Europe, and of infecting her with a sectarian enthusiasm infinitely more soul-absorbing than any that her lukewarm allegiance to the old faith had been capable of engendering. The last thing that Elizabeth wanted was to escape from the Roman frying-pan into the fires of Geneva. Her only interest in the conflict of faiths was to disengage herself from it as cheaply and completely as possible. About the choice of means she may have been no more scrupulous than Machiavelli himself, but the end in view was not one of power, imperial or spiritual, but simply of freedom; and her policy was neither Protestant nor Catholic, but English—and subconsciously at least inspired by the principle of 'a plague on both your Faiths with a big F'.

Thus we find that Elizabeth and her counsellors were engaged in a task of infinite delicacy. It was not enough to fend off the enormous menace of a militant Catholicism that made no secret of its intention to bring back the rebellious province to its proper allegiance, and showed its hand openly when Pius V fulminated his Bull excommunicating the Queen and absolving her subjects from her allegiance—and it must be borne in mind that the adherents of the old faith formed a potential fifth column variously estimated at anything up to half the population. It was essential to do this without allowing what one might call the left wing of Protestant extremism from getting out of hand and sweeping Church, Throne, and Government down a torrential spate of Protestant intransigence. So we find that the hand of constituted authority was hardly less repressive of the hundred-per-cent Protestants—the Calvinists or Puritans who ought to have been the spearhead of an anti-Catholic resistance—than of the Catholics themselves.

It was not the way of Elizabeth, or of the great Cecils, father and son, who for more than half a century were the effectual heads of the longest and most successful Government the country has ever had, to formulate the principles of their policy even to themselves. It was enough for them to adopt it empirically from day to day to an ever-changing situation in the English way of intuitive practicality. But its guiding principles, viewed in the light of events, were both simple and constant, and may be briefly summed up in a twofold determination—firstly to keep England as much as possible in a state of insular detachment from the secular and still more the spiritual imbroglio of European power politics, and secondly to purge the virus of sectarian enthusiasm as far as possible from England's own body politic.

The keynote of her whole policy was set by the form and spirit she imparted to a Church no longer styled Roman or Catholic (except that the latter epithet remained incongruously embedded in the Creed) but specifically that of England. Its function was to act not as a stimulant but as a tranquillizer. A too militant zeal for either of the contending ideologies was calculated to divide the realm hopelessly against itself, and bring it to an only too foreseeable desolation. Crusades were therefore off, as far as Elizabeth's staff of Anglican bishops was concerned. Their main objective—as formulated by the leading Anglican divine, the judicious Hooker—was to establish a reign of law such as would provide a framework within which the maximum number of sober Christians, as distinct from faith-drunken zealots, could accommodate their differences sufficiently to allow of their presenting a united front, in the name of Queen and country, to aggression from overseas. Here was a form of enthusiasm, not religious but patriotic, in which Protestant and Catholic could join forces—and which, when the supreme crisis came, did in fact prove to have permeated the national consciousness to at least a sufficient extent for the purpose in hand.

But it was a patriotism of a very special, not to say unique, nature, such as could have grown up only in an island community and such an island as Britain. It had in it scarcely the faintest tincture of that urge to collective power and expansion that is almost inevitable in states with open land frontiers, and compels them to organize themselves on what is really a footing of potential imperialism, in which every other consideration is subordinated to that of disciplined efficiency under a sovereign commander—a process that we see consummated in the post-Reformation struggle for survival on the Continent.

But the England of Elizabeth developed in the opposite direction. The Queen was in perfect agreement with her subjects that a standing army was not worth the cost of its keep—soldiers meant taxes—and rather than touch her Parliaments for an avoidable penny she was prepared to let military efficiency go by the board, and trust to her diplomatic finesse and in the last resort to the strip of water that lay between the island and the mainland.

Through all these years of mortal peril, during which she was employing every twist and subterfuge in order to spin out time, never for a moment did the Tudor Queen make the least effort to turn her threatened realm into an armed, let alone an imperial, power. Never, even when those mighty captains the Duke of Alva, Don John of Austria and the Prince of Parma were mustering their invincible *Tertias* within striking distance of her shores, notoriously with the intention of landing them there at the first convenient opportunity, did it even occur to her to provide herself with a similarly trained force of regulars. What sort of a show the enthusiastic militia assembled in the camp at Tilbury could have put up against the professional army that it was the task of the invincible Armada to convoy across the few miles of water that separated it from the Kentish coast was, thanks to the sea power that had been England's salvation ever since the Conquest, never put to the test. And yet even sea power had to be maintained, as best it might, subject to the same overriding necessity of making do on the wholly insufficient resources at the disposal of the Crown.

That maintained it was when the supreme crisis, after thirty years' successful postponement, could no longer be averted, was an achievement so amazing in itself and so momentous in its effects on a long-term reckoning, that it seems almost ungenerous to point out the inevitable limitations that on a short-term reckoning robbed the defeat of the Armada of the consequences that might reasonably, from the English point of view, have been expected to ensue from it. The supreme fact of England's immunity from invasion, now of over five centuries' standing, had indeed received its most dramatic confirmation, though even so King Philip was by no means inclined to accept this setback as a final decision. But when it became a question of passing over from the defensive to the offensive, it soon became apparent that England had not the military power behind her punch to enforce a decision on her own behalf—nor could have, without losing her distinctively English soul.

This was what Elizabeth, in the depths of her own Tudor soul, realized as none of her subsequent critics, and few even of her professed admirers, have succeeded in doing. For good or otherwise, England had embarked on a course of unqualified political and spiritual independence that, by taking her right out of the family of European nations, cut her off from membership of any wider union, political or spiritual. And it equally caused her to shun, to the best of her ability, participation in the bloody anarchy of power politics and religious conflict which the nations of the Continent seemed doomed to endure, until some one of them, on the Roman precedent, should wax strong enough to impose its imperial peace and sovereignty upon all the rest, but from which England, so long as she could keep her shores inviolate, might hope to insulate herself.

But such a policy of non-involvement, pursued to the limit, is almost equally bound to be one of non-aggression, especially when it is conditioned by the necessity of keeping expenditure down to a peace-time minimum. There was not the least question of England reverting to such a course of adventure on the mainland as she had pursued in the late Middle Ages, and any idea of her playing a dominating role in that power competition from which she was seeking to detach herself was ruled out in advance. England could not have it both ways. Elizabeth, with the backing of her Cecil advisers, was too clear-headed to be swayed by the voices of those brilliant or specious thrusters who were constantly at hand to urge her to take a strong line in this, that or the other field of policy. But the leading lady of England understood her part too well to double it with that of war lady until she was positively forced to assume it, and she had even less desire to supplement her royal crown with an imperial diadem.

Which brings us to the second, and more insidious, of the fallacious assumptions in vogue about the Elizabethan age, and one that is largely coming to supersede that of the Queen as a crusader for Protestantism. It is to the effect that the most significant achievement of Elizabeth and her Government was to have laid the foundations of the British Empire by fostering the beginnings of imperial expansion.

Nothing can be more directly the reverse of the truth. No régime was ever less imperialistic either in spirit or practice. It was just here that the English concept of civilization had come to stand in greatest contrast with that bequeathed by Rome to the nations of the Continent—that which envisaged the Head of the State as gathering all the threads of power into his own hands, making his will his law, and imposing it with a sway more or less benevolent over as wide an area as possible. Such was the idea that had gained almost unchallenged acceptance among the States, great and petty, of the Continent, whose Sovereigns were engaged in setting up as divine Caesars to the limits of their capacity and resources. And where these were great enough to permit of expansion overseas, as most notably of all in the case of Spain, their realms blossomed into genuine empires in the full Roman sense of the word.

But nothing could have been further from the desire of Elizabeth than to harbour such ambitions for herself or her realm. Her inherited wisdom was enough to warn her off anything so contrary to the grain of English sentiment as the imperial idea in any guise whatever.[1] For a virgin goddess her subjects might willingly fall, but anything resembling a divine Caesar, male or female, they were not prepared to stand. And rather than arm the Head of the State with the necessary means of becoming one, or foot the bill for such a purpose, they would go to all lengths, and incur all risks, even of foreign conquest. For that was what it plainly amounted to.

In any of the sovereignties of the mainland such a determination, pushed to the verge of unilateral military disarmament, would have been suicidal. But so long as England could count on retaining control of her sea approaches—though how long would that be?—there would be at least a chance of her preserving uncut the frayed lifeline of her independent existence. On that chance Elizabeth had no hesitation in gambling. She made not the least attempt to arm herself with a power capable of answering, in its own terms, the only too obvious challenge from overseas. She continued to cut down expenditure on defence to a peace-time minimum, and exhaust every device of procrastination and evasion to prolong the double labour of appeasing her enemies abroad and her subjects at home. And in default of

---

[1] It was his failure to understand this that caused Froude, a hundred-per-cent imperialist, to be perpetually nagging at Elizabeth, of the first principle of whose Tudor statecraft he seems not to have had the faintest inkling.

asserting the national will to power in the time-honoured imperial fashion, she maintained, as long as she could, an attitude of ostensible non-belligerence, keeping up a masquerade of friendly relationship in which her good brother and brother-in-law, Philip, was prepared, for his own reasons, to play his part—so long, at any rate, as he could make his game on the expectation of Elizabeth's failing to survive her Catholic and captive cousin, and presumptive heiress, Mary of Scotland, a failure that he and his Church would stick at no means to expedite. Both parties were, in fact, playing for time, Elizabeth from necessity and Philip not only by temperament, but from a rational calculation that the time factor was at least three quarters on his side.

His Catholic Majesty was an imperialist through and through, a Caesar in everything but name, and the Spanish Empire,[1] already far more extensive than any that the classical Caesars had dreamed of, was an *imperium* in the most unqualified sense, of being to the remotest fringes of its vast circumference controlled from the centre at Madrid or El Escorial. And to this Empire of the New World that of the Old might soon be added—so far, at any rate, as Christian Europe was concerned. Indeed the way might be considered clear to such a consummation,[2] provided only that the chief limiting obstacle, constituted by the persistence of this intractable island power on the flank of King Philip's sea communications, could be removed.

This his sluggish but formidable mentality was fully capable of apprehending. What he was less capable of realizing was that he was confronted with a phenomenon radically different in kind from anything with which he or previous aspirants after empire had had to reckon: not merely a rival power in a competition for empire, but— though hardly more than in embryo—a new order of civilization, inspired by the direct opposite of the imperial principle.

Elizabeth, unlike Philip, had not the least wish to rule other peoples with her sway, or even to impose a pattern of life on her own people; it was as the visible embodiment of their own will that she strove to put herself, as England's virgin Gloriana, across the footlights. It was for their liberties and not for her own power to ride her will roughshod over them after the manner of her fellow Sovereigns that she elected to stand; and to anyone hardy enough to assert that this was after all a stage pose, it can be replied that it was a pose so consistently maintained and lived up to as to be practically indistinguishable from the reality.

'Let tyrants fear' was what she said in the hour of greatest crisis— and it was the constant note that she struck throughout her reign—'I

---

[1] Particularly after the annexation, in 1581, of Portugal and her empire.
[2] Even if, for the nonce, the *imperium* might have to be shared between two Caesars of the House of Hapsburg, an arrangement for which there was sufficient Roman precedent.

have always so behaved myself that under God I have placed my chiefest strength and safeguard in the loyal hearts and goodwill of my people.'

And in fact she played up to this precept of trusting her people to an extent that would have been suicidal in any realm less fortunately circumstanced. It was not that public opinion would have stood for any relaxation of Tudor firmness in enforcing the reign of law, the Common Law that was part of a common heritage, and that the common Englishman cherished as the safeguard of his liberties. A short way with even the potentiality of treason—as short as her father's—was what he expected and even demanded of his Sovereign; and not from any sectarian motive, but as a matter of simple expediency, he would support her in taking no chances with priests, Jesuits or even captive royalty, who might be suspected, under the cloak of religion, of undermining the security of the State.

On the home front, then, there was no question of shortening the arm of the Queen's Government.| It was only where foreign and defence policy was concerned that she found herself hamstrung and handicapped at every turn by the unwillingness of her subjects to trust their own Sovereign with money in her coffers or arms in her hands, such as might conceivably be employed in setting the power of the Crown above that of the law, at a time when Rome and Philip, with the armies of half Europe and the wealth of the Indies to dispose of, were notoriously biding their time for the conquest and enslavement of the recalcitrant island.

Thus deliberately skimped and starved of the power to make head against this overwhelming combination, Elizabeth and her advisers faced up to the situation in a spirit of cheerful realism. Even her loyal subjects could not have it both ways, and in so far as they grudged her the means of providing for their common salvation, it was plainly up to them to shoulder the burden from their own individual resources and in their own way. This amounted to pitting an anarchic individualism against the disciplined might of empire, in an undeclared war that, though formally disowned by constituted authority, set loose a host of adventurers, ranging from such inspired enthusiasts as Drake at one end of the scale to pirates ruffianly and unashamed at the other, to serve the double purpose of filling their own pockets and draining the resources of imperial Spain.

This is not the place to repeat a story that has been told so often. Here it is only necessary to emphasize that far from laying the foundations, in any conceivable sense, of a British empire, the Elizabethan way was to counter the imperial idea by a spirit not only its direct opposite, but one of specifically native origin. To say that it was the spirit of English freedom at war with that of Spanish or Roman despotism would be putting it too baldly; but rightly understood, it would be no less than the truth. But it does not follow that the first-fruits of this spirit were of a uniformly edifying order.

No doubt a fire of the noblest patriotism was blended with an enthusiasm genuinely religious in the breasts of very many of these indomitable heroes, but there were few, if any of them, who were not in their respective ventures primarily for what they hoped to get out of them, and few indeed who were inhibited by any scruples in their way of getting it. The most important of their voyages were capitalized on a joint stock basis in which not only the wealthiest magnates but, on occasion, the Queen herself, did not disdain to acquire a stake. The principle of every man for the main chance and devil take the hind-most might, when given unlimited scope, be productive of the most amazing triumphs of courage and initiative, but it was not, on the face of it, calculated to engender such self-effacing co-ordination as the discipline of a competently run imperial system.

Nor did it. Elizabethan individualism had its weak as well as its strong side. The liberty that was its driving power only too easily ran to licence. The most supermanly of its adventurers were erratic and self-willed to a degree calculated to imperil the success of any com-bined enterprise in the common cause. Even the supreme national effort against the Armada was not exempt from this handicap. For the Armada, with all its defects, was at least, on its voyage in close forma-tion up the Channel, more of a united fleet, continuously responsive to the control of its commander, than the fleet that outgunned, outsailed, and outfought it, but whose most renowned captains, and even supreme commander, were liable at the most critical junctures to quit station to fulfil their own chivalrous or even predatory instincts, and who, like Frobisher and Drake, were not above marring what ought to have been a united team spirit by unbrotherly wrangling. No one indeed could ever have described the chiefs of any Elizabethan joint operation on land or sea as a band of brothers, and this alone would be enough to account for the disappointing outcome of so many promising enterprises.

There is no need to melodramatize the conflict between the time-honoured power complex of imperial civilization and this new intran-sigence of freedom that, though unformulated and less than half realized, animated the English resistance to it. Whatever the future might hold in store, it would have taken an incurably biased contem-porary observer to have regarded it as a sort of Ormazd-Ahriman duel in which the forces of light were at variance with those of darkness.

Here we shall be best advised to record the simple fact that the imperialism that was taken for granted as the be-all and end-all of political aspiration among the Sovereigns of the European mainland had come up, in England, against a wholly unprecedented and incompatible phenomenon, a polity that did not even aspire after imperial status, whose methods and aims were fundamentally opposed to those that were Caesar's. The discipline of Spanish-Roman imperialism had set itself to crush the nascent spirit of English anti-imperialism, and signally failed to do so. What was decided in the defeat of the Armada off Gravelines, a battle incomparably more decisive than that of Trafalgar, was not the triumph of a British empire, actual or potential, over its Spanish opposite, but simply that a British non-empire or anti-empire had come into existence, and had come to stay.

That was the secret that had been intuitively grasped by the Tudor Queen and her government, and inspired their technique of husbanding the country's resources by rationing war-time expenditure to a peace-time minimum, and avoiding open hostilities with England's continental neighbours by hook or by crook, until the island had built up its strength to a degree sufficient, though as yet no more than just sufficient, to ensure its unconditional political and spiritual emancipation from the powers of the mainland. No super-national combination would force her into its orbit. No power but her own should have the shaping of her destiny. But to go beyond that and impose her power on other peoples was a wholly different and, as it soon appeared, impracticable proposition.

Neither the men nor the means were available for a policy of imperial expansion, either on the European mainland or in the New World; nor, in the most responsible quarters, was there the remotest inclination for it, though there were never lacking spectacular personages about court to press for equally spectacular lines of action. But it was not to the Leicesters, the Essexes and the Raleighs that the Queen confided the shaping of her policy, and the Cecil administration never swerved from what in a later age would have been stigmatized as one of uncompromising isolationism and Little-Englandism.

Even the opportunity of adding the Dutch provinces to her dominions at their own request was a bait for which Elizabeth refused to rise—she doled out just enough grudging help, and no more, to suffice to keep Philip's Dutch ulcer in a distracting state of malignancy, without involving England more than was absolutely necessary in military commitments on the Continent, or prejudicing the chances of an early settlement with Spain. It was a policy calculated to madden hundred-per-cent imperialists like Raleigh, who believed that by throwing all her resources into an all-out offensive it would be possible to bring the unwieldy fabric of the Spanish Empire crashing in ruin, and to plant an English empire in its stead. There was nothing chimerical in the project from a purely military standpoint, but its pursuit would have involved a political *volte face* that would have precipitated a domestic revolution. The last thing for which Parliament or people would have been prepared to stump up would have been a policy that, even if successful, would have brought the English monarchy into line with the despotisms of the Continent, and put the whole trend of national development violently into reverse. England had no use for an empire because England had no use for a Caesar, even of the female sex, and no one knew this better than Elizabeth herself, who continued to wage open, as she had undeclared, war, on the limited liability principle and without taking any steps to provide herself with its military sinews.

The result was what might have been expected by anyone not sanguine enough to imagine that it is possible for a nation to keep its own soul as well as gain a world empire. Elizabethan England did succeed in the former, but failed in the remotest approach to the latter objective. The climax of the invasion was followed by the long frustrating anticlimax of a war that went on and on, without the faintest chance of a decision, until both of its sovereign protagonists were in the grave, and it petered out by mutual exhaustion, with the Spanish Empire still formally intact and an English empire—except for a few fishermen's huts on the shores of Newfoundland—not even started as a going concern, the attempt to plant a colony on the North American seaboard at Virginia having proved a fiasco. As an imperial power England had not even begun to exist, and as a military power she was negligible; but in rather more than compensation she had kept not only her freedom from foreign coercion but her own domestic liberties, in a way that the sovereignties, great and petty, of the Continent had signally failed to do.

C

5

EXPANSION
WITHOUT EMPIRE

THE ACCESSION of the House of Stuart may be taken as the starting point for the history of British expansion overseas. But to lump together the results of this expansion under the collective designation of the British Empire—which is the usual practice—is to rob an invaluable word of its hitherto accepted content. An empire without an emperor is certainly conceivable, in the sense in which we might talk of an Athenian or Venetian empire, but an empire that omits to imperialize is no empire at all. The Vergilian touchstone, *regere imperio populos*—to rule the peoples with its sway—holds good for the Roman and pre-Roman empires of antiquity, and the Spanish, French, and even the Dutch and Portuguese empires of the modern [1] age. But a British empire? That remains to be seen.

One might be tempted to characterize Britain as the latest starter in the imperial handicap. But that would have been to assume that she was ever a starter at all. We can talk of conquering an empire, or of building an empire—but hardly of an empire just happening, without any significant foresight or assistance on the part of the State or Sovereign. And yet, by and large, this is just how British expansion overseas did happen in the formative epoch before the colonial wars of the eighteenth century, and as, given the unique physical and spiritual circumstances, one can almost say it was bound to happen.

Provided only that Britain was able to maintain the sea power that was the indispensable guarantee of her freedom, the overflow of her vigorous, growing and largely seafaring populace into the virgin territory overseas could hardly have been prevented, in one form or another. It was merely a question of what form it would take, and whether it would be a planned and directed effort, under state supervision, or the spontaneous product of individual energies forcing their own explosive outlet.

[1] Modern—in the sense of post-medieval.

Now in Britain, by virtue of her insular self-sufficiency, state action was rationed to a minimum that would have been inconceivable in any of her continental rivals. With them it was a life-and-death necessity to strengthen to the utmost possible extent the hands of the sovereign power that was their only defence against subjugation and conquest, in a perpetual anarchic struggle for national survival. But in the ordinary Englishman's consciousness the danger of invasion, in normal times, had almost ceased to count. He had been free from it for so many generations that he had got into the habit of sleeping quietly in his bed, so far at any rate as visions of an invading army were concerned. And in consequence he was less concerned with strengthening the hands of his Sovereign to protect his liberties, than with binding them from infringing them. He would keep him in a state of military impotence, and ration him to the barest necessary minimum—if that—of peace-time expenditure. And even when, as at the time of the Armada, invasion was actually threatened, he was still only ready to dole out funds for his own defence like water from a squeezed sponge—a fact that Elizabeth and her advisers understood a good deal better than some of their latter-day critics.

Such an attitude was flatly prohibitive of state-sponsored imperialism in any form whatever. That classic definition of imperial functioning, *regere imperio populos*, postulates the imposition of power by compulsion. It is in the imperative mood that Caesar is bound to express himself. But a Caesar without man-power or money-power to implement his will is no Caesar at all, and it was just the unique feature of the English constitutional set-up that for both of these powers the executive organ was dependent on the legislative—or in plainer English, the monarch had to come hat in hand to a Parliament that was more and more openly determined to starve him of both. To cry for a British empire in these circumstances was to cry for the moon.

But there are other ways of expansion than the imperial one. The Elizabethans had already shown how much could be achieved by individual adventurers, or combinations of them, with the state refraining from any overt participation, though continuing within very elastic limits to act in a supervisory or restraining capacity and not disdaining to acquire a stake of its own in certain of the ventures. But in Elizabeth's time none of these had been on a scale big enough to bear fruit in colonial, let alone imperial expansion, except of the most ephemeral description. Attempts to plant a colony of Virginia on the North American mainland, though sponsored by no less a genius than that of Raleigh, had at the time of Elizabeth's death resulted in evacuation by one relay of colonists and the disappearance without trace of a second, though time was to prove that the plan had been soundly conceived, which was more than could be said of the numerous attempts to open up a north-west, or even a north-east passage to China, or of Raleigh's mirage of fairy gold by the banks of the Orinoco.

It would have taken a singularly clairvoyant observer to divine in the England to which James I succeeded the promise of overseas expansion in any form whatever, least of all under a Sovereign who possessed neither the means nor the ambition to enter into competition of this sort with rival sovereignties. And up to that date it might have seemed as if the unco-ordinated efforts of privately sponsored enterprise lacked the force or persistence to effect anything lasting, without such material backing as all genuine imperial powers were ready to give as a matter of course.

And yet even thus early conditions were set that were bound in the long run, if Britain were only to prove capable of profiting by them, to give her a winning advantage over these others. For in turning her back on the Old World she had come to face outward to those new lands of undreamed-of opportunity, along the paths by which she could radiate freely under the protection of her sea power. And if her Sovereigns had other tasks more urgent to occupy their energies than that of empire building, her people more than made up for it by their far greater measure, compared with others, of expansive potentiality. Centuries of constitutional development on principles exactly the reverse of those consecrated by Roman Law had engendered in the English habits of self-help that had blossomed out in the wild exuberance of Elizabethan individualism. They did not look instinctively to the State to take the initiative in or take over the controls of even their most ambitious undertakings. Given the maximum of liberty from governmental and above all foreign interference, they were fully capable of setting forth to any of the still unappropriated fields of expansion and striking root there.

The factors that had inhibited the Elizabethan adventurers from doing this were steadily weakening in the new century. The claims of imperial Spain to an absolute monopoly of the New World, though never formally relaxed, were becoming more and more of a dead letter outside the area of her effective occupation, and beyond these limits still stretched a vast no man's land that included the greater part of the North American continent, which was to prove the most favourable area of all for white colonization, but of which Spain, with all the New World to pick and choose from, had so far not troubled to possess herself.

For we must remember that the value of overseas possessions for imperial Spain was not, primarily, as a field for colonization, but as a source of wealth—and wealth most preferably of all in the form of the precious metals and, next to these, such tropical products as could be shipped and sold on the most lucrative terms in the European markets.

And since the fecundity of the soil in such commodities was in almost inverse proportion to its suitability for permanent settlement by men of European stock, it may perhaps be accounted as a blessing in disguise for England that she started in the race for colonies so handicapped by the lack of state support for her efforts that most of the more obvious plums had been snapped up by her rivals before she really began to get under way.

Other competitors were beginning to enter the field, and in particular the newly formed Republic of the United Netherlands, whose amazingly swift and brilliant efflorescence put it in the leading rank of maritime and commercial Powers, and bade fair to eclipse Britain's utmost achievements in both these capacities. Nothing but an almost superhuman toughness and drive, engendered in the desperate struggle for independence against Spain, could have enabled this small nation, or rather federation of provinces, to plant its dominions far and wide in the two hemispheres wherever the richest opportunities presented themselves. For with the Dutch there was no alternative. Their own flat and niggardly soil was not capable of sustaining the swelling poulations of their newly planted cities. A trading empire, with a sea power equal to maintaining its communications, was the only apparent solution to their problem, and they did not shirk the challenge. Britain was faced with a similar challenge, but fate had dealt the cards more kindly to her. Her sea power was capable of affording her complete protection—Holland's was not. The Dutch had an open land frontier to defend against far more powerful military neighbours, and even if they could hold them at bay, the effort must needs put an intolerable strain on energies that were already sufficiently taxed in overseas enterprise. And even Dutch sea power was liable to be hamstrung by the way in which Britain was spread out on the flank of her communications, a fact that would be bound to tell as decisively against Holland in the event of hostilities supervening between these two Protestant allies of the Elizabethan age, as it was against Germany three centuries later. Long before Britain became an unsinkable aircraft carrier she had been an unsinkable blockader.

Holland entered the competition for overseas possessions well in advance of Britain, and with an organized efficiency that was conspicuously lacking in the undisciplined heroics of the Elizabethan and Jacobean men of action. A Dutch admiral succeeded in carrying off the supreme prize of war that had persistently eluded the English, in the shape of a complete Spanish treasure fleet. It seemed as if these indomitable seamen had only got to single out the most profitable sites of the Eastern and Western hemsipheres in order to appropriate them; or, where conquest was out of the question, to establish trading monopolies. They were as ruthless in the pursuit of the main chance, and as totally lacking in scruple, as ever the Carthaginians had been in the ancient world, and so lacking in dignity as to be ready to kowtow and abase themselves in the presence of oriental potentates where it was a question of turning an honest, or even a dishonest, guilder. The 'no money, no grovel' of Pooh-Bah would perfectly have defined their attitude. Finally, as some of their English competitors were to find to their cost, no religious or humanitarian inhibitions would debar them from eliminating competition in their chosen preserves. Supremely and unconditionally, business, with them, was business.

But in their heyday, which we may roughly take as covering the first half, or perhaps three-quarters, of the seventeenth century, they did succeed in delivering to themselves the goods, in fabulous quantity. Fully convinced that their national existence depended on trade, they made trade the basis of a life of such overflowing opulence, while it lasted, that no other nation on earth could produce anything to compare with it.

In what sense can we talk of a Dutch empire or of Holland as an imperial Power? Naturally not in the full-blooded Roman sense which postulates an *imperator* or Caesar imposing his will over the circle of his dominion—a sense that would hold good for the great despotisms of antiquity. But there is a cognate sense in which we can talk of an Athenian, or Carthaginian, or Venetian empire, in which the part of Caesar is played by some sovereign body more or less genuinely impersonal. The real test is in the way it functions—empire is as empire does.

Judged by that test we can place the Dutch dominion in a class somewhere between the Roman Empire and the British non-empire— call it, perhaps, a commercial empire. The extraordinarily able series of princes of the House of Orange, though that House was destined to outlast all its European rivals, were at best never in anything corresponding to the position of the ordinary continental Sovereigns—they were like managing directors of a flourishing business concern, kept in more or less tight leading-strings, and at one time dispensed with altogether. Even the style of United Netherlands was to a certain extent a misnomer. For big business, in the shape of the moneyed oligarchs of Amsterdam, had often a greater say in the actual running of the concern than either the nominal director or all the six other provinces combined. This is not the way of empire; but then on the other hand few Caesars have wielded a more despotic sway than the central Dutch authority over its possessions overseas, a fact that largely accounts for the failure of the Dutch to make good their conquest of the great Portuguese province of Brazil, where the enlightened efforts of their governor on the spot, Prince João Maurice, to win the goodwill of the original colonists, were contemptuously swept aside by the greedy directorate of the Dutch West India Company.

But the fact is that the Dutch were not out for expansion, but for profit pure and simple. They were not a colonizing folk, looking for homes overseas, but for trading posts, for plantations and other quick-yielding fields of exploitation, human no less than material; though in their settlement planted at the Cape of Good Hope for the purpose of serving as a port of call for Dutch shipping on the way to the East, they did achieve the unforeseen and unintended result of planting the seeds of a national community that, at the present time, asserts a precarious and it may be tragic dominion over the southern part of the African continent. But no such development was dreamed of in the palmy days of Dutch efflorescence, or for two centuries after. It remains broadly true to say that the Dutch trade empire, so far as we can describe it by that name, signally failed to develop into a colonial empire, or a colonial Power in any sense whatever. Holland, with the small population and area of her utterly insecure European base, was even less capable than Portugal had been of more than strictly commercial expansion. Even when she had acquired such prizes as Brazil, and what was then called New Holland but is now New York, she could not find the manpower to hold them—nor perhaps even the will. For with her feverish, but necessary, obsession with trade, quick returns were what she had to go for, and these do not come from the long-term, gradual process of colonial expansion.

It may perhaps be said that there was little enough to choose between the English and the Dutch in their concentration on the main chance, except that the Dutch in these early days pursued it with more success; and in so far as a significant part of English emigration overseas was undertaken not in the service of Mammon but of God. Apart from this, however, it might fairly be said that the planting of British communities overseas, when they did at long last begin to get a precarious footing, was organized and financed by way of commercial speculation, often of a highly dubious character. In Elizabeth's time the failure of such enterprises to establish themselves on a permanent footing had been mainly due to the fact that such joint stockholders as clubbed together for particular enterprises seldom, if ever, commanded the capital resources adequate to the establishment of colonies, or even permanent trading posts. And the monarchy, though it might do its best to encourage or regulate these activities, was itself in too needy a condition to remedy the deficiency.

Not so the Dutch who, fully conscious that with them it was a question of trade or perish, put the resources even of their imperfectly cemented state behind their commercial expansion. Thus the Dutch East India Company, which was almost entitled to rank as a state enterprise, started off, in 1602, with a capital of no less than the then equivalent of £540,000, while its English opposite number, which had been incorporated two years previously, had to make do with a beggarly £30,000.[1] It is therefore in no way surprising that in the first quarter of the seventeenth century the Dutch should have practically cleared their English competitors out of the coveted spice islands of the East Indies, with the paradoxical result that the English were driven to try for such pickings as they could get on the mainland of the Indian Peninsula, by favour of the Great Mogul. They little realized what was destined to grow out of these humble beginnings.

Thus we find a state-sponsored purposefulness in the Dutch expansive activities that was conspicuously lacking in their British counterpart. And this still more applies to the other European Power that was now coming into the colonial competition. France, like Britain and Holland, relied at first on the expedient of chartered trading companies for her expansion; but the instinct of imperialism pure and simple had been implanted in this most Romanized of all the classic provinces, and during the seventeenth century it was carried to its logical completion under the auspices of the two great Cardinals and finally of that quintessential type of divine Caesardom, Louis XIV. The French colonists who fastened on to the islands and mainland of the North American continent had no desire for, or idea of setting up independent house for themselves. Quite as much as their fellow Latins of the Iberian Peninsula, they looked to their European Sovereign to govern their destinies, by ruling them with his sway through his proconsular emissaries in the authentic Caesarian way. If there was going to be French expansion on a world-wide scale, then beyond all shadow of doubt the result would be an empire in the full imperial sense—a new Rome, or, if possible, super-Rome.

Such would have been the conclusion even thus early of any observer capable of plumbing the depths of national psychology and reading the signs of the times. Such an inconceivably gifted intelligence would have needed no foreknowledge of the then future to divine that by no possibility would, or indeed could, British expansion ever take place on these lines. Just as any sort of Greater France was bound to take the form of a French empire, so it could be predicted with equal certainty that there would never be, in anything like the same sense, a British Empire. Nor even, for that matter, anything so closely partaking of the nature of empire as the trading dominion of the United Provinces.

It would be a next to hopeless undertaking to furnish an account that would make dramatically intelligible sense of the unfolding plot of British expansion. There is indeed no apparent thread on which such a plot could be strung. It followed no coherent plan—one can best say of it that it happened because it was ripe to happen, and happened in

[1] *Cambridge Modern History*, IV. 232.

all sorts of different ways. It is only in the light of subsequent developments that we can see all these disconnected events beginning to fit
themselves into a pattern of their own that even after the passing
of so many generations posterity is but imperfectly beginning to
apprehend.

When we say that Britain—or more specifically England—was ripe
to expand, at the beginning of the seventeenth century, we have in
mind a convergence of apparently disconnected factors, but each the
outcome of those special conditions which, as it has been the object of
the preceding pages to demonstrate, resulted in England breaking
loose from effective membership of any civilization wider than her own.
For what we speak of as a civilization is by definition super-national.
An insular civilization is a plain contradiction in terms. If England
were to make good her implied challenge to the old civilization, she
must, in one way or another, succeed in evolving a new communion
or commonwealth of peoples, inspired by her own new-born and itself
evolving concept of civilized existence.

It would be ridiculous to pretend that any of the actual pioneers of
British expansion were consciously inspired by such visionary notions.
Most of them were very much more down to earth. But the hand of
destiny was upon them, guiding them to ends that were not theirs. The
mere fact of Britain becoming a demilitarized but at the same time an
invasion-proof island had a logic of its own. Speaking very broadly we
may say that in comparison with European Powers it greatly increased
her expansive potentiality. Whereas something like half of *their*
energies had to be devoted to the business of keeping up (not to
speak of using) great military establishments, Britain, after satisfying
—and that grudgingly—the modest requirements of her fleet, was free
to allow her resources to accumulate at home, and for the most part
in the coffers of individuals, since it was both in the will and power of
these propertied individuals to keep the State, as represented by the
Sovereign, on a starvation ration.

The effect of this was inevitable, and except for its being flatly
incompatible with established mythology, should have been obvious.
Though one hesitates to employ a word that itself has become so
notoriously a reaction stimulus, one can best put it by saying that, in
comparison with the militarist Powers of the Continent, it had the
effect of imparting an increasingly capitalist complexion to the social
order in Britain.

For capital is merely wealth that, instead of being consumed as
soon as it is got, is retained by its owners either, as in the parable of
the talents, in order to fructify and produce more wealth in the future,
or simply wrapped up in a napkin in the form of savings. And it will
easily be seen that the greater the proportion of wealth that a country

* C

can afford to hold back in this way, the stronger and more expansive will be its economy, even if this wealth is distributed in a number of private hands, and is not, as in the ultra-capitalism of latter-day Marxian economy, concentrated in the hands of an all-powerful state, or of the one or more individuals who, for practical purposes, constitute the state.

No nation or empire can eat its cake and have it, and the more it consumes of its wealth the less there will be left to fructify as capital. And in the Europe of the seventeenth century, torn asunder as it was by wars of which the alleged religious motive became a more and more transparent camouflage for anarchic mass-egotism, there was small chance for wealth to fructify in private or any other hands. As in ancient Rome, the State or Sovereign became a gigantic vampire, sucking up the lifeblood of the people. It was one of those simple facts that, even though the course of history is determined by them, hit nobody in the eye. And yet the state of Spain after the wars of her most Catholic, or of France after those of her most Christian, Kings, and still more that of the Nordic or Central European combatants in the all-against-all killing match of this most unhappy century, ought to have been enough to convince anybody of the futility of trying to get rich on a diet of glory. A capitalist economy, whether you like it or not, does not have a chance to get started in such circumstances. And ill fares the land, on a strictly economic reckoning, where wealth does *not* get a chance to accumulate.

It was just in this particular respect that Britain's peculiar circumstances gave her a winning advantage. She had next to no army to keep up, and such wars as she did wage were of that maritime kind of which, as Bacon truly remarked, she was able to take as much or as little as she chose. And instead of the Sovereign being in a position to bleed his subjects white, in parliamentary England it was just the other way about. And consequently, in England, wealth was bound to accumulate at a much greater rate than it did anywhere on the Continent, except perhaps for a time in Holland. But precisely because Holland did not enjoy the advantages that nature had conferred on England, that time was not destined to be long.

An economy of this kind offers no theme for panegyrics. Wealth, though a means to not a few desirable ends, is hardly to be described as an end in itself except by those who push avarice beyond the bounds of sanity; least of all when it tends to become concentrated in the hands of a minority, who themselves are determined to take full advantage of the power it confers to seize in their own interests. But whatever may be our final verdict on these men and this system, we have got to face the fact that capital does possess an expansive force of its own, and is the master stimulus not only of overseas trade, but also of colonization, which could not thrive at all without its backing. And it is the nature of capital to be continually seeking new and profitable fields for its own exploitation.

This progressive accumulation of wealth and the unevenness of its distribution was certainly *a*, and not impossibly *the*, determining influence in both the domestic conflicts and the overseas expansion of Britain during the first half of the seventeenth century. To say that the Great Rebellion, and its parliamentary prelude, boil down to a conflict between the old merry and the new moneyed England would be too rhetorically sweeping, though it may come as near to hitting off the essential truth as any such brief statement could. But it is not with the domestic situation that we are more than indirectly concerned in these pages. What we have to consider is the way in which the injection—if we may put it that way—of capital into the social system acted not only inwardly as a stimulant of revolutionary upheaval, but also outwardly as an expansive force driving men to radiate outwards along the sea paths, to plant communities on any still-unoccupied territories of the New World.

This had proved beyond the capacity of the Elizabethans, because the Queen would not, and her subjects could not, supply the financial backing needed to carry them beyond the particular voyage, ending with its return to port and share-out of the profits, to the permanent trade post or colony whose profits, though they might be delayed, would be in the nature of a perennially fructifying investment. It was not that the Elizabethans had lacked the idea of doing this, but that none of their efforts in this direction had taken root. Even the most hopeful project of all, that of establishing a colony on the North American seaboard, had, it will be remembered, petered out miserably, bequeathing only its name, Virginia, to inspire subsequent and more successful efforts in the post-Elizabethan age.

For the time was coming when such precariously planted communities of British settlers would no longer be doomed to extinction, though in the first stages only a very few of the toughest of the pioneer founders would stand the least chance of survival. Such grim statistics as we have of these first experiments in colonization would suggest that this form of activity carried about the highest occupational risks on human record. But this was a consideration hardly calculated to cause undue anxiety to the wealthy promoters who adventured their capital in the business, but only quite exceptionally their skins.

This is not the place to tell, even in outline, the complicated but always thrilling story of the beginnings of what is commonly described as the British Empire. Not that it would be too easy a story to tell, for it has none of the purposeful unity that characterized the expansive activities of the Iberian monarchies, of France, or even of the loosely United Provinces of the Netherlands, which, being frankly out for whatever they could get in the way of territory or trade, and determined to employ all necessary means to get it, were in the fullest sense imperialist.

But that was just where they differed from the British monarchy and its Government. This was not for any lack of sympathy with their subjects overseas—the attitude of the Stuarts, and particularly of Charles I, towards the colonies, was one of consistent benevolence—but simply from lack of means. Even if, in their condition of chronic semi-bankruptcy, they had been able to run to the luxury of an imperial or even expansive policy, they would have had things of more immediate urgency to monopolize their attention. The domestic conflict was so plainly working up to a revolutionary crisis as to absorb most men's attention almost to the exclusion of foreign and wholly of colonial matters. Consequently there could be little choice but to suffer overseas expansion, if any, to develop on its own lines.

But that was not enough to stop it happening. Capital was piling up all the time, and needing outlets for profitable investment. The technique of joint stock enterprise, that was in course of rapid and extremely flexible development, could be readily applied to the exploitation of any territories or trade routes that offered the prospect of increasing returns in a not too distant future.

Offered—but to whom? To Caesar? For in genuine empires this is what may be assumed to take place. Not even the Pharisees and Herodians dared dispute that the image and superscription on the tribute money put it in the category of things that are Caesar's. And the tribute of the Indies, that came in the Spanish treasure fleets, bearing, or destined to bear, King Philip's image and superscription, might fairly be classed among the things that were Philip's. But though King James's image, or King Charles's, might be stamped on their coins, neither of them was a penny the better for the expansion of their realm overseas, though this was precisely the bait that a genuine imperialist like Raleigh could hold out to his Sovereign. The whole idea of his last expedition was to open up a source of wealth that would relieve the Crown of the necessity of applying to Parliament to balance its account—a prospectus on whose soundness the royal bargainer was ready to allow the promoter to stake his already forfeited head.

But the Stuarts were no Caesars—quite the reverse. For it was their tragedy that while their subjects, or a fortunate minority of them, were piling up wealth at an unprecedented rate, the monarchy was sliding faster and faster into bankruptcy, which its faithful Commons were all out to precipitate by docking it even of such traditional sources of revenue as might just enable it to scrape along on a peace-time basis.

In these circumstances there could be no question of a State-sponsored policy of colonial expansion. The utmost that the King could do was by way of trying to regulate such expansion as did take place, and even here his powers were in practice more apparent than real. There was never the least question of his imposing his imperial will on his subjects overseas, who for their part were not in the least inclined to dispute an authority by which they were not seriously inconvenienced, and with whose protective offices they did not as yet feel themselves in a position to dispense.

Expansion thus came about not because it was willed but because, in the existing circumstances, it was bound to happen. The section of the community at home that, economically and politically, was making the pace, was that capitalist minority to which I have already referred, whose newly acquired money power was more and more coming to overbalance the equilibrium of the social system, and which numbered among its ranks the heads of those aristocratic houses whose rise dated from the grand share-out of Church property in the Reformation, and who, in consequence, tended to form a sort of left-wing pluto-puritan spearhead of opposition to Church and Crown.

It was this new money power—not all of it as yet directed into revolutionary courses—that provided the sinews of both colonial and trade expansion, no less than of civil war. For it is a gross but seemingly impregnable fallacy that persists in regarding the revolutionary protagonists in the great constitutional drama of the time as if they were simple folk to the point of *naïveté*—honest idealists even in their errors, and incapable of double talk or sharp practice, still less of making their political or religious professions a smoke-screen for cunningly organized conspiracy in pursuit of their own individual or common advantage.

And yet if we turn from the field of domestic politics to that of overseas expansion we shall be presented with a background pattern of adventurers, as they were then called, sitting pretty at home, while a different sort of adventurers set forth overseas to suffer in their own proper persons incredible hardships, and more often than not to perish miserably, but if all went according to plan to reward the enterprise of the promoters with an answerable profit It was all in the recognized way of business. Capitalist investors, who found their pockets bulging with money that they preferred to use in making more money, were performing a highly necessary service and might fairly expect to have it made worth their while. They might even have put in a claim to be esteemed the original founders of the Empire, so far as the results of British expansion may be lumped together under that more than questionable designation.

The picturesque and heroic episodes of which the time is prolific have naturally tended to draw the limelight, but we have not far to penetrate below the surface of events to realize how expansion abroad and revolution at home were equally the effect of new-gotten money power in the hands of a comparatively small number of ambitious individuals. In a surprising number of cases, in both connections, the same names keep cropping up. And we can go further and say that those who were most deeply involved in subversive conspiracy at home are found, more often than not, to be behind the least scrupulous forms of overseas enterprise.

For honest colonization was not by any means the only way in which the getters of this new form of fluid wealth might hope to reap quick profits. The Elizabethan tradition of freedom, in the most aggressive sense, on or across the high seas, particularly where it was a question of poaching on the King of Spain's preserves, was too deeply ingrained for even a pacifist king to uproot. No man of the time was more active in promoting colonizing activities than the immensely wealthy Earl of Warwick, the descendant in the fourth generation of Richard Rich, the most Gargantuan of all the racketeers who had founded noble houses on the proceeds of the Reformation. The great-grandson, in spite of his Calvinist professions and patronage of dissident preachers, was a worthy chip off the old block, besides being a ringleader in every sort of seditious activity, largely because the strictness of the Crown in enforcing its few remaining claims upon its most powerful subjects constituted a rich man's grievance.

Warwick's vast fortune was continually being invested in projects of colonial expansion and kindred ventures of a more dubious, and some of them of a nakedly piratical, order. We find his name linked with those of nearly all the leading 'patriots' in the drive against the monarchy, in the promotion of the notorious Providence Island project, whose London headquarters was in Warwick's own town mansion and whose treasurer was that formidable Commoner, John Pym. This experiment in company promotion was one that would have suited the genius of Horatio Bottomley. The island, lying off the 'mosquito coast' of Central America, was duly stocked with a credulous or predatory populace of settlers, who soon found it to be unsuited for any other profitable purpose save that for which its proximity to the Spanish trade routes rendered it suitable. Even so the promoters were not long in discovering that the whole project was a financial blind alley, and that it was time to cut their losses, and switch over to the exploitation of a larger island than Providence, leaving the miserable settlers, or such of them as had survived, to be rounded up in due course by a combined Spanish military and naval force, dispatched at last to liquidate what had become an intolerable nuisance. But their fate had ceased to interest Warwick, Pym and company, who by this time had found fatter fish to fry.

This is admittedly an extreme and far from favourable example of the sort of financial activity that was the impelling force behind so much of British expansion overseas. In one sense it might, in comparison with that of other nations, have been described as a sort of capitalist anarchy, in which State policy played only the most indirect and insignificant part and which had hardly any patriotic and still less imperial inspiration, but was conditioned by the urge of moneyed individuals, singly or in combination, to find means of putting their wealth to the most profitable use. And wealth, as I have already explained, owing to the special conditions arising from Britain's invasion-proof isolation, was piling up there at a substantially greater rate than in continental countries.

In all this there is no need to impute any necessary moral delinquency to these backers and organizers, beyond the fact that like other men of business they were in it for what they hoped to get out of it. They were performing an indispensable service in providing the motive power without which there could have been no question of British expansion, either of colonies or trade; their standards were those of their age, neither better nor worse—and it was an age not distinguished by delicacy of scruple. If they included a fair proportion of slippery characters pursuing projects that went beyond even the most elastic limits of honourable trade, they included also such statesmanlike projectors as George Calvert, first Lord Baltimore, a former Secretary of State (who if he had lived would have ranked as the founder of the colony of Maryland), who were cast in a large, even if not specifically heroic, mould.

And it would give quite a false impression if we said that the peopling of these new lands overseas was dictated solely by economic considerations. History seldom, and British history never, lends itself to such clear-cut generalizations. It is one thing to say that capitalist backing was a *sine qua non* of expansion, and quite another to talk as if the rank and file of colonial settlers were impelled by no other motive than the desire to earn a profit or even a living. For religious motives could, and sometimes did, act with as compelling a force as economic ones. The story of the Pilgrim Fathers is known to everyone, and these devoted and mostly obscure sectarians were impelled by a desire, not only to flee from persecution of which they had had no very hair-raising experience, but also to set up a community in which they would be free not only to practise, but forcibly to standardize, their own particular brand of Calvinist ideology. And this small settlement was soon overshadowed by the group of Puritan colonies known by the collective name of New England, in which the imposition of holiness and the pursuit of the main chance were reconciled with characteristically Puritan facility, and in which religious zeal was sharpened to so fine a point that a new colony had to be founded by the professors of one brand of godliness fleeing from the persecution of those of a different brand.

More space would have to be allotted than can be afforded here to record all the various fortunes of the different ventures in colonization or in the enlargement of trade, and even so no very connected story would be likely to emerge. Certainly—as far as my experience goes— such histories as there are of early British expansion make very disjointed and fragmentary reading, in which we find a whole hotchpotch of different arrangements and relationships between colonists on the one hand, and originating companies or individual proprietors or royal govenors on the other, with every colony constituting a disparate law unto itself, and the regulating authority of the Crown more apparent than real. Though all was done in the most law-abiding way, the spectacle presented is one of chaos, with hardly the least semblance of the sovereign planning that was the mark of French or Spanish or even Dutch—and as it must needs be of all—imperial expansion. Empires do not spring up of their own accord wherever their seeds happen to fall, as those first upshoots of a greater Britain did.

There is, about all these budding communities, a unifying sameness underlying their apparent diversity that already puts them in a class apart from the provinces of genuine empires. The habit of freedom, according to the distinctively English notion that had grown up in the course of centuries, was so deeply implanted in the national subconsciousness that wherever a few score or hundred Englishmen set up house for themselves in a distant land they instinctively began to form themselves into a self-governing community on the English model, with rights and liberties safeguarded by the Common Law taken for granted, and with a model of representative government springing up approximating to that with which they were already familiar. It was so much a matter of course for them to conform to this pattern that they were seldom conscious of any particular need for revolutionary self-assertion. Nor did kings, proprietors or companies make any prolonged or convinced attempt to ride their authority roughshod over what was now tacitly admitted to be the basic right of Englishmen, and particularly of Englishmen whom there were no very apparent means of bringing to heel, to run their own affairs in their own way.

It all developed so naturally, and with so few dramatic highlights, that it seems to have struck hardly anyone that something of even profounder significance was taking shape in the New World than any conceivable outcome of the civil strife that was convulsing Britain in the mid decades of the century. For since the days when the Greek cities had sent forth the overflow of their swelling populations to found independent replicas of themselves on distant shores of their great inland sea, no comparable phenomenon had been witnessed to this of the transplanting of social organisms on a far more prolific and extensive scale, to spring up as at least potentially independent national units bound together in bonds not of a common subjection but of a common spontaneity.

They were hardly in the least conscious of this newness, this break with the past. Such self-consciousness as any of them had was more of a religious than of a political nature. The Declaration of Independence was still in the distant future. Loyalty to the sovereign Power, even in such intractably self-willed colonies as those of New England, was in theory at least taken for granted. The colonists, so few in proportion to the vast spaces in which they were precariously opposed to the forces of nature and man, had no time for the niceties of political theory. They were practical Englishmen wrestling with practical problems, living, as it were, from hand to mouth, and therefore, of necessity, extroverted to an even greater extent than the national average. They consequently tended to make the best of the existing framework of things, and go their own way in contempt of logic, and by any practical compromise that suited the needs of the moment.

The result did not work out too badly for them. They were after all not ready to stand entirely on their own feet. They could not have got started at all without capitalist backing, and proprietors and joint stock companies were a necessity, if an onerous one, and there was as yet no idea of openly defaulting on the stipulated *quid pro quo* for their services, though the honest pilgrims of the original Plymouth settlement made it a first call on their energies to buy out the speculators who had invested in the fruit of their labours. But as the century progressed, these initial differences and handicaps tended to straighten themselves out, and the colonies, particularly on the North American mainland, to approximate to the same form of nominally Crown-governed, but in practice self-governing communities, each with its Parliament conforming more or less closely to the English pattern —most of all in the determination to gather the effective powers of sovereignty into its own hands, a task that its transoceanic distance from the nominal seat of supreme authority rendered easy of accomplishment.

This is admittedly to give a very simplified rendering of an almost infinitely complicated story—or number of stories. It would be true in a sense to say that the dominant theme is one of evolving liberty, but only if we keep in mind that the British notion of liberty is something very different from that of liberty in the abstract. We should be nearer to the mark if we were to talk of the building up of a structure of concrete liberties, or of basic rights whose existence was their own sufficient justification. These tough and practical colonists were the last people to harbour sentimental aspirations after liberty in the abstract, or indeed for any liberties but their own. The rights of the original inhabitants of the land, the Indians, to possess it—in spite of such honourable attempts as those of the original Quaker settlers to deal with them on Christian principles—were on the whole, and in the long run, as little regarded as those of the inhabitants of Canaan by its Chosen invaders.

Nor did any regard for human liberty prove the slightest bar to the exploitation of slave labour to an extent and with a ruthlessness that was tempered by no other consideration except that of pure business expediency. At first there was a refreshing absence of racial discrimination, and any white slave labour that could by any means be procured was grist to the mill. But white, and in particular British, bondmanship proved too intractable, and in too short supply, to provide more than an ephemeral makeshift, and as the century progressed the designation 'slave' became practically synonymous with that of African Negro. The Dark Continent offered an inexhaustible supply of this easily conditionable human material, whose fitness for manual employment in conditions too onerous for the European labourer had first been discovered by the Spanish American colonists. But their example was eagerly followed, and even improved on, by their British and other European rivals, and on the horrors and cruelty involved there is no need to expatiate. But it is as well to remember that the principles of freedom and self-government to which the Englishman overseas clung as the most precious part of his national heritage, he did not dream of extending to cover these chattels in human form. That Britons never should be slaves was not, at the time of which we are speaking, held to be the least bar to their being slavemasters. On neither side of the Atlantic was there any tendency to dissent from the opinion one day to be formulated by James Russell Lowell's presidential candidate, that freedom is the sort of thing that don't agree with niggers.

When we talk of a world order of free civilization as being in process of gestation, we must look such facts as these in the face. The manure of the seed bed may exude a less alluring odour than that of the mature blossom. It would be worse than futile to try to make a patriotic song or a libertarian epic out of the story of British expansion during the age of religious wars, or the following age of reason. There is no lack of soul-stirring episodes, nor of gallant and forceful personalities but, take it for all in all, it was a hard and mercenary time in which money values reigned supreme, and, after the cooling of ideological fervour, enthusiasm of any sort, most especially of an altruistic nature, came to be regarded with contempt. Even if Puritan zeal did act as a stimulant in these early stages, it is notorious that the Puritan mentality, however deeply stamped with the image of Jehovah, seldom failed to bear the authentic impress of a bourgeois Mammon on the reverse face of the coin.

Even so this day there is such signal lack of comprehension among Englishmen themselves of what was taking place, that they habitually go on applying the jargon of continental imperialism to these proceedings of their ancestors, and fling about the grotesquely inappropriate designation of 'Empire' in connection with this essentially spontaneous proliferation of communities united, if in nothing else, by an unconditional determination to preserve intact those concrete and inherited rights and liberties which summed up their all-sufficient notion of freedom.

It was no planned edifice that they were engaged in constructing, no journey by map and compass on which they were faring. Reflection would follow in the wake of achievement, but their plotting of their route would be in retrospect, and progress would continue to be by the same blind and cumulative instinct into a still uncharted future. This may account for what, if it had been intentional, would have eclipsed all records of self-depreciation. Far from thanking God that they were not as other nations, far from suspecting that they were engaged in raising civilization to a new plane, they persisted, and even gloried, in degrading themselves to the common level and ruck of empires.

This was perhaps a fault in the right direction, for however much cause there may be for thankfulness, there is nothing, or less than nothing, to boast about in the unique combination of circumstances by which greatness was thrust upon England's unwilling shoulders.

6

CAESARIAN INTERLUDE

DURING THE first half of the seventeenth century the process of expansion had got fairly under way and quite a number of British communities had sprung up, principally on the North American seaboard and in some of the lesser islands of the West Indies, but nothing had appeared that by any conceivable stretch of imagination could have been described as an empire, or that showed the least signs of developing into one. The impression one gets from such records of the time as have survived is that, except for those of them who had an axe of their own to grind, the British islanders were too much absorbed in their own domestic conflicts to have time and thought to spare for what was happening on the other side of the Atlantic.

Even Charles I, who was far in advance of his time in his consistent endeavours to foster colonial development, was without the means to implement his good will, or to run an imperial policy even had he so designed, and it is significant that even though in the course of a futile war with France into which his minister Buckingham's spirited policy had landed him, the glittering prize of Quebec actually fell into his hands, he was fain to hand it back tamely as the price of peace.

But now a revolutionary change was about to transform the domestic situation, and did seem as if it were destined to reverse the whole course of British history, and to bring the phenomenon of empire within the scope of practical possibility.

It will be remembered that the governing factor of England's historical development had consisted in her ability to insulate herself behind the barrier of an invasion-proof sea power, so as to work out her destiny in her own way, without burdening herself with the upkeep of a permanent military establishment, or of a strong monarchy on the continental model.

It now seemed as if all this was to be altered as the result of the Civil War, and England provided with an army and empire all complete on the Caesarian model. For the very name of Emperor, or Imperator, signifies Commander-in-Chief.

Here we can only dwell as briefly as possible on what is essential for the elucidation of our present theme.

In the first place it must seem an extraordinary dispensation of luck or providence that this should have fallen out at the one time in modern history that Britain could have afforded to be violently divided against herself for a matter of practically nine years, without any European power cutting in to decide the issue one way or the other in its own interests—as Spain would certainly have done if it had happened a little earlier, or France if a little later. The fact is that the nations were so murderously involved in what in one sense might be regarded as civil war on a continental scale that they had none of their strained energies left over for further commitments. And besides this, the crisis in England happened to coincide with the time when the competition that was perpetually going on for European supremacy was in temporary abeyance owing to the fact that no immediate candidate for supreme honours was in the field, since the power of Spain was finished without that of France having fully matured. The vital problem, for Britain, of preserving the anarchy of nations—or as it was soon to be called the balance of power—on the Continent had thus solved itself for the nonce without any need for British intervention.

Britain was therefore left with a free hand to fight her way to a solution of her own domestic problem. But the solution at least provisionally arrived at as the result of the Civil War was one that neither of the original contending parties had foreseen, still less desired. As in the battle of the frogs and the mice, a third party entered on the scene and proceeded to swallow up the other two. It ceased to be even in form a contest of monarchy against Parliament—the monarch was butchered and Parliament reduced to a picked handful of stooges, who were, in due course, ignominiously driven out of doors. And for the first and last time since Britannia had ceased to be a Roman province the stage was set for the advent of a Caesar, in the person of the Imperator, or Commander-in-Chief, of the victorious army.

For the war had taken a course outside the calculations of the parliamentary bosses who had engineered it, and who, with the overwhelming economic advantage springing from their control of London and the chief sea ports and industrial centres, had had every reason to count on bringing their Sovereign to heel in a matter of weeks or, at most, months. But instead of the expected walk-over, by the end of a second campaigning season a situation of deadlock had been reached; and though Pym, by a masterpiece of diplomatic finesse, had sought to end this by throwing the sword of Scotland into the scales, another campaigning season passed without the rebel combination being able to clinch its advantage, owing to the cold-footed incompetence of commanders with political axes to grind and only half a will to an all-out victory. The logic of the situation was now irresistible. The way of total war was indicated—that of a professional army under commanders wholly intent on a final knock-out, and a rank and file inflamed by a spirit of ideological fanaticism.

Such an army was indeed formed and, by intensive training and propaganda, worked up to the desired pitch of efficiency. The knock-out blow was duly administered, and the result of the war appeared to be, on the face of it, to lodge the sovereign power unconditionally in the hands of Parliament, or rather those who survived of that formidable group of wirepullers on whose strings what was left of Parliament danced.

Those who thought so were soon to be undeceived. Something had happened utterly foreign to English experience, though only too congruous with that of Republican Rome in its last stages. Parliament had ceased to be its own master. A new military power had been called into existence that, once it became conscious of its own strength, would be capable of overriding every other authority in the country—even that of the law itself. It followed that the man who controlled the army, its commander or *imperator*, would be what no English Sovereign had ever dreamed of becoming, the supreme authority in the state, with a power limited only by the necessity of retaining the goodwill of his own soldiers, just as the early Caesars had been dependent on that of their pretorians and provincial legionaries.

It so happened that the commander, whose prowess in the field had marked him out as the only possible candidate for the part of English Caesar, was qualified for it by an overplus of that demonic energy, so characteristic of the dictatorial personality, which enabled him to put himself across the footlights of history as one of its heroically strong men. But, like Mussolini in our own time, Oliver Cromwell was signally lacking in those qualities of intellect and will that are needed to sustain such a part. Like so many other successful men of action, he was essentially an opportunist, and he was one of a particularly dangerous kind, since he had developed the faculty of dramatizing his opportunist hunches as divine inspirations. The joker in Cromwell's psychological pack was something he called the Lord, and this he produced from his sleeve on every critical occasion of his life, and played, in pious good faith, to any required value. The Lord was with Cromwell, ordering all things together in the interests of his servant Oliver, because, without Cromwell being in the least conscious of it, the Lord *was* Cromwell.

A demonic personality thus capable of deifying its own demon may be of a forcefulness more than human, but a mind so constituted is incapable of shaping a fixed course of principle, rational or moral. It is only natural that Carlyle, the apostle of violence, should have been spellbound by the pathological explosiveness of his hero's outpourings, but that our own generation, that has seen enough of this sort of thing and where it leads, should fail to see through it passes comprehension.

It has been necessary to draw attention to this weakness of Cromwell's mentality because perhaps the greatest peril that has ever threatened Britain—certainly from within—was lest this middle-aged civilian, who had had a record of success equalled by few soldiers as a commander and trainer of armies, should have grasped the opportunity he himself had created of raising his country to full-blown imperial status, with himself in supreme control, either as its actual Sovereign or—what he would almost certainly have preferred—as the all-powerful Mayor of the Palace to a *roi fainéant*. That this would have involved a violent reversal of the whole course up to date of Britain's evolution, and the exchange of her own unique selfhood for the standardized pattern imposed on the despotism of the Continent was the last thing that Cromwell's chaotic intelligence would have been capable of appreciating. As an opportunist and man of action, his instinct was all for getting things done, to the glory of the Lord, and damning the consequences. No man, as he himself put it, ever rises so high as he who does not know where he is going.

Cromwell was consistent in this, if in nothing else. To talk of him, as is sometimes done, as a subtle and far-sighted schemer, possessed by the same sort of ruthless ambition for absolute power that has possessed some modern dictators, would be to miss the essential point about him. Subtle indeed he was, and ruthless, a perfect combination of lion and fox, in compassing visible and immediate ends; but far-sighted he was not, and did not aspire to be. He was, in the field of statesmanship, a tactician without a grand strategy.

Consequently he plunged deeper and deeper into difficulties, and with each successive mastery of the immediate situation he allowed the overall situation to master him. This army that, by his shaping, had become the most formidable military force in Europe and, under his leadership, succeeded in imposing its yoke on the whole of the British Islands, was no ordinary army, but one of Englishmen, with the instinct for self-government in their blood, and worked up to a fever heat of ideological fanaticism by only-too-successful propaganda. And on such a force not even the most dynamic commander could count on imposing his will after the manner of the Roman centurion's 'go, and he goeth; and . . . come, and he cometh'. It was an army with a will of its own that it was fully capable of imposing on its commander, an army that required to be humoured, and was never very far from breaking loose and taking its command into its own hands from leaders of its own choosing.

This army was now the supreme governing factor of Cromwell's, and England's—as it might soon be of Europe's—situation. The effect of the war had been to impose it on the already exhausted country like a huge, blood-sucking parasite that demanded to be maintained and—still worse—employed at the public expense, but whose removal from the scene, even had that been possible, would more and more probably every year have opened the floodgates of counter-revolution. And probability was changed to certainty when the parliamentary bosses who, deprived of their ablest heads, were still under the delusion that they had won the war and had only to garner its fruits, perpetrated the crowning folly of seeking to break up or disband their presumably loyal forces after bilking them of their pay. The army, in consequence, broke loose from the control of the politicians; and it was now only a question of whether it would remain under the control of its own leaders—which boiled down to that of the only leader conceivably capable of making his authority respected. Cromwell was a man of action, but that he had founded any long-term plan of action is to the last degree improbable. From what we now know of the remarkable debates on matters of fundamental principle that were going on at headquarters, it would seem that the Lord General's ideas were more than usually chaotic, and that his political line was laid down for him by his lawyer nephew Ireton, who wanted at all costs to prevent the extremist elements in the rank and file from pushing the rebellion against authority to the length not only of a political but a social revolution, in which, as one of its leaders said, the poorest He that was in England should have a life to live as much as the greatest He, with its only-too-obvious corollary of a levelling of incomes. It was accordingly decided to transfer the effectual sovereignty of the realm from the parliamentary chiefs to such of the higher commanders as were prepared to stand in with Cromwell and Ireton in arresting this drift to democracy among their followers, and they sought to camouflage this virtual military dictatorship by a cleverly drafted paper constitution that would sweeten the pill to the defeated royalists and churchmen. The success of the plan depended on securing, as they did by a military coup, the person of the captive monarch, and inducing him to sponsor the venture as its crowned figurehead.

It was just the sort of unprincipled expedient to appeal to an opportunist like Cromwell, and its effect would have certainly been to set England and himself on the broad road to empire. But he had misjudged his man in the King, who, with nothing of Cromwell's demonic energy, was nevertheless prepared to die rather than swerve a hair's breadth from such principles as he had elected to walk by. He saw that to stand in with a military plot to override the law and dragoon Parliament would be a betrayal of his office, and one that neither threat nor cajolery would induce him to be party to. This refusal certainly cost him his life, but it almost equally certainly preserved his throne, and may well have been the means of saving his country from incalculable disaster. The fate of the House of Savoy in our own time suggests what might have been the result of a willingness to collaborate in remarkably similar circumstances.

But this determination of his unarmed captive to offer himself as the sacrifice in his own gambit had wrecked Cromwell's clever combination in a way that threatened him with actual checkmate unless the sacrifice were accepted. The mere suspicion that their commanders were truckling for terms with the bogey man of their propagandists was enough to inflame left-wing sentiment among the soldiers to—and in fact beyond—the verge of mutiny. No one but Cromwell would have been capable of quelling this, as he did, sword in hand, by the tempestuous impact of his personality, but no one knew better than he how urgent it had become for him to conform to the temper of what, if he had not, would soon cease to be his command.

A mind habitually bent on thinking up solutions for the problems of the moment could hardly fail to deduce that the need of this one was to annihilate this opponent who thus persisted in confronting the physically irresistible force with the morally immovable obstacle; and this conclusion was overwhelmingly strengthened by the event of a second civil war, in which a desperate attempt of a disarmed majority in the country to throw off what had now become an intolerable yoke was crushed by the ruthless application of professional force by the now propaganda-drunken soldiery, whom nothing would now suffice but the royal blood sacrifice for which they had stipulated in advance of the campaign as the reward of victory.

Cromwell, though an opportunist, was no fool. He must have had at least some inkling of the desperate nature of the course to which this surrender to his followers would irrevocably commit him. To lift his hand against the Lord's Anointed would be not only a crime—and the most heinous of all crimes in the eyes of the law—but a colossal blunder. For no conceivable advantage he would be perpetrating what in England had always been the unpardonable sin of setting himself openly above the law, and by one blow of the axe making himself, in the regard of a suppressed but ever-strengthening public opinion, an arch-felon whom only the muskets and pikes of his myrmidons kept from the gallows and the quartering block. However little he may have intended it, it would be thenceforth, with him, a case of *aut Caesar, aut nihil.*

That Cromwell ever designed it to come to this is quite out of keeping with his character. He was no Hitler to harbour megalomaniac hankerings after absolute power, and even though his naturally overbearing temperament saddled him with an explosive power complex, he preferred to mask it even to himself under the forms of godliness and legality. But, like other men of similar temperament and merely physical courage, he was too practical to share King Charles's capacity of taking his stand unconditionally on a fixed point of moral principle, and damning the consequences. He was too much afraid—and with reason—of what the consequences might be of setting himself in head-on opposition to the sentiment of his army. He therefore decided to seek the Lord with more than ordinary fervour; for the Lord was more to be relied on than the New Model Army to take His orders unconditionally, once their nature became apparent, from His servant the Lord General. The required release was granted and Oliver drove straight ahead with furious, not to say hysterical, vehemence on the new path of military violence naked and unashamed, that involved not only the cold-blooded slaughter of the King, but the shameless coercion followed in due course by the expulsion of Parliament, and the overriding of every inhibition of justice or legality. The sovereignty of the sword was now openly set up in England, and if the experience of such conditions in other countries was anything to go by, the commander of the controlling army would become in fact, if in not form, emperor of what it would no longer be an abuse of language to speak of as the British Empire.

It might have been thought that, having gone so far, Cromwell's best chance would have been frankly to accept the logic of the situation, and seat himself on the vacant throne. But things were not so easy. After his great surrender he was more than ever bound to defer to the wishes, and even the whims, of this unique army that was ready to take no orders, even from him, that it was not prepared to endorse. And no one knew better than Cromwell that sentiment in the army was dead against the setting up of an open monarchy to take the place of that which it had been at such pains to demolish. Nor is there any reason to believe that Cromwell himself was not of the same mind. With his somewhat muddled intelligence, and his avowed aversion from setting his course towards any fixed goal whatever, he was capable of dramatizing himself in the part of a plain, law-abiding citizen—no Caesar, but just Lord Protector of the Realm, as the Duke of Somerset had been in almost living memory; though the good Duke, having no army to back him, had after a short time parted with his head.

But it is not given to any man to evade the *karma* of his actions by declining to be bound by it. It was no more open to Cromwell to settle down to constitutional courses than it is for a gangster chief to retire into private life on his takings. The yoke of the army was on the neck of the country and it was he who—whatever his intentions—had been the prime agent in riveting it there. What could fairly have been described as the classic imperial situation was in being, and it was up to Cromwell, as it had been to Julius and his nephew Octavianus, and as it would be to Napoleon and to Hitler, to master or be crushed by it. There was no other choice.

Government must be either by force or consent, and the possibility of consent by the English people, in any normal circumstances, to a régime that was in flat defiance of all their inherited traditions and instincts, as well as imposing an unprecedented burden on everyone with a material stake in the country, was unbelievable. The first task of any genuinely representative assembly would be to get the army to disband. The next would be—as the event was to prove—to restore the law and the constitution to as near as possible their pre-war working. And what sort of a reckoning the law would then demand from one who had for years trampled it underfoot and superseded its reign by one of the sword would have been obvious to a meaner intelligence than that of Cromwell. Even if he did not choose to know where he was going, he must have known well enough that there was neither halting nor turning back on this road that for him had become more one of escape than of triumph—escape from the vengeance that was indeed destined to overtake what was left of him *post mortem*.

Some dictators achieve empire, others have it thrust upon them, though it is not always easy to place any particular individual in his proper category. But Cromwell, if anyone, belongs to the second. He was the most unwilling of imperialists, but he dared not be anything else. Not ambition but sheer lust of self-preservation hounded him up the ascent to the imperial summit.

Militarism was in the saddle, and it was not in its nature to remain static. This splendid force equipped and trained up to the highest fighting pitch of efficiency, and already employed in holding down the three realms it had conquered, was not there for ornament, or for vegetating in barracks. If not disbanded it would have to be used. Such fulfilment was the law of its being.

This proved to be the case even before Cromwell was constrained to jockey himself into supreme power. The so-called Parliament, now devoid of any semblance of representative character, that existed by favour of the army that it still cherished the illusion of commanding, could not even wait for the domestic struggle to be over before it had committed itself to a course of imperialistic bellicosity. And it is significant that in its choice of an enemy it proceeded to make nonsense of those ideological professions that had been the driving force of the Roundhead propaganda, and were no doubt sincere enough on the lips of plain Ironsides and buffcoats. But even to this day the distinction has never been sufficiently drawn between the simple and single-hearted enthusiasts—the type of John Bunyan or John Bunyan's Mr Greatheart—to whom the religious issue was all in all for its own sake, and for those magnates and politicians who, whatever their private beliefs, were in the religious racket for what they could get out of it. It was these pluto Puritans who were pulling the strings of the provisional Government that was set up after Pride's Purge and the killing of the King. It was the least that could be said against this gang of notoriously corrupt adventurers—denounced as such by Cromwell himself in his memorable dismissal of them—that their policy should have been dictated by entirely material considerations. So long as they had this incomparable martial organization at their disposal, it was only natural that they should have sought for the most lucrative way of using it. But it might have seemed the limit of cynicism that they should have pitched for an enemy not on Catholic France or Spain, but on England's old Protestant ally and the bulwark of the Calvinist cause in Europe—the sister Republic of the United Netherlands. There is only this to be said: that the Dutch themselves yielded to no people on earth in the unconditional and unsentimental priority that they accorded to business considerations over all others.

That it was very much a case of diamond cut diamond between the authorities at Westminster and those of Amsterdam does not alter the fact that what is known as the First Dutch War involved a complete stripping of the gilt from the Puritan gingerbread, and a new departure in British policy that in tendency, at least, might be described as imperialistic. But it was imperialism that lacked the martial glamour of the traditional pattern, for, though its origin was militaristic, its purpose and spirit were those of a bourgeois commercialism. No difference of religious or ideological principle was involved or even alleged; it was simply and avowedly a fight for trade between two rival firms, though whether fighting for trade was the best way to promote it for either party might have been open to question.

The origins of the conflict are too complex to be unravelled here except so far as to say that the success of the Dutch in securing a lion's share of the European carrying trade had aroused a jealousy in the rival maritime Power that had expressed itself in an attempt, by legislative action, to bar English ports to all but English-built and English-manned ships, and to make trade with the English plantations overseas as far as possible a national monopoly. This, if it could have been got to work, contained the principle of a closed commercial empire, though in point of fact it never did get to work much more effectively than Simple Simon's project of carrying water in a sieve. But the attempt to put it into practice involved trouble and bloodshed culminating in the eventual, though not necessarily the ultimate, separation between the two main constituents of British-born civilization.

It is hard to specify any one cause—even that of the so-called

Navigation Acts—of the war that broke out by a sort of spontaneous combustion in the Channel. The fact is that the parliamentary bosses, whose authority commanded no respect in any quarter whatever, were only too glad to cash in on the popular urge to settle up a number of long-standing scores with this grasping trade rival, and it must be admitted that on a purely material calculation they had—whether by design or not—chosen their ground shrewdly. The two fleets, commanded on the English and in at least one case on the enemy side by landsmen, indulged in a mere slogging match, in which the floating gun-platforms duly pounded each other into shambles, whilst the advantage enjoyed by Britain owing to her straddling of Holland's sea approaches enabled her to impose a lucrative strangle hold on the trade that was all in all to the Netherlanders. On a short-term calculation the war might have been reckoned a profitable venture in *realpolitik*, and its tendency, if prolonged, to knock the linchpin out of any possible Protestant combination in Europe, signified little enough to the authorities of Westminster in comparison with its effect in diverting public attention from the domestic situation. Even so, it was not enough to prevent their own Commander-in-Chief, in due course, from sending them packing and taking the reins of power into his own hands.

Now Cromwell, for all his capacity for masking his real motives even from himself under a religious smoke-screen, was not consciously a cynic. He quite sincerely believed himself to be a soldier of that somewhat questionable entity he personified as the Lord; and however pliable the Lord may have been in other ways, even Cromwell entertained no doubts about His patronage of the Protestant cause in Europe, and consequently of the obligation laid on His servant, on coming into power, to make the advancement of this cause a main plank of his foreign policy.

Consequently he lost no time on coming into office in winding up this unnatural conflict by granting easy terms to the Dutch who, with ruin staring them in the face, were ready enough to close. But this did not mean that the new dictator of British policy was able, even if he had been willing, to give the country the rest it so urgently needed, and renew those times of peaceful prosperity it had enjoyed under the dead King's régime. There was no peace for this compulsory usurper, who was now more than ever the prisoner of his own army that he dared not for the life of him disband, and that he was consequently bound to humour and impose on the civilian population with whose consent he aspired to govern. No wonder that five years of floundering from one foredoomed attempt to another, to find an acceptable way of squaring this constitutional circle, wore him quite literally into the grave.

Like it or not, he could make good in only one capacity, that of a conqueror, cutting all knots by the sword, and hypnotizing the populace by the glamour of his triumphs. He was committed by the logic of his situation to a way of out-and-out imperialism now that the path of constitutional monarchy, that he would much sooner have trodden, was barred by the plain intimation he received from his own officers that his acceptance of a crown would be wholly unacceptable to this obstinately intractable army that might eventually prove less squeamish about enthusing for the dictatorship of its conquering hero. For armies are like that, and it is doubtful whether even a Caesar, or Napoleon, could have put himself across the footlights in the style and trappings of formal kingship.

Cromwell may not have known, or cared to know, where he was going, but so far as he could be said to have had a policy at all, it was certainly not lacking in vigour. If anyone had been under the illusion that his winding up of the Dutch war signified an intention of giving his war-weary country the boon of rest and recuperation that it now so desperately needed, they were wishfully mistaken. With his army as much in occupation of the country as that of a foreign invader, any sort of government save one by martial law—which indeed was imposed openly for a few months and then in its turn dropped—was doomed to collapse, and with his administration sliding uncontrollably down towards the abyss of bankruptcy, the one thing that Cromwell dared not do was to call a halt to his imperial stampede from one dazzling coup to another. Like a cleaned-out gambler, who dare not rise from the table, he was constrained to go on plunging deeper and deeper on the chance of recouping his losses. He had still his army and his fleet to make play with, and his flair for their inspired direction was no less than on his former battlefields. It would have been surprising in these circumstances had Cromwell not had a good run, while it lasted, for his—or rather the nation's—money.

Few could deny that the fleet was more profitably employed in extending British sovereignty of the seas to the Mediterranean—thereby singeing the Pope's beard and knocking the forts of pirate Tunis about the ears of its Bey—than in swapping broadsides with fellow Protestants in the Channel. And it was a gesture of a kind at least calculated to enhance British prestige when he espoused, not without effect, the cause of the 'slaughtered saints' of the Protestant Waldensian community in the Alpine valleys.

So far, so good. Warlike action is even at its rare best a necessary evil, but, assuming that it has got to be taken at all, it is best applied with honour, intelligence and economy, and these requirements may be said to have been fulfilled by this first Cromwellian essay in a strong foreign policy. But no such plea can by the remotest stretch of imagination be advanced for the reckless plunge that followed into the blood-bath of continental power politics, from which England had so far happily kept aloof, and on what, by every sane and established canon of British policy, was the wrong side at that. For to back the rising power of France against the falling one of Spain was not only a crime—since no conceivable point of principle was involved in taking sides in a duel between two Catholic Powers—but also a suicidal blunder from the national standpoint. But it would have been suicidal for Cromwell personally to have let up for a moment on this violent and desperate course, which he was now irrevocably doomed to pursue in the name of the Lord, to its glorious or bitter end.

If the revival of the pre-Reformation struggle between the Houses of Hapsburg and Bourbon, which had so largely come to supersede the religious issue as the determinant of European power politics, Cromwell was characteristically engaged in sitting armed to the teeth upon the fence before making up his mind or getting the Lord to make it up for him on which side to come down. Though every rational or patriotic consideration was for tilting the European balance in favour of the weaker Power, his own emotional bias was rootedly and traditionally anti-Spanish.

It was this, combined with his ingrained fashion of riding roughshod over weakness, that had the effect of driving him into what proved to be his only serious essay in the art of empire-building. For in spite of his having been said to have toyed, at one time, with the possibility of emigrating to America as a political refugee, Cromwell would seem to have been Old-World-minded in comparison not only with the Stuarts, and with their keen interest in colonial expansion, but also with such then unfledged revolutionaries as the Warwicks, the Pyms and the Sayes, who had been neck-deep in the promotion of more or less legitimate projects on and beyond the High Seas before they diverted their talents to subversive activities on the home front. But the war with Spain, into which he now plunged, was in its very nature global rather than European.

There is something both surprising and significant in the extent to which, during long domestic agony of the civil war, the colonies contrived to keep out of the picture. In spite of the fact that they varied in sentiment for or against the monarchy almost as much as districts in England, there was a sort of tacit agreement that such differences of opinion were not worth coming to blows about, and that these budding communities were capable of minding their own business until such time as the mother country had succeeded in putting her own affairs into a shape that they could, and would, recognize. Meanwhile such grip as the home Government or individual proprietors—some of whom were pushed out altogether as supporters of the losing side—had on the domestic affairs of the colonists was naturally weakened. The latter had still too much to gain from the British connection to want to get free from it on any ground of political difference, but they had not the remotest intention of submitting to any sort of imperial dictation, monarchist or republican. It would hardly be too much to say that in substance, though not in form, something very like a budding commonwealth of nations had begun to take shape. Certainly this designation is nearer the mark than such a flagrant misnomer as that of British Empire. Cavalier Virginians were no more minded than Puritan New Englanders to come within the orbit of any imperial system.

It was of course necessary for the republican régime to mop up such islands of royalist resistance as held out in the West Indies—no very difficult task—and to find a more profitable use for some of these same islands as dumping-grounds for the British and Irish prisoners of war who were shipped off as white slaves to the local planters.

And it was in the direction of these islands, more coveted for the richness of their tropical products than were the comparatively temperate and habitable fields for colonial development on the mainland, that Cromwell looked, as soon as his mind turned—as it was bound to do—to projects of imperial expansion. For this 'strong' foreign policy that he had got to fulfil, or collapse, bound him to go on striking out and scoring successes with these great armaments of his in every feasible direction. He had only got the Dutch War off his hands in order to clear his decks for action of more ambitious scope, and, if possible, more in harmony with his innermost longings. Indeed what he at first planned to do, if he could have got the Dutch to stand in with him, would have been to switch over to a grand alliance between those two maritime Powers which, by an amicable scheme of partition, would have enabled them to turn the tables on Spain and substitute a Protestant for a Catholic monopoly of overseas empire. But such grandiose combinations were not of a sort of appeal to the stolid burgher mentality. Crusading enthusiasm had no affinity with Dutch commercialism.

Cromwell was therefore driven to shelve, for the nonce, his darling project of a grand Protestant alliance, and to grab what quick returns he could out of making friends with the Mammon of unrighteousness in the shape of one of the high contending Catholic Powers on the Continent. But which was it to be? He had at first inclined to the side of Spain, and it was only after an undeclared naval war in the Channel had failed to exhaust the long-sighted patience of Cardinal Mazarin's French diplomacy that he had turned to even more aggressive action against Spain herself, after his terms for a formal alliance had been rejected at Madrid.

This action took the form of a combined military and naval expedition, with a roving commission to seize as much as it could of the Spanish possessions in the West Indies, in the faith that Philip IV's tottering Government would make a virtue of necessity, and put up with any outrage rather than bring in England on the side of France in the European conflict. And perhaps, if that much-tried monarch had been swayed by realistic calculations, that is how he would have reacted; but Philip, futile and feeble though he was, had still too much of the pride of a high-hearted Castilian to submit to open bullying; so Cromwell found his choice of sides in the European war made up for him, and made up in what, from the British standpoint, was palpably the wrong way. For to back the stronger power against the weaker was to wage indirect war against Britain herself, a policy of long-term *felo de se*. But even had he been capable of doing so, Cromwell could not afford to look beyond the needs of the moment, and to play from strength against weakness at least gave him promise of those quick and spectacular returns of which he was most urgently in need.

This expedition to the West Indies possesses a special importance for us, since it may rank as the first British venture in out-and-out imperialism,[1] certainly since the opening up of the New World. And no doubt, if all had gone according to plan, it would have been the first move in the creation of a British Empire, with Oliver as the first British emperor. As it was, it did succeed—though not according to plan—in accomplishing the most authentic feat of empire-building, properly so called, on British record, before the conscious experimentation in that style of architecture in the later nineteenth century.

Not the least significant part of the episode is the hopeless and almost ignominious way in which the whole affair was, from the start, bungled. This at least would seem to be flatly out of character with the Cromwellian technique. For not even Cromwell's bitterest detractors have ever taxed him with inefficiency within the opportunist limits which he habitually set himself. Once launched on any undertaking, few men have ever combined greater energy with a more consummate faculty for oganization. It would have seemed the simplest thing for the creator of that finest force in Europe to have detailed a sufficient number of its formed units for this important service. Whereas we find Cromwell, of all people, shipping off into the blue a scratch force made up of drafts from different regiments, and a sweeping of such toughs and down-and-outs as could be pressed into the venture. No wonder that even the voluminous Gardiner, Cromwell's devoted kinsman and panegyrist, is moved to admit that 'it had not been by gathering a mob and styling it an army that Oliver had beaten down his

[1] I do not count Raleigh's foredoomed last expedition, which was more the desperate last fling of a private individual than an act of state policy.

D

enemies at Marston Moor and Naseby' [1]—and leaves it at that, without pausing to account for this extraordinary lapse on the part of his hero.

And yet the dispatch of this ill-commanded, ill-organized and ill-staffed expedition does need to be accounted for, though perhaps not quite in a way that Gardiner would have found congenial. For no other explanation seems possible than that of what Cromwell might himself have described as cruel necessity. However much he may have desired to embark on projects of imperial expansion, he dared not weaken his army of domestic occupation to any substantial extent by detachment overseas. His New Model Army had its resources stretched to the limit in holding down the conquered realms on the outer fringe of the British Isles, and above all in keeping the civilian English population from any hope of shaking off the chains that bound it to the existing régime. With all military or totalitarian usurpers it is a choice between governing by the sword or perishing by means less honourable.

Cromwell's expeditionary rabble, swelled to nine thousand by West Indian volunteers in quest of loot, failed ignominiously, and most fortunately, to accomplish the purpose eventually agreed on by its commanders of seizing the island of Hispaniola [2] from its Spanish garrison. But by a strange irony these same leaders, who knew only too well what sort of thanks they were likely to get from the Lord Protector for staging this total fiasco, acting on the principle that any results were better than none, sailed off in the direction of the hitherto unregarded island of Jamaica, whose sole garrison of a few hundred Spaniards they overwhelmed by weight of numbers, thus securing for Britain a possession of incomparably more value than ever Hispaniola would have been. But so little was this appreciated by Cromwell that he relieved his feelings by clapping both commanders into the Tower for their pains.

This conquest, inglorious though it was, might well, if Cromwell and his successors could have succeeded in holding the course, have ranked as the first episode in the formation of an authentic British, or more properly speaking un-British, Empire. But it was the dictator himself who was approaching his point of 'thus far and no farther!'

He was now less and less the shaper of his own policy. The war with Spain, which he had precipitated in his own despite, virtually forced him into alliance with France, and a division of the New Model, shipped across the Channel to co-operate with the French army, played a leading part in a major victory under the eyes of the great Turenne, one result of which was to put Britain into possession of the fortress and harbour of Dunkirk; thus, after the lapse of almost exactly a century, providing her with a sally port on to the Continent

[1] *History of the Commonwealth and Protectorate*, IV, 129.
[2] Haiti and San Domingo.

such as she had not possessed since her loss of Calais. No achievement could have been better calculated to boost the crumbling prestige of the Protectorate.

But Cromwell was too great a soldier to sacrifice blood and treasure merely to secure what, unless he had intended to use it, would have saddled him with an expensive liability. He could not afford to tie up men or further deplete his bankrupt finances in maintaining an advanced base merely for its prestige value. It is only too evident in what direction his course was shaping. He was fast approaching the end of his constitutional tether. No juggling with the franchise would give him a Parliament that would not prove obstructive to the limit, or one that would vote him the funds that he so desperately needed to maintain his enormous martial establishment. He had dissolved the latest of these bodies in a flaming rage. The time was approaching when he would have no choice but to set up a tyranny of the sword, naked and unashamed.

One resource, and one only, would have been open to him, and he had plainly adumbrated his intention of using it. The Swedish Gustavus Adolphus had already showed what could be achieved by military action on the Continent in the role of Protestant champion. The events of the recent campaign had shown that the prowess of the New Model was in no way diminished. Britain's mastery of the Channel and her possession of Dunkirk ensured her the power of striking out in any chosen direction, and the first spectacular victory would be the surest means of whipping up patriotic sentiment in the country. Cromwell's situation was strikingly similar to that of Henry V, who had gambled successfully on the prestige of a victorious war to rally support for his dubious title and shaky administration. It would have been the tragedy of the Hundred Years War re-enacted on a more grandiose scale, with the same inevitable result of Britain exhausting her strength and bleeding herself to death in an endeavour to sustain herself in a capacity to which her resources were not equal—that of a first-class continental military Power. The more gloriously she might have contrived to prolong the agony, the more surely would she have been reduced in the long run to the same state of played-out insignificance on the fringe of Europe that was to be the fate of Sweden.

That Cromwell had even at this stage formed a master plan of continental intervention is not in character. He had never been one to command his destiny. Since the time of his weathercock veering from constitutionalism to regicide he had been driven forward by an urgent instinct of self-preservation from one forced move to another—a series of desperate and generally violent adaptations to the need of the moment, each of which left him less in control of the overall situation than ever.

Quite plainly the time was at hand when the logic of events, or the *karma* of his own actions, would have driven him to his last fatal resource, to which indeed—as no one was better capable of realizing— he had already committed himself decisively by his occupation of Dunkirk. With his whole edifice of government on the verge of collapse and bankruptcy staring him in the face, there still remained his dream of a grand Protestant combination, and the fact of his hitherto unbeatable army. How these two could best be translated into warlike action would be a task of adaptation peculiarly suited to his opportunist genius. No doubt he was already in process of seeking the Lord about it.

If ever there was a time when the fate of British civilization can be said to have trembled in the balance it was surely this fifth year of the Protectorate. If events had been allowed to run their course—and who was capable of stopping the mighty war lord in his career?—it would have been goodbye to any prospect of a commonwealth of free nations, or even of more than the most ephemeral of British empires. It may have been the Lord after all who, in His mysterious way, decided the matter on Cromwell's lucky day, the day of his 'crowning mercy', which perhaps after all was not that of the Worcester fight, but of his removal from the scene with his fame at its height and the *karma* of his actions unfulfilled.

One can think of other more recent dictators to whom, and to whose reputations with posterity, death has proved less timely—and less merciful.

7

VETO ON CAESAR

THE CHURCH of England was more profoundly right than it realized in making the anniversary of the Restoration a day of national thanksgiving. But what rendered this event the decisive landmark it was in British evolution was not the restoration of a monarch or a dynasty, or even a system of government, but the fact that it signalized the irreversible consummation of the process begun at the Reformation of Britain's severance from membership of any civilization but her own.

Her subjection to the yoke of an irresistible army had rendered it only a question of time before she fell into line with the armed autocracies of the Continent, and conformed to the common pattern of European Powers, the imperial pattern that was the heritage of Caesarian Rome. However little Cromwell may have intended it, the successful consolidation of his régime would have entailed as an inevitable consequence that there would cease to be, in the true—or Shakespearian—sense, an England, even though there might be, not only in name but in literal fact, a British Empire. The shameful conquest of herself would have been brought about. However much of the world without she might succeed in bringing under her sway, she would have lost her own soul.

And in addition to this, the fever of ideology, Protestant or Romanist, so long as it continued to rage in her blood, would have rendered it doubly impossible for her ever to rest true to her own self—because it is in the nature of an ideology to be imposed from outside, and to prohibit the spontaneous development of any native-born civilization. As part of a Protestant *bloc*, or as one or more provinces of a Roman empire, however holy, Britain could never have expanded freely into Greater Britain.

It bears tribute to the demonic forcefulness of Cromwell's personality that the effect of his death should have been to recall England to herself, and to bring the whole seemingly inviolable edifice of military rule crumbling in ruins. Even the soldiers themselves, though their

93

power to suppress even the faintest incipient stirrings of revolt was more unquestionable than ever, lost the will to stand up against the current of popular feeling that was setting in with irresistible force towards a return to the old ways of constitutional liberty whose continuity had been so rudely interrupted, and whose resumption was symbolized by the return of a legitimate monarch to Whitehall. That the still embattled hosts of the Lord should have allowed the Abomination of Desolation to be set up under their very eyes, and then have disbanded peacefully to their homes, is surely a phenomenon more extraordinary and significant than any of those famous victories whose effects were thus suffered, without a blow, to be signally reversed.

What had been decided irrevocably—as it proved—can best be defined in the words of a popular refrain current during the last war:

There'll always be an England . . .

so long at least as England continued to be physically capable of shaping her own destiny.

To put it with somewhat greater precision, it was humanly speaking certain that henceforward she would never have it in her to grow into anything else but her own proper self, even though the full realization of the self she had it in her to be might always lie in the future, beyond the scope of any present generation.

Henceforth, for two centuries at least, the course of her development proceeds on comparatively simple and what, from the standpoint of a perfectly well-informed and superhumanly gifted contemporary observer, might have been almost predictable lines, a thing that could hardly, by any stretch of imagination, have been said of the period of religious and civil strife that had gone before, in the course of which it is scarcely too much to say that anything might have happened.

It will be the purpose of the ensuing chapters to elucidate as far as possible these broad lines of development, always bearing in mind the unique relationship in which Britain was henceforth to stand to the Continent, independence of whose civilization she had effectually, though not formally or even consciously, achieved, and that it henceforth rested with her to perpetuate.

It cannot be too emphatically reaffirmed that independence need not carry with it the least implication of the hermetically sealed national self-sufficiency that is signified by insularity in the pejorative sense. It is one thing to be unreceptive to ideas and influences from without, but quite another to be receptive to them on one's own terms, to master instead of being merely conditioned by them.

And it was decidedly in this latter way that, in the highly sophisticated age that was now dawning, the cream of the European intelligentsia may be described as positively and consciously anti-insular—and nowhere more so than in Britain.

But in the political field, and most particularly that of foreign policy, the downfall of military rule signalized a whole-hearted determination to return to the so rudely interrupted continuity of constitutional development on specifically insular lines behind the shield of an impregnable sea power, and a consequent maximum detachment from the power politics and armed militarism rife on the Continent. Nothing would have been more in accord with popular sentiment than to have carried the revulsion from Cromwell and all his works to the extreme of total military disarmament. The very idea of a standing army, and almost the sight of a uniform, had become enough to start the bogey of military tyranny. What could have been more satisfactory than to trust exclusively to the moat and the wooden walls, and concentrate all the energies thus set free to the pursuit of honourable trade, leaving rival nations to exhaust theirs in the task of mutual destruction?

Unfortunately this counsel of perfection had a flaw in it. No doubt, in the time between the Elizabethan age and the Restoration, a policy of rigid isolationsim had been fully practicable. Both James and Charles, except during the catastrophic Buckingham interlude,[1] had put it into practice with the happiest results. Their walls and their moat had been sufficient guarantees of immunity from foreign invasion. But their hundred-per-cent effectiveness had been largely thanks to the conjunction of circumstances that had prevented the emergence of a Power on the Continent capable, as Philip II's Spain had been, of becoming a menace of the first order. Capable, that is to say, of becoming so much the dominating Power on the Continent as to be able to unite its forces, or at least an overwhelming proportion of them, for a second Roman conquest of the island on its fringe.

There are certain deep-seated instincts that grow up in the course of generations, and though they may never be formulated in word or print yet become as deeply implanted as the inherited wisdom or prejudices of individual men. It would be strictly true to say that in the course of many generations England herself had arrived at the firm conviction that certain eventualities would be fatal to her very existence, and therefore she must go to all lengths to prevent their materializing.

She had at a very early date got it firmly implanted in her that her salvation lay in fostering her domestic liberties behind the barrier of sea power, and keeping the military power of her Sovereigns rationed to a controllable minimum and, most preferably of all, to a ceremonial

---

[1] That of the Duke of Buckingham's fatal and foredoomed policy of European involvement, that cost him his life and Charles, ultimately, his throne.

bodyguard. The experience of six centuries had shown the fleet to have been fully capable of shouldering this responsibility. The fate of the Armada might have been considered the crowning proof of this.

But could the moat and the wooden walls provide a completely invasion-proof guarantee in *all* circumstances? In most, no doubt—in all perhaps that *had* arisen so far—but in all that *might* arise? The English mind was not disposed to take it for granted that continental land power could never succeed in proving more than a match for insular sea power. Hence its chronic sensitiveness on the subject of the Low Countries, which were felt to provide the jumping-off stage from which an invasion could be most easily mounted by a first-class military Power.

But this particular anxiety was part of a wider apprehension of which this was the most proximate and obvious manifestation. It came to this: England with her sea power was fully capable of preserving her shores inviolate from invasion by even the most formidable of continental Powers, provided only that it was not the *sole* Power. That was the one contingency with which, rightly or wrongly, she did not feel sure of coping. A new Roman Empire might proceed to effect a new Roman conquest. The situation to be avoided at all costs was that which actually materialized on two separate occasions, when an *imperator* or Caesar [1] had united all, or nearly all, of the land mass west of the Scythian plains under his sway, and it became a choice for Britain between wrecking this new European empire before it had time to consolidate, or herself perishing miserably.

And let it not be forgotten that, by a process as sure as that of gravitation, such a situation was always tending to come about—nay, was bound to do so sooner or later if left to work itself out without interference. For a thousand years after the fall of the Western Empire the ideal of a Europe united under the sway of a spiritual Caesar, and even, in some vaguer degree, of a temporal one, had persisted. All roads still led to Rome. But the event of the Reformation, following on the emergence of the great national sovereignties, had brought Europe to a state of naked anarchy, an all-against-all wrestle for supremacy with no holds barred. But no one involved dreamed of accepting this as a permanent state of things. Rome was more Rome than ever: the only question in dispute was whether Rome happened to coincide for practical purposes with Vienna, or Madrid, or Paris, or Berlin—or even, ultimately, Moscow. Nor had Caesar abated one jot of his pretensions—once it could be decided who Caesar was, or was going to be, he intended to rule the nations with a sway compared to which the ancient *imperium* would be child's play.

[1] Napoleon and Hitler.

Europe might therefore have been regarded, as indeed she may be said to have regarded herself, in the light of a number of temporarily detached members of an as yet undefined but all-inclusive imperial super-organism, in which all believed, but with which each severally sought to identify itself. Underlying all their differences was a fundamental sameness. And where all were striving among themselves to bring about the similar circumstances, the presumption was overwhelming that between them they would eventually succeed, unless some disruptive force from outside were brought into play to prevent the conflicting forces within from ever resolving their differences in the unity of a common subjection. Such a solution, whatever it might signify to Europe, would be the beginning of the end for Britain. The task of British policy was therefore plainly defined. It was not enough to stand aside and allow Europe to stew in her own juice. Means must be applied when, and to whatever extent they might be required, to keep the witches' cauldron unceasingly on the boil, and maintain a chronically unstable equilibrium—in short, to perpetuate European anarchy.

That and nothing less was what it signified, and what it was bound to signify. It was the necessary price of England's momentous but unformulated decision to repudiate membership of any civilization but her own, and to work out her own destiny in unqualified independence. She would no doubt have found it an ideal policy to dissociate herself entirely from the power politics of the Continent, to mind her own insular and transoceanic business, and leave these other nations to mind theirs—but however well this might and did answer for a time, it proved in the long run an unattainable ideal. Britain could not afford to leave Europe alone unless she could be sure of Europe leaving her alone. A Europe divided against itself could be held at arm's length with comparative ease. But a Europe effectively united in the bonds of empire would, it was instinctively felt, have both the power and the will to bring back the rebel island to its proper allegiance. 'Then'—as was said in reference to the original Caesar—'lest he may, prevent!' There was British policy defined in a nutshell.

As we have already seen, the struggle for power in Europe preserved a rhythm of unfailing constancy though varying tempo. From the general *mêlée* some one participant would stand out as the strongest, and would continue to thrive on its own success, until it threatened to become stronger than all the rest put together, and therefore capable of drawing them all to revolve like satellites in its orbit, if not of absorbing them in its own mass. Sooner or later one point of decision would be reached, beyond which the process would either be carried on to a now inevitable conclusion, or, by a supreme effort, be so signally frustrated that the almost successful aspirant for imperial supremacy

* D

could be not only halted, but flung back, baffled and exhausted, either to drop out of the running for good or at best to undergo a period of recuperation more or less prolonged before venturing a renewed bid for supremacy.

Up to the present there have been five such almost successful bids for European or world supremacy. These will be found to have conformed to an almost unchanging pattern. Each of them—one Spanish, two French and two German—culminated in a violent act of expansion or annexation by which an already ostensibly strongest power aspired to seize a position of overwhelming preponderance. And each of them—to adopt an appropriately nautical metaphor—came to grief on the selfsame rock:

(1) The absorption by the Spanish of the Portuguese world empire was followed by the catastrophe of the Armada, which in the event proved to have marked the point at which the hitherto rising curve of Spanish greatness bends over to its even longer decline.

(2) The attempt by the French Sun King, Louis XIV, in 1702, to convert Spain itself, with all its continental and overseas provinces, into so many satellites revolving in his imperial orbit, was sufficiently foiled at Blenheim, which similarly, though less irrecoverably, marks the transition from rise to decline of French military predominance on the Continent. And Blenheim, if only partially a British victory, was indisputably the result of British intervention, failing which Louis's gamble would almost inevitably have come off.

(3) Napoleon's temporarily successful attempt to annex or dominate all that mattered of Western Europe was similarly foiled by his failure to subdue Britain or break the strangle hold of her sea power.

(4) The German seizure of Belgium in 1914 and subsequent violent expansion were foiled not only by British but in the long run by united Anglo-Saxon intervention.

(5) The same process is re-enacted on an even grander scale in the Second World War, whose decisive turning-point proved to be the frustration, by British air power this time, of the customary armada which, like all its predecessors, except the first, never got to the stage of leaving port.

Anyone who casts his mind's eye over this sequence, as rhythmical as that of Channel waves, one after the other, rolling in and gathering and breaking against the white English cliffs, may well be inclined to query the dogmatic assumption of the textbooks, that these things chanced to happen as part of a struggle for power in which Britain is involved on no different footing from that of other European nations. Yet this is what is implied by the customary verbiage about something vaguely referred to as the balance of power, which all, including Britain, are supposed to have had an equal interest in preserving and which each was severally doing its best to tilt to its own upsetting advantage. It would pass the wit of man to make intelligible sense of such a story.

Whereas once the special part of Britain, standing, as it were, not in but over against Europe, is fairly recognized, we see the lineaments unfolding of a stupendous drama—though it may depend on the audience's point of view whether the part in question is to be regarded as that of hero or villain.

But regard it from what angle we will, there is no excuse for blinking the facts. And the more these are examined, the more clearly it stands out that it has tended to become the aim of British policy to hold aloof from involvement in the power politics of the Continent, except to the extent judged necessary to prevent Europe from becoming united under the sway of any one of its competing sovereignties. To do this successfully demanded the application, by a subsconsciously evolved technique, of just the amount of force that might be needed from time to time to avert this contingency.

To say this is neither to justify nor condemn conduct that is as natural as breathing. To ask whether this one insular community had the right to impose its veto on the coming together of the ancient civilization from which it had elected to break off is to ask what no community is capable of asking itself. The urge towards self-preservation is basic. *Il faut vivre*, and the necessity is not argued about but acted upon.

The plain fact of the matter is that Britain came instinctively to realize that the survival of her independent civilization was incompatible with the emergence of a united Europe, a resurrected Western empire, in sight of her shore. And she would not stick at doing her best—or damnedest—to stop it. Would not, because she could not. It was a matter not of moral choice, but of primitive and fundamental necessity. *Il faut vivre*.

But waiving all considerations of right and wrong, the profounder question arises whether it is to be accounted, on the most comprehensive reckoning, a *good* thing that Britain should not only have embarked on, but succeeded, in this policy of preventing Europe from emerging from the condition of international anarchy into which she had fallen after the final breakdown of her medieval attempt to maintain at least the framework of a united civilization.

And the answer—even supposing one to be possible on the strength of our experience up to date—will depend on answers to two other questions. Whether, in the first place, even a divided Europe might not have been a lesser evil than the only kind of unity by which it was likely to be superseded—that of an imperial, culminating in a Totalitarian, despotism? And again whether the free growth and expansion of British-born civilization might not have been fraught with such consequences to mankind as to justify any measures taken to safeguard its continuance?

I merely state these questions, leaving the facts, so far as I am capable of supplying them, to answer for themselves.

I am not seeking to imply that British policy was ever consciously directed to such ends, or that those responsible for framing it would ever have dreamed of formulating it in these terms. They were bound by its preconceptions and thinking in its terms, feeling their way empirically. But there are modes of thought and action that grow up in communities, apart from and above those of the individuals composing them, and by which the reactions even of their leaders are determined to a greater extent than even the greatest of them consciously realize. Thus it is permissible to regard these statesmen, not only as framers each of his own policy, but to a greater or less degree in proportion to the integrity and vision vouchsafed them, as the trustees and agents of an overriding national or eventually super-national policy.

But we cannot be too much on our guard against attributing to it the precise and logically defined outlines that any attempt at lucid exposition must constantly tend to assume. We are dealing with deep-seated habits of thought and action formed in the course of many generations, that are in no sense planned, and seldom acknowledged, and that can be known—but even so are rarely recognized—only by their fruits. They are born, after much prolonged travail, of trial and error, and their first surface manifestations are ambiguous and often contradictory. And we must bear in mind that of all national mentalities the English is that which is the most addicted to going forward on the strength of its intuitions, and is the most allergic to the clear-cut processes of self-conscious reason. It is therefore only by a long, patient discipline of factual and, as far as possible, unbiased observation that we can hope to see the lineaments taking shape of an evolving pattern, a dramatic unity, into which all the otherwise confused incidents of the story are seen to fit themselves with some approximation to inevitability. It is only then that history begins to make sense, and history that does not make sense had better not be written.

BOOK THREE

1

ENGLAND GOES
OUT OF ORBIT

WE MAY LOOK upon the Restoration as the point of no return in British history. It is from then onwards that the *decree nisi* of divorce between the British and continental ways of civilization, pronounced by Henry VIII and confirmed by Elizabeth, may be said to have become absolute. As long as Cromwell survived there was a real danger that at the last moment Britain might be pulled back from the path of her almost accepted destiny to go whoring after stranger gods of European imperialism, to her incalculable loss, temporal and spiritual.

Not that even so she can be said to have blossomed out into her true self, or struck out a decided line of her own. The period that follows, of over a quarter of a century, covers a drama of violent vicissitudes in which none of the leading characters appears to be impelled by any motive not entirely self-regarding, and in which no point of public principle appears to be involved. And yet, if we examine the plot from the standpoint of mass psychology, we shall discover a definite thread of purpose binding it together. The nation, if not fully conscious, was at least becoming incipiently subconscious, of a destiny that it was determined at all costs to fulfil.

A new international situation had developed of ominous import. For though Cromwell was dead, he had not died soon enough to prevent his reckless and suicidal policy from bearing fruit. For by backing the rising power of France against that of declining Spain he had helped to bring about the very situation that Britain had most cause to dread—of one Power, and that the most dangerously sited for offensive action against her, threatening to draw all the rest into its imperial orbit. From henceforth to the end of the seventeenth century and beyond, the France of Louis XIV, a far more efficiently organized empire than that of Spain had ever been, towered like a Colossus above the other nations of Europe with its magnificent army, for long unbeatable in the field, and its limitless expansive ambition not only in Europe but overseas.

It was now, if ever, if might have been thought, time for Britain to have seen the red light, and to have devoted all her energies to providing against this vital menace. But it was at this very juncture that, owing to an ill-advised royal marriage, the Sovereign himself was, half by birth and almost wholly by temperament and inclination, a Frenchman, and a secret addict of the Roman Catholic and—as such—militantly anti-British ideology. The second Charles, a brilliantly astute politician and no more unscrupulous than most others of his time, made no conscience about bypassing the constitutional difficulties that had been the death of his father, by allowing Britain to revolve in the French Sun King's orbit for a consideration—in cash down. He played this game on a Parliament that developed the same disposition to starve and blackmail the occupant of the throne that its predecessors had done, and whose leaders had no more scruples than he about lining their pockets from the same source.

It was a continuation of Cromwell's game of playing for his own hand at the expense of that of Britain. Both were impelled by a similar and understandable fear, the one of being brought to book for the crime of high treason, the other of being sent, as he put it, 'on his travels'; and though Oliver, in his English way, preferred to go ahead in the strength of the Lord without knowing where he was going, and Charles, with his French lucidity, knew very well indeed where *he* meant to go—and where to stop—it worked out to essentially the same conclusion of throwing the weight of British support on to the side of the acting candidate for European empire.

Charles played his hand with subtle plausibility, by enlisting patriotic sentiment on his side, and selecting for Britain's enemy number one, not the land power of France, but the sea power of the United Netherlands, thereby reverting to the Rump Parliament's policy of a frank trade war in which Britain's geographical position and superior resources were bound to give her a winning advantage. This indeed worked out more or less according to plan until, after the Dutchmen had resigned themselves to making the best of a bad business and giving Britain more or less what she wanted by way of a peace treaty, an incident occurred of a kind that seemed fated to bedevil Anglo-Dutch relations, for it was curiously the same in principle as that of Majuba Hill, two centuries later.

While the negotiations for peace were actually on, a professedly hundred-per-cent loyalist Parliament, taking their conclusion for granted, actually cut off from the Crown the bare minimum of supply necessary for keeping the hitherto on the whole victorious fleet in commission. Charles, who did not resemble his father in making a patriotic conscience of such things—for indeed he was little troubled with a conscience of any sort—just shrugged his shoulders in his French way, and constitutionally obliged by laying up the ships, washing his hands of the consequences. And the Dutch Admiral is hardly to be blamed for taking what, on a statesmanlike reckoning, was a most unwise advantage of an obvious opportunity, by making a bonfire of the helpless ships at their anchorage in the Medway, and towing off in triumph the pride of the King's navy, the flagship *Royal Charles*. It was a fool's mate, as neat and sensational as the storming of Majuba, and like that, it hardly affected the already virtually concluded peace settlement. Charles, who was not the man to allow the booming of distant cannon to interrupt his evening's enjoyment, probably registered nothing more emphatic than a cynical 'I told you so'. But those who are old enough to remember the part that the 'Avenge Majuba' slogan played in inflaming the South African war fever will realize how the man in the London streets, who had experienced for himself the panic and humiliation of that memorable night, must have felt about getting even with *Mynheers* over the Medway. It was a sentiment that Charles did not need to share to exploit it in due course to his own advantage.

So far no irreparable harm had been done. At least a plausible case might have been argued, on Machiavellian principles, for this second Dutch war, which had undoubtedly tended to confirm the supremacy of British sea power and might have been considered to have justified itself—if anybody of the time had been capable of appreciating its significance—by the handing over to Britain of the under-colonized Dutch settlement on the Hudson River, that now became the English colony of New York, thus linking up the northern and southern areas of British expansion on the North American seaboard.

But though dangerously irrelevant to what ought to have been the essential aim of British policy, this war between the two Protestant sea Powers had involved no direct collusion with the overshadowing menace of French imperialism, and indeed had been followed by the formally correct move of an alliance between them that helped in effecting a temporary hold-up of France's expansion on her vital north-eastern frontier.

But this merely served as a camouflage for what, from the British point of view, amounted to a criminal conspiracy, promoted by the monarch himself, to accept French collaboration in putting England back under the yoke of the Catholic ideology. How far Charles himself ever took this scheme seriously is at least doubtful. He was fully as capable of treble-crossing his cousin Louis as the latter was of double-crossing him. And by secretly pledging himself, as and when it might become feasible, to an undertaking that he never made the least serious attempt to honour in practice, he did at least succeed in touching him for just the amount of cash he needed to render himself, at a pinch, more than a match for the blackmailing tactics of his own faithful Commons.

It was a policy as brilliant as it was cynical, and at a time when almost everyone in political life was playing for his own hand, without inhibitions of any kind, not abnormally immoral. But it was, in the most dangerous sense, not only un-British but anti-British; all the more so because it played up to the basest form of patriotic sentiment in the desire to get even with the Dutch over that coup of theirs in the Medway.

The third Dutch war, into which England allowed herself to be drawn in junior partnership with France, sounded the lowest depth of the policy of collaboration, and, if all had gone according to plan— Louis's plan—would have precipitated the very disaster that it had been the prime object for centuries of British policy to avert, for it would have involved the extension of the Sun King's *imperium* over the United Provinces, which would certainly have paved the way for its absorption of the Spanish Netherlands, and the inclusion of the whole of the Low Countries in the dominions of a potential Caesar. And yet it was hard to see how anything short of a miracle could have averted such a catastrophe, when the combined navies prepared to sever the vital Dutch sea communications, while the magnificent French army, under the leadership of those two mighty captains, Condé and Turenne, swept round in overwhelming force on Holland's open eastern flank, carrying all before it.

That the miracle did in fact happen was no thanks to Britain, though it saved her from the pit that she had dug for herself. Holland's finest hour did produce the men. For no naval victory has Britain ever had more cause to be thankful than for her frustration at the hands of the great de Ruyter, while the temporarily eclipsed ruling House of Orange produced the latest of its series of patriot heroes who, as if to the manner born, took charge of the situation, and saved it in the only way possible, by cutting the dikes and turning the capital and heart of the Union into an island. This last-ditch expedient gave him breathing space, by a masterly diplomacy, to rally other (now thoroughly alarmed) European Powers to his support in fighting Louis to a stand-still. This young hero, the third of the Orange Williams, though no more personally attractive than the heroes of real life are apt to prove, had the advantage—as might have been noted for future reference— of having just as much British blood in his veins as the reigning King, and of being in the legitimate line of succession.

It may be asked how this signal failure of Britain to rest true to herself in her official policy is to be reconciled with the statement made at the beginning of this chapter about the Restoration having constituted the point of no return in British history. Here was surely a turning of her back on what we have indicated as the path of her true destiny as ominous as any associated with the dictatorship of Cromwell. It may fairly be conceded that the policy of either of these two strikingly contrasted characters, if carried through to its logical conclusion, would have been equally catastrophic in its effects. But it is just in that 'if' that the fundamental difference between them lies. Cromwell had possessed the means for implementing his policy in the shape of the finest army, for its quality, in the world, and one that held the country in a grip of iron and had been in a position to override public opinion.

But that army was now dissolved, and Charles was—except for a mere token force of the one or two regiments that he had succeeded in retaining—without an army at all, and consequently in no position to defy a public opinion that, once roused, was capable of dispatching him on his travels at short notice. And, public opinion in England being intransigently Protestant, he was shrewd enough to realize that he was as capable of giving Louis the moon as of handing him a Catholic England on a plate, whatever it may have suited his book to promise.

There was never the least serious question of his putting back the religious clock, or of turning Britain aside from the path of her self-chosen destiny. Even her participation in the conspiracy to annihilate the Dutch Republic had been an act of self-betrayal into which she herself had been betrayed by a royal appeal to her own baser impulses; and it was only a short time before she came to her sober senses, and forced her monarch to realize that 'this dance'—to anticipate a phrase of Sir Robert Walpole—would 'no further go', and to get out of a now thoroughly unpopular war as quickly and unobtrusively as possible.

England, we may say, was becoming intuitively apprised of what was involved in the independence she had in effect declared at the crisis of the Reformation. She reacted violently and blindly against any suspicion of an attempt to bring her back into membership of a wider civilization than her own. This must be held to account for the extraordinary outbreak of mass hysteria known as the Popish plot scare, worked up, as it was, at the instigation of political gangsters like Lord Shaftesbury, by professional perjurers like Titus Oates.

But there was something more to it than mere criminality. If the public mind had not been in a ferment of genuine apprehension, men like Oates and Shaftesbury would never have been able to take advantage of it as they did. England had seen the red light, even if she could not pinpoint the danger. The Popish Plot was no chimera. The King himself was in it as far as he dared, and had indeed undertaken to sell the pass to the enemy, though whether so slippery a customer could be relied on to honour his side of the bargain was another matter. But the King's brother and heir made no bones about his conversion to the Faith, and James, Duke of York, was notoriously the sort of man who would go to all lengths in any cause to which he had once committed himself.

It was therefore with some formal justification, in the light of events, that Shaftesbury, now plainly committed to mobilizing Parliament against the Crown in the same way as Pym had done in the former generation, switched over from the played-out stunt of crude Catholic baiting to the more subtle device of carrying an Act of Parliament, excluding James from the succession in favour of the most immediately available Protestant candidate, who happened to be the feather-brained bastard whom his alleged father had created Duke of Monmouth and whose patent inadequacy, on every ground, was the weak point of the whole scheme.

The country was thus presented with a choice of alternatives each equally unacceptable, and it is fascinating to observe how that impalpable but very real entity of English mass consciousness did in practice contrive to react to the challenge, by hitting on a solution precisely as if it were endowed with an intelligence and volition of its own. This is a faculty that, however we may, or may not, be capable of accounting for it, is inherent in the English political genius, and has more than once, in such times of crisis, enabled the people to take the game out of the hands of its politicians and dictate its own solution.

Here was conspicuously a case in point. England was getting more and more restive and dissatisfied about the way in which her affairs were being conducted. Public opinion was becoming increasingly suspicious of collaboration in high places, not only with the spiritual bogey-man at the Vatican, but with the far more formidable temporal Caesar whose imperial palace at Versailles was just rising to its symbolic completion. But there was one thing that the country dreaded even more, and was determined to avoid at all costs, and that was any repetition of the armed rebellion and revolutionary violence of the previous reign, which was what Shaftesbury and his Whig party (as it was now named) were plainly heading for. It was this that enabled the most astute of monarchs, fortified by just enough of what was in effect a satellite retaining fee from Louis, to call the revolutionary bluff and dish his Whigs at what appeared to be the height of their success, without forfeiting one jot of his personal popularity—rather, if anything, enhancing it.

The country was well satisfied to allow the King a free hand to suppress the revolutionary menace, which had now reached frightening proportions, and to allow him to carry on for the rest of his reign without parliamentary assistance. There was all the difference in the world between this state of suspended constitutional animation and a real absolutism on the continental model. Charles was forced to make do on a starvation revenue that he dared not augment except by such niggardly doles as he might from time to time get out of his cousin, and he had to mind his step the whole time, since his lack of military force left him wholly dependent on the goodwill of his subjects. It was also a breathing space of comparative non-belligerency on the Continent. The makeshift arrangement in fact suited everybody concerned, except the Whigs, and the royal voluptuary, who desired nothing better than to enjoy a peaceful existence, was not the man to upset it. He had learnt his lesson, and as long as he lived could be trusted to steer clear of popish conspiracy at home and martial commitments on or over the seas.

This was well enough as far as it went, and might have passed for a reversion to the traditional principles of British policy, but there was a flaw about it—it was tending to become out of date. Defence by sea power alone, backed by such levies as could be improvised to cope with any particular emergency, had indeed sufficed for all practical requirements in Elizabethan or early Stuart times; but to prevent the domination of Western Europe by so highly organized a military power as that of Louis XIV some comparably trained military force, though on nothing like the continental scale, would be called for. When it was the question of tilting a nicely poised balance a little British army would still—in the words of the old music-hall song—go a long, long way; but no British army would go no way at all.

The easy-going solution of the constitutional problem arrived at in the last years of Charles II's reign, which involved such a calculated rationing of sovereign power as to keep the Head of the State in a condition of military and financial impotence, might thus prove to be a suicidal gamble. But it is characteristic of the English mentality to avoid meeting trouble half way, and consequently to neglect making any provision against it till it has actually materialized. It was, however, brought up against reality in a way it had little expected.

When Charles died, fortified by the rites of a Church to which he had prudently abstained from rendering any practical support, and his brother James took over, the country was on a rather shamefaced rebound from its recent bout of anti-Papal hysteria, and few Englishmen were likely to think the worse of their sailor Prince for his honesty in standing up for the faith that was in him. He had only to run reasonably straight for them to accord him as much loyalty as they had given to his brother. But they had the misfortune to be dealing with a man who, if not certifiably insane, was incapable of a normally factual adaptation of conduct to circumstances. James II presents a problem for the psychologist that has hitherto evaded his biographers, none of whom has ever seriously attempted to account for the change or collapse of personality that transformed a naval commander of the first rank and a naval administrator second to none on British record into a cold-hearted and pig-headed reactionary, ignominiously devoid (most amazingly of all) of the redeeming gift of kingly courage. It would seem that something must have snapped in the man when, by the operation of an act of precautionary or panic legislation, he found his honourable career cut short and himself dismissed from all his offices on the ground of his religion.

However we may account for it, the fact is glaring that James, once in the saddle, started riding for a fall at a breakneck gallop, as none saw more clearly than the Pope himself, who was as powerless as anybody else to make this impossible convert listen to reason. The Popish Plot was now an open conspiracy flaunted by the monarch in the sight of the whole nation, and it was in such circumstances that James chose, with the uncompromising logic of insanity, to proceed, bull-headed, to confront a hitherto loyal and largely packed Parliament with a demand for the regular army of expeditionary dimensions, that nobody but so experienced a fighting man was better capable of realizing was a prime necessity of national self-preservation. But anybody less obtuse than James would have realized that such a demand, coming at such a time and from such a source, would mortally affront the most rooted convictions of all but the small Catholic minority of his subjects. What Parliament had gone to all lengths to deny to James's father, what it had wrought its own destruction by conceding to Cromwell—the power of the sword—was the last thing it was ever likely to entrust to a prince who was openly determined to fashion the new force into the armed spearhead of his popish crusade, and a means of providing himself with an arbitrary mandate to override both the liberties of his subjects and the independence of his realm.

Here was a worse dilemma for the country than ever, and not for the first time, nor the last, England demonstrated her capacity for preserving her loyalty to the throne by transferring it from a legitimate to a practicable incumbent, with the least possible breach of formal continuity. The public consciousness was dead set against any fresh unloosing of the subversive forces that had brought about the Civil War; it was still as loyal as it dared to be to the reigning dynasty, and had given proof of its readiness to leave its King to the enjoyment of his private religion if he would only leave his subjects to the enjoyment of their own religious and civil liberties—a thing which James was fully convinced and determined that he would be damned if he did. His elimination had thus become a surgical operation, to whose urgency public opinion had become alive, and the only question was how to get it performed as cleanly and painlessly as possible. It was accordingly decided to call in the Anglo-Dutch specialist who had so signally demonstrated his competence in performing a similar operation for his own country.

To talk of the successful performance of this necessary act as a glorious revolution is disingenuous. There never was, in fact, a less glorious episode in the history of this or any other country than that of the unopposed landing on British soil of a mixed invading force composed of Dutchmen, Prussians, Swedes and other foreign mercenaries; the ignominious failure of a superior British force to check its progress to the capital, through the treachery and double-dealing of everyone responsible, from the Commander-in-Chief downwards; and finally the unkingly readiness of the once-gallant Sovereign to allow himself to be shooed out of his realm with his tail, metaphorically, between his legs.

Nor was there ever a person less calculated to appeal to the British of all temperaments than the cold and calculating realist who put through the business with such unromantic efficiency. Never in the long and varied line of English Sovereigns had there ever been one who was less liked by his subjects than William of Orange, or one who was at less pains to conciliate their affections. Though he might, not implausibly, have been described as the saviour in turn of both the countries whose blood he shared in equal proportions, he was neither an English nor a Dutch patriot, but something more cosmopolitan and impersonal that might best be defined as a European patriot. He had an obsessive conviction that the ambition of Louis XIV would stop at nothing short of the subjection of the whole Christian West to his imperial sway, and he had dedicated himself, with frigid concentration, to frustrate this purpose by binding as many as possible of its scattered sovereignties into a close-knit alliance for their common safety. They were the pieces on his board, and with a single eye to the eventual checkmate, or failing that, stalemate, of this latest attempt to unite the West under a resurrected Caesardom.

It will be seen that this wholly fitted in with what had long been the prime objective of British policy, of preventing the domination of Europe by any single Power. But there was a subtle difference of standpoint between that of the good European, who was wholly concerned with the preservation of a *status quo* that to him signified a free Europe, and that of the basic Englishman, who was primarily concerned with the freedom of his own country to develop and expand in unconditional independence of any civilization except her own, and to whom this *status quo* of a divided Europe signified the essential condition of that freedom.

That was an attitude from which, to the time of the World Wars, Britain was never to swerve to any serious extent. It is essential for us to realize what this attitude was, and to what extent it represented an advance on what had hitherto been her policy of insulating herself behind the protection of her sea power, and depriving her Sovereigns of the possession of any regular army of more than token or ceremonial dimensions. This problem the parliamentary coalition that had engineered the revolution proceeded to solve in a characteristically English way, by putting the army in constitutional leading-strings, and making its maintenance and discipline dependent on annually renewed parliamentary sanction. Even so the idea was to improvise an army for this special emergency of a European war, and for that only. Since the lesson taught it by Cromwell, the country was not as yet able to stomach the idea of providing the Head of the State with an effective peace-time army, even under the strictest constitutional limitations.

It was not altogether to Britain's disadvantage that her Dutch Sovereign should have been interested in her internal politics only to the extent of getting the maximum contribution out of her to his grand European strategy, and a consequent free hand for himself in his military and foreign policy. Provided he got this, he was content to leave the politicians to hammer out among themselves the various constitutional adjustments called for by the new domestic situation, which meant that Britain was able to evolve on her own lines in entire freedom from foreign and with the minimum of royal interference. The process of her development was by no means edifying, since the political game had never sunk to a lower level of corruption and sharp practice; but the fundamental liberties were at least preserved, and the thread of their vital continuity remained unbroken in an age of practically standardized imperialist absolutism among the Powers of the Continent.

So much Britain may be said to have owed to the intervention of her Dutch liberator—but as an unintended by-product of his dedicated task of liberating Europe from the tyranny of the Gallic Caesar. And hence the reflected coldness towards him of his British subjects was in the circumstances inevitable. The difference between their respective standpoints was felt rather than defined, but it was fundamental. He was seeking to bring Britain back to Europe in membership of his anti-French crusade, and to get the maximum effort out of her in membership of a grand continental alliance. Her purpose, on the other hand, was to limit her contribution to the common cause to the bare minimum necessary to safeguard her own freedom from European interference. Her involvement in continental power politics was a necessary evil, to be kept within the strictest limits imposed by necessity. Her attitude was 'isolationist' in the sense in which the

word was coined to denote American policy in the early years of this
century.

And hence, throughout the century that follows the Glorious
Revolution, we find her tending to act in a way that explains, whether
or not it justifies, the epithet of 'perfidious Albion'. She is constantly
found in alliance with the weaker Powers against the big bully of the
Continent, but she is an undependable ally, as she engages herself on
the limited liability principle and pulls out of the hurly-burly as soon
as her own limited objective is achieved and the bully of the moment
neutralized.

Britain was thus able to exert a decisive influence on the European
situation without the total commitment of her resources that was
imposed on the competing land powers, allies and enemy alike. Her
sea power, as Bacon had foreseen, allowed her to take as much or as
little of the war as she chose, and she chose the latter. Consequently,
while they were bleeding themselves and each other to death, she was
able to keep the major part of her energies in hand for more profitable
employment elsewhere, whether for expansion overseas or industrial
development in the security of her wooden-walled insulation. This
depended on the existence of so nice a balance of contending forces on
the Continent that a comparatively small increment of strength to one
side or another would give it, if not a winning advantage, at least
security from defeat. And this condition was in fact fulfilled after
William had brought Britain into the anti-French coalition. The
French armies still maintained their ascendancy in the spectacular and
almost ceremonial general actions that were the rare highlights of their
almost static campaigns, while all the time Louis was being held to a
standstill and exhausted in the process. After nine years of this unprofitable clinch, he gave it up and concluded a peace that practically
amounted to restoring the *status quo ante bellum.*

Britain's weight in the scales had thus proved fully effective, and
William, with her aid, had once again succeeded in frustrating, if not
yet of removing, the threat to the liberties of Europe. But he got little
enough thanks for this from his English subjects, whose constant
anxiety was lest he should be planning to involve them more than
absolutely necessary for their own safety in the pursuit of his essentially
European aims. The longer the war went on, the stronger became their
desire to get back to the old traditional isolationsim.

Their natural instinct was therefore, as soon as peace was concluded,
to get Britain permanently free of her European entanglement, to
demobilize this instrument of potential despotism constituted by a
war time army, to get every Dutch or foreign soldier shipped overseas,
and in future to leave the other continental nations to settle their own
accounts with France, which they appeared capable of doing without

British assistance. William, whose thankless exertions in the common cause were wearing him into a premature grave, and who knew that Louis was only biding his time for his supreme bid for European supremacy of virtually extending his *imperium* to embrace the vast Spanish dominions, could only bow to the storm. Though he had at one time been on the verge of resigning his crown and shaking the dust of England off his feet, he stuck with invincible patience to his dedicated task of saving Europe. When the expected crisis burst he had at least, before closing his eyes, the satisfaction of seeing Britain adding her whole-hearted, and what was to prove decisive, support to his reconstituted grand European alliance—fully decisive this time.

For now Britain had the opportunity of giving an almost classic demonstration of her European technique of limited intervention. The grip of her sea power at once closed on the Franco-Spanish seaboard, while an English army, exiguous in comparison with the Dutch and other allied forces, but under a commander of supreme genius, resumed its old station on the northern flank of the alliance. But the conditions of the former, static warfare were relaxed; this time Louis was going all out for a decision. By getting the alliance of Catholic Bavaria he had opened up what was subsequently to prove Napoleon's route down the Danube to Vienna, the seat of the Hapsburg Emperor, a scion of whose House was the rival candidate for the Spanish throne. That in exploiting this route he was exposing his flank to a counterstroke from the Anglo-Dutch-German forces strung out along the northern theatre was so contrary to all the established conventions of military science that it never occurred to the French high command as a practical possibility. But it did occur to Marlborough, the English generalissimo, who, by a masterpiece of deception of his own allies no less than the enemy, and an unexampled combination of strategic and tactical brilliance culminating in what has been rightly classed among the decisive battles of the world, not only threw France on to a precarious defensive, but for three generations put paid to any conceivable chance there might have been of a French domination of Europe. Such was the effect of British intervention on the Continent, without which there could never have been the least question of such a result, and Marshal Tallard's Franco-Bavarian army might as likely as not have knocked the keystone out of the alliance by smashing its way to Vienna. And yet the British contingent had been, in point of numbers, as contemptible a little army as that which turned the balance in the crisis of 1914.

It is arguable that if Britain could have got out of the war as soon as possible after Blenheim she would have done so, if not with honour, at least with her main object achieved. But it would have been hardly thinkable for her to miss the opportunity of following up her success, in conjunction with her allies, by driving the French armies out of the Low Countries and sending them reeling back behind their own frontiers. England had never had such a surfeit of military glory since the days of Agincourt, and it seemed that there was nothing that her army, under its invincible commander, was not capable of accomplishing in conjunction with its allies. But it was at this very high-water mark of success that the tide of public opinion began to turn against the war and even its leader. And nothing is more distinctive of the British way of civilization than the power that public opinion, once it has been fairly aroused, has time and again shown itself to possess of imposing its will on Parliament and government, in spite of the most corrupt and illogical system—or lack of it—of parliamentary franchise.

It was conspicuously so on this occasion. Just as England, in despite of all apparent probability, had made a complete *volte face* from her pacifist isolationism to enter the war as a united nation, so now, after half a dozen years of unprecedented military success, she decided that she had had enough of involvement in European quarrels and alliances, and that the time had come to get out of the war on the most favourable terms that she could get.

Accordingly there took place something equivalent to what in twentieth-century terms would be called a Tory landslide. It is fashionable to demonstrate that nothing equivalent to the modern party system did, in fact, exist under the auspices of Queen Anne; we do not need to be reminded of the Duchess of Marlborough's falling out of favour, and the excitement worked up over the comic-opera martyrdom of the egregious Dr Sacheverell, and all the other incidents in the criss-cross of personal intrigues that were the ostensible means of bringing about this result, reinforced by one of the most skilfully conducted propaganda drives on all record, headed by the redoubtable Dean Swift. Are not these things the commonplaces of the textbooks? But the effect of it all was precisely as if a working majority of Englishmen—as if Britain herself—had decided that the war was being needlessly prolonged, and that her interests were being sacrificed to the greed and selfishness of her European allies. Like a winner in a party of card sharpers, she decided to gather up her winnings and retire from the contest with the least possible delay.

This is what the very able and wholly unscrupulous bosses of the victorious party succeeded in effecting for her, by a deal with the common enemy behind the back of her allies, And an uncommonly successful deal it was for both parties concerned, since it gave Britain all she could reasonably have hoped to get out of the war, and left France a great deal better off than she would have been if the terms she had been willing to concede four years previously had not been thrown back in her face.

It is impossible to justify such a transaction in terms of ordinary morality. The leaders of the now dominant faction were troubled with no more scruples than Machiavelli's Prince—they were out for number one first, and were playing their country's hand in the same diamond-cut-diamond spirit that they were playing their own. But they were playing it correctly, in the sense that they were accurately conforming to the will of the impalpable entity that we personify as Britain. They harboured no latter-day illusions about her membership of the European family—their aim was as frankly isolationist as that of the Republican party of the United States in 1919. And this represented not a passing mood, but what had now become the settled and basic determination of Britain to cut down her European commitments to the extreme practicable limit. But with only the Channel instead of the Atlantic Ocean between her and Europe, to define that limit would not be easy.

Certain guiding principles did however emerge, that will be found to hold good into the present century:

(1) Britain would regard it as a life and death matter, and go to all lengths to prevent the domination of the Continent by any single Power.

(2) She would also regard it as a life and death matter to maintain control of her outward radiating seaways, and consequently her own freedom to expand, and incidentally to trade.

(3) If forced, in pursuit of either of these aims, to resort to military intervention on the Continent, she would do so with the utmost economy of manposer and expense, and pull out of it at the earliest practicable moment, without too nice a regard for entangling alliances or engagements.

Only by holding fast to these threads shall we be able to make intelligible sense of Britain's seemingly ambivalent relationship to Europe in the modern age. It might be defined in these three words:

Isolation to capacity.

2

IMPERIUM
A NON IMPERANDO

SUCH WAS the relationship in which England had, by her 'Glorious Revolution', signified her determination of standing towards Europe. From that choice she was never to swerve—least of all in the century that lies between that and a very different sort of revolution on the opposite side of the Channel. It is a time in which Britain is involved in no less than five major wars, in all of which she finds herself with France as an opponent and, in all but the last, opponent in chief. According to the conventional account, these are, to an ever-increasing extent, wars for empire. There is a French Empire pitted against something of the same nature called the First British Empire. The latter succeeds in demolishing the former, and then itself comes to grief through internal dissension. The collapse of this first British Empire is held to date from what is described as the loss of the American colonies.

But this orthodox and plain-sailing version will be found, if we come to examine the facts, to depend on the more than questionable assumption that there ever was a British in the sense that there was a French Empire. Of course we can, as in fact most writers do, lump together the results of British expansion overseas under the designation of empire and leave it at that. But in that case we are emptying a necessary and irreplaceable word out of its proper context, by equating an empire that *is* an empire, and functions as such, with one that has nothing imperial about it except the name.

It would indeed be permissible to proceed on the analogy of the famous seventy-second chapter of a certain History of Iceland, and say (speaking of empires instead of snakes): 'Concerning empires, there is no British Empire to be met with during the period specified.'

We might even go on to question the precise sense in which the American colonies may be said to have been 'lost' to this alleged empire.

But of the French Empire, as it took shape during the great age of

Louis XIV, there can be no more question than of its Spanish predecessor and contemporary. There never was a more authentic emperor
in everything except the title than this officially styled Most Christian
King. Of him it can truly be said that his imperial capacity was limited
only by his power. He had entered into the inheritance of a State
organization fashioned on autocratic lines by the two great Cardinals,
Richelieu and Mazarin, and of which he himself could truly say,
'L'État, c'est moi!' And he discovered a minister, in Jean Baptiste
Colbert, of a genius ideally calculated to give practical expression to
this idea. Under this upright and devoted but inhumanly efficient
bureuacrat—men called him the North Star—the Latin instinct for
imperial centralization was given unlimited scope. Every department
of national activity was taken in hand and regulated so as to function
with the precision of a vast machine, under the control of a single
operator. Not only the political but also the economic life of the
community was subjected to this royally sponsored form of totalitarian
State socialism.[1] Manufactures were forced and fostered with all-
embracing energy. And the same urge for centralized regulation was
applied to the management of the French Empire overseas. Though
orders might take months to transmit, it was sought to hold the
French settlers on the St Lawrence or Mississippi in as tight leading-
strings as the courtiers at Versailles. And incredible as it may sound to
English ears, there is no doubt that the system did work, as far as the
colonists were concerned, without friction according to plan.

That is just where these real empires differed most fundamentally
from the British non-empire. The French, like the Spanish and
Portuguese colonists, wanted nothing less than to be saddled with the
responsibility of conducting their own government. They expected,
on the broadest lines, to have their affairs ordered and settled for them
by a paternal sovereign Power. They would have regarded it as a
gross betrayal to be turned loose to their own devices. For the imperial
coin has two faces, of mastery in the ruler and obedience in the subject
—the will to power and the willingness to be governed.

Now, in the minds of the British settlers overseas, this reverse face
of the imperial coin did not exist. They felt fully capable of running
their own affairs for themselves; they had in their blood the tradition
of doing so, and believed that when they went abroad they took their
liberties with them—their Magna Charta and Common Law and
associated privileges and habits of self-government—which they
assumed the right of exercising, quite regardless of forms of government, which they preferred to ignore rather than dispute.

[1] Though not completely enough; for Colbert, who was essentially an opportunist going for quick returns, never succeeded in cutting out of the system two
besetting evils of provincial customs barriers and discriminatory taxation.

For they were practical folk, pioneers of civilization in a new world, with all their energies engaged in their struggle with wild nature and savage men, and with little time or inclination for discussing nice points of constitutional procedure. They were content to take things as they came, and carry on as best they might within the framework of the existing system, since it was a physical impossibility for the Crown, or any capitalist proprietor, to come the tyrant over them, or subject them to any more pressure than they were ready to endure for the sake of peace—which as a rule amounted to precious little.

Indeed it is difficult to form any clear picture of the patchwork evolution of what is so often miscalled the First British Empire in the century preceding its collapse. Each of the thirteen colonies along the Atlantic seaboard functioned as an almost independent entity, with hardly the least consciousness of membership in any wider union—indeed they might plausibly have been referred to as the *Dis*united States. Each of them in its own individual way contrived to assert its liberties and work out its own constitutional salvation, if not without friction, at least with a marked absence of sensational incident, and it would be safe to say without the knowledge of at least 99 per cent of the home population, to whom colonial affairs, except from a purely commercial standpoint, were a matter of profound indifference.

Certainly, until things began to boil up to the final crisis, it hardly occurred to anyone, even in the colonies themselves, that there could be the least question of open revolt, or of severing connection with the mother country. Considerations of loyal or patriotic sentiment may have weighed lightly enough on the colonists, but they had a shrewd enough sense of their own interests to realize that they had far more to gain than to lose by keeping the bond of allegiance formally unbroken. They had not yet arrived at the stage of being able to stand on their own feet and go it alone. The protecting hand of British sea power was performing as indispensable a service for them as it was for Britain herself. Isolated communities as they were, whose populations were numbered only by thousands, they were sandwiched between the two mighty empires of Spain to the south and France to both north and south of them. This latter, incomparably more united and efficiently organized than the loose federation of British colonies, formed an ever-present and increasing menace, as it threatened to execute a vast pincer operation behind them, by joining up, by a chain of forts, its settlements on the Mississippi with those on the St Lawrence, and thus pinning the British colonies to the narrow strip between the Alleghany Mountains and the sea, sealing them off from what they were afterwards to claim as their manifest destiny of peopling the vast continental hinterland between these mountains and the Pacific. And in addition to this, there was the problem of the undefined and shifting frontier between themselves and the wild Indian tribes to whom these lands were the hunting grounds over which they ranged in a perpetual state of warfare with each other and the Palefaces. Incapable as they were of combining together, or pursuing a united policy, without British support their case would have been desperate.

But on what terms was this support likely to be forthcoming? We should be deceiving ourselves if we thought of the mother country being moved by a national solicitude for these pioneers of her civilization overseas. Of no time in her history could it have been said with less qualification than in this so-called age of reason that the cult of Mammon, uncomplicated by any emotional or moral infusion, was more openly in the ascendant. The spirit of that age might, for purposes of practical policy, have been crystallized in Iago's maxim of 'put money in thy purse'. It is only by keeping this firmly in mind that we shall be able to understand the rise and collapse of this first British Empire that was in fact no empire.

It was the profit motive that made British statesmen, with the backing of public opinion, desire to retain the colonies, and not only to retain them, but to maintain Britain's authority to regulate their economic activities in what purported to be the common interest. And her attempts, however sporadic and ineffective, to assert such authority, constitute the only plausible excuse, though a thin one, for applying the term empire at all to the results of British expansion in the eighteenth century.

To understand just what this amounted to, we must make a distinction that is seldom drawn, between what such regulation sought to effect, and what it in fact did. We hear a great deal in the textbooks about something that is dignified with the name of the Mercantile System, though anything less systematic than the hotchpotch of Parliamentary ukases by which it was sought to apply it, it would be hard to imagine. But its governing idea is that international trade is less than a mutually profitable exchange of goods and services than— to adapt a phrase of Clausewitz—war carried on by other means. Nations are supposed to be engaged in a perpetual struggle to thrive at one another's expense, and therefore need to organize themselves as effectively for trade as for any other sort of war. It is therefore to any nation's advantage if it can extend the range of its control over as wide as possible an area, within whose pale economic activities can be co-ordinated on a footing not of mutual hostility but of fruitful co-operation.

It being taken for granted on both sides that the colonies and mother country were good to each other only for what they would fetch, something had to be done to put the connection on a business footing. The obvious way seemed to be to render this world-wide association, if not hermetically sealed, at least as self-contained as possible. The trade of the colonies was therefore to be directed into the courses most profitable for the mother country, and therefore—so they were asked to believe—for themselves. Britain was to be made the great emporium, or staple, for their products, which products were to consist of such raw materials as simple hewers and planters, working under relatively primitive conditions, might ship thither in British-manned vessels to be worked up—except when, like tobacco, they could be passed on direct to the consumer—into finished products. And therefore, in order to maintain this profitable apportionment of function the colonists were to be gently but firmly restrained from setting up manufactures of their own. As Lord Chatham put it in his magnificent hyperbole, if the Americans should manufacture a lock of wool or a horseshoe, he would fill their ports with ships and their towns with troops.[1]

This is putting very baldly what in practice was more often left to be deduced from a whole complex of legislative Acts by Parliament and administrative Acts by the Crown adapted to the needs of the moment rather than forming part of any master plan. But this was its general effect and, in theory at least, it cannot be denied that an element of imperial purpose entered into it.

If the system could have been got to work, of a world-wide economic organization, directed from a centre at Westminster, with all the constituent members functioning in ordered unison for their mutual advantage, then indeed it would not have been straining language to talk of a British Empire, even if it were not an empire in the unqualified Caesarian, but in a strictly business or commercial, sense.

But the plain fact of the matter is that such an empire never got into existence at all, in the sense that it did in the French or Spanish dominions. The psychological conditions were dead against it. *Regere imperio populos* had no application to British peoples, who totally lacked the instinct for being regulated or regimented as part of an imperial set-up. Of the Mercantile System, so far as it can be called a system at all, they were prepared to take just as much or as little as they found suited their convenience. As long as the shoe did not pinch too tightly they were content to go on wearing it, even if they had to slash and cut it so as to convert it into the equivalent of a sandal. For the home Government could do no more than enact laws and regulations that it lacked the machinery to enforce, and that could be rendered virtually dead letters by evasion or smuggling with the ill-concealed connivance of the colonists and their representatives. A system that can be made to work only by a tacit agreement to connive at its wholesale infraction is no system at all—least of all an imperial system;

[1] Quoted in *The Causes of the War of Independence* by C. H. van Tyne, p. 65.

unless indeed we elect to apply that title to an *imperium a non imperando* which is all that the First British Empire ever succeeded in being.

We have to realize, in dealing with the history of these times, by what crude and childish notions even the choicest minds were apt to be possessed, particularly where commerce and industry were concerned. Since the discovery of the New World the economic structure of society had been changing at a rate that had outrun the capacity of the human mind to keep up with it. Consequently we find public opinion and State policy possessed by a spirit that often, in the event, seems one of sheer lunacy, chasing will-o'-the-wisps, and basing calculations on what now seem demonstrable fallacies. It was in the heyday of this age of reason that statesmen and public alike allowed themselves to be stampeded by such transparent bluffs as that of the South Sea Bubble in England and Law's Mississippi Bank in France, from sheer inability to realize that money is incapable of multiplying itself indefinitely without a tangible backing in the way of goods and services. Indeed the whole attitude of the age of money was determined by a superstitious belief, inherited from the alchemists, of the magic properties supposed to be imparted to these so-called precious metals by the fact of their having been adopted as the medium of exchange, and this confusion of thought was worse confounded by the superstructure of faith, or credit, imposed upon it.

The temptation to simplify or rationalize the facts of history is too often the bane of those who write it. It is so fatally easy to take the notions of our forefathers at their face value, and to conjure up the picture of an ordered and controlled system of economic co-operation, which we can, with apparent plausibility, dignify with the title of Empire, whereas what we actually find is an unplanned chaos, with nothing imperial or systematic about it, but whose very ineffectiveness was the sole guarantee of its continuance.

Intuitively, at least, this was sufficiently realized on both sides of the Atlantic. And so long as British policy was in such hands as those of Sir Robert Walpole, whose considered principle was to avoid trouble at all costs, or of the Pelham brothers,[1] whose instinct it was to follow on all occasions the line of least resistance, there was no serious tendency on the part of the colonists to challenge openly rights and regulations that could be almost as easily honoured in the breach as in the observance.

Seldom can there have been a case in which the ostensible face of things corresponded so little to the reality. While the fabric of royal government and commercial regulation remained formally intact, the individual colonies had accomplished all but the final stage on the road to independence before there was any question of declaring it. There

[1] Henry Pelham and the Duke of Newcastle.

might indeed be individual Governors who tried to throw their weight about with tactless arrogance, but in the resultant friction and squabbling the colonists, with their power of the purse, had the whip hand. In New England two of the colonies, Rhode Island and Connecticut, had actually attained the equivalent of dominion status by electing their own Governors, and over the whole of this northern area, with its Puritan and radical tradition, there was hardly the pretence of *de facto* recognition of, or loyalty to, any outside authority. And here, at any rate, the sole inducement for remaining in even formal allegiance was supplied by the overshadowing proximity of the French province of Canada, whose military potential rendered British military and naval support a positive *sine qua non* of colonial survival.

In even the briefest survey of British expansion overseas in the century preceding the War of Independence, one's attention inevitably tends to become monopolized by the colonies on the North American mainland. But they did not stand out so prominently in the eyes of contemporary Englishmen, few of whom, to judge by the records of the time, condescended to bother their heads about them one way or the other. From the strictly utilitarian standpoint that was assumed as a matter of course, these settlements were regarded as an asset of less value than tropical islands whose cultivation by slave labour under the control of a small planter aristocracy offered such rich returns.

As for the colonists themselves, in so far as they were thought of at all, it was without any feelings of pride or brotherhood, but with a certain superiority or even distaste as a barbarous sort of folk, judged by the standards of a polite age, whose proper function it was to perform the necessary spadework of civilization. Not everyone was as brutally frank as a certain colonial Governor who asserted that the King's subjects in New England did not differ much from the slaves, the only difference being that they were not bought and sold,[1] or of Dr Johnson, who regarded Americans as, if possible, worse than Scotsmen, and would explode at the very mention of them; but such ebullitions were at least recognizable caricatures of prevailing opinion. And in William III's reign no less a dignitary than the Attorney General, on being asked to draw up a charter for a religious college in Virginia, on the ground that the Virginians had souls, had retorted: 'Souls! Damn your souls! Plant tobacco!'

It is not necessary to have a very exalted or even complimentary notion of the term 'empire' to say that it was never more preposterously applied to the process of national expansion than to that of Britain beyond the western ocean. But if we turn our regard eastward during the same period we should have to make an exception, for there the

[1] Governor Joseph Dudley in 1702—cited by C. H. van Tyne in *The Cause of the War of Independence*, p. 38.

E

imperial spirit was not only lacking, but specifically opposed to British sentiment. Never was there a plainer case of business for business' sake, without any tincture of patriotic and imperial aspirations, than that of the British East India Company, which had no corporate ambition except to produce dividends for its shareholders, though its individual servants were commonly even more concerned to feather their own nests than to make profits for their employers. There was nothing that either the Company itself or its servants desired less than to have any other form of power than that of the purse thrust upon them, and not in their wildest dreams or nightmares would any of them have envisaged laying the foundations of an empire that should embrace the Indian subcontinent. That it should ever have gone to India at all had formed no part of the Company's original intention. The islands of the East, like those of the West Indies, were the commercial plums of their respective hemispheres, and the Asiatic mainland was not, like the North American, free for European expansion, but was already densely populated and under the sway of potentates as outwardly formidable as those of Europe.

In the first century of the Company's existence nobody could have foreseen the circumstances that were to turn the Indian Peninsula into a vast political vacuum and a field of limitless opportunity for economic exploitation. But such was the effect of the dry rot of the Mogul Empire during the long reign of the last of the really great Moguls, Aurungzebe, whose death in 1707 was followed by the collapse of the only native power capable of arresting the fragmentation of his empire into an anarchy of provincial despotisms. In face of this breakdown of central authority, even a company of peaceful merchants was forced to stake out its own claim to sovereignty over however limited an area, if it was to remain in business and pay dividends. But this was a business to which the principle of limited liability did not apply. Having committed itself so far as to grasp the sword and the sceptre, John Company—as it was to be called—was to find no practicable limit to its commitments short of that set by nature in the mountain chain of the Himalayas. To expand thus far or to collapse—such was the accepted, if not the manifest, destiny of even the most unwilling entrant in what was to prove essentially a knock-out competition for the Raj that even the Moguls had failed to consummate, and that no native Power was strong enough to achieve.[1]

No more paradoxical event has ever been recorded than that this enormous prize should have ultimately fallen to the latest come and most unwilling of the European competitors, and that the wholly

---

[1] This was finally proved when the Hindu Maratha confederacy was knocked out of the running on the historic field of Panipat, the Indian Armageddon, in 1761.

commercially minded British Company whould have proved strong enough to sweep the board of all its genuinely imperial rivals—one of whom, France, which had enlisted some of her ablest warriors and administrators in the venture, had seemed at one time on the point of carrying all before it, and had even in 1746 secured local command of the sea for long enough to capture the seat of the British Company's government at Madras. And yet within fifteen years of this event the French power in India was to all practical intent finished, and the British Company was already in control of the opulent and fertile province of Bengal, which was the first stepping-stone towards the sovereignty of India.

3

WINNING ADVANTAGE

THE TWO MID decades of the eighteenth century were big with fate. They saw two major wars in which the| European Powers were involved in varying combinations, and which were separated by an interlude of peace that was no more than a truce, and an imperfect one at that. They were, in one aspect at least, wars of empire. But, as far as overseas empire was concerned, it was the least imperially minded of all the Powers involved that eventually triumphed all along the line from Quebec to Calcutta. It was not a British Empire that had profited by the downfall of the French and the repulse of all the others, but was on the one side of the world a complex of as yet disunited and potentially independent states that were now less inclined than ever before to defer to Britain's imperial mandates, and on the other a trading company as anxious to evade imperial responsibilities as its now extruded rivals had been to assume them. Whatever it was that all this added up to, time would reveal, but what nobody, even among her sometime opponents, doubted was that Britain had emerged from the long struggle at a pinnacle of world power undreamed of and unsurpassed.

It was as if fate had dealt her a winning hand that only in the concluding stages of the game, and under the inspired leadership of the elder Pitt, she had found the secret of playing. For, pending his advent to power, her career had been anything but glorious. In the first of the two great European wars in which she was engaged she had cut a sufficiently inept figure, not only on land but even on her own chosen element, where it seemed more than once as if her command of the sea was about to be lost from sheer slackness on the part of her commanders; though in the concluding stages the navy had recovered its traditional stranglehold sufficiently to induce Louis XV's flabby administration to purchase a breathing space by disgorging such vital conquests as those of Madras and Flanders. But the second and ultimately victorious war opened in such ignominious fashion that it proved necessary to make a public example by shooting a typical slack admiral in order to encourage the others, which was just exactly the effect it had, for from that time forth it was all out to win with the rest of them.

Once, under adequate leadership, Britain had found her true form, she had comparatively little difficulty in driving home her winning advantage with scientific precision, so as to sweep the French navies from the sea and most of the French overseas possessions, with a pick of the Spanish thrown in, from the map. And it is important to realize just what that advantage consisted in, for it went much deeper than mere success in war.

Briefly it consisted in the freedom that Britain had acquired to develop her own way of civilization in effectively sheltered independence of that followed by the nations of the Continent, and in consequence to devote a decisively greater proportion of her energies to its natural expansion or outflow. This freedom was conditional on her ability as an island Power to command her own sea approaches and to control her outward radiating seaways.

It would have been an ideal solution of her problem had she been able to take refuge in a policy of unconditional detachment from the rivalries of the Continent—in other words of insular isolationism. But it was only in face of a divided Europe that her freedom had been, or could have been, won in the first place, and it was her deep-rooted conviction that only in face of a divided Europe could it be maintained. In the depths of her being she was haunted by the fear of the old Roman Empire reincarnating under some new Caesar of a transplanted Rome, and reclaiming the lost province of Britannia. To prevent such a contingency needed a perpetual vigilance, and the diversion of just as much, though no more than that much, of her energy as was needed to prevent such a contingency from ever materializing. During the eighteenth century such a policy was known as that of the balance of power, which is a more polite way of describing one of keeping Europe continually on the boil in order to free her own hands for the task of overseas expansion. But that was what it undoubtedly worked out at during those two great wars of the middle of the century.

The luck of dynastic succession provided Britain with a *pied à terre* on the Continent in the shape of the Electorate of Hanover which, though its maintenance in the interest of whoever happened to be the reigning George was apt to be regarded by his English subjects in the light of an entangling commitment, gave her just the opportunity she wanted of drawing out the energies of her chief opponent, with the utmost economy of her own. The elder Pitt, an anti-Hanoverian himself when on the political make, switched over, when in office, to

the exploitation of this technique, in order—as he put it in his magni-
loquent way—to conquer America in Germany. It was only part of a
grand political and diplomatic strategy that Britain had muddled into
more by instinct than calculation in the first of the two wars, but which
Pitt taught her to pursue with masterly intent in the second, of keeping
the European Powers with their hands full and their veins bled white
in a murderous agony in which Britain was concerned to intervene only
to the extent necessary to prolong it. Hence the master-stroke of her
alliance with Frederick the Great of Prussia, whose armies, in their
struggle against colossal odds, were doing their essential bit for Britain
of conquering America in Germany—and India too for that matter—
just as much as the small but highly efficient British contingent that
fought at Minden to cover his western flank. And Britain, under Pitt's
successor, threw him over in due course with as little sentiment as she
had evinced in playing the same trick on her allies of the Spanish
Succession War, but on no more cynical a calculation than Frederick
himself habitually acted in betraying anyone who ever trusted him the
moment it suited him. War is a dirty business at the best of times, but
there was never one in which it was pursued with less tincture of
morality or elementary decency than in this age of polish and reason.

When we say that Britain's triumph proved in the long run one of
the principle of free civilization over that of imperial tyranny, it is with
no implication that this was the spirit in which even the best of contemporary Englishmen went about the task of winning it. A crusade
for liberty, or anything else, was fantastically allergic to the spirit of
the age. You were in wars for what you could get out of them in the
most material sense—on that there was no dispute even among the
combatants themselves. And to Britain in particular, with her world-
wide commercial interests, all wars were apt to present themselves
primarily as wars of trade, though even her efforts were apt to be
marred by unbusinesslike maladjustment of means to ends, and she was
largely ignorant of the real sources of her strength.

For the winning advantage that she had over her European rivals,
in that amphibious sort of war in which she specialized, applied equally
to the fields of industry and commerce. It sprang from the freedom to
which I have already referred, of being able to build up her own way of
life behind the protection of sea power, so as to keep the maximum of
her energies and resources at her own disposal for peaceful employment in the most profitable channels. And that was just what was
lacking to the chronically embattled land powers of the Continent.
They had need for all their expendable energies in the struggle for
existence on the one hand and power on the other, and it was the
prime business of their more or less benevolent sovereigns to mobilize
all the resources that their subjects could be made to yield for this

purpose. We who have lived through an anxious struggle for our own existence realize how thoroughly the national resources can be combed when such a crisis is on. But in the nations of continental Europe such a crisis was always on, or sensibly impending. And where the national resources are drawn upon to the limit for the most unremunerative of all forms of activity there can be no scope for building them up for any more constructive purpose. You cannot spend and save at the same time—you have got to choose between guns and butter, between arming to the teeth and stocking your trade and industry.

It was upon the horns of this dilemma that Colbert had found himself impaled in his heroic efforts to make France as great a commercial and manufacturing as she was a military Power. Whether or not such hothouse forcing by state action as he relied on was the best way to go about it, what is certain is that industry can no more thrive without its sinews than war. These sinews of industry consist of capital, by which name is signified those products of industry which, instead of being consumed as fast as they are produced, can be set aside, like seeds, to fructify and multiply production in the future. Once the Sun King had fairly committed himself to his grandiose policy of imperial expansion, everything in the way of money and manpower that could be soaked out of the nation was bespoken by the insatiable demands of Louvois, the war minister, for the maintenance of those armies strung out along the frontier, that though so long invincible could never achieve decisive victory—so that Colbert's plans for industrial supremacy died of capital starvation. Even the navy, that by a supreme *tour de force* he had built up almost to the point of achieving command of the Channel, lost control of it after one battle, and the means were lacking for even an attempt to regain it. He died a baffled and a broken man, having been set to wrestle with a task that he was denied the means to accomplish.[1]

And what was true of the France of Louis XIV was true to a greater or less extent of all the jarring continental imperialisms in the 'balance of power' era. They were compelled to expend such an overwhelming proportion of their available energies in raising themselves up to the highest pitch of military efficiency in the struggle for power and survival that they were forced to starve themselves of the necessary means of economic supremacy.

Now Britain's advantage—reckoned in those unblushingly material values that all alike took for granted—consisted in her ability to cut

[1] The finishing touch was supplied, after his death, by the insanely consistent effort of Louis XIV to round off the imperial unity of his realm by persecuting and driving out the Protestant subjects, who supplied the most valuable element of his industrial manpower. Spain, earlier in the seventeenth century, had perpetrated the same blunder in expelling her Moriscoes.

down her military commitments to a jealously rationed minimum, and consequently to devote a far greater proportion of her energies to the building up of her economic resources, behind the invisible wall of her sea power. Instead of her industries being starved in order to feed her armies, with her it tended to be the other way about. It was only during the burst of martial enthusiasm inspired by the magnetic leadership of Pitt that the Parliamentary guardians of her purse-strings could be induced to damn the expense and go all out for victory—and that only for the briefest period.

But dating roughly from the second quarter of the eighteenth century, Britain was undergoing a revolutionary change, resulting ostensibly from a series of discoveries and inventions that altered and eventually mechanized the whole structure of her industry, and put her on a level of productive capacity that, until later in the nineteenth century, remained far above that of any of her European rivals. But this is not to be credited to any special faculty she possessed of producing inventive geniuses, in which it would be absurd to claim that she was more prolific than contemporary France, but simply that the conditions existed in her (as they did not on the Continent) in which such genius could be turned to profitable employment on an adequate scale. Invention has to wait on capital quite as much as capital on invention. If the looms of Lancashire, let us say, had not been hungry for mechanization, there would have been no Arkwright, no Crompton, no Cartwright, to devise means of mechanizing them. It is a case in which ripeness is all. The idea of the steam engine is as old as the Ptolemys, and the principle of it was well grasped before the eighteenth century, but until the conditions were ripe for the firm of Boulton & Watt to commercialize it, the steam engine was no more than an expensive toy. And England was the first country in which such conditions were realized—the first country, that is to say, that could afford to put aside a sufficient proportion of her material wealth for the creation of more wealth, instead of consuming it up, or firing it off, as fast as she got it.

It was really as simple as all that. Of all her conscious efforts to foster her industry and equate her trade that figured so largely in the calculations of the time, and are even now accorded such importance in textbooks of economic history, it is at least a moot question whether —in so far as they were ever got to work at all—they did not do more harm, in the long run, than good. Certainly this applied to such clever political coups as that of Queen Anne's Tory Government bargaining at the peace with France for a monopoly of the African slave supply to Spain—a move that turned out to be as unprofitable as it was immoral.

The dogs barked—the caravan moved on. Parliament fussed and

legislated; Adam Smith's predecessors spun their theories, the colonies made nonsense of the Mercantile System, and all the time the steady process went on of a multitude of individual Britons, each of them intent solely on feathering his own nest, building up the mounting resources of capital that were to enable Britain to become the workshop of the world.

It was one result of her separation from Europe—a result on the lowest plane. But at least, on that plane, it did pay dividends.

4

THE NEW ORDER
COMES OF AGE

IF THE NET results of Britain's break away from the civilization of the Continent, and her determination to strike out her own line in unqualified independence, had produced no better results than those already recorded, it might have been thought little enough to boast about. To have feathered her own nest at the expense of her neighbours, and to have made her own profit by exacerbating their differences, might seem a course hard to justify even by success. The same question that was originally supposed to have been put about the most striking of her victories might be asked of her performance over the whole epoch: *But what good came of it at last?*

Not that it would have occurred to any contemporary critic, British or European, to ask it. Whether or not we can endorse the description of the age as one of reason (it was one almost equally of muddled thinking and pompous superficiality), no one would ever dream of describing it as an age of morals. Material standards ruled the roost as they never have succeeded in doing even in the heyday of Marxian communism, which does at least manage to stoke up an inverted sort of idealism. But in the age of wigs and perukes, before the romantic revival began to get under way, no more than the most conventional lip homage was paid to any pursuit but that of success, and success reckoned solely in terms of 'things that you can touch and see', with spiritual values barred. It was a time when even poets could see nothing inappropriate in writing odes to commerce, though they would have blushed to stoop to the display of naked emotion. This attitude was in no way peculiar to the English. However much the insular civilization may have diverted from that of the Continent in other respects, whatever moral blight may have affected it lay at least as heavy on the lands adorned and symbolized by such figures as those of the Pompadour, Frederick the Great and Casanova.

And yet I would dare to submit that it is from a time quite early in the eighteenth century, or late in the seventeenth, that we ought to date not the birth, but the visible coming of age of an order in being of civilization embodying a new principle of freedom, and capable in process of time of a world-wide expansion so far above and beyond its insular seedbed as to supersede the very designation of 'British'. And the first inklings of such a development were observable not so much in England as—what is even more significant—in the most enlightened minds on the Continent.

It is true that if we were to judge by the conventional patriotic out-pourings of those coarse-spun days, we might be inclined to imagine that the sole basis of the average Englishman's claim to superiority over all foreigners consisted in his alleged capacity to match his jolly self triumphantly against any 'two skinny Frenchmen and one Portuguee', which is the attitude of the perennial schoolboy towards the inmates of rival establishments which he believes, in kind, to differ in no way from his own.

For patriotism itself, in those days when the stoutest patriot of all could describe it as the last resort of a scoundrel, was a very *ad hoc* and straightforward assertion of 'better than thou', based on an under-lying assumption of 'the same as thou'. And in an epoch dominated by the enormous bulk and wig of Sir Robert Walpole there was no difference to speak of between 'better' and 'better off'.

Even Hogarth, the great delineator of that age, dropped his pose of *censor morum* when he gave rein to his own meaty patriotism—not to speak of that of his prospective buyers—and contrasted the beef-guzzling John-Bullishness of his English types with the frog-fed scarecrows who stand for their opposite numbers in such pictures as that of the typical French scene of Calais Gate.

'The first time'—to quote his own words—'an Englishman goes from Dover to Calais, he must be struck with the different face of things at so little a distance. . . . Poverty, slavery and innate insolence, covered with the affectation of politeness, give you even here a true picture of the manners of the whole nation.'

From this the natural reaction of most modern readers will be one of aversion from the spectacle of so consummate an artist prostituting his brush and pen to this sort of mud-bottom patriotism. And yet, if we look into the matter a little more closely, we may find reason to suspect, even thus early, an incipient cleavage between the British and continental ways of civilization that it only needed time to widen into a gulf deeper than the Channel.

Even these words that I have just cited from Hogarth, and still more the pictorial matter that they are intended to elucidate, may be found to carry an implication that is not entirely materialistic. Poverty is linked to slavery, and Hogarth clearly means to rub it in that the connection is causal, that it is just because those scarecrow soldiers and peasants lack the Englishman's birthright of freedom that they are condemned to a diet of frogs instead of the roast beef of old England: a lampoon on whose *suppressio veri* and *suggestio falsi* it would be superfluous to enlarge, but, for all that, giving authentic expression not only to what in Hogarth's day was the rooted faith or prejudice of his own countrymen, but was even coming to be regarded with a certain sympathy among the high intelligentsia of the so-called Enlightenment on the other side of the Channel.

For whatever may have been the shortcomings of the British way of life judged by twentieth-century standards, the contrast between its effects and those of the sort of autocracy that was standardized on the Continent was palpable. On a diet of freedom concocted to their own insular specification the English did visibly thrive and prosper, if not quite to the extent indicated by Hogarth, at least so as to impart a certain plausibility to such strains as those of his almost equally admired contemporary, James Thomson, the bard of *Rule, Britannia!*:

> The nations, not so blest as thee,
>   Must in their turns to tyrants fall,
> Whilst thou shalt flourish great and free
>   The dread and envy of them all,

or even such roaring belly-catches as that subsidiary national anthem about the glories of England's roast beef.

It is true that this brave façade masked a background of brutal injustice and squalid misery. For this we can have no more damning testimony than that of Hogarth himself, when he is not composing patriotic advertisements and can give full rein to his native realism, and it is fully borne out by that of Fielding, Smollett and a host of contemporary witnesses. But the tough guts and coarse-spun nerves of the early Georgians enabled them to take in their stride accompaniments of their daily life the very thought of which are enough to turn the average stomach of our less robust days, and rendered them perfectly capable of believing that England was the veritable Utopia of freedom and prosperity compared with her continental rivals generally, and France in particular. And incredible as it may seem to us, there is no doubt that this belief was to a greater or less extent shared by the most advanced leaders of French thought, who were the last people to be carried away by even their own patriotic propaganda, let alone that of a traditional rival.

Voltaire, for instance. Witness the remarkable series of letters that was the fruit of his enforced sojourn in England, whither he had been practically banished, after having been sent to cool his heels in the

Bastille for having demanded the satisfaction of a gentleman from a nobleman who had first grossly affronted him at the dinner table and afterwards had him beaten up by his lackeys. Just the sort of thing that Volatire thought could not have happened in England.

But Voltaire was more in his element in noting down the visible benefits of British freedom—and particularly as they affected a free-thinking young Frenchman of letters—than he was at diagnosing its causes, or even its precise nature. It was not his way to delve deep enough below the surface of things to diagnose the workings of a mentality as different from his own as growth is from planning.

But it was this very task to which another almost equally famous leader of the French intellectual revival, the Baron de Montesquieu, set his hand. In contrast to the dazzling impressionism of Voltaire's sketches of English society, he sought to comprehend its workings scientifically and to weave the result into the pattern of by far the most ambitious attempt at a social philosophy that the so-called Enlightenment managed to produce.

A more unqualified Anglophile than Voltaire, he had no doubt that England owed her unique constitution to the freedom that it embodied, and the account that he gave of it to the world did at least— if only by dint of its errors—play a notable part in shaping the course of future events.

Relying largely on the writings of John Locke, the philosopher evangelist of the Whig party in England and of its Glorious Revolution, Montesquieu imagined he had discovered the secret of this freedom in the separation of powers—executive, legislative and judicial —that had been the theory and very largely the fact of the constitution under the Tudors, who had really governed as well as reigned through ministers of their own choosing, with Parliament making the laws and controlling the purse-strings. It was this theory of the constitution that the tragic Sovereigns of the House of Stuart had fought a losing battle to retain as its fact, but that the Glorious Revolution had finally exploded into fiction. Henceforth the tendency was for the legislative body, the Parliament, to swallow up the executive, by lodging the controls of State in the hands of a committee or cabinet representing its own dominating faction, though the House of Hanover fought a long, dogged rearguard action to delay, or prevent, this ultimately inevitable consummation.

Montesquieu had, in fact, allowed his Gallic instinct for neat and logical solutions to betray him into a signal misunderstanding of the way that the facts of English political life have of taking on shapes that nobody had planned or foreseen. He had thus, like so many foreigners who take the Englishman's account of his own proceedings *au pied de la lettre*, mistaken the form for the fact. But this very misunderstanding was itself a fact that was fraught with momentous and even revolutionary potentialities, when propagated with facile eloquence and swallowed hook, line and sinker by those who, like the founders of the American constitution, had the power to put them into nation-wide operation.

But however fortunately or fatally Montesquieu may have gone astray in his explanation, we can at least credit him with having grasped, more firmly even than Voltaire, that there was a fundamental difference between the British order of society and that standardized on the Continent, and that this difference was summed up in the idea of liberty. That was after all the root of the matter, even if the nature of that liberty was still far from being adequately realized. For it was no abstract conception, but liberty of that concrete and uniquely English brand, that had been the theme of so much patriotic bombast, but whose underlying reality no Englishman had been as yet much more successful than these continental critics in defining or appreciating.

And yet if Montesquieu had only had the insight to follow up the clue afforded by his own title, *The Spirit of the Laws*, it might have led him to realize how profoundly the distinctive quality of the English social and political system, and the unbridgeable cleavage that separated it from those of its continental rivals, was due, in the last resort, to the spirit of that law, the English Common Law, of which the constitution itself was the outward and visible embodiment, and of which the spirit of empire and autocracy was the irreconcilable antithesis.

That there could have been any special magic of freedom enshrined in the English legal system (or chaos) might seem a claim beyond the limits of paradox, about this of all times when judges did not turn a hair at packing the Tyburn cart with men, women, or even children, who had committed the most trifling offences against the rights of property, when whole estates were swallowed up by the law's proverbial delays, when lawyers grew fat while debtors rotted alive, and when poor men found the scales of justice mercilessly tilted against them by technical quibbles. Yet in spite of all these things, that are the commonplaces of the textbooks and are summed up in the title of the original John Bull saga, *The Law is a Bottomless Pit*, the evidence is overwhelming that the early Georgian Englishman, even of the lower classes, was robustly satisfied with what he regarded as his heritage of freedom, and looked on most if not all foreigners as slaves by comparison.

The common Englishman was in fact satisfied, on the whole, with a *status quo* in which his wholly illogical liberties were guaranteed by his equally illogical law, and this hedgehog-like attitude was respected by those in authority who knew him best. And it was, to say the least, shared by his kinsmen who had emigrated overseas, not only taking their liberties with them, but transplanting them to soils on which they sprang up and luxuriated with rank exuberance. This was a state of things the reverse of that which obtained in the overseas provinces of such genuine empires as those of France and Spain, where the ingrained habits of obedience which had been fostered at home by military necessity and a legal system inherited from imperial Rome engendered loyalty to more or less benevolently paternal sub-despotism.

5

THE PRICKING OF
AN IMPERIAL BUBBLE

VERY DIFFERENT was the spirit of British colonists, who had not the least wish to have their liberties cut down to the pattern of Empire, but were prepared to stretch a few points of nominal obedience provided they were conceded at least nine-tenths of their own way in practice. And that was a state of things that Walpole and his immediate successors in office were prepared to wink at, and connive at, rather than run the slightest risk of a head-on collision with those intractable subjects of His Majesty. It was thoroughly of a piece with their attitude to the unenfranchised but hardly less intractable 'mob' of common citizens at home, and was dictated by an instinctive determination to jog on in the accustomed grooves, and avoid trouble at all costs.

It was a system, or rather a lack of system, that worked to the reasonable satisfaction of all parties concerned, until what appeared to be its crowning and triumphant success in the virtual annihilation of French imperial rivalry in both hemispheres. It would seem only natural to conclude that the British Empire, presided over by its new King, George III, was now on the top of the world, and had only to harvest the fruits of its victory. Whereas, far from having any empire to imperialize over—barring possibly the imperial province which she had just taken over from France—Britain now found herself confronted with a number of nominally subject but practically independent communities of her own stock whom, at a vast expense of blood and treasure, she had contrived to relieve of their principal reason for wanting to remain in connection with her.

It had been seriously proposed that, as part of the peace settlement, she should have handed back Canada to France in exchange for the rich West Indian island of Guadaloupe, just as fifteen years previously she had got back Madras by restoring the French fortress of Louisburg, at the mouth of the St Lawrence. Had this been done it is to the last degree improbable that the colonies would have dared sever connection with the mother country. But such a Machiavellian masterpiece was out of keeping with the intelligence or even the morals of George III and the ministerial team presided over by that dimmest of amateur mediocrities, Lord Bute, who had set their hands to the ungrateful task of liquidating the policy of imperial conquest regardless of expense, to which that most dynamic of war ministers, Pitt, was irrevocably committed. Pitt was in fact shelved, as Marlborough had been half a century previously, in order to wind up a ruinously expensive war policy that was being pursued à outrance simply for victory's sake, and to come to a practical business arrangement that would allow Britain to gather up all the winnings she could reasonably hope to get, and retire from the contest. If this involved leaving her allies, and particularly such an ally as Frederick of Prussia, to shift for themselves, it was part of a perfectly understood game in which everybody was equally out for his own advantage.

Those much maligned personages, George III and Bute, could at least claim to have successfully sponsored the most glorious peace settlement on English or British record—judged at any rate by conventional standards. To all ostensible showing, it was the British Empire—the first British Empire—that had sensationally vanquished its Gallic and Iberian counterparts, and now, with its control of the seas firmly assured, saw opening before it a vista of power and expansion such as Rome herself had never dreamed of. And yet, within a mere decade, the process had visibly begun that was to precipitate a collapse even more sensational than the victory had been, and to write *finis* to this same alleged Empire.

The bare facts of the story are—or ought to be—notorious: the Boston Tea Party, the first hostilities, the Declaration of Independence, the surrender of two British armies, the belligerent intervention of the other imperial Powers and the all-but-belligerent hostility of most of the rest of Europe, and finally a peace as humiliating as the one twenty years previously had been glorious. All this needs no retelling. It is only its significance that is open to dispute.

It is but fair to acknowledge that the myth that once set the ever-changing fashion of historic orthodoxy is now largely discredited on both sides of the Atlantic. In reputable circles no one clings any longer to the simple explanation of George III as a reactionary tyrant goading his simple and loyal subjects overseas into rebellion—though no doubt it was precisely in this way that their leaders did melodramatize the situation. George III was a pathetically well-intentional sovereign, with no grain of the tyrant in his composition. He was endowed with outstanding talents both as a political tactician and still more as a promoter of scientific agriculture. But he had a mental twist that was almost certainly due to his German origin, and might be best described as a sort of earnest literalness. He was a man not only of principle, but also of preconceived and cast-iron principle. He had none of the Englishman's instinct of compromise, or of adapting his principles to practical necessity. For instance, he considered himself quite literally bound by the terms of his coronation oath to maintain the Protestant ascendancy in Ireland, regardless of consequences. It was an honourable, but to an Englishman would have been an impossible, attitude. And in just the same way he took the British Empire, and his own responsibility to maintain it, literally. However benevolently he might be disposed towards his subjects overseas, he had a known system to operate, and lawless defiance of it was more than any lawful sovereign had the right to tolerate. There was a fatal logic in his 'Rebels must be made to obey'. But it was an imperial logic, and as such, flatly un-English and Teutonic.

If George had had a greater infusion of English blood in his veins, he would have taken a leaf out of the book of Sir Robert Walpole, who had, when the mobs at home had started rioting against his own attempt as Premier to launch an excellent excise scheme, thrown logic to the winds, and dropped the whole project with the remark that 'this dance will no further go'. If King George and his government had been equally wise in their generation, the American crisis might at least have been postponed, and the dance that followed the Boston Tea Party prevented from developing into a dance of death.

But that is not to say that any conceivable effort of statesmanship could have preserved the semblance of a British Empire in any form that would have included the North American colonies. It is easy to censure the ineptitude of the royal and ministerial handling of the situation, and to demonstrate the folly of niggling attempts to force the colonists to foot some fraction of a steadily mounting bill for imperial —or at least common—expenses. But we should find it less easy, with all our advantages of hindsight, to suggest any alternative line of policy that would have offered a feasible solution to a problem that was perhaps in the last resort insoluble—and fortunately so in the interests of all concerned.

For it is tacitly assumed, at least by all British commentators on the subject, that what is described as the loss of the American colonies was in the nature of a tragedy that ought somehow to have been prevented; and this involves the further assumption that these colonies were in fact 'lost' when they asserted, and made good, their political independence of the British Sovereign and Empire—assuming again that there ever was such an empire. And certainly if we are to think imperially—in terms, that is to say, of power—we should have to account any daughter community as 'lost' that openly set up house for itself and signified its intention of becoming, unconditionally, its own mistress. But bonds of family union are not always necessarily severed —and sometimes are even strengthened—by this natural and healthy process of development. Membership of a common civilization is in no way affected by the really irrelevant consideration of who governs whom. And it is at least arguable that the British-born order of civilization was both confirmed and strengthened by an event that set each of its constituent members free to ensue a common destiny in its own individual way.

The more, indeed, we consider the situation in the light not only of what we know of its essential factors, but also of what experience of the subsequent two centuries has revealed, the more we shall realize the utter impossibility of 'keeping' America in any sense that the men of that time would have found acceptable or even intelligible. It must be remembered that up to, and even beyond, the turn of the eighteenth century, sentimental considerations had been explicitly barred from any consideration of the colonial question on either side, and that to Britain, by dint of the elaborate apparatus of tariffs and restrictions that constituted the mercantile system, the colonial empire was believed —on more than doubtful grounds—to constitute a rich, dividend-paying asset. But after the great victory it became apparent that, from the colonial point of view, the connection was worth maintaining only on terms that would offset these largely imaginary British assets by a crushing liability.

Britain had already saddled herself with what by the standards of the time was a swingeing burden of debt, in a war which the colonists had done their best to prolong by illicit trading with the enemy; and now that the menace of French encirclement had, chiefly by force of British arms, been finally dissipated, not only did they make it clear that they expected the British taxpayer to foot every penny of the bill, but also that they intended to go on taxing him, in effect, without representation, by piling up fresh bills, regardless of expense, on his account. For not only did Britain provide the free services of her navy to endow her colonists with the same invasion-proof security that she enjoyed herself, but her army was also expected to be at their disposal against any lingering threat from European rivals and also against the aboriginal denizens of the vast continental hinterlands. The least that the British authorities might have expected in these circumstances was for the colonists to refrain from stirring up trouble by wantonly impinging on these immemorial hunting-grounds, and allowing the King's government—which was the only possible co-ordinating authority—at least some power of frontier supervision. But this was the last thing the practically independent and mutually hostile individual colonies were prepared to concede, even had they been capable of setting limits to their own expansion. For indeed the Americans had already begun to feel the urge of what they were subsequently to describe as their manifest destiny. The most lawless and criminal elements of the population gravitated to a West whose wildness has become legendary, an irregularly advancing outer fringe in which white toughs and red savages vied with each other in the blackest extremes of treachery and cruelty.

Whether this drive to the Pacific, involving the dispossession and all but extermination of the tribes in possession, was America's destiny or not, it could not in any sense have been described as that of Britain. The war with France had barely been concluded when the Indian frontier flared into a conflagration that swept like a prairie fire over the white settlements, and was brought under control only by the help of King George's redcoats, whose very presence, when billeted in the coastal towns, was resented as an intolerable grievance, as was every effort of the home government to enforce a peaceful *modus vivendi* with the Indians, by putting some curb upon the anarchic aggression of the whites. The whole problem of controlling colonial expansion was—if anybody in Britain or even America could have realized it— fantastically beyond the physical and mental resources of the Hanoverian Sovereign and the aristocratic amateurs out of whose shifting combinations he had to form such governments as he could get, and none of whom had even set foot in the colonies, or had more than the vaguest notions of actual conditions there.

The more one comes to survey the brief interlude between what is usually presented as the triumph of the First British Empire and its downfall, the more it will be borne in mind that here is far less a tragedy of high principles in conflict than a glorified case of mental deficiency. It is a record of the muddled and blundering impingements upon each other of men who had not the wits to know what they were up against, whose thoughts moved in out-dated grooves, and whose actions were adapted to a world of their own imaginative reconstruction.

This might not have mattered so much had such substitutes for reality, from which after all few minds are wholly exempt, been framed on generous lines or determined by a high sense of values. Even the folly of Don Quixote may be fraught with greater promise than the realism of the man with the muck-rake who can look no way but downwards. And the idea of an empire that was no empire in the ordinary sense, that functioned by a complex of unprofitable and unworkable commercial regulations, and was united by no other bond than a fallacy of mutual self-interest, was not even realistic, and was bound to burst like the bubble it was by dint of its own expansion. The first attempt to make it a working reality would be the end of it.

And this is what the King and his ministers, in a very gingerly and hesitant way, attempted to do, almost inevitably, from their point of view, since the American connection had come to involve a back-breaking burden with the whole of which the colonies, in the sacred name of liberty, were determined to saddle the mother country. Such administrative fleabites as George Grenville's abortive Stamp Act, or young Charles Townshend's tariff jugglings, which even if they could have been put into force would hardly have paid the cost of their own collection, were no doubt of the nature of pills to cure an earthquake; but the earthquake was on, pills or no pills, and it was no cure to sit still and be engulfed by it. It is easier to blame these well-meaning and averagely competent Jacks in office for what they did, or tried to do, than to suggest what they conceivably could have done, short of scrapping the existing system and dropping the pretence of an imperial or even sovereign dominion, which the citizens of Boston proved to be no more than a gigantic bluff by pitching a cargo of the East India Company's tea into their harbour.

A statesman as wise in that generation as Walpole had been in the previous one would have seen the red light at once, and recognized that this latest dance 'would no further go'. But honest George, who, with his obsessive sense of his kingly duty, had not the least conscious-ness of bluffing, proceeded to take up the challenge and oppose force with force. And the discharge of the first musket signified the collapse of the imperial façade beyond hope of recovery. It was with no mere rhetorical flourish that the great Chatham proclaimed, 'You cannot conquer America', but a statement of simple fact, even if it took several years of futile slaughter to bring it home to the satisfaction of all concerned.

Looking back on it now it is overwhelmingly obvious that the imperial solution of the American problem, in any form whatever, was barred. Britain was wholly lacking in the physical or human resources for imposing her will for any length of time on her colonists. Even if by some miracle she could have succeeded in crushing the rebel armies in the field, she would have found herself committed to the permanent military occupation of the whole country—a feat of which she was even less capable than she had been of holding down France in the Middle Ages, and in attempting which she would have bled herself to death.

It is plain that the only conceivable alternative solution to this problem of keeping America loyal to the British connection would have been one that had not in those days become associated with the word 'commonwealth', that still retained its Cromwellian associations. But could the last pretence of empire have been dropped, could the colonies have been accorded what we should now call dominion status, and the whole Mercantile System scrapped altogether or superseded by some freely negotiated form of tariff union, it is just conceivable that a *modus vivendi* might have been patched up that would have left the two main branches of the British order of civilization still formally joined in allegiance to a common sovereign and united by no other bond than that which Burke was to describe as thinner than gossamer but stronger than links of iron—the invisible bond of common sentiment.

Unfortunately sentiment of any kind was clean contrary to the spirit of an age of reason. But the mere fact that such sentiments could have been uttered on the eve of the separation shows that a spirit was beginning to stir that, if it had only had time to gather head, might just possibly have averted or at least postponed it.

But the question still arises whether this, in the long run, would have been such an unmixed blessing as is commonly assumed. It is more than doubtful whether any formal Anglo-American partnership, even on the basis of the freest co-operation, would not have proved too ruinous a commitment for at least the British partner. It is easy to imagine not only what might, but what in some form was bound to have happened. The responsibility for America's westward expansion was one that King George's ministers had already found themselves equally incapable of assuming or evading, and this responsibility was bound to go on growing, and to impose an intolerable strain on Britain's physical—and what was even more serious, her moral—resources. The expansion to the Pacific may have been inevitable, but it involved methods of conquest that would have been impossible to reconcile with the most elastic notions of British freedom or fair dealing. The Wild West and its ethics were America's business: the best that Britain could do was to wash her hands of it. She was in no position to dictate to the colonists how they should comport themselves in face of difficulties that were beyond the experience and comprehension of even the best informed stay-at-home Englishman. It was at least a moot point whether it was right for the continental spaces between the Alleghanies and the Rockies to be maintained in perpetuity as the hunting-grounds of nomadic tribes who themselves recognized no right to them but that of the strongest, who dealt with rivals of their own race with a ruthlessness that no white frontiersman could surpass, and with whom anything like a stable relationship was, with the best will in the world, an impossibility.

But for England to lend her active support to this process of eliminating the Red Man and his quarry, the bison, from the prairies, which was undoubtedly what the colonists would have stipulated for in the event of union, was more than she could in any sense have afforded, and for her to have seriously attempted to exercise a restraining influence would in itself have been enough to precipitate a secession.

And it was not only the red man who stood in the path of the 'manifest destiny'. The drive to the Pacific involved the eviction from the southern and western part of the area of its Mexican possessors on no other principle than

> The good old rule . . . the simple plan,
> That they should take, who have the power
> And they should keep who can.

This again was a quarrel into which a Britain formally united with America could hardly have failed to be drawn, with results perhaps as damaging as those of Napoleon III's Mexican adventure.

But far more serious would have been her having to take sides in the great civil war that was the nemesis of the persistence of a slave economy within the framework of a libertarian democracy. With what grace could Britain have taken the uncompromising world lead which we shall see she did in the next half-century against both the traffic and the institution of slavery, if it had continued to flourish and expand under the aegis of her own sovereignty? And with what tolerance would the 'deep South' have regarded her efforts to stamp it out in the islands that formed almost, as it were, an outlying fringe of its own system?

It was by the narrowest of margins that, even as it was, Britain escaped the immeasurable disaster of being drawn into the conflict, and on what, by all the standards fostered by her own civilization, would have been the wrong side. It was only her starting on a footing of neutrality that enabled her to preserve it. But had even the fiction of a common sovereignty been maintained, it is almost inconceivable that she could have succeeded in doing so. And the event of her armed participation might have found Britain hardly less divided in sympathy than America herself, between the respective causes—to give them their nearest British equivalents—of Northern Whiggery and Southern Toryism.

It seems clear that there was no conceivable way in which Britain could have been yoked in any sort of double harness with her gigantic offspring—at least until the latter had grown to its full stature—without wrecking freight and passengers. It was eminently a case to which the saying would have applied: 'He travels fastest who travels alone.'

On this reckoning, what is usually described as the loss of her American colonies and the downfall of her empre ought to be counted to Britain for a blessing in disguise; assuming, that is to say, that she had ever had an empire to lose, or that, in the deepest and permanent sense, the political separation signified the *loss* of these daughter communities.

Looking at it from the standpoint not of insular nationalism but of the new world order of British-born civilization, might it not have been said that the colonists, in the stand they took up, were vindicating British principles against Britain herself in the face of the whole world? Indeed it actually was said, in the most explicit terms, by such leading spirits of the colonial resistance as John Adams, who laid it down, ten years before the Declaration of Independence, that the British Constitution differed from all other forms of government in the fact that 'liberty is its end, its use, its designation, drift and scope, as much as grinding corn is the use of a mill', and it was by the desire of giving practical definition to such principles that the founding fathers of the American Constitution were actuated.

These were no philosopher guardians, laying the foundations of an ideal republic, in detachment from workaday considerations, but practical men faced with the task of a gigantic improvisation at the shortest notice, and they were men of their time and environment blazing a path like the pioneers they were through an uncharted wilderness. In their endeavour to formulate in set terms constitutional principles that their fathers had allowed to grow up, as the spirit moved and the needs of the moment modified, they blundered, sometimes, into courses the exact reverse of those they had intended to take—not necessarily with unhappy results Thus they contrived to put back the clock to where it had been before the Glorious Revolution and the Great Rebellion, and to restore what was substantially the constitution as it had been under the Tudors, and as the Stuarts had vainly striven to maintain it, with the Sovereign in effective control of his own Government, working in such harmony as he could with a representative body in control of legislation and finance. And that happened substantially to coincide with the notion that George III had formed of the constitution, and which he consistently tried to realize in practice. Whether or not he had actually come under the influence of Lord Bolingbroke's celebrated piece of political propaganda entitled *The Patriot King*, it was in that capacity that George III undoubtedly wished to figure, and not as a rubber stamp for the managing committee of whatever faction might have secured a controlling majority in Parliament. He was, as far as Britain was concerned, fighting, with great skill and determination, what was at best a delaying action in which the odds were so heavily weighted that the Crown was bound to lose in the long run.

The fathers of the American Constitution however decided that, in what might (as Adam Smith already had the insight to foresee) become the predominant member of the Anglo-Saxon partnership, the principles of George III should be established, consecrated and guaranteed, as far as this could be done by the written word for all subsequent generations. The immediate result of their labours was to unite the thirteen States under the sway of a George who was no longer a remote figurehead but a fully effective Sovereign, and none the less so because his other name happened to be Washington and not Guelph, and because his mandate was conferred not by the anointing of his own head, but by the counting of other people's. And it only strengthened the position of the American Sovereign that he was not subject to the accidents of hereditary succession, but was renewable every four years like a key part of some continuously functioning mechanism. The patriot King came into his own at last under the style of President, and which of the two Georges he happened to be was a matter of comparatively superficial import.

What did matter, above everything, was that in spite of the errors and omissions incidental to the attempt to freeze the spirit of the Constitution within the letter of this written code, that spirit was in fact its inspiration, and all the basic elements of the old unwritten Constitution were sufficiently preserved in the new to make it a faithful alternative rendering of the order of civilization whose birth-place had been on English soil. Parliamentary government, the Common Law, what had at least come to stand for the principles of Magna Charta, the priority accorded to the rights and liberties of the individual citizen before any reason of state—all these things were duly preserved as part of the American system, and a new extension of the same principle was contained in the guarantee to individual states of all those collective rights and liberties that were not specifically reserved to the Federal Government, each of them thus receiving a charter of subordinate independence, inviolable within its own limits, and with a supreme, independent court of judiciary to keep those limits from infringement. A more Caesar-proof safeguard against any attempt to reproduce in the new world the imperial pattern of State architecture that had become standardized in all but one of the leading Powers of the old, it would pass the wit of man to conceive.

But it must not be forgotten that even the inherited tradition of British civilization would never have been enough to render such an adventure in freedom a practical proposition, had not the same essential conditions that had rendered it possible in the British Isles been in effect reproduced on the American mainland. But paradoxical as it may seem when set down in cold print, the effect of the victory over France and the conquest of Canada had been to confer on the American colonies, for a quite unforeseeable period, the equivalent of insular status. For all practical purposes they might regard themselves as no less proof against invasion than Britain had been since the Conquest. The threat of encirclement from the land side had been finally dis-sipated, and no European Power was as yet capable of fitting out an expeditionary force to reverse, in its own favour, the verdict of Saratoga and Yorktown. Consequently they were no more forced than Britain herself to subordinate every other consideration to that of military prowess, and were able to get on well enough without any regular army to speak of, or much more of a regular navy. They could thus concentrate on the development of their own special form of civilization with an almost complete freedom from distraction by external affairs. This tended to engender an attitude of what, if the United States had happened to be surrounded by water, would have been called insularity. But since its logically appropriate equivalent, continentality, did not admit of linguistic coinage, the world had to wait until, more than a century later, the term 'isolationism' was pressed into service. But from their first formation up to and even beyond the First World War, not only the policy but also the mentality of the United States might have been described with little exaggeration, in what came to be the twentieth-century significance, as uncompromisingly isolationist, at least as far as the nations of the Old World, not excepting their own mother country, were concerned. But for their ability to maintain this convenient detachment, and to take it (as they did) for granted, they might and did come in time to be more dependent on external—and specifically British—assistance than they would be willing to admit.

For pending the fulfilment of her ex-colonists' 'manifest destiny', not only to occupy but to people their self-promised land between the Atlantic and Pacific seaboards, Britain had a vital interest—however little she might consciously realize it—in American isolationism. It was, as I have tried to show, utterly beyond her physical and moral resources to have part or lot in the fulfilment of this colossal undertaking. But that it should be substantially fulfilled—not in the British but in the American way—and within a time limit set by the ripening of a different and more sinister form of destiny, was, as the event was to prove, literally a life and death matter not only for Britain herself, but for the whole order of civilization in which Britain and the United States (and not only they) were in membership. It was necessary that the two should part only that they might meet again on a higher level and in a more fruitful form of association.

There could surely be no better way of putting it than in the words of the Apostle Paul:

For perhaps he therefore departed for a season, that thou shouldest receive him forever; not now as a servant, but above a servant, a brother beloved . . .

6

ORDERS OF CIVILIZATION
IN CONFLICT

'BUT YESTERDAY and England might have stood against the world: now none so poor to do her reverence,' were the words in which the aged and fast-failing Lord Chatham thought fit to describe the situation of 'this late flourishing empire', now 'reduced to ruin and contempt' in November 1777, when her power was still ostensibly intact, before the news of the wiping out of a main British army at Saratoga had had time to cross the Atlantic. Worse—far worse—was to come upon her in the ensuing years before she was forced to throw up the sponge and conclude a humiliating peace, comprising her complete severance from her American colonies, and the docking of some of her few remaining overseas possessions.

To outward appearance it was disaster shattering and unmitigated. Lord Chatham's words seemed to have been fully borne out by the event. The bursting of her imperial bubble might indeed have been thought to have reduced Britain to the lowest depth of ruin and contempt, and degraded her—if the journalese term had been coined— to whatever might have been considered the status of a second- or third-rate Power.

So it might have seemed, and so there is every reason to suppose it did seem to contemporary observers. And yet once the bitter pill had been swallowed, and the political upheaval had had time to subside, it might have been said with perfect truth that, as in the sequel of the bishop's curse,

> What gave rise to no little surprise,
> Nobody seemed a penny the worse.

It was not only that it would have passed the wit of man to discover in what tangible way either Britain herself, or anybody in it, was worse off without an empire than with one, but that she was entering on a boom period of strength and prosperity under the strongest government of the century, with the monarch more firmly established in the affections of his subjects than ever before, and a young and supremely capable Premier of his own choosing firmly established in office. And that this recovered prosperity was no illusion was shown when, at the end of a decade of peace, Britain was called upon to face a longer and sterner ordeal than the American War had been, her resources proved equal to the test.

It was by not the least of the ironies of history that the Bourbon monarchy, that had seen in Britain's trouble with her colonists a heaven-sent opportunity of evening up the score of France's recent defeat, had, by its decisive intervention in the American War of Independence, been engineering not its rival's downfall, but its own; and this in two ways, each sufficient in itself. It was not only that by committing itself to a war in two hemispheres, the royal Government, with its resources already strained to the limit, was depriving itself of its last chance of pulling up on the inclined plane to bankruptcy, and thence to revolution, but that contact with British principles, in that most advanced form in which they had been enlisted against Britain herself by her own rebellious children, had infected with the revolutionary virus the officers and men of the French expeditionary force that had been the spearhead of the colonial resistance in its latter phase. And it was a virus that, once it had got a lodgment in an organism like that of a Latinized autocracy, would be free to proliferate with unchecked virulence, since it was liable to encounter no resistance.

With the Americans it had been otherwise. Nurture in the British constitutional tradition had, in effect, immunized them. In the stress of the rising conflict with the mother country their leaders had waxed eloquent, as their manner was, about liberty, and appealed to the laws of God and nature as justifying their resistance to any authority but their own. But once these fundamental rights and liberties that they claimed had been vindicated in arms, the last thing that any of them wanted was to see liberty run riot. They were solid, practical men, faced with a job of constitution-drafting, and they got down to it in a spirit that was fundamentally conservative. The principles to which they were giving outward and visible form were bred in the bone— they were *there*.

It was in 1787 that the Constitution of the United States was signed, and the first President elected, in the person of George Washington. It was in March 1789 that the first Congress was convened, and in May of the same year that the States-General of France met at Versailles. The libertarian and democratic idealism that had inspired the American constitution-framers was freely, and there is no reason to doubt sincerely, professed by those enthusiastic and more than averagely intelligent Europeans, who had come together for the express purpose of performing the selfsame task for their own country, and who had all the advantage of the American model to inspire them. The result might have been foreseen by anyone capable of realizing what sort of consequences were likely to ensue from the attempt to apply British principles—or the formulae by which they were expressed—in the environment of that very order of civilization of which Britain had abjured membership, and whose law and tradition she had superseded by one which was its direct negation. The American Constitution, like the British, was based on a solid foundation of the Common Law and the rights of the common man. The French or continental system was steeped in the tradition of an imperial law, and resembled a majestic arch whose keystone was the head of the state—Imperial Caesar. Louis XVI may have been as subnormal intellectually as his predecessor had been morally, but he *was* Caesar, and to knock him out of his place would be to start the collapse of the whole structure. Moreover, as the imperial system of architecture was the only one to which the French political mentality was conditioned, it would have been safe to predict that any reconstruction was bound to result in a similar arch, on a possibly grander scale, with perhaps an even more imposing imperial keystone.

This not only might have been foreseen—it actually *was* foreseen almost from the first with the most astonishing accuracy, by the very man who had been foremost in championing in Britain the cause of the American Revolution. Edmund Burke is as much entitled to rank as a major prophet of British, as Isaiah or Ezekiel are of Hebrew civilization. To say this is to pass no verdict on his record as a man or a politician. To be inspired in principle is one thing, but to apply such principle to the concrete issues of workaday life demands qualities of which the prophetic afflatus is no guarantee. And in these qualities Burke was lacking—too often conspicuously. The further we get from him in time, the more his genius seems to raise him above the level even of his greatest contemporaries; but on those who saw him at close quarters he signally failed to impress himself as the sort of pilot on whom anyone would instinctively rely—as almost everyone did on the younger Pitt—to guide the Ship of State through stormy or dangerous waters. His failure to make good as a practical statesman was no accident, even of birth.

We must take him for what he was—for what he still is—the man in whom the distinctive genius of British-born civilization first became consciously articulate. He, more than any other man, taught the as yet unchristened Commonwealth to know itself—to look unto the rock whence it was hewn and go forth in the strength of its own spirit, a spirit not of imperialism or power politics, but of free and spontaneous co-operation.

It was by relying wholly on this spirit that he sought to perpetuate the association, strained almost to breaking point, of Britain with her American colonies:

> My hold on the colonies [he said] is in the close affection which grows from common names, from kindred blood, from similar privileges and equal protection. These are ties that, though light as air, are as strong as links of iron. Let the colonies always keep the idea of their civil rights associated with your government: they will cling and grapple to you and no force under heaven will be of power to tear them from their allegiance.

This is the flat negation of the spirit of empire. In so far as there was ever such a thing as the First British Empire, Burke's remedy for its mounting discontents would have been to let it go by the board. To rule the nations, and in particular those budding daughter nations, with her sway, was no object that he envisaged for Britain. Power, in so far as it was to be sought by her at all, was no end in itself, but a means for asserting and defending those concrete rights and liberties that had grown up in the course of ages, and were guaranteed by the British Constitution as the common heritage of Britons.

> As long as you have the wisdom to keep the sovereign authority of this country as the sanctuary of liberty, the sacred temple consecrated to our common faith, wherever the chosen race and sons of England worship freedom, they will turn their faces towards you. The more they multiply, the more friends you will have; the more ardently they love liberty, the more perfect will be their obedience. Slavery they can have anywhere. It is a weed that grows in every soil. They may have it from Spain, they may have it from Prussia. But until you become lost to all feeling of your true interest and natural dignity, freedom they can have from none but you.

Here we have, in brief, the whole gospel of the British or Anglo-Saxon order of civilization, and it holds as good now as it did the best part of two centuries ago.

It is true that Burke's practical grasp of the American problem can, in the light of events, be shown to have been far short of ideally comprehensive. He seems to have imagined that the system of commercial regulation might, in some form, have been kept in being with the colonists, and he was not enough of an economist to have arrived at Adam Smith's common-sense conclusion that it was not enough of a paying proposition to be worth keeping, but that everyone concerned would be much better off—as indeed they actually proved to be—by setting their trade free to thrive in its own natural channels. And

Burke, who had never crossed the Atlantic and whose knowledge of the colonial situation was necessarily of the vaguest, had an all-too-imperfect conception of the nature and magnitude of the problems that were bound to arise out of the continued association of Britain and her colonies even on a voluntary footing. He had only his principles to go upon, and to apply even the soundest of principles without knowledge of the facts of each particular case is a perilous undertaking. It may well be that the forces making for political separation had acquired too great a momentum to make their arrest possible or even desirable on any terms whatever.

But this in no way affects the question of principle, and the principles laid down by Burke stand for all succeeding generations on both sides of the Atlantic as those basic to the new order of civilization that was destined to rival, and perhaps in time to supersede, that of imperial domination. A younger contemporary of Burke, a seer with no suspicion of a political axe to grind, forminated the gist of the whole matter in one terrific, if gnomic, pronouncement: 'Empire is no more, and now the lion and the wolf shall cease.'

But no one, even among the few who had heard of him, paid serious heed to the outpourings of such an obscure and eccentric personage as William Blake.

Such visionary geniuses were fostered by a spirit that was astir over the whole civilized West, continental no less than insular, and has been called—not altogether adequately—Romantic. Pyschologically, it was a simple and almost inevitable reaction against the tendency, in the age of reason', to rely exclusively upon those processes of conscious rationalization that had always been more characteristic of the Latin than the Anglo-Celtic mentality. With the Romantic age it might be said that the subconsciousness, even if its existence had not been formally recognized, came into its own, though at the best of times there was a formidable lump that proved resistant to the Romantic leaven. The age of Blake and Byron was also that of Bentham and Castlereagh.

The cult of feeling and sentiment was as rife on the Continent as it was in England, and it also had its prophet in Jean-Jacques Rousseau, whose writings were so largely the inspiration of the French Revolution and, in particular, of Robespierre, and are no less eloquent and persuasive than those of Burke—not to speak of the founders of the American Constitution.

But these latter were inheritors of an age-old tradition, and one diametrically opposite to that which had been inherited from Imperial Rome, to which the Governments of the European Powers conformed, and by which their legal systems were pervaded. Rousseau himself worked out his system of ideal democracy on a foundation of abstract principle and (as it were) in a vacuum. When it came to be applied by men who had been born and bred in a tradition of imperialistic autocracy, and had no sort of experience in the working of free institutions, it was capable of becoming a blueprint of pure tyranny. Burke divined this in the first optimistic phase of the revolutionary dawn, and saw where these fine theories were bound to lead when such men, in such an environment, sought to put them into practice. The original tyrants of Greek city states had been swept into power on the crest of democratic upsurges, and the will of the people only too readily crystallizes into that of a Caesar or Dictator. Just as the democratic sequel of a King Log by divine right proved to be the highly efficient divine Caesar whom Burke had perceived at the end of the revolutionary road, so does a neurotic Kaiser give place to a maniacal Führer, and White Tsar, by the logic of ultra-democratic socialism, to Red super-Tsar.

Burke then, as the prophetic mouthpiece of the British-born order of civilization, has been more than vindicated in his diagnosis of its predecessor and rival. The cult of power and empire was not changed, but carried to its logical, or—as it came to be styled—totalitarian conclusion, by being democratized or eventually communized. Even in the first exuberant outbreaks of French revolutionary fervour it became apparent that to liberate peoples at home or abroad, according to the revolutionary prescription, was merely to substitute King Stork for King Log, and to render the little finger of an up-to-date Caesar thicker than the loins of any Caligula or Constantine of an unmechanized age. If it could be granted to Burke to reconsider his philippic in the light of subsequent events, he might well stand astonished, like Clive, at his own moderation.

It is not on that side that he is vulnerable to criticism, so much as in his failure to apply his own principles with corresponding emphasis to the order of civilization that he defines as 'a partnership in all science, a partnership in all art, a partnership in every virtue and in all perfection', which, since 'its ends cannot be obtained in many generations . . . becomes a partnership . . . between those who are living, those who are dead and those who are yet to be born'. Such a partnership, by plainest implication, he sees to be embodied in the British Constitution.

But in his passionate revulsion from the proceedings of the French constitution-makers, Burke did tend, if not to create, at least to confirm, an impression that the British Constitution was something finished and perfect already, and consequently petrified, like the proud keep of Windsor to which he likened it in the most superb of all his flights of rhetoric. Its ends would on this showing have been sufficiently obtained already to render any attempt to expand or improve upon it, by those who were living, or those who were yet to be born not only superfluous, but treasonable. Burke never actually said or even implied this in set terms, but the emotional effect of his exhortations on lesser minds was to harden them in opposing the immovable obstacle of a purely static conservatism to the otherwise irresistible force of revolutionary dynamism. That was a flat contradiction of Burke's own essential precept of conformity to nature in our artificial institutions, since the way of nature—or at least of healthy nature—is a way of growth, of vital as opposed to mechanized energy, and consequently of freedom as against compulsion. But Burke was a prophet who, like Jonah, experienced considerable difficulty as a man in living up to the height of his own vision.

It was after all too much to expect of British, or any other human nature, that with red ruin threatening to undermine and overwhelm it, it should have continued on the positive course of its own development at the former tempo. The wonder is that, in a struggle for survival extending over nearly a quarter of a century, Britain did not harden herself into the likeness of her adversary, and become an armoured monster, an empire in good earnest at death grips with others of its own species. On a superficial view this might have seemed the course to which she had, by force of circumstance, become irrevocably committed. The fear of letting in the thin end of the revolutionary wedge had caused even her previously liberal-minded Premier, William Pitt, followed by his war-time successors in office, to fall back on an attitude of pure negation towards reform or progress of any sort on the Home Front, an attitude that survived the war and that under the existing electoral system nothing short of a revolution seemed capable of modifying.

Humanly speaking, this was no doubt inevitable, deadly though its effects may have been at a time of all others when the social environment was changing with unprecedented rapidity, and consequently the need for adaptation was greatest. But in a contest of such length and against such odds, to stand fast was the utmost that could be hoped for. The land had to be made to yield its utmost if the continental blockade was to be broken, however many commons had to be enclosed; production in the fleet-protected factories, that was the decisive factor in the war effort, had to be maximized at all costs, even to the workers themselves; and to maintain the domestic *status quo* was matter of such vital urgency as to preclude attempts to reform it. Pitt was characterized in a famous metaphor by his colleague and disciple Canning, as the pilot who weathered the storm; but in a storm the vessel has to be brought safely to port before there can be any question of subjecting her to even the most belated overhaul. And in such circumstances it is only too easy for the war-time urge for stability to harden into a peace-time obsession.

F

The price of victory, reckoned in spiritual no less than material terms, was indeed grievous, and there is no point in trying to minimize it, but it is missing the essential point to talk as if it were more than temporary and, in the long run, reparable. What counts for infinitely more is that Britain, through all these critical years, matched, as she eventually was, against the Caesar of an almost united Continent, did in the long run succeed in saving herself and Europe without losing her own soul, or compromising that truth to herself that, though obscured and retarded in its unfolding, preserved uncut the lifeline of its evolving vitality.

7

VICTORY WITHOUT SPOILS

I T IS NATURAL that patriotic pride should fix upon this time of ultimately victorious conflict, with its highlights of Trafalgar and Waterloo, as almost—if not quite—the most glorious epoch of British history. And yet it is a pride conspicuously devoid of imperial tincture. It is true that in respect of art and culture it is customary to talk of the opening years of the century as the Empire period, but the Empire in question was that which the British monarchy was out to de-imperialize and reduce to its former limits, not a rival empire that it aspired to supersede. Search the records of the time as we will, we shall find hardly the least disposition to talk, let alone boast, about such a thing as a British Empire, though in the brief blaze of glory after the triumphs of the Seven Years' War the term had been coming into fashion. But the cold douche of the American fiasco had put a damper on imperial ambition, and though Britain had no intention of parting with such of her possessions overseas as she had not been forced to disgorge, she regarded them more in the light of detached properties, good for what they would fetch, than as parts of a great imperial entity.

And yet if we look into the facts of British expansion overseas, we can hardly refuse to consider these years of imperial eclipse between the surrender of Yorktown and the victory of Waterloo as the great, formative period of the British Commonwealth of Nations. Almost without realizing it, Britain emerged from her continental struggle with the foundations of three of the four great dominions well and truly laid, and her mastery of the Indian Peninsula, which she had never sought nor wished to assume, if not an accomplished fact, at least one in process of foreseeable accomplishment, under whatever forms she might seek to disguise it.

All this had come about not only without her intention, but almost without her knowledge. After her decade of peaceful recuperation under Mr Pitt's auspices, her attention became more and more monopolized by the European agony. It is true that when Pitt was forced to turn his civilian talents to the uncongenial task of conducting a war, he could think of no better way of leading off than on the conventional lines of appropriating colonies for use as eventual bargaining counters in a peace settlement. This merely resulted in the all-but-annihilation of the occupying forces, not by enemy action but by that of disease germs. And in the second, or Napoleonic, phase of the struggle, the colonies faded out of the picture. It is surely not without significance that the fascinating and erudite study of the reign of George III, which is the latest volume to be added to *The Oxford History of England*, should contain in its index no reference to Australia, as if the addition of a mere continent to that monarch's dominions were an event that called for no special record; an estimate that would certainly have been endorsed by contemporary opinion—at any rate in Britain, where there was an almost complete absence of any desire for, or even interest in, imperial expansion. And yet expand she did, on a world-wide scale, not only without willing but almost without knowing it.

The same thing could not be said of her arch-opponent. Not only did the French Revolution, after the passing of its first brief phase of pacifist idealism, become militantly and uncompromisingly expansive, but Napoleon was imperially minded, long before he assumed the imperial title, to an extent that the most ambitious of his monarchal predecessors had never approached. Quite at the dawn of his career he had decided that 'little Europe' did not afford him the scope he needed, and it was this conviction that drove him to the hare-brained project of invading Egypt without previously securing his own sea communications, and with the idea, amongst others, of marching in the tracks of Alexander to wrest the lordship of India from British hands. But though the 'gorgeous East' made the most compulsive appeal to his imagination, there was no quarter of the world to which his imperial cupidity did not extend. He had visions of world-wide colonial expansion; with him to dream was to plan, and to plan was to act. But he might as well have lusted after the moon. His empire stopped short at the beaches of Europe. Thus far might it expand and no farther, and beyond the limits thus set, not a foothold, let alone a colony, could be got or kept for it, owing to the fact that Britannia did effectually rule the waves that broke on those beaches.

Thus the continental Caesar found himself debarred from the overseas expansion that he so desperately needed for the fulfilment and even the survival of his *imperium*. Though an islander by birth, Napoleon had the mentality of a landsman. Almost his last coherent words were reported to have been 'tête de l'armée'. He thought and acted in terms of the land warfare of which he was a past master, but as regards sea power, he himself was, in the metaphorical sense, hopelessly at sea. He started by ignoring it altogether, when he succeeded in marooning his whole command, minus its commander, in the sands of Egypt. That lesson did at least open his eyes to the urgency of the naval problem, and it was rubbed in by the demonstrated impracticability of his idea of forcing the Channel with a flotilla of troop-crammed barges in the face of an unbeaten fleet. But the intelligence that could conceive of such strategic masterpieces as those of Marengo and Ulm had no doubt of its capacity to think up an even more grandiose seaborne combination that should ensure the command of the Narrows for long enough to ferry the expedition across. The whole thing had turned out a landlubberly fiasco, months before the will-o'-the-wisp of French sea power was dissipated for good and all at Trafalgar. This drove Napoleon, who, like his opponents at Waterloo, refused to know when he was beaten, to embark on an even more desperate and grandiose plan of conquering insular sea power by continental land power that committed him, by an inexorable logic, to unite the whole Continent, from the Atlantic to the Urals, under his imperial sway—an effort to which even his physical and mental resources proved inadequate. Thus as powerful a will as any on historic record, backed by a corresponding intelligence, and with all the tempestuous forces unloosed by the Revolution at its command, set itself to the achievement of a world-wide empire which, in the event, completely eluded it.

Napoleon himself was under no illusion about the identity of his arch-enemy, though he had only the vaguest conception of the might of industrial power behind the protection of sea power, with which his armies were powerless to cope, and which constituted that opponent's ultimately winning advantage. For that matter, its real nature was no better understood by those who possessed it. They were practical politicians, carrying on or muddling through, in their instinctive English fashion, from one day's task to another's. There is no reason to credit them—as in the knowledge of the event one might be tempted to do—with a sort of jiu-jitsu strategy for compelling their adversary to bring about his own destruction. But in his desperate efforts to shake off the stranglehold of British sea power, Napoleon was in fact to go to all lengths of military violence in order to compel the nations of the Continent to subject themselves to the full rigours of a maritime blockade. But this was to cut off the Continent from the cheap manufactured goods that were being turned out in peaceful security and in ever-increasing quantities in the British factories, a proceeding calculated to make his yoke so intimately grievous as to turn every home into a focus of potential resistance.

Not only that, but the megalomaniac consistency with which he sought to seal off the whole European coastline impelled him to go on from one act of territorial brigandage to another, culminating in the attempt to impose his sway, in the true Caesarian tradition, on the Iberian Peninsula, thus opening to Britain an opportunity for the landward application of sea power under ideally favourable conditions. It was now possible to exhaust the new Caesar's military potential with the minimum expenditure of human and material resources; to compel him to fight, when the European resistance had gathered to a head, on two fronts, and with a Grand Army diluted to a cosmopolitan horde by the pinning down of its best elements to the Peninsula. It needed only persistence on Britain's part to bleed her enormous and triumphant adversary surely and scientifically to death. And persistence happened to be the strong suit of the otherwise far from spectacular ministerial team that guided her destinies.

Thus the duel à *outrance* between the continental empire and the insular non-empire proceeded to its inevitable conclusion like the clash—to adopt a famous Arnoldian image—of ignorant armies by night. Nobody on either side, not even the Emperor himself, had more than the foggiest conception of the underlying forces at issue. Their attention was absorbed by the conventionally obvious aspects of the struggle—by the sensational victories that only weakened the victor's power by inflating it nearer and nearer to bursting-point, and by annexations and conquests that only added crushing weight to the burden under which the conqueror was self-doomed to stagger, and to fall. Not even to this day is there much more apparent comprehension than there was at the time, of the highly unromantic factors that were ultimately decisive of what was in the last resort a process of attrition and exhaustion.

Nor is this to be wondered at when we consider that historical fashion is still set upon the assumption that the whole conflict was a sort of family set-to between a number of European Powers, in varying combinations, but all on the same qualitative footing, Britain being one and France another; and that what was really decided and confirmed at the Congress of Vienna was to reduce France to her proper place in this family of European nations, and thereby restore the pre-war *status quo*, or balance of power. This indeed is true enough as far as it goes and, if we narrow our perspective to the confines of a Europe which we insist on regarding as a single family unit, might pass for the whole truth. But if we enlarge our horizon to the extent, already suggested, of envisaging a potentially world-wide dialectic of two fundamentally incompatible orders of civilization, we shall see that the whole and essential truth comprises far more than can be comprehended in this limited, and by comparison provincial, setting.

The tendency to ignore all but the European aspect of the struggle with revolutionary and imperial France is at least understandable. The three previous wars in which Britain had participated had been to a large extent motivated by the urge for overseas expansion. In that sense at least they could be described as wars of empire. But in this sterner conflict such motives played hardly an ostensible part at all—not at least after the collapse of Napoleon's Egyptian adventure. All the highlights of the drama were turned upon the European stage, on which all the leading characters performed their parts; and this for the sufficient reason that the side that lusted after imperial expansion was debarred from using the necessary seaways to it, while the one that controlled them was to all intents and purposes devoid of imperial ambition. The one side that wanted empire could not get it, and one that could have it did not happen to want it.

This refusal of Britain to exploit the opportunity that presented itself, for building up a bigger and better empire than that which she was supposed to have lost in the previous generation, constitutes a revolutionary departure from international precedent. To judge her by the conventional standards of European power politics had ceased to be relevant, and those who, like Napoleon himself, had no others to apply, failed to make sense of her proceedings.

There is indeed something a shade ludicrous and more than a little pathetic in the spectacle of the fallen Caesar holding forth in captivity on the ineptitude of his vanquishers. Admittedly it is hazardous to swallow all the conversational sallies attributed to him by his *entourage* of would-be Boswells, but all accounts are in convincing agreement about this reaction to British policy and statesmanship, and it is no more than we might have expected from one so totally obsessed by the will to power of which he was the quintessential embodiment.

He was consistent enough in this cult of power to respect it even when it broke him. England he recognized, and hated, as his mortal enemy, and yet he could not withhold from her an uncomprehending admiration. With an English army, he declared, he could have conquered the universe! But the thing about England that he could not get over was that having, in the end, so signally triumphed, she should never even have stooped to gather up the fruits of victory that were to be had for the asking. To her war-time policy he could accord a disgruntled appreciation, but her conduct at the peace conference was something outside the scope of his comprehension. By the only standards he recognized, those of power politics and imperialism, it amounted, as he logically concluded, to sheer lunacy.

It was therefore only natural that he should have discovered the villain, or zany, of the piece in the man who more than any other had been responsible for his own downfall. This was the British Foreign Minister, Lord Castlereagh, without whose diplomatic binding the final combination against him could never have been carried through to the ultimate victory, and who owed largely to this the dominating influence he was able to exert in the framing of the peace settlement. 'What sort of a peace is it', Napoleon asked, 'that England has signed? Castlereagh had the Continent at his disposal. . . . The peace he has made is the sort of peace he would have made if he had been beaten. . . . Thousands of years will pass before England is given a second opportunity equal to this opportunity to establish her prosperity and greatness. Was it ignorance, was it corruption, that induced Castlereagh to take the line he did?' [1]

Liar though Napoleon habitually was, in this outburst at least there can be no doubt of his sincerity. It was a cry, wrung from the heart, of amazed, and one might almost say sympathetic, bewilderment. He made no secret of the line he would have taken if he had been in Castlereagh's shoes and the fortune of war had given him England's hand to play. He would have proceeded, as a matter of course, according to the rules and rigour of the only game he knew—the European family game of imperial grab. Having got France down, he would have taken steps to keep her from ever getting up again, by detaching whole provinces from their allegiance to the central government to revolve in the British orbit [2]—which would have put back the clock to the days of the old feudal Angevin empire. He would have made an imperial annexe of Belgium, he would have enlarged King George's German dominions to take in the great commercial depot of Hamburg, he would have helped himself right and left to whatever he happened to covet in the way of ports and naval bases, and he would have made a clean haul not only of the French, but also the Dutch overseas possessions, including the fabulously rich East Indian Islands—for had not Holland, by virtue of having been forced into the French Empire, become technically an enemy and, as such, lootable? What other explanation could there be of Castlereagh's neglect or refusal to take any action of this kind, except that he must have been either a traitor or a lunatic?

Napoleon, being what he was, and believing in what he did, could have come to no other conclusion; nor could any other consistent imperialist; and it is not without its significance that the biographer of his captivity, the British ex-Premier, Lord Rosebery, who was at least as much Imperialist as he was Liberal, writing as late as 1900, should in principle have endorsed his verdict on British policy.

He [Napoleon] thought well and justly of our blockade . . . but ill and with even more justice of our diplomacy. He could not understand, and posterity shares his bewilderment, why the British had derived so little benefit from their long struggle and their victory.[3]

---

[1] Quoted in *The Congress of Vienna* by Harold Nicolson, p. 237.
[2] Ibid., p. 236.   [3] *Napoleon, the Last Phase*, p. 269.

But had they? After all, on any factual reckoning, Britain may be considered to have benefited to a quite extraordinary degree from the effects of her victory, and her statesmanship in the hour of it. She entered on a long period of peace and mounting prosperity. The nineteenth proved, by almost universal agreement, pre-eminently the British century. She continued to rule the waves, and came to be not implausibly considered the workshop of the world. And the peace settlement, that she had laboured so hard and sacrificed so much to bring about, proved—as such settlements go—an outstanding success. Europe did, for more than a generation, secure a breathing-space of comparative peace and stability. And if Britain failed to exploit to the full whatever opportunity may have presented itself to build up an empire of her own on the ruins—and model—of Napoleon's, it was because she did not happen to be thinking on those lines. It was not that her statesmen or that public opinion were lacking in patriotism— there was never a time at which it was more exuberantly rampant— but simply that they were not in the least degree imperially minded. Nobody who mattered tended to enthuse about, or even to be much interested in, the idea of a British Empire. In so far as British expansion was thought of at all, it was under the heading of 'colonies', a subject of secondary interest and rather prosaic calculation.

It was not as if British war or peace policy had been in the hands of quixotic idealists. The crusading afflatus of Burke, its power as a national stimulant, would probably in itself have been a sufficient disqualification for ministerial office. Certainly neither Mr Pitt nor any of his colleagues or successors had shown any obsessive signs of it, and those two eminent products of the Anglo-Irish aristocracy, Castlereagh and Wellington, who had carried on their shoulders the burden of her policy at the Vienna Conference, had been throw-backs to the purest eighteenth-century pattern of unemotional realism— what Jane Austen might have defined as sense as opposed to sensibility.

But it was sense moulded by the magnanimity proper to their breeding and tradition as English gentlemen. It was not in their nature, even in matters of policy, to stoop to conduct that they would have instinctively felt to be common or mean; and colony-grabbing, or any other sort of imperialistic pushfulness, would undoubtedly have struck them in that light. Typical of their attitude was the letter (quoted by Sir Harold Nicolson in his admirable account of the Vienna Congress) written by Castlereagh to his Premier, Liverpool:

I still feel doubts about the acquisition of so many Dutch colonies. I am sure our reputation on the Continent as a feature of strength, power and confidence is of more real value to us than any acquisition thus made. [1]

[1] Op. cit., p. 98.

*F

Magnanimity in fact was, by Castlereagh's reckoning, not only the best but in the long run the most paying policy—as, on a long reckoning, it has surely proved to be.

But it was a sensible and objective magnanimity, with no flourishes or theatrical gestures. While handing back the French and Dutch overseas possessions otherwise intact, Britain did stand out for, and got, certain—from her standpoint—necessary adjustments, by way of securing her overseas communications and trade routes. The chief of these was the port and harbour of the Cape of Good Hope, which she regarded in no other light than that of an ideal half-way house on her sea route to India, and which she acquired, not by right of conquest, but for an honest (if compulsory) consideration in cash down.

But the rest of the far-flung colonial empire that she might have had she cheerfully sacrificed as so many expendable counters in a greater or, what was at least felt by her representatives to be a more gentlemanly, game than that of imperial power politics. She had fought her twenty-three years' war to avert what to her had always stood for the supreme danger of the imperial dominance of one Power over the whole of Europe.

But if we are to follow the prevailing fashion of lumping together all the results of British expansion overseas under the question-begging designation of Empire, then indeed we should have to admit that in spite of all her efforts to divest herself of imperial responsibilities, Britain found herself with an empire thrust upon her of greater extent and potentiality than that which she had declined to achieve. It was a destiny that she may be said to have imposed on herself. By cutting off rival Powers from access to as yet unexplored or unexploited fields for profitable expansion, her command of the seas imposed on her almost a necessity of filling them. I have referred to the case of Australia, whose south-eastern coast Napoleon's eye had already marked down as part of the overseas empire that he so greatly longed after, but that lay so tantalizingly beyond his reach. In a map [1] that was actually printed under his auspices, this, which is now the most flourishing region of the Australian Commonwealth, is marked as *Terre Napoléon Nouvelle*. But by the ordinary or even the official Englishman, these Antipodes were thought of (if at all) as a convenient dumping ground for the toughest of the criminal population, under what was in principle and intention—however differently it may have worked out in practice—a humane and hopeful scheme of penal reform, but one hardly conducive to imperial pride and affection towards the regions thus selected or their inhabitants. It will be remembered how Charles Lamb, writing to a friend who was supposed to have emigrated to

---

[1] It is reproduced in J. H. Rose's *Life of Napoleon I*.

Sydney, had no hesitation in bombarding him with such witticisms as: 'Tell me what your Sydneyites do. Are they th**v*ng all day long?'

It is safe to say that there can seldom have been a community on historic record less ambitious of laying the foundations of a world-wide dominion or commonwealth than Britain in the dawn of the nineteenth century, let alone conscious of having done so. And yet this was just what she had done, with a success that could hardly have been bettered by the most far-sighted calculation.

Even by the crudest imperial reckoning she might have been considered well advised in laying off from what had hitherto been thought of as the most rewarding form of colonial enterprise, which had envisaged the exploitation, mostly by slave labour, of tropical islands— the Indies in either hemisphere. This was really, as it proved to be in subsequent generations, a wasting asset, tending in the long run towards dead loss, whereas these unsought-after regions with whose possession or control Britain had, in her own despite, found herself saddled, were, whether she wanted it or not, instinct with the potentiality of growth on a continental or national scale into dominions far transcending colonial proportions.

This, which in the light of subsequent events might challenge recognition for the most pregnant outcome of the great peace settlement, passed—and one may almost say still passes—practically unnoticed. Imperial expansion had formed no part of Britain's war aims. The peace which, with consummate diplomatic skill, her representatives at the conference had striven at the cost of almost any necessary sacrifices on her behalf to bring about, had been the one best calculated in their opinion to secure a stable settlement in Europe based on the immemorial British *sine qua non* of keeping the Continent divided, in order to prevent it from becoming united under the domination of a single Power, concentrated in the hands of an imperial autocrat.

That was the danger that she had fought her twenty-three years' war to avert; to safeguard against its recurrence by stabilizing, for as long as was humanly possible, that equilibrium of independent sovereignties, or balance of power, that constituted her notion of European freedom. That freedom she sought to perpetuate as the necessary condition of her own. To that extent it might be said that her policy was self-regarding.

But of seeking her own aggrandizement, above and beyond freedom, she can by any reasonable test be acquitted. Her attention was to all intents and purposes monopolized by the European aspect of the situation. To no subject could public opinion have been more indifferent than that of the revival or even the existence of a British Empire.

From what might have been the expansive repercussions of her war effort behind the back of her blockade, Britain was content to avert her eyes. She had more important things to think about than Colonial Office matters that could be left to straighten themselves out in due course.

8

THE BIRTH OF
A PUBLIC CONSCIENCE

S O FAR WE have considered Britain's conduct of the war and of the peace negotiations without any specific reference to its moral aspect. And indeed even the attempt to do so involves a challenge to the conventional assumption that nations, in their dealings with each other, are actuated by purely self-regarding motives, an assumption basic to the whole conception of power politics and empire. An order of civilization based on the will to power is one that from the moral standpoint has made evil its good. But one based on the will to liberty is committed to honouring the liberties of others as its own, and to that extent, to the Golden Rule.

During the greater part of the eighteenth century it would be no exaggeration to say that from European (including British) policy the moral factor had been to all intents and purposes eliminated. Not only did the will to power rule unchallenged, but it tended constantly to do so on its lowest level of a grovelling materialism, with commerce assimilated to war in a game of universal beggar-my-neighbour that ruled out in advance the least tenderness of sentiment or delicacy of scruple. Certainly there had been little enough of either *en evidence* in the politics or statesmanship of the early Georgian age.

But the principle of Newton's law, that to every action there is an equal and opposite reaction, holds good in the world of mind as well as that of things. A swing back was bound to come from an exclusive reliance on the processes of the self-conscious and unemotional reasoning faculty to an equally one-sided submission to impulses arising from the hidden or subconscious depths. To an age of reason the predictable sequel is a renaissance of sentiment, and it might equally be expected that this latter would be carried to much greater lengths in England, where it accords with the grain of the national disposition better than with that of the more logical and lucid, though perhaps more superficial, Latin mentality. In France the revival of sentiment produced many colourful and extravagant phenomena, but it never seemed to penetrate so far beneath the surface, or perhaps it never found such congenial material to work upon, as in England.

There was nothing in France or anywhere on the Continent in the eighteenth century that corresponded to the great religious upheaval, associated in the first instance with the evangelizing genius of the brothers John and Charles Wesley, that, not only on one side of the Atlantic, operated with the effect of a moral revolution, and may even have contributed towards averting a revolution of a different sort.

When we talk of a moral revolution, we are by no means begging the question of its healthiness or desirability. All morals are not necessarily good morals, and some, like those attributed to the scribes and Pharisees, may be rooted in a profounder immorality. John Wesley has been equalled by few as an evangelizing and organizing genius, but he hardly aspired, except in the most perfunctory sense, to be a thinker, even if his non-stop proselytizing activity had left him leisure to reflect. The tenets advocated by him and his followers, who differed violently and often venomously among themselves about their precise nature, will hardly stand up to serious examination, even by theologians. Their propaganda derived much of its force from what it would be an understatement to describe as Devil worship, for by no milder name can we describe the cult of an omnipotent Sadist of ungovernable wrath and more than fiendish vindictiveness, who is supposed to have conceived so indiscriminating a hatred of the unhappy creatures He has created in His own image, as to have decided to turn them all over to His agent the Devil to suffer the most exquisite tortures for all eternity, even though He may eventually be bribed into a grudging remission of sentence to an elect minority, by the sacrifice of His blameless and beloved Son, on some principle of divine justice incomprehensible on the human level. It is no wonder that illiterate audiences, who took these terrific assertions literally, could be thrown into paroxysms and convulsions by such rabble-rousing shock tactics as the mere impassioned repetition of 'the wrath to come! O, the wrath to come!'

But we should be perversely wide of the mark if we were to insist on applying purely rational standards to what was essentially a pheno-menon on the emotional plane, and in its very nature a revolt against reason. Judged not by its logical implications but by its psychological effects, it will be seen that the religious movement originally sponsored by the Wesleys, with its collateral and derivative strains of evangelism, is to be judged not on the strength of what is fantastic or even revolting in its mythology, but by its power to quicken in the mass of the popu-lation at least the rudiments of a common conscience—a conscience all too constrictive and warped, but even so better than the dormant or frozen one of the Age of Reason.

An agonized preoccupation with the idea of sin was an essential feature of the movement, and sin was supposed to consist largely in breaches of taboos of a more or less arbitrary nature, imposed by wrathful Omnipotence, prohibitive of many, if not most, worldly pleasures and recreations. But the net of sin was cast wide enough to include things that by all sane human as well as divine standards are in themselves evil, and the Hell-thundering God of Wrath was, without the least sense of inconsistency, allowed to double the part with that of a loving Father, or what John Wesley described as 'the God of Love, of pardoning mercy', and whose elect children are enjoined to 'carefully abstain from all evil and labour . . . to do good to all men, friends or enemies'. It was indeed this rigid adherence to the principle of non-violence that, though it was already honoured by the Quakers, most sharply distinguishes the evangelistic revival of the eighteenth from the Puritan belligerency of the two preceding centuries.

Like it or not, there is no denying its power not only to change, to the extent of revolutionizing, the lives of countless individuals, but even to infuse public policy with notions of Christian morality and elementary human decency that had hitherto been conspicuously absent from it; most conspicuously of all in regard to the traffic in slaves, and indeed the whole institution of slavery, which had been pursued and promoted by all European Powers, with Britain in the van, as the mainstay of their colonial economy, with no other thought save of the profits believed to accrue from it.

What lends its greatest significance to the change of national heart and policy on this particular subject is that the approach to it was not only, or even in the first place, from the religious angle. The holding of property in human beings was discovered to be not only repugnant to the law of Christian charity, but also to the Common Law of England. And the judges who arrived at this conclusion were not, to any perceptible degree, swayed by religious or even humane considerations. They had less than no desire to alleviate the sufferings of the unhappy blacks—indeed they would have much preferred to wash their hands of their grievances. But they were single-hearted in their service of the law, and their judicial honour forbade them to play fast and loose with its principles, if it came to a direct issue, however much they might try to evade or postpone doing so.

Chief Justice Holt, who had been appointed to the office by William III, and ranks as one of the greatest of legal luminaries, had long ago pronounced that such a thing as a slave was incapable of legal existence on English soil, but it was not until as late as 1772 that an even greater judge, Lord Mansfield, put the matter beyond all doubt by a famous decision which he had done everything in his power to avoid having to pronounce, as the last thing he wanted to do was to deprive thousands of slaveholders at a stroke of their human property. But there was no getting round it, and all he could do was to confirm Holt's decision that short of a positive statute, the Common Law did not recognize and could not be wrested into the recognition of anything so plainly contrary to its own spirit as the rightlessness of any individual within the sphere of its jurisdiction.

The spirit of the time was ripe, as it had not been in Holt's day, for the assertion of such a principle. Slavery, which earlier in the century had been accepted without a qualm, and exploited for all it was supposed to be worth, had begun to stink in the nostrils of more and more ordinary British folk with no immediate vested interest in it. And naturally the quickening of conscience brought about by the religious awakening tended to reinforce the respect for the liberty and dignity of the individual man which might be specified as the basic, distinctive principle underlying the literal formalities of the English Common Law. And indeed, the course of time has shown that the best and most enduring effect of the evangelical revival, and most particularly of Wesleyan Methodism, has been to foster this very sense, in each individual convert, of a sober self-respect, 'humble to God, haughty to man', that in turn seeks fulfilment in a corresponding neighbour-respect, which is incompatible with slavery; or, if the same logic is pushed far enough, the assertion by man over man of arbitrary power in any form.

But it would be wrong to imagine that these principles were obvious from the start. It took John Welsey's massive integrity to grasp the plain incompatibility of slavery with anything professing or calling itself Christian. It was less obvious to his fellow evangelists. George Whitefield, for instance, who has had few equals as an emotional spellbinder, had no difficulty in justifying an institution fraught with such practical benefits to Christian planters, by citing biblical and particularly Old Testament authority. But in the Wesleyan movement, and still more emphatically in the evangelical revival that took place within the bosom of the Anglican Church, Christian principles came to prevail to the extent of recognizing all God's children, without distinction of race and colour, as fundamentally equal in His sight, and therefore equally within the pale of Christian brotherhood. The result was to render the flagrant and obvious violation of these principles even more odious to the evangelists than it had been to the judges, and to work up a crusading fervour against slavery that spread with astonishing rapidity to all ranks of society—all the more rapidly perhaps, owing to the dawning consciousness that what was bad in morals was almost equally bad for business.

Adam Smith, though he was in the front rank of British moralists, and recognized as such before he ever turned his attention to economics, pricked the bubble of slave economy with true Scottish canniness, by pointing out that slave labour is of all forms the most expensive and inefficient, if only because the slave's only interest is to work as little and eat as much as possible. And the impact of Adam Smith on concontemporary thought it would be hard to exaggerate. But to double the service of God with that of Mammon has seldom presented any insuperable difficulties to the British temperament, provided that all is done on the principle of not letting the left hand know what the right hand doeth.

Space does not permit of recording even in outline the story, of which the main facts are notorious and indisputable, of the long and ultimately victorious campaign which resulted in the conversion of the nation of all others that had been the ringleader in this inhuman traffic, to setting her face like a flint first against the trade itself, whether conducted by its own or foreign nationals, and following this up by a second root-and-branch offensive against the very institution of slavery in those selfsame colonies whose prosperity had been founded on it.

It is a story thrilling enough in itself, and embellished with a galaxy of personal highlights, but of a kind that runs directly counter to the current assumptions of power politics, which rule out any sort of disinterestedness as a motive of national policy. Indeed it would tax the resources of casuistry to make out any remotely plausible case for maintaining that any material British interest—except on an impossibly speculative long-term calculation—could be subserved by Britain's taking her stand on this particular issue. Even if it had been merely a gesture, it would have been of a sort to make Niccolo Machiavelli turn in his grave. But it was much more than a gesture. It formed an essential object of national policy that once adopted was unswervingly pursued, even at the cost of substantial sacrifices, including those of other ostensibly profitable objectives. And this is more remarkable when we consider that this change of heart was consummated during the strain and stress of a long conflict against seemingly hopeless odds and under a régime whose general tendency was to freeze the existing social system for—and beyond—duration.

The crowning proof of British disinterestedness was at the Vienna Peace Conference, and is all the more remarkable considering that British policy was in the hands of the coldly unsentimental Castlereagh, who, before he had assumed ministerial responsibility, had been anything but favourable to the anti-slavery cause. But nobody could have stood more loyally for the policy on which the national will was now irrevocably set. In fact, amid all the diplomatic imbroglio of greed and sharp practice that made up the practical reality of the Congress, Britain, through her representative, showed an almost fastidious determination to keep her own hands clean for a nobler purpose. She was prepared to forgo any claims she might have staked out to rich colonial acquisitions, in order to get the other nations to join her in formally closing the high seas to this inhuman traffic that was equally the disgrace of civilized Europe and the scourge of uncivilized Africa.

I have singled out this episode of the anti-slavery crusade, not so much on account of its intrinsic importance—momentous as that is—but because it displays England as assuming a moral role that would have been sheerly inconceivable before the loss of her so-called First Empire, and to which it would be hard to discover the remotest semblance of a contemporary parallel. Both in the long series of wars and the subsequent peace settlement, it would be no exaggeration to say that the Powers of the Continent had been without exception determined to stick at nothing calculated to advance their own several interests or enlarge the scope of their dominions. Even the pettiest Sovereigns were imperially minded to the limit of their capacity, and the French revolutionary bosses, in spite of their resounding professions of love for humanity, were soon eclipsing all records of predatory aggressiveness, before these in turn were surpassed by Napoleon. It was power politics pure and simple, and moral considerations did not come into the picture.

But this could not have been asserted, to anything like the same degree, of Britain. She had proved herself capable of taking a disinterested standpoint, and of pursuing a demonstrably ethical and even Christian line of action. But here we must be careful not to overstate the case. Sudden changes of heart are seldom to be depended on even in individuals, and national character is the cumulative growth of many generations. It would be absurd to deduce from the fact that Britain did actually undergo something equivalent to conversion in this one matter of the slave trade—which after all could hardly have been said to have affected her vitally—that she had blossomed out into a policy of unadulterated idealism, unswayed by mundane or selfish calculation. The hard-bitten men of the world who guided her destinies were scarcely of the sort, even in that age of sentiment, to let their hearts take control of their brains, and the criss-cross of petty and often cynical intrigue that even in the direst national crisis governed the permutations and combinations of the political game were not exactly of the sort to foster a high standard of national morality. The miracle was that in such circumstances, in spite of all lapses and shortcomings, any moral standard should have been maintained at all, and that England alone among European nations did to however limited an extent succeed in rising superior to the immorality of pure power politics.

And it is surely not without its significance that this change of heart, or quickening of conscience, may be roughly dated from the pricking of the imperial bubble by the secession of the American colonies. The effect of that shock had been to exorcise whatever incipient power complex might have been engendered in Britain by her sweeping victories in the middle of the century, and to set her free from the pursuit of British power for that of British principle. That, at any rate, is what we do find developing—and in more than one direction. Her revulsion against slavery had, as we have seen, been influenced by the sense of its being un-British even before it was found to be sinful, and though the evangelical motive entered so prominently into the crusade for emancipation, it is at least doubtful whether it would ever have taken such a hold unless it had accorded with the trend of British inherited sentiment.

But the emotional revival also affected policy through channels that, though moral, were not specifically evangelical or even religious at all. Now that the American nucleus of a British Empire was not only lost, and that the loss had begun, in view of the subsequent recovery, to be thought of rather in the light of a good riddance than otherwise, what survived of British expansionist activity came to be regarded from a different viewpoint from that of imperial power politics. Public opinion was less concerned with the acquisition of territory, or even the imposition of commercial restrictions, than with the maintenance of that liberty, or those liberties, soon to be regarded as the most valuable part of the national heritage, and which liberties not only the rebellious colonists but even the domestic opponents of King George's American policy had made it their ostensible business to vindicate, regardless of more crudely patriotic considerations.

Nowhere was this new spirit more manifest than in the awakening of public conscience to the responsibility of the Government and people of Britain for the proceedings of their compatriots who were in process of acquiring a *de facto* supremacy over the Indian Peninsula. Until well on into the second half of the eighteenth century nobody had dreamed of regarding the East India Company's operations in any other light than that of a commercial venture, whose success was to be measured by the profits accruing directly to its shareholders, and indirectly to the nation. The last thing that either of them wanted was to acquire sovereign power over any part, let alone the whole, of the Indian subcontinent. They had gone there to trade, and not to rule; and everybody in the business, whether on the Board of Directors at home, or in the killing circumstances of an Englishman's life in an oriental environment, was out to exploit all the numerous opportunities that presented themselves not only of swelling the Company's profits, but still more of feathering his own nest. India was a country where bribery and corruption were practised by everyone, from the highest rulers to the humblest officials, to the limit of his capacity, and it was an order of things to which the Company's servants had adapted themselves with true Western efficiency.

The inevitable result, therefore, of Robert Clive's conquest of Bengal, followed by the elimination of the French Raj in the south, was to let loose an orgy of plunder and tyranny hardly to be paralleled even on Indian record upon the defenceless population of the newly won province. Every Englishman who could get the chance eagerly rushed to take his part in what came to be known as the shaking of the pagoda tree. Fortunes proliferated with fungoid exuberance. A new breed of moneyed vulgarians, known as nabobs, bought its way into the ranks of English upper class society, sensibly lowering its tone in the process. The miserable people of Bengal, forced below the level of human subsistence, and with famine to aggravate the rigours of human exploitation, died in uncounted multitudes.

Such were the first-fruits of the Company's rule in India on a sovereign as distinct from a merely factory basis. They were those of anarchy rather than deliberate wickedness. Certainly no other European nationals of the time would have behaved better in similar circumstances, and many might have behaved far worse. There was no deliberate conspiracy to starve or tyrannize; it was simply that a trading company was actuated by business to the exclusion of philanthropic motives, and that in a general scramble for wealth in which— as Bernard Shaw said of marriage—the maximum of temptation was combined with the maximum of opportunity, every separate individual was too busy filling his own pockets to bother about at whose expense this vast racket was being carried on. The impact of white civilization was proving as deadly to the native of the Indian subcontinent as it had to those of the African and American continents, only in a different way, and one that could not by the utmost stretching of language be described—so far at least as Britain was concerned—as one of empire. There was not the least question of a British *imperium*, and the Hanoverian monarchy had less than no desire to saddle itself with the territorial commitments that the Company had been forced in its own despite to assume. The natural and obvious thing, according to eighteenth-century standards of morality, was for the home Government to leave it the freest possible hand, and to wash its own hands of responsibility for their proceedings.

But moral standards were imperceptibly changing, and the tough-gutted materialism of the age of reason was on the way to be superseded, or at any rate modified, by the emotional upsurge which was its almost inevitable sequel. When we consider the length, in space and time reckoning, of communication with India, it is extraordinary that the first stirrings of public conscience on British dealings with her inhabitants should, if anything, have preceded those about the slave trade. Almost from the beginning of George III's reign, records of parliamentary debates show that the British governing class, or the most dynamic section of it, was troubled by the Company's assumption of power without responsibility, and that when reports began to filter through of scandalous abuse of that power they felt the honour and good name of the country to be involved. But the obvious and imperial solution of the Crown frankly substituting its own sovereignty for that of a mere trading corporation, though already favoured by such bold spirits as those of Chatham and Clive, was one that it would take a century of cumulative experience to force within the sphere of practical politics. Far from wishing to set up a British Empire of India in place of the Company's rule, the statesmanship of the time sought, by a series of compromises, to make the best of both worlds by maintaining the Company in formal control of its expanding dominion, while keeping it in Government leading-strings.

It is by no means an edifying story, as far at least as its political underplot is concerned. But it is one, for all that, into which the moral element does enter to an ever-increasing extent. The economic aspect was no longer the only one to be regarded. It was felt that no considerations of profit could render tolerable such reckless shaking of the pagoda tree; that the Company's affairs needed putting in order and its agents calling to account as a matter of plain national honour.

It was only to be expected that this newly awakened concern with the wrongs inflicted on the Indian subjects of British rule should have sought a scapegoat in the man to whose military and administrative genius the British ascendancy in India was so largely owing. He was now, as Lord Clive, living in honoured retirement on the wealth that he could hardly have prevented from sticking to his fingers in the course of a career which, if it had not been hampered with a more pedantic nicety of scruple than that of any other conquering hero, was at least such as to justify his professed astonishment at his own moderation. It was only fitting in the circumstances that Parliament should have shown its concern by appointing a committee of inquiry into the whole question of the Company's proceedings which, though it put on record the enormous sum that Clive had in point of fact succeeded in pocketing, had the restraint to let the facts speak for themselves, and the grace to acknowledge the great and meritorious services he had rendered to the country. No censure or punishment could have emphasized more impressively the determination of Parliament to enforce a standard of conduct on Britons overseas that conformed to moral, as distinct from merely business or imperial, requirements. This was a revolutionary declaration of principle that would have been inconceivable anywhere in the first half of the century, and would have no relevance even today to more than a minority of ostensibly civilized communities.

It is a far cry from laying down principles to putting them into practice, and the purity appropriate to a censorship of morals was not to be expected of so venal and faction-ridden an assembly as the Unreformed Parliament. But it was an incalculable advance that unanimous and even passionate lip-service should be paid to the claim for moral principle to have precedence over calculations of interest in determining the course of British expansion overseas. And, in theory at least, the basic requirement exacted by Britain from her sons over-seas who, in any capacity whatever, had to deal with subject or backward races, was henceforward to be that defined by the time-honoured formula: 'To do justice and love mercy.'

An even more impressive opportunity of vindicating these same principles was afforded fifteen years later by the impeachment of Warren Hastings, the Governor-General who, in circumstances of almost unimaginable difficulty, had succeeded not only in maintaining but confirming and strengthening the ascendancy in India that the British Company, and Britain herself, had owed so largely in the first instance to the genius of Clive. But Parliament emerges with a less unequivocal record from its dealings with Hastings than from its treatment of Clive.

I have no wish to be drawn more than necessary to my theme into the discussion of a *cause célèbre* on which no agreed verdict is ever likely to be reached. Few however are likely to dispute the essential integrity of the accused or fail to recognize the 'great and meritorious services' that he, no less than Clive, had rendered to his country, and not only to his country but to India herself. And even those who take the most uncompromising view of the much-tried Governor's pro-ceedings can hardly fail to be shocked by the factious vindictiveness that drove his accusers, unlike those of Clive, beyond all bounds of decency, and signally obliterated the distinction between prosecution and persecution.

We need to put a severe curb on our own feelings to stomach the paradox that an attack of this kind on a great and, according to the eventual verdict of the tribunal, innocent public servant, may have provided the occasion for as memorable an assertion of fundamental principle as any on British record. But that is the sole aspect of the trial which has any present concern for us.

Even at the time it was doubtful whether the aristocratic and cultural *élite* of the realm, that packed the galleries of Westminster Hall on the opening days, was inclined to regard the prosecution's heroics in any other light than that of a superb display of rhetorical fireworks provided for its entertainment, with little relevance to the guilt or innocence of the accused.

But even if it be doubted whether the Tiger, whose lineaments Burke and his fellow managers of the impeachment have etched so indelibly on the imagination of their own and subsequent generations, had enough in common with the Warren Hastings Esquire of real life to pass for so much as a recognizable caricature, their invention and dramatization did serve, as nothing else could in this time of critical transition, to focus attention upon those essential principles by which the process of overseas expansion must needs be governed, if it were to retain its specifically British quality.

And how could they have been better defined than in such a typical passage of Burke's indictment as this?

My lords, we contend that Mr Hastings, as a British Governor, ought to govern on British principles; not by British forms—God forbid; for if ever there was a case in which the letter kills and the spirit gives life, it would be an attempt to introduce British forms and the substance of despotic principles together into any country. No. We call for that spirit of equity, that spirit of justice, that spirit of protection, that spirit of lenity, which ought to characterize every subject in power; and on these, and these principles only, he will be tried.

Principles, one might add, which apply not only to one but to every British subject in power, in however exalted or humble a capacity. And, no less, to Britain herself.

It would be possible, after eliminating all references to the ostensible issue before the tribunal, to compile from Burke's philippics an exposition of this theme fit to rank with his even more famous pronouncements on the American Secession and the French Revolution.

Here, however, I will only ask leave to subjoin one more quotation, and this from Burke's hardly less famous colleague in the prosecuting team, Richard Brinsley Sheridan. The reference is to the visionary form of British justice in specific application to the peoples of India:

Enthroned by the sovereign hand of Freedom and adorned by the hand of Mercy . . . not arrogantly scorning to stoop when listening to the voice of afflicted innocence—and in its loveliest attitude when bending to uplift the suppliant at its feet.[1]

It is tragic that such sentiments should have been wrested to the service of a cause so dubious, but that they should have been uttered

[1] Quoted from *Sheridan*, by Walter Sichel, Vol. II, p. 168.

at all, and in circumstances calculated to impress them indelibly on the national subconsciousness, is what matters most.

To the accused himself our sympathies go out, but in moderation. He would have been the last person to claim a martyr's crown. The result of the long ordeal, which he sustained with such unruffled dignity, was in the long run to confer on him an historic standing he would never have had otherwise; and even on the shorter view his ending may be counted as happy as Job's, for with his cause vindicated and his colossal costs reimbursed, he settled down in sufficient affluence, in the long-coveted ancient seat of his family, to the enjoyment of a ripe and honoured old age.

He was unfortunate, certainly, in being cast for the villain's as he has been since for a hero's part, in the pageant or mystery one day to be entitled *British Empire in India*. It was the weakness of his chief accuser on the philosophic as it was his strength on the rhetorical level, that his genius was so incurably dramatic. Just as Edmund Burke needed a tragedy queen to put across the footlights the profound political philosophy embodied in his *Reflections on the French Revolution*, so he could not awaken his countrymen to the tyranny of the Company's rule in India without having, or inventing, an actual tyrant to focus their indignation. He himself was the first to be swept away along the spate of his own passion. In this he was a true product of the emotional revival. And in the main, it would seem, this was understood by his audience. They watched the superb performance staged in the building that had witnessed so many other historic dramas with critical appreciation, but without the least impulse to rush out after the fall of the curtain and put the villain under the pump. The histrionics were just a little too gorgeously spectacular to carry entire, or at any rate criminal, conviction.

Indeed, if the indictment had been sponsored solely by these high-lights of the political opposition, whose enthusiasms, however sincere, did notoriously follow party, not to speak of personal, lines, it would have stood no chance, in the House of Commons, of being pushed to the length of impeachment. Though there was nothing resembling the soul-purging strictness of party discipline in later times, the young Premier, Pitt, did have the situation enough under control to ensure that no step should be taken against Hastings without his own active intervention, and though he was careful to preserve an attitude of strict impartiality, the shelving of the first and apparently most damn-ing count by a two-to-one majority appeared to make it certain that all the rest would be similarly voted down. And then, to the general amazement, Pitt himself, who had voted with that majority, came down, on a second charge, at the end of a carefully balanced speech, sufficiently against Hastings to make it obvious that in his opinion there was a case to go to trial, and this decisively swung the House in favour of the impeachment.

This *démarche* of Pitt's is, from our point of view, of an importance not less than that of Burke's more direct and colourful denunciations. It is true that Pitt's sober periods have none of the visionary quality that emanated from Burke. But though he rarely soared above the clouds, the young Premier had his feet firmly planted on the earth. If he had little flair for abstract principles, he saw straight to the concrete reality of every one of the multitudinous problems with which he had to deal, and he could be relied on to do so fairly and without bias on its individual merits. That is why his countrymen reposed an instinctive confidence in his judgment and leadership that they would never have dreamed of according to Burke. It was conspicuously so in this instance. The fact of Mr Pitt having come down so unexpectedly on the anti-Hastings side in respect of his treatment of a not specially important and wholly unattractive minor Indian potentate produced an effect on the House that the combined efforts of a galaxy of some of the most brilliant men who ever adorned it had utterly failed to do.

And indeed, if we pause to consider it, we shall see that a principle of vital importance was at stake. The matter at issue was extremely simple. It was in the year 1781, when Britain had been fighting for her life against not only her American colonies but a belligerent and non-belligerent coalition of practically the whole of Europe, and when her power in India seemed about to be overwhelmed, that, by a miracle of nerve and strategic insight, Governor Hastings had contrived, with the fantastically exiguous resources at his disposal, to ride out this storm and preserve the British Raj from seemingly inevitable shipwreck. It was only natural that in such a crisis he should have grasped at every means of replenishing his depleted war chest, and that he should have taken the perfectly legitimate step of calling on Zamindar Cheyt Singh of Benares for a substantial but not unreasonable wartime increase to the tribute he in any case owed to the suzerain Power. This arrangement had worked smoothly enough for two years, but now the time-serving Oriental had evinced plain symptoms of an intention to rat from an apparently sinking ship. Without a moment's hesitation Hastings had imposed a swingeing fine equivalent to approximately half a million sterling, and hastened to the Holy City, with only a handful of followers, to bring its ruler to his senses. He had nearly paid with his life for his rashness, for he had found himself besieged by a horde of insurgent soldiery, but he had been eventually relieved by the nearest British contingent, and followed up his work by sacking the defaulting zamindar and appointing a more amenable tributary at a considerably increased assessment.

No fair-minded person—and certainly not Pitt—could dispute that in circumstances of unexampled difficulty Hastings had displayed the highest qualities of courage and statesmanship. And Pitt himself had, in the first part of that crucial speech, gone out of his way to defend Hastings from the charge of having exceeded his powers in demanding an increased contribution from one of the Company's vassals, or even in imposing a fine on him for incipient contumacy. But a fine of half a million—roughly equivalent to a year's total revenue of the zamindarate [1]—that, in Mr Pitt's sober judgment, consituted a plain violation of those rules of justice and liberty by which England expected her representatives abroad, in whatever capacity, to be bound. And 'on this ground', he said, weighing his words with palpable reluctance, 'I feel it impossible to acquit Mr Hastings of the whole of the charge brought against him; for I feel in my conscience that he has pushed the exercise of that arbitrary discretion which, from the nature of the Eastern Government, was entrusted to him, to a greater length than he was warranted to do by the necessity of the service.' [2]

Hard measure it might seem—even though it involved no final condemnation—to mete out to the good and faithful public servant who, on his Indian, no less than Pitt on his subsequent European, record, is entitled to the proud designation of 'the pilot who weathered the storm'. Less imperially minded critics than Thomas Carlyle may be tempted to conclude the whole matter in the famous metaphor that he coined in justification of the Victorian Governor Eyre's imcomparably less defensible conduct in office than any charged against Hastings.[3] This is to the effect that a captain, who by bold and resolute action has succeeded in putting out a fire at sea, ought not to be called to account for having flung a bucket or two of water on the hold beyond what is necessary. Even if he has damaged some of the cargo, he has saved the ship. And if in the process of saving India for a future British Empire Hastings had applied the financial screw, without too scrupulous a regard for the niceties of justice, to such crooks in high places as Cheyt Singh, who should blame him? Mr Pitt, for one; and on a principle formulated with classic lucidity by his biographer, Holland Rose: [4]

Not only did the conduct of Hastings far exceed the limits required by justice; it was also bound up with a question on which the stability of our

---

[1] Which the ruler, in his turn, would have proceeded to sweat out of a peasantry never far from the verge of starvation.

[2] See *Pitt and the National Revival* by J. Holland Rose, p. 233, to which the reader may be referred for by far the best and most comprehensive account of this episode.

[3] In stamping out, by methods of calculated frightfulness, a Negro revolt in Jamaica in 1865. See p. 259.

[4] J. Holland Rose, op. cit., pp. 239-40.

Indian Empire has ever rested. So long as the feudatories of the British Raj feel confidence in his sense of justice, India is safe. Whenever they have cause to believe that injustice and oppression are the charactcristics of his rulc, the foundations of the Indian Empire are shaken to their base.

It might indeed be questioned how far such unconditional sub-ordination of power to morality can be reconciled with the imperial principle at all. Certainly, at the time at which we are speaking, John Company's rule had hardly begun to be viewed in the light of a British Empire, or its Governor-General, even with the greatly en-hanced powers conferred on Hastings's successors by Mr Pitt himself in his later India Act, in that of a Viceroy.

Some apology I feel is needed for the space devoted to this episode. But the principle involved is of the highest relevance to our theme. Burke, from his visionary standpoint so far above the clouds as too often to cause him to lose his mundane bearings altogether, and Pitt, at ground level, burning out his candle at both ends in grappling with the innumerable demands of quotidiañ urgency that crowded upon him, were each in their different but complementary ways playing an essential part in the handling of this same test case, which involved so much more than the fate of one individual, and was pregnant with that of Britain herself.

It is as if, at this crucial phase of her development, she had arrived at the parting of ways not yet signposted as those leading respectively to the goals of Empire and Commonwealth, and that she had un-wittingly and irrevocably made her choice for the latter. That was, or rather is, the supreme issue at stake at the Hastings trial, and what gives it its supreme historical importance.

BOOK FOUR

1

RENEWED EXPANSION
WITHOUT EMPIRE

NEVER HAD any people or nation been less ambitious of world-wide dominion than the British in the dawn, or indeed for the greater part of, the nineteenth century. And yet if we were to follow the fashion of lumping together all the results of overseas expansion under the question-begging designation of 'empire', we should be forced to admit that despite all her efforts to divest herself of imperial responsibilities, Britain emerged from her struggle with imperial France saddled with an empire of unrivalled extent and potentiality. Such greatness, however little she may have designed to achieve it, she may be said to have thrust upon herself. Her conquest of sea power, by cutting off her European rivals from fields of profitable expansion, imposed on her almost the necessity of enlarging her own orbit to include them. It was a process as natural as the flooding of a blocked-up river over the surrounding level.

But it was not one that ever had been, or could be, conducive to the making of the empires that expand and burst on the stream of historic time with bubble-like frequency. For there was one way in which they resembled the bubbles of children rather than those of nature. They had all hitherto, without exception, been the result of strenuous, planned effort. Empires do not just happen, or fall to the lot of those who do not particularly want them, any more than races are won by somnambulists—not at least before this alleged Second British Empire came about as an unintended and almost unrealized by-product of Britain's efforts in the great European war.

On the conclusion of peace, three of what were to be the four leading white dominions were already firmly planted under the sovereignty of the British Crown, two of them acquired after the loss of the American colonies.

I have already referred to the case of Australia, the land of promise that Napoleon had marked down for the overseas empire that lay so tantalizingly beyond his reach, but that the ordinary Englishman was more apt to regard in the light of a social convenience, a sort of human sewage farm—an attitude that could hardly in the nature of things have been conducive to pride in or affection towards the land thus selected and its inhabitants. But given the land and immigrants of British stock or tradition to develop it, the plant of Australian nationhood could be left to grow up in its own time and way from this gratuitously manured soil, and all the more vigorously from being left alone.

What was one day to be the Dominion of Canada stood on quite a different footing towards the mother country, for it was all that on the North American mainland had survived from the ruin of the so-called First British Empire. It was the very fact of the United States having seceded from the British connection that had the effect of binding this newly won northern province to its recent conqueror by those very ties, 'thinner than gossamer but stronger than links of iron', by which George III and his ministers, if they had been advised in time, might have held the States themselves in a few more years of formal allegiance.

If this had been done and the counsels of men like Burke and Chatham had been allowed to prevail, the hour in which the colonies decided to set up house for themselves could hardly, in the nature of things, have been postponed indefinitely. But a United States that ripened peacefully into independence would surely have included the whole of the North American land mass from the subarctic to the subtropical. There would have been no attempted invasion by rebel levies of the Lower Province of Canada, nor flooding of the Upper Province by fanatically pro-British loyalist refugees, and consequently no stimulus forcible enough to provoke the counter-militancy of Canadian independence.

As long as Canada had remained a French province, capable of linking up with the other French possessions in the south, it had been the standing menace that more than anything else had kept the American colonies loyal to the British connection. Now it was just the other way about. The menace of forcible absorption by their overweening neighbour was one that made not only the British but even the French Canadians lean as heavily upon British support as the Americans had done during the struggle with Bourbon imperialism.

Britain herself had contributed to this result by displaying as much wisdom in ordering her relations with Canada as she had ineptitude in her dealings with the original American colonies. She had given as free a scope to the still nascent and unformulated spirit of her own civilization as the circumstances allowed. Obviously the time was not ripe for the grant of anything like commonwealth or dominion status. Such revolutionary action would have been quite contrary to the British way of feeling forward by intuition and experiment, as it would have been to the notions of paternal government inherited by the late subjects of the French monarchy. But it is to the credit of Lord North's ill-starred administration that in the year following the Boston Tea Party and previous to the outbreak of the War of Independence, they dealt with the Canadian situation by an Act deliberately calculated to confirm these new British subjects in a way of government, and even of law, adjusted, in the main, to their own and not to British notions.

Mr Pitt's Government dealt in the same spirit with the enlarged post-war Canada that had continued in the British allegiance, by granting separate constitutions to the British Upper and the French Lower Provinces, on the traditional British lines of keeping the executive power in control of the Crown, and giving that of the purse to a more or less representative assembly—a working arrangement of predictably unstable equilibrium, but one that succeeded, despite the inevitable growing pains of political factiousness and unrest, in securing the overall loyalty of both provinces to the British connection, even if the attachment of the French one may have had a certain resemblance to that of the child who

> Always keeps a hold of nurse
> For fear of finding something worse.[1]

That something was absorption—or what today would be called liberation—by the United States. This matter was put to the test in the scrambling, fratricidal and otherwise pointless war that broke out between Britain and the United States over the ostensible issue of the British maritime counter-blockade to that of Napoleon's continental system. The only issue at stake that relieves this inglorious squabble from the reproach of criminal futility is whether the new republic had a manifest destiny to fulfil, of northward as well as westward expansion. It is curious that the chief impetus behind this northward drive should have come from the Southern States of the Union, whereas those nearest to the Canadian border had no heart in a struggle that put a stranglehold on their developing commerce, and from which they virtually stood aside. This Canadian War of Independence, though fought on a much smaller scale than the American one of the previous generation, ended in an equally clear-cut decision, that there could henceforth be no more serious question of the United States conquering Canada than of England conquering the United States. And by some this might be accounted a worthwhile compensation for the waste of

[1] See H. Belloc's *Bad Child's Book of Beasts*.

wealth and loss of blood in what were happily destined to be the last formal hostilities ever to be waged between the separated main branches of the Anglo-Saxon family.

But it would be too palpable an absurdity to talk as if Canada had been saved from forcible republicanization to be swallowed up in a British or any other empire. It is true that her advance to complete self-government within the Commonwealth covered a period of over a century from her original conquest, and was accompanied by a fair amount of incidental friction, and even one or two damp squibs of rebellion. But there was never the least serious intention of holding it up indefinitely, or of treating Canada in the light of an imperial province. It really boiled down to a question of when, and by what means, the young daughter nation would be of age to assume unqualified mistress-ship of her own house. And that depended chiefly on when the representative body, or bodies, would be ripe for following the British example of adding to their legislative functions the effective control of those executive powers formally vested in the Crown and its nominees.

It is true that progress was slowed down, and threatened at times to be bogged down, by the inertia of the home authorities in dealing with colonial matters, and what a later age might have described as the blimpishness of some of the battled veterans who were thought fit to be rewarded for their past services with provincial governorships. But the innate constitutional genius of the British order of civilization, though it might have evinced some slackening of its dynamism in the period of recuperation from the long war effort, was only gathering fresh momentum, and took on a new strength in the age of middle-class ascendancy that was ushered in by the passing of the first Reform Bill. A spirit of progressive liberalism was brought to the solution of colonial problems, and there was s sufficiency of eager enthusiasts in high places to give it practical application, the most notable of these being the Radical plutocrat, Lord Durham, who with the backing of an extraordinarily brilliant team, was sent out in the capacity of Governor-General to report on a situation that seemed to have reached the point of hopeless and explosive deadlock, and who in the course of a few brief months gathered the material for the famous report which, as one of its chief authors, Durham's right-hand man, Charles Buller, truly predicted, would be the textbook of the colonial reformer, until it became the manual of the colonial government of Great Britain,[1] and certainly forms a decisive landmark in the evolution of Canada to complete self-government.

Twenty-seven years had still to elapse between the publication of

[1] *The Cambridge History of the British Empire*, Vol. VI, p. 301.

this report and the achievement by Canada of virtually complete domestic self-government, or what we should now call dominion status, within the framework of a free British commonwealth, and there were to be times of friction and maladjustment when the bond of loyalty seemed perilously frayed, largely owing to differences between the two national strains in Canada itself. But what we might describe as the gravitational pull of this new order of civilization was too strong to be denied. Never would any British Sovereign or statesman dream of reverting in any circumstances to the firm line of George III with his subjects overseas. British forces might indeed be called in, as they actually were in Canada, to assist in the police work of putting down sporadic and sectional revolts. But nothing could be more certain than that any serious attempt by one of the major colonies to walk out of what passed for the British Empire would find itself pushing at a door already ajar. Neither the soldiers of a British Sovereign nor the money of the British taxpayer were expendable in a second war of colonial independence. The imperial bluff was one that was notoriously liable to be called at any moment.

But it would have been premature to deduce that any alternative principle of association had as yet been consciously envisaged either by those in authority or the public at large. The seeds of a free commonwealth of nations were no doubt sown, and needed only time to ripen to maturity, nor was Burke the only visionary to have had a Pisgah view of that not quite so distant prospect; but the whole idea of an empire that was in fact no empire at all in any hitherto accepted sense of the word, and with nothing to hold it together except the free will of its constituent members, was a notion too contradictory of all that had hitherto been taken for granted to find an easy lodgment in a mind so temperamentally conservative as that of the normal Englishman.

The choice, as he saw it, in dealing with the colonies, was not one between compulsory and free association, but between tutelage and independence. And since it was tacitly agreed that there could be no question of preventing the daughter communities from taking over full control of their own destinies as soon as they judged themselves to be of an age and capacity to do so, their complete independence of and separation from the mother country seemed, in the course of nature, only a matter of time and convenience.

Still, though the results of separation from the United States seemed to show that, on a purely material calculation, the burden of colonial sovereignty was one that could profitably be dispensed with, there was no disposition to lay it down prematurely. It would have been out of keeping with the British character to take the initiative in parting with anything whatever that was held in even nominal possession. Canada for instance, might be visibly heading for her own declaration of independence, and though nobody would lift a finger to stop her, still less would anybody want to hurry her. The later the better, might be felt by those whose reason had convinced them that the parting was bound to come, and would be all for the best when it did come.

What the Englishman feels is apt to be more important than what he thinks. It is seldom his way to formulate his theories in advance and apply them logically, and we shall get the story wrong if we simplify it by crediting him with doing so. It matters much less what he thought about the colonies than that he hardly thought about them at all. In this booming period when Britain really ruled the waves and was establishing herself as the workshop of the world, he was content on the whole to let Colonial Office matters take their course. That office was notoriously the Cinderella of ministerial appointments, a fact that accounts largely for the hamfisted treatment meted out to the captive Napoleon by its worthy but almost monumentally undistinguished incumbent in the long Liverpool administration, when it was not even the sole province of its chief, who bore the title Secretary of State for War and Colonies. Not that this restriction of the political limelight was necessarily a bad thing, since it allowed full scope, in the shaping of colonial policy, to the administrative genius of the Permanent Under-Secretary, James Stephen—'Over-Secretary', as he was sometimes called—who was credited by one of his colleagues, not implausibly, with ruling the colonial empire.[1]

Though indeed anything less fitted to be associated with the name of empire than the story of British colonial expansion from the late Georgian to the height of the Victorian age it would be hard to imagine. That story may now be studied in voluminous detail by anyone with time and patience to wade through the relevant compilations, but it would pass the wit of man to find any thread of unifying purpose binding it together, even to the extent of a determination to leave well alone and trust the colonists to work out their destinies in their own way. It is true that in the long run they generally succeeded in getting it, but too often after niggling interference by the home authorities, or the efforts of reactionary or incompetent Governors to stand on the letter of their authority and hold up their advance to self government; though it is remarkable how in every case, before things had been allowed to get irremediably out of hand, the right man proves to have been forthcoming to make British principles prevail.

But we shall seek in vain for any line of colonial policy persistently followed towards a consciously envisaged goal. The overall impression that one gets is that colonial affairs were not considered of sufficient

[1] See his Life in the *Dictionary of National Biography*.

importance to engender the necessary concentration. They were
accordingly suffered, for the most part, to shape their own course, as
is the way of streams that fall and trees that rise, but assuredly not that
of empires, that are the products of conscious volition.

Hence we find ourselves confronted with a paradox. It is this very
time in which imperial ambition was most in abeyance, and in which
Britain was more concerned to limit than to expand her overseas
commitments, that saw the expansion of what subsequently came to be
known as the British Empire on an unprecedented scale. What at the
beginning of the century had been barely fit to be dignified by the
name of colonies had blossomed out, by its third quarter, into communities that were already plainly destined to stand in their own right
in the peerage of civilized nations. This in addition to the sovereignty,
shortly to be proclaimed as the empire, of the vast Indian subcontinent,
and an already world-wide assortment of possessions sprinkling the
map with points and patches of red.

And yet one has only to delve into the records of the time to
realize how insignificant a part what we should now call imperial
matters played in the thought and calculations of Englishmen, particularly if we leave out the obviously spectacular subject of India, and
confine our attention to what were still lumped together under the
designation of colonies.

Though political consciousness among the educated classes was
very much alive, and most of all in the heyday of middle-class supremacy between the first and second Reform Bills, it would be only a
slight exaggeration to say of the vast majority of intelligent citizens
that all they knew, or cared to know, about the future dominions was
the bare fact that they existed, reinforced by a vague conventional
notion of the rough and ready folk who inhabited them and the sort
of life they led. It was a subject in which few were sufficiently interested
to demand more exact information. Except on very exceptional
occasions, as of a native war, or a flare-up of civil disturbance, colonial
affairs were not what, in the modern journalistic phrase, would be
accounted news. Still less were they capable of ranking as live political
issues about which passions were engendered and the fates of governments swayed.

In the biographies of leading contemporary statesmen, voluminous
as they are, it is remarkable how few and far between are references of
any sort to colonial matters. Lord Palmerston, for instance, with his
wide-ranging interest in world affairs, from America to China, who is
generally regarded as the embodiment of rumbustious patriotism, was
hardly what we should now call empire-conscious at all—certainly not
in so far as the daughter nations were concerned. His attitude towards
them may be judged by one of the rare occasions on which he

condescended to dwell on colonial affairs, when in March 1838 he intervened in reply to a motion of censure moved on the colonial administration of his Cabinet colleague Lord Glenelg, the head and front of
the charge against whom he alleged to be: 'What?—why, the demoralized state of the penal colony of New South Wales. So, forsooth, Lord
Glenelg is unfit to conduct the administration of the colonies because
the settlers of New South Wales have not yet attained the perfection
of angels.'

His dismissal of the 'settlers' at the Cape in the course of the same
speech was almost equally contemptuous, though time would appear
to have vindicated his judgment on those of them who had taken their
departure (in the Great Trek) 'because they were prevented from
continuing a system of persecution they had followed against the
aborigines'.

One's general impression is that a great gentleman like Palmerston,
steeped in the traditions of the old civilization, viewed these dwellers
beyond its pale in the light of outsiders with whose affairs he found it
beneath his dignity to be more involved than necessary, and was more
interested in the fortunes of Hungarians, Turks, Neapolitans or
Portuguese. But though the imperial aspect of colonial affairs left him
cold, he was full of enthusiasm on behalf of the peculiarly British
campaign for the suppression of slavery. For with all his faults, 'Old
Pam' did believe in liberty, according to his lights, and thought nobly
of Britain and her mission in the world.

In the pre-Victorian part of the nineteenth century the average
Englishman's interest in colonial matters had tended to be monopolized by those West Indian possessions which were the last strong-
holds, under British auspices, of the institution of slavery. And here
the imaginative impact was the reverse of imperial. For these islands
were thought of as opulent salvage from the shipwreck of the British
Empire in the West. They were not peopled by rough pioneers, but
were the domain of a planter aristocracy resembling that of the
Southern States of the mainland, and the vast fortunes that were made
out of sugar and slaveholding caused the penetration of British society
by a species of moneybug corresponding to the nabobs from India,
and of the rise of families—Beckfords, Barretts, Gladstones—who
were to play a conspicuous part in the shaping of the new order of
society in England.

Imperial interests therefore would plainly seem to have called for
the fostering of these rich island estates, slavery and all, as a first call
upon policy, and it was in pursuit of this notion that the West Indies
had been allowed to become the grave of whole armies of British
soldiers during the war with revolutionary France. But both during its
Napoleonic sequel, and still more the peace that followed it, public

opinion at home came to be swayed, in the vital matter of slavery, by moral to the almost complete exclusion of imperial considerations. It was a heavy enough blow when the supply of slaves, on which the planters had hitherto relied for the maintenance of their hitherto expendable labour force, was cut off by the suppression of the trade. But, from the planters' point of view, it was the climax of outrage when the reformers and evangelists went on to stir up the people to demand the root-and-branch extirpation of slavery itself, which signified the confiscation of the human property that was the indispensable foundation of their prosperity, and, as they saw it, their own isolation as a white minority in an anarchy of emancipated savages. And this at a time when the ruling classes in Europe were gripped by an obsessive fear of even the thinnest end of the revolutionary wedge.

No wonder that the planters dug in their toes and developed an extreme form of what has since become an only-too-standardized pattern of settler mentality, and roundly notified their determination to abate no jot of their right to wallop their own niggers at their own sweet will. For after all, like other colonists, they were merely asking to be left alone to mind their own business in their own way, which was no more than George Washington and his compatriots had demanded from George III, or that the Southern States, in the next generation, would demand from President Lincoln.

But the reformers and evangelists were not to be denied in bringing to the volitional surface what was now the fully formed national conviction, to the effect that slavery was such an abominable thing in itself—and most of all under British auspices—that its root-and-branch extirpation had become an imperative necessity to which every other consideration had got to give way, even those of imperial welfare and the sacred rights of property. And this demand became irresistible when the carrying of the Reform Bill, on the crest of what had threatened to be a revolutionary upsurge, let loose a spate of reforming activity, directed by the triumphant and newly enfranchised upper bourgeoisie, who were solidly determined that emancipation had got to come, and come at once, and that the planters would have to like it or lump it. A cynic might have remarked that these crusaders in top hats turned a Nelson eye on conditions just as atrocious as any in the plantations that obtained in the mines and factories at home, or the Bumbleized workhouses whose rigours they themselves spared no pains to intensify. But the planters were after all the last folk to whom this humanitarian line of counter-attack was likely to occur or to appeal.

To them it was as plain a case of arbitrary interference with the rights of Britons overseas as could well be imagined, and the planters had shown themselves to be in a mood of militant intractability. But these obstinate men submitted if not exactly without a murmur at least without a struggle—a thing so different from the common form of colonial reaction that one can only account for it by the fact that, being after all themselves British, they could not work up any convincing enthusiasm in the defence of so plainly un-British a thing as slavery. Accordingly they acted in a thoroughly British spirit by striking the best bargain they could with the home authorities who, for their part, were ready to temper the wind of change to Massa turned Boss by a generous plunge into the pockets of the British taxpayer, as well as by an interim arrangement for binding the ex-slaves to their jobs in the capacity of apprentices, a form of compulsion that in many instances proved more onerous than slavery itself, and that a now vigilant public opinion at home caused to be swept away in its turn after a very brief trial, in favour of unconditional emancipation.

2

UNDER WHICH CIVILIZATION?

THIS WORKED well enough in British colonies where the
settlers, however callous and obstinate, had enough of their
native spirit in them to conform to rules of the game sanctioned by
immemorial tradition. But such compliance was not to be counted on
from folk, equally stubborn, brought up in a different tradition of
civilization, as were the Dutch, with an infusion of Huguenot and
German colonists, who peopled the colony that had grown up around
the port and harbour at Table Bay that His Majesty's Government had
purchased with a sole view to the convenience of their shipping,
without the least afterthought of territorial expansion into the vast
hinterland that stretched on and on like the American prairies, without
even such obvious limits as the Rockies and the Pacific. If there had
been an unswerving determination from the first to limit British
responsibilities to the harbour settlement and its supporting farmlands,
it is possible that today there might be still one patch of red on the
map of South Africa. But such clear-cut decisions are not in the British
way of proceeding. A Governor was appointed and the usual arrangements made for running the newly acquired Cape Colony with the
stolid apparent acquiescence of its white occupiers, and things were
allowed to take their own course without anyone at home knowing or
caring much about it—at least as far as its mundane problems were
concerned.

Little did the home authorities, or public, realize the nature of the
problem they had set themselves in assuming responsibility for this
community of farmers, or Boers, one of the toughest races on earth, of
largely nomadic habits, each dwelling or wandering in more than
patriarchal isolation, each a law to himself and his household, and
already scattered abroad over an area wider than England. These
uncompromising individualists, who had often in the past proved too
tough a nut for even the Dutch authorities to crack, and who were
brought up in the combined tradition of Roman Law and Calvinist
religion, were utter strangers to the way of British civilization, and

would obviously require the most tactful restraint in handling if they were to be fitted somehow into the British pattern. It is possible that under some easy-going Governor who was out to avoid trouble at all costs, and capable of preventing others from making it for him, some sort of a *modus vivendi* might have been evolved between Briton and Boer.

But a spirit of reforming earnestness was abroad that went straight to its end regardless of consequences, and the crusade against slavery had got a grip on the British mind that imparted to it a religious—not to say fanatical—momentum. And ironically enough, the impelling religion happened to be of a kind essentially similar to that of the Boers themselves. For the great evangelical revival which was at its height in the years following the great war had made this cause peculiarly its own, and lent it all the force of a wealthily backed and highly organized missionary organization whose emissaries penetrated into the wildest parts of a still imperfectly explored world with an apostolic zeal rivalling that of the primitive Christians. And naturally they found no more congenial field for their activities than the newly acquired colony, where they could be sure of a prestige and authority that hardly the local or even the home government would be willing openly to challenge.

Unfortunately this zeal was not apt to be tempered by discretion. The revulsion from the horrors incidental to the slave traffic had engendered a resolve to espouse the cause of the native races in the spirit of that noble and Christian motto of the Anti-slavery Society: 'Am I not a man and a brother?' Unfortunately this did not always stop short at a resolve to recognize the equality of all men without distinction of colour before God and the law, but resulted in a sort of inverted partisanship of black against white, and a wildly unrealistic view of the savage as a grown-up and responsible brother.[1]

Even apart from this disturbing factor, there were the seeds of irreconcilable difference between Briton and Dutchman in their respective attitudes to natives. The Boer, in his lonely isolation, and environed by an indigenous population of a less than averagely prepossessing kind—Hottentots and Bushmen—had acquired his own way of dealing with creatures whom he regarded as hardly men and not brothers at all, but as the divinely appointed hewers of wood and drawers of water for God's elect, among whom he included (as who does not?) himself. He too, like the West Indian planters, claimed the right to wallop his own niggers, whose lot was at least preferable to

[1] It is frequently asserted that this was the effect of Rousseau's idealization of the savage. This is easier asserted than proved. The impact of Rousseau on the English mind was chiefly that of a revolutionary bogey, and even Blake knew so little about him as to equate him with Voltaire as a 'mocker'.

that of the slave gangs on the plantations. Tough as he was, and bully as he could hardly help being, there is no reason for believing the Boer to have been addicted to unnecessary cruelty. In his God-fearing self-righteousness he lived up to his own standards.

But they were irreconcilably different from British standards, and from that difference stems the great South African tragedy whose *dénouement* still awaits fulfilment. It is as easy as it is obvious to say that, given wise handling from the start, there need have been no tragedy, and that the two white peoples might have blended harmoniously in the larger unity of a free commonwealth. And certainly nothing could have been more inept than the way in which the originally not unfriendly Boers were rubbed up the wrong way by well-meant official and private British interference. But the cleavage of principle was fundamental, and so long as that remained unabridged it would have been hard to conceive how any effort on the British side, short of total surrender, could have joined together in perpetuity that which inherited tradition had put asunder. And in any case we are concerned with what did happen, and not with what might have happened.

The native problem was one that in South Africa was bound to dominate the situation, the more imperatively with every fresh bout of white expansion, if—as proved to be the case—the solution was ruled out that obtained in the United States, and in the other three eventual dominions, of the virtual elimination of the aboriginal population, or its reduction to an insignificant and controlled minority. This did actually happen in South Africa to the original Hottentots and Bushmen with whom the first settlers were confronted, but the more vigorous and virile Kaffir and Bantu stocks that were pressing down from the north were not to be disposed of so easily. Thus it came about that, to an ever-increasing extent, the white man was doomed to find himself in a minority in what, as far as numbers were concerned, was a preponderantly black man's country. In what relation was this white minority to establish itself towards the indigenous majority?

Seen in its naked reality, there were two, and two only, alternative solutions of this problem, the one on imperial and the other on what we should now define as commonwealth lines, and these were too flatly divergent to admit of any permanent compromise or middle way between them. Was the white man to assume from the first membership of a master race, and maintain that status unconditionally and at all costs? Or was he to regard every human being, whatever his race or colour, as on a footing of at least potential equality with himself as a man and a brother, even if he were not yet a grown-up brother?

The former assumption was that which was unquestioningly

adopted and acted upon by the Boer, and if there had been a British Empire in anything but name, would have been equally so by his British partner. But though there was nowhere as yet a clear conscious-ness of it, the spirit of British civilization had already taken a decisive turn towards acceptance of the latter. Briton and Boer had thus early taken their respective stands on positions that were bound to bring them into conflict.

And to complicate the matter still further—if the settlement at Cape Colony were to be the starting-point of an expansion over the whole of South Africa, it was overwhelmingly probable that the Boer, who had started expanding already, would maintain his lead, so that the majority of the white population would be of Dutch and not British origin. And thus it might have been foreseen that with every fresh radiation outward, the temptation would be increased for the Boer majority to constitute itself not only the master race, but the master white race, of an ultimately completed South Africa; for, failing the miracle of the two European stocks uniting voluntary allegiance to a common—or commonwealth—ideal, the numerical preponderance would be bound, in the long run, to entail political domination. Unless indeed the numerically inferior of the two breeds could succeed in frankly mobilizing all its forces, world-wide as well as South African, and imposing its imperial suzerainty by force on the other—but to what permanent advantage if the imperial solution should prove to be ruled out by the very nature of British, though not of Dutch, civilization? Thus it was possible for Dutchman to impose his yoke on Briton with as clear a conscience as on Kaffir, but the Briton could only return the compliment by making a shameful conquest of himself.

The proof of these things was still in the future, but the elements of the tragedy were there, and an observer of superhuman penetration might even then have been capable of foreseeing the overwhelmingly probable (to say the least of it) manner of its unfolding.

But any remote chance of things working out differently would have been frustrated by the way in which the British control proceeded to ride its own principles roughshod over those of the Dutch settlers on whom it had been superimposed. That these principles were incom-parably more liberal and humane than those of the Dutch master breed in dealing with its African dependants, did not make them any more palatable when imposed by an alien and unsympathetic administration which itself was continually being kept up to the mark by hot-gospel-ing evangelists who could command the full backing of public sentiment. For the emotional revival was now in full spate, and by no channel did it find more congenial vent, to the British temperament, than that of apostolic propaganda among the heathen, the more

* G

heathen and primitive the better. The missionary was abroad, and the new African colony soon became a prime field of his activities. And with the powerful and wealthy London Missionary Society to organize them, these acquired a compulsive force that few Governors abroad or Governments at home would be hardy enough to set themselves against.

And the missionaries themselves, by the very nature of their calling, must needs be single-hearted enthusiasts, with no material axe of their own to grind, though not necessarily exempt from such occupational defects as ignorance, fanaticism and spiritual pride. But they had a high and holy concern for the natives whom they made it their dedicated task to bring within the pale of the Christian fold on a footing of equality with all God's children. And this, with men whose bigness of heart was seldom matched with a proportionate intelligence, was capable of developing a bias none the less dangerous for being on the right side.

The missionaries soon discovered ample reason to be shocked and scandalized at the methods of the Boers—and particularly those farthest from the seat of government—in imposing their yoke on the fast-disappearing Hottentots, and any other black Africans with whom they had to deal; nor did the Boers themselves make matters any better by their uncompromising opposition to missionary interference either with themselves or the natives. The result was a violent and undiscriminating pro-native partisanship on one side and (since the missionaries were known to have the support of authority) anti-British as well as anti-missionary on the other.

The missionaries were not in a mood to stick at anything in pursuit of their ideal, not even, in some instances, of taking to themselves Hottentot wives. One of them in particular, John Philip, was a Scottish Congregationalist, inspired by a militant Calvinism not very different from that of the Boers themselves, which did not prevent him from moving heaven and earth against them in a propagandist offensive conducted with the holiest zeal and corresponding absence of scruple, both on the spot and by stumping Britain itself, where the public, and even the authorities, were ready to take his wildest denunciations for gospel. Not that there was any lack of only too genuine material for Philip's muck-raking assiduity.[1]

The situation was still further exacerbated when a Whig Government came in, full of reforming notions that it had no inhibitions whatever in exporting. Slavery was swept away with even less compensation to the South African farmers than to the West Indian

---

[1] Curiously enough, the solution for which Philip was pressing was that of the segregation of the natives in separate reserves, so that in a sense he may be said to have been the apostle of *apartheid*.

planters, and to make matters worse, at the height of the harvest season.

The climax came when the Kaffir advance guard, of a far more formidable breed of natives than the Hottentots, launched a sudden invasion of the white settlements in the east of the Cape Province which, after sending hundreds of farms up in flames, was only suppressed after hard fighting by British troops under the redoubtable Sir Harry Smith. The universally respected British Governor, another Peninsula veteran, Sir Benjamin d'Urban, followed this up by an expansion of frontier that was approved of by the missionaries themselves on the spot. But not by Philip, who worked on the well-meaning but gullible Colonial Secretary, Lord Glenelg, to convince him that the Kaffirs were the innocent victims of white aggression, to such effect that the new frontier was contracted to its former limits; and when Governor d'Urban proved unco-operative he was given the sack.

This proved the last straw for the Boers. Large numbers of them abandoned their homes and, packing all their possessions into their great ox-wagons, inspired by the Old Testament example of the exodus from Egypt and equally believing themselves to be the Lord's chosen people, set forth in quest of whatever Promised Land they could find in the vast grass spaces of the interior beyond the now hated British rule. Among them was a wiry youngster of ten called Paul Kruger, whose impressions, thus formed, were to set the cast of his mind for the remainder of the century.

Nobody at the time thought of attaching any decisive significance to this undoubtedly picturesque episode, which seemed more likely than not to end in the swallowing up of these devoted bands, one after another, by the hordes of ferocious warriors whose lands, for the most part recently acquired by conquest and extermination, they had marked down for the Canaan of their wanderings. Nobody dreamed that a train of events had been set in motion by which the fate of South Africa would in the course of generations be determined, and that the irrevocable step had been taken by which, in all human probability, an ultimately united South Africa was bound in advance to be lost to what in those days would have been called, if it was called anything, the British Empire.

Yet so it was, and so it proved, for two definite and sufficient reasons. The great Boer exodus—or rather a series of exoduses that took the *trekkers* beyond the Orange to the Vaal, and thence across the rolling expanses of the veldt to impinge on the tropical zone of Africa, parcelling out the country as they went into the enormous farms in which each owner reigned in a patriarchal isolation—set the seal on a manifest destiny' on the same lines as those of the United States, except that the Limpopo River was a less indubitable terminus than the

Pacific Ocean. But it also ensured that the stamp of that seal should be Dutch and not British.

It is true that the British authorities, who were taken by surprise and were at a loss what attitude or policy to adopt in face of this new development, did make an instinctive effort to head off the *trekkers* from penetrating to the shores of the Indian Ocean, and to shepherd them northward in the direction of the interior. With what more resembled a considered policy than most of their reactions, they contrived, not without fighting, to bar their access to the sea at Port Natal or, as it came to be rechristened, Durban, which itself came to be the nucleus of a British colony extending to the foot of the Drakensberg Mountains, over whose passes the *trekkers*, or such of them as had escaped massacre at the hands of the ferocious Zulus, made their sullen and weary return to the veldt. But this did not prevent the grasslands of the central plateau, which formed the heart of South Africa, from falling under the rule of these dour pastoral folk of non-British origin and anti-British tradition.

Anyone who even thus early had considered the simple fact that in three of the four white man's provinces of which an expanded South Africa had come to consist, in only one, and that the smallest, the British were in a majority, and that in two of them they were not even in a perceptible minority, might have deemed it rather much to expect these unlikely elements to evolve into unity as part of a British empire or even commonwealth; for what reason could a Dutch South Africa have for remaining in the British orbit for a moment longer than necessary?

It might have been objected that the French of Lower Canada found no insuperable difficulty in remaining loyal to the British connection. But here neither the material nor spiritual set-up offers a true parallel. In an expanded Canada it was the British and not the French who did the expanding, and consequently formed an increasing majority. And from the start the handling of the French Canadians by the British had been, on the whole, as wise and tactful as that of the Boers had been the reverse. And above all there had been no overshadowing problem of an aboriginal majority to bedevil Anglo-French relationships. Nobody was likely to quarrel about the impotent and scanty Canadian Indians. But the native problem, in a land in which the black enormously outnumbered the white population, had come to stay, and on this the conflict of principle between the Boer and British way of approach was direct and fundamental, though it might come about that in course of time some of the British settlers would turn traitor to their own tradition. But apart from the wound being thus perpetually open, enough had happened already to plant the germs of an inextinguishable hatred of everything British in those indomitabl *voortrekkers* who, like the Kruger family, were the Founder-Fathers of the Transvaal and Orange Free State.

Still, even in South Africa, these conflicts, though working up beneath the surface, delayed coming to a head. The practical Boer, certainly in the Cape Province, was far from wanting to embark on a wave of liberation from the clumsy but far from tyrannous yoke of British sovereignty. Even the *trekkers* themselves had been glad to have British help against the Zulus, and the red coat of the British soldier formed a welcome and almost necessary insurance against the menace from the militant Bantu peoples who had taken the place of the Hottentots, and against whose encroachments it seemed more than doubtful whether the scattered denizens of the veldt would be able to hold out indefinitely.

The story of the attempts of Briton, Boer and Bantu to arrive at a mutually acceptable *modus vivendi* in the mid part of the nineteenth century is one that it does not fall within our province to narrate, except so far as to say that it follows no clear-cut or obvious lines, but is a tangle of confused cross-purposes in which the heroic aspirations of the original *voortrekkers* seemed to have been almost eliminated, and which is marked on the British side by an almost complete absence of any more definable policy than one of opportunism on the cheap. The impression one gets is that the British Governments of the early and mid Victorian age, while unwilling to be responsible for abandoning any part of the Queen's sovereignty, were chiefly concerned to relieve themselves of all the trouble and expense possible in dealing with colonial matters, and would have been ready to connive at any arrangement that would divest them of responsibility for what went on in the remote hinterland of Cape Colony, even if it amounted in practice, where the emigrant Boers were concerned, to taking a leaf out of Dogberry's book:

> Take no note of him, but let him go, and presently call the rest of the watch together and thank God you are rid of a knave.

However, after every conceivable shift of policy, including the temporary annexation of the Orange River, or southernmost of the two new Boer states, the British Government did, in the early fifties, adopt this very solution, by formally recognizing the complete independence of them both. But if it thought to be rid of them on such easy terms, the event proved it mistaken. White South Africa was in the nature of things an organic whole. Already the vision was taking shape of a federation, from the Limpopo to the sea, of all these spread-out communities, and the real question at issue was whether it should materialize under the flag of the British monarchy or of a Dutch republic. And behind this loomed obscurely a further question—of the part or lot of the great African majority in this foreshadowed new order of a united South Africa. Was its evolution to be on liberal and—in the English sense—constitutional lines, towards an ultimate full-fledged majority control? Or would it take the form of an imperialist conspiracy of the white race, or perhaps even a ruling majority of that race, to fasten its yoke inexorably and permanently on the African majority of the population?

3

THE WAY OF
FREE DEVELOPMENT

THE OVERALL impression that one gets of the attitude of the mother country to the major colonies during this period when they were advancing with giant strides from colonial towards national status, may best be defined as one of indifference tempered by benevolence. It would be quite wrong to say—though it is sometimes implied—that public opinion on the policy of responsible statesmen was, in general, desirous of turning the colonies loose, like those of the ancient Greek cities, to carve out their own destinies in entire independence of the mother country; but it would be true to say that the preponderant attitude was one of resigned acquiescence in the idea that this separation was, in the natural course of things, bound to come about sooner or later—though the later the better. And it was tacitly agreed that, after her experience with the thirteen American colonies, Britain would make no serious attempt, when the time came, to oppose their departure.

But it is essential to appreciate what was the idea of colonial status that was more or less taken for granted in the first half of the nineteenth century. A colony, by its very nature, was under the sovereignty of the Crown, and sovereignty, so far as it implied anything, implied power—'supremacy; highest place; supreme power', according to Dr Johnson's definition, which nobody at that time would have been likely to challenge. Power, we might say, was the essence of sovereignty—which answered to the Roman conception of *majestas* and *imperium*. However much, therefore, the power of sovereignty might be watered down or waived in practice, it was inseparably bound up with the conception of empire. And so long as even Englishmen allowed their minds to be bound within the pale of these assumptions, so long was the idea of a colony that set up to be its own Sovereign and a law unto itself a flat contradiction in terms. Such a colony would be no colony at all. No empire, no colony. The idea of a free commonwealth was thus automatically ruled out in advance.

This did not however mean that Britain was wedded to the alternative conception of empire—very much the reverse. Hardly any British civilian, until the Victorian age was well past its meridian, was sufficiently enthusiastic about the idea of a British Empire to be willing to shed a drop of his own blood or to have his taxes raised on its behalf. But there were, particularly in the early part of the century, quite a considerable number of old-fashioned Tories, and others, to whom it seemed obvious that there was no sense in hanging on to colonies at all if you were going to disclaim all responsibility for governing them; whereas what we might call left-wing—liberal and radical—opinion welcomed on principle any advance towards colonial freedom and self-government.

The practical effect of both standpoints was the same. Nobody wanted to cut the colonies adrift a moment sooner than necessary, but if and when the colonies decided to take over the management of their own affairs, there was nothing that the mother country could, or ought to do to stop them. She saw her children growing up to independence, and wanted to put off the hour of separation as long as possible, feeling all the while in her heart that it had got to come.

Not that anyone in England was likely to put it as plainly as all that, even to himself. That would have been out of keeping with the national character. The instinct for carrying on, or muddling through, without any clear conception of an end in view or plan for getting there, was especially marked in the handling of colonial matters by what the colonists themselves were wont to refer to bitterly as 'Mr Mother Country'; though the creative energy that was so conspicuous in all departments of national life in this age of progress and reform manifested itself in a sufficient number of such outstanding individuals as Durham, Buller, Elgin, Grey and their like, to provide a *deus ex machina* for every strained situation before it had got irrecoverably out of hand.

And yet the fact remains that if we are to follow the prevailing fashion of lumping together all territories formally in allegiance to the British Crown under the designation of empire, we should be forced to reckon this half-century between the conclusion of the struggle with Napoleon and the formation of the first of the great dominions (that of Canada) as the golden age of British imperial expansion. And the more closely we follow the unfolding of the story, the less we shall be able to resist the conclusion that this came about not *in spite of*, but *because of* Britain's lack of any positive or consistent colonial policy, and of any imperial policy or ambition whatever. It was just because she was on the whole content to let expansion take its own course while keeping down her own trouble and expense with it to a minimum, that she set it free to take the course it did.

It is a common fallacy to regard this whole process of British expansion from an exclusively British standpoint, as if it were, in fact as well as in name, one of deliberate empire-building. And it would be only natural to regard the building of a house—or of an empire, for that matter—from the standpoint of the builder. It is the product of his volition—the work, in a double sense, of his hands. We are not absurd enough to take the alternative standpoint and speak of the house as having sprung up of its own accord while the builder was engaged on more pressing business elsewhere.

But the case is reversed when instead of bricks and mortar we are speaking of social organisms that are capable of growing up spontaneously from their own roots, all the more luxuriantly from being set free to follow their own natural bent, instead of being forced into some preconceived pattern of formal gardening. A British empire must, by its very nature, be a British achievement; but a free, British-born commonwealth of nations may owe to the initiative of the daughter nations as much as or more than to that of the mother country. In practice it will seldom be possible, with any approach to certainty, to determine the proportions.

This at least we can say: that Greater Britain (to avoid the question-begging term of 'empire') was never less bitten with the lust to expand than during what must surely be accounted its period of maximum expansion. If Britain evinced no willingness to part with her colonies, she could hardly have shown herself less actively concerned to bind them to her, or to put herself out for them in any way. Her emancipation of the slaves, noble and disinterested as it was, had, as we have seen, been carried out in such a way as to be ruinous to the white community in the West Indies, and to have planted the seeds of deadly antagonism between Briton and Boer in South Africa. Her conversion to free trade in the middle of the century involved a clean sweep of those preferential tariff arrangements that had been the last relics of the old mercantile system. This was naturally a heavy grievance to the colonists, but free trade had been raised from the status of an economic expedient to that of an ideological panacea, which the dominant British middle class was determined to apply with totalitarian thoroughness regardless of every other consideration.

But nothing that Britain could do, or neglect to do, could shake the loyalty of the British colonies to the British connection. The wider the door was held open for their departure, the less willingness they evinced to avail themselves of the opportunity. And though sentimental considerations undoubtedly played their part, it is reasonable to conclude that such a tough and practical breed of men as colonial life engendered must have deemed it to be substantially in their own interests to remain in what was soon, for want of a better word, to be misnamed the Empire.

It is only true to national form that this attitude should have been rather the result of deep-seated instinct than reasoned calculation. But it was an instinct engendered by centuries-old experience of the advantages accruing to Britain from the peculiar geographical circumstances which had enabled her, behind the shield of her sea power, to render herself sufficiently invasion-proof to dispense with the burden and tyranny of militarization, and had thus set her free, as none of her European rivals were, to evolve her own order of civilization. And it was this advantage, or its equivalent, that Britain, as long as she remained in effective control of the linking seaways, was in a position to pass on to the communities overseas that were growing to nationhood in membership of this same order of civilization. How long it would last in a changing world no man could say, but last it did throughout this critical century, and while it lasted these budding dominions were in enjoyment of a demilitarized status substantially equivalent to that which Britain herself had enjoyed throughout the centuries of her constitutional development. Though each of them had its manifest, if self-imposed, destiny of expansion at the expense of uncivilized aborigines, all of them shared in the effectual enjoyment—so far as civilized Powers were concerned—of the King's (or Queen's) peace. Under that overshadowing guarantee they could devote the whole of their overflowing energies to the task of peaceful development, without having to divert and overstrain them in that of arming themselves to the teeth against potential invaders; they were at liberty to build up a fabric of free institutions without any inhibitions about tying the hands of the executive, and therefore military, power. They could almost as easily dispense with the luxury of armies as the Swiss Republic with that of a navy, for even in their struggles with the natives they could usually rely on the services of the British regular soldier—with however grudging or niggardly a hand doled out—to do the main part of the business for them; and as for ships and forts, why go to the expense, so long as Admiral Napier, K.C.B.,[1] and his fellow inheritors of the Nelson tradition were on deck looking to their oceanic moat for them, and more than capable of shooing off any intrusive Frenchman, German or other foreigner from their shores?

Australia and New Zealand were not only islands in the geographical sense, but were also politically and strategically insulated. Each of them had been saved from the predatory clutch of French imperialism by the long arm of British sea power; and to the end of the century they had

---

[1] As in Thackeray's ballad of 'Little Billee'.

taken their peaceful immunity as much for granted as if they had been spirited away to another planet. South Africa, with her open frontiers to the north and her unresolved antagonisms between white and black on the one hand, and white and white on the other, was at times more like an arena than a haven of peace, but it was an arena in which British sea power held the ring, and prevented such bedevilment and exploitation by outside interference as was the only-too-common form in the civil conflicts of Europe; and its right to do so passed unchallenged, if not quite, yet almost to the end of the century.

The case of Canada is the most significant of all. Here, as in no other of what were still called Britain's colonial possessions, there was a land frontier of enormous length, and in part undetermined, with a civilized Power—a Power, moreover, that had only recently been repulsed with difficulty from an attempt at all-out conquest. Here, if European experience were anything to go by, was a situation as explosively belligerent as that of France and Germany glaring at each other across the Rhine, or Russia and Austria each grimly set on the reversion of the Turkish empire in the Balkans. It might, therefore, by anyone versed in technique of international power politics, have been laid down with an approach to mathematical certainty that Canada's sole chance—and that not a rosy one—of preserving her colonial or semi-independent status within the British orbit would be by subordinating every other consideration to that of a Spartan efficiency in arms, by virtue of which, with the support of British sea power, she might hope to repeat her defensive success of 1812–14.

Such a calculation would have left one vital factor out of account. These rival Powers were not nurtured in the European, imperial tradition, but were equally in membership of another order of civilization, a membership that was in no way impaired by the accident of their political separation, because it had its roots in a past common to both—in a common tradition and, in more than one sense, a common law. And though to outward appearance the breach between monarchical Britain and republican America might seem absolute and final, and though in America a pose of uncompromising and strenuously vocal Anglophobia had become a patriotic imperative, none the less, underlying this superficial advertisement of difference there was a sense of fundamental unity, an unformulated conviction that Anglo-American differences were after all family quarrels that must never again, after one distressing experience, be allowed to pass from words to blows.

Only such a conviction could account for the unprecedented and unpredictable steps that were taken to prevent the most obvious and seemingly inevitable occasion of quarrel from ever erupting into war. This was the result of no treaty or formal agreement, except for a mutual undertaking, four years after the conclusion of peace in 1814, to demilitarize, or rather denavalize, the Great Lakes. But from this small beginning followed the uncovenanted and effectual demilitarization of the whole Anglo-Canadian frontier, to the advantage of both parties concerned. It was henceforth simply and tacitly taken for granted that for members of the same family to fight out their differences, or even to arm themselves for the purpose of doing so, would be as unprofitable as it was wicked. A policy of spontaneous neighbourliness, with respect for existing landmarks,[1] is a dictate of plain common sense that needs no treaties nor diplomatic paraphernalia to put into effect. But in countries bred in the imperial tradition, to act on these lines would be to fly so directly in the face of all accepted notions as to pass, even if it could ever have been perpetrated, for treasonable lunacy.

This psychological sealing of the world's most vulnerable frontier, which came about with such unobtrusive informality as to be passed over in most records with the most casual (if any) reference, is surely, when we consider its implications, to be accounted the most momentous new departure in the sphere of international policy in this age of steam-powered progress and liberalism. It represents the first application on a wide scale of a new technique of free co-operation that is distinctive of the new order of Anglo-Saxon civilization, and may be said to be inspired by the new commonwealth as contrasted with the old imperial principle.

It is true that in this particular instance the requirement of neighbourly respect for landmarks was complicated by the fact that for a considerable length at either end of the long frontier there were, to start with, no agreed landmarks at all, but conflicting and overlapping claims as to where it ought to run, involving very large and important stretches of territory, and indeed, on the west, Canada's access to the Pacific. To find a peaceful solution was about as delicate and dangerous a task as could be imagined, especially as the United States, who were proud to see their symbolic prototype in the lean and acquisitive Uncle Sam, were unashamedly hard bargainers. Here was a problem that did not lend itself to settlement by spontaneous goodwill, and called for diplomatic negotiation, complicated by easily frothed-up patriotic effervescence in a democracy clamouring for a tough line. But even here there was an overriding consciousness on both sides that by one means or another a peaceful solution had got to be found, and that it was unthinkable that a boundary dispute should be allowed to boil over into fratricide. And so, in spite of tension, the two main sectors of disputed boundary, those of Maine and Oregon, as well as others of minor importance, were marked out by diplomatic

---

[1] The agreed line of demarcation coincided roughly with the forty-ninth parallel of latitude.

compromise—involving a good deal of horse-trading and grumbling on both sides at what would now be called appeasement—but at least definitely and finally, which was what most mattered. And the long, unfortified frontier settled down to an existence as uneventful and unchallenged as if it had parted two American States or English counties.

This, if anyone at the time had been capable of appreciating it, might have served to indicate that the formal severance of Britain from the United States, which had been solemnized by the Treaty of Versailles, might not be so absolute or so fundamental as had been assumed. There is a unity of the spirit that has no relevance to forms of government or to the letter of treaties. The forces that had been shaping a common destiny for these two branches of the Anglo-Saxon community had been at work centuries before the muskets had started popping at Lexington, and they were no more halted than hurried by the alarums and excursions of the ensuing years. The order of civilization to which the old monarchy and new republic equally belonged needed time to bring itself, if not to birth, at least to maturity, and to the realization of its own purpose and potentiality. And if this could be better accomplished by the unqualified freedom of either main branch to work out the application to its own special circumstances of principles common to both, then nothing was lost by their formal separation, provided only that if such freedom of either were seriously challenged, the party not immediately concerned should recognize the challenge as offered equally to itself. England was submitted to this test in the early eighteen-twenties, and America's turn came a little less than a century later, and neither can be said to have been found unequal to it.

4

A NEW WORLD
SAFE FOR FREEDOM

I HAVE TRIED to show how the prime condition that had
enabled Britain to develop her order of civilization in the first
place had resided in her invasion-proof insulation under the protection
of sea power, and how, by her control of the world's seaways, she had
been able to pass on an equivalent advantage to the incipient nations
that were growing up in her formal allegiance overseas. But the United
States was in just as much need of this same freedom to fulfil not only
the 'manifest destiny' of territorial expansion that she had marked out
for herself, but also to do so in accordance with those principles that
the Founding Fathers of her constitution had laid down for her. But
in her still immature condition it was at least open to question whether
this freedom would be granted her.

By a dispensation of fate or providence almost unparalleled in the
records of historical coincidence, the essential situation of the United
States happened, in the most important of all respects, to have reproduced (only on a greatly magnified scale) that of the island that had
been the generating source of her own budding order of civilization.
For just as Britain had been an island whose whole potentiality of
development had depended on its ability to insulate itself effectively
from the political or spiritual domination of what for her had constituted the Old World, so the Americas themselves might be regarded
as a vast island, enclosed by the Atlantic and Pacific oceans, in which
the United States had the 'manifest destiny' to play the same leading
part as England in her more limited insular environment.

One of the least regarded by-products of the long English struggle
with, and blockade of, French imperialism, had been the virtually
complete emancipation of the mainland of both American continents
from the shackles of Old World imperialism. The French Empire,[1]
the Spanish Empire, the Portuguese Empire, had ceased to exist except

[1] Except for the practicably negligible French footing in Guiana.

in outlying islands. But how long would this state of things be guaranteed to last, once the iron clamp of British bloackade had been relaxed, and the seaways once again opened? How long could the insulation of America from the Old World be maintained? And by whom? For it was asking a great deal of the still immature and imperfectly consolidated republic on the gradually expanding hinterland of the Atlantic seaboard, to impose its single-handed veto on the only temporarily frustrated lust for imperial expansion of the Old World Powers.

This was all the more dangerous, as after the fall of Napoleon these Powers showed every disposition to act with concerted unity in support of their own authoritarian and imperialistic principles of government, that were the direct negation of those embodied in the American Constitution, and to impose a similar yoke on the New World to that which they were already engaged in riveting on the Old under cover of the nebulous but formidable manifesto known as the Holy Alliance. And even if the United States itself were to maintain its own independence of such domination, its application to the rest of America would beyond doubt have imposed a crippling handicap on her own freedom of development by dragging her into that very competition of armaments that she had most need to avoid.

It was Russia—which had emerged from the struggle with Napoleon as the most formidable of the European land Powers, and had already, after absorbing the whole northern part of Asia, clawed out to obtain a footing on the North American mainland—that started the ball rolling by an imperial ukase, whose literal effect would have been to appropriate the whole north-western seaboard down to the fifty-first parallel, and all trading and fishing rights within a hundred miles of the coast. This terrific gesture was in fact bluff, but it was enough to show the way the wind was blowing from the direction of Europe and the Holy Alliance of despots.

It was a more serious matter when France, under her restored monarchy, and eager to restore her tarnished martial prestige, threatened to take a hand in the game. A French army had already marched to Cadiz, as if no Peninsular War had ever been fought, to restore that almost subhuman tyrant, Ferdinand VII, to the throne on which he had quickly exhausted the patience even of his Spanish subjects; and the next move indicated was to reach out a hand across the ocean and perform a similar operation on the revolted provinces of the Spanish Empire in America, which were threatening to set up what to the leagued sovereigns constituted the abomination of desolation in the shape of republics. A glorious and by no means unprofitable undertaking, with French princes, backed by French arms, more than ready to take up the burdens of sovereignty; but a most unwelcome proposition for the United States, who, for their part, regarded the abomination of desolation as consisting in the importation of European power politics to American soil. A restored Spanish empire, including Mexico, would have stretched right across the path of the 'manifest destiny' of expansion to the Pacific. But it was more than doubtful whether the United States had as yet the power to impose an effective veto on a really determined attempt of the Holy Alliance to impose the same shackles of legitimacy and imperialism on the whole of South and half of North America, that they had on the states of central and south-western Europe.

The determining factor, it might confidently have been predicted, would be the attitude of Britain. If she were to elect to stand in with her late allies, against the kinsman who had sought to stab her in the back in the hour of her direst need, nothing that the Americans could have done would have prevented the stamping out of the republican principle over a vast recolonized area stretching from California to the Horn.

But providentially Britain, though under a Sovereign who might have been thought an only too worthy yokefellow of the leagued despots, and a reactionary administration that was engaged in sitting tight on the safety-valve of reform, had the conduct of her foreign affairs in the hands of two men of the highest and—above all—authentically British genius, that soared above party considerations. Lord Castlereagh, who had carried the alliance against Napoleon almost on his shoulders to victory, had been quick to take the measure of its transformation after it into a conspiracy of autocrats inspired jointly and severally by principles of which British civilization was the flat antithesis, but he had played his country's hand with an agonizing restraint, and an exquisite appreciation of the limits set by Britain's dependence on sea power. So long as its action was confined to the Continent, Castlereagh could only stall on the alliance without opposing it head on. But his nerve broke down under the strain, and he took his own life on the eve of the last of a series of international conferences in which it was proposed to regulate the affairs of Europe by a league, not of nations, but of sovereigns, and which did actually provide for the French invasion of Spain. But before it assembled at Verona Castlereagh's mantle had fallen on the shoulders of George Canning, whom he had once nearly killed in a duel, but who was the one man alive capable of carrying on his work, without breach of continuity, and crowning it with a success whose hour had never struck for Castlereagh.

For the march to Cadiz, that Britain lacked the means to oppose, was in itself a profitless gesture unless by way of providing a jumping-off platform for the reconquest of the New World by European imperialism. But here, as the new Foreign Secretary at once perceived, was the long-awaited chance for Britain to intervene with decisive effect on her own element. For the way to America was by sea, and since the United States had a more immediate and vital interest even than Britain in keeping the New World—to anticipate the phrase of a twentieth-century President—safe for democracy, so clear an intelligence as that of Canning could hardly have failed to perceive that the sure way of checkmating the despots was by reinforcing America's incipient naval power by that of Britain in order to render the Atlantic, and if necessary the Pacific, Ocean, closed highways for any other purpose than that of peaceful commerce.

This was obvious, perhaps, to an intelligence like Canning's, but by no means easy to bring home to that of the average American citizen, or for that matter, statesman. The worst legacy of two wars within living memory had been to implant in the minds of the Americans a militant obsession of Anglophobia. England was melodramatized in the role of national enemy, and one of those myths of which the voice of history at any given time is usually the mouthpiece had grown up almost unchallenged about the process of political divorce in which George Guelph had figured as the tyrant villain and George Washington as the patriot hero, each at the head of a team of his own kidney; and this was not only taken for gospel by every good American citizen, but had almost as unchallenged a reception in England itself, where it was woven into the texture of the all-conquering Whig mythology. It would never have done, therefore, to suggest to Americans of that generation, or even that century, that the mere fact of their having elected to take over the control of their domestic affairs had in no way altered the permanent considerations that made it imperative for Britain and America, as sharers of the same spirit and inheritors of the same tradition, to stand together in the maintenance of their common civilization against the outer imperialism to which it was anathema, and which might well take advantage of its division to bring overwhelming force to bear on whichever happened to be its more vulnerable half. In the eighteen-twenties this was certainly America, though the time would come when the proportion would be reversed.

The question on whose answer the future destiny of mankind might conceivably depend was, if anyone at the time had been capable of formulating it, whether the old order of civilization was to confine itself to the Old World in which it had originated, now that the Iberian empire of the New had dissolved itself into self-governing fragments which, even in the event of their ever-developing imperial ambitions, would be incapable of gratifying them; or, to put it in a nutshell, whether Blake's visionary dictum, *Empire is no more*, might not henceforth apply in sober fact to the Western Hemisphere?

That was what we can see now was really at stake, and why a common policy towards the imperialist Powers of 'Hands off the New World' was of such common and vital urgency for the Anglo-Saxon communities. And the means of realizing it were transparently simple. The American continents were, from the European stand-point, islands. The only access to them was—though it might not always be so—by water. The United States, by itself, had not yet developed the capacity of effectively policing the seaways. But Britain had. And Britain in conjunction with the United States was capable of denying the use of the Atlantic and Pacific to any European armada or expeditionary force bound for American soil.

No one saw more clearly to the heart of the situation than America's grand old man, ex-President Jefferson, whose advice had been sought by his acting successor, President Monroe, on what ought to be America's reaction to a proposal that Canning had made for a joint Anglo-American declaration of policy in this critical situation.

Jefferson was the last person anyone would have suspected of Anglophile leanings, and yet he at least had no shadow of a doubt about what America's response ought to be.

One nation most of all [he wrote] could disturb us in our endeavor to make our hemisphere that of freedom; she now offers to lead, aid, and accompany us in it. By acceding to her proposition, we . . . bring her mighty weight into the scale of free government and emancipate a continent at one stroke. . . . Great Britain is the nation which can do us the most harm of any one or of all on earth; and with her on our side we need not fear the whole world.[1]

Another ex-President, Madison, professed himself of the same way of thinking, and one would have thought that this might have resulted, if not in a formal alliance, at least in a close and permanent *entente*, on a basis of common principle, involving a spontaneous coincidence in the broad essentials of foreign policy with the equally spontaneous backing of such combined forces as might, in case of need, be available. This, which would merely have been giving its logical effect to the advice of the two ex-Presidents, was an arrangement that the logic of events might yet be destined to bring about, and which would have redounded to the advantage of both parrners, if it could have been come to when it was first mooted, and if the hand held out by Canning had, as a preliminary, been frankly grasped.

But this was not to be, and perhaps could not have been, in the then attained stage of psychological development. Wisdom, in masses of

[1] Quoted from *The Relation of British Policy to the Declaration of the Monroe Doctrine* by Leonard Axel Lawson, Ph.D., p. 126.

men, is the fruit of long and painful experience, and the war-time legacy of distrust and hostility was a fact of American psychology that could not be argued away by one or two enlightened spirits. The American mind was simply incapable of conceiving that Britain differed in any essential respect from the other European Powers against whom her aid might be proffered, and therefore to be openly beholden to such aid would be galling to a thin-skinned national pride. The real directing mind behind American policy was that of the Secretary of State and future President, John Quincy Adams, who was no lover of England, and though ready to pursue a common line of policy with her, was determined, as he himself put it, not to allow his country to figure as a cockboat in the wake of a British man-of-war. It was essential therefore that America, even while availing herself in fact of British support, should seem to be going it alone.

The result was that after some intricate diplomatic manœuvring the purpose common to both parties of warning off the Holy Alliance was achieved with the desired saving of American face. Canning's proposal for a joint *démarche* was turned down, but President Monroe, at his Secretary's prompting, defined America's attitude in the historic statement of principle that has been canonized under the style of the Monroe Doctrine, which amounts to a notice to all whom it may concern of a United States' veto on any further colonizing activities or attempt to alter the political *status quo* in the New World by any European Power whatever, not excepting Britain; since Adams was determined that the warning, instead of being sponsored *by*, should be ostensibly directed as much *at*, her, as against the most full-fledged member of the Holy Alliance.

But—as no one can have realized better than Adams himself—to the hard-bitten ministerial directors of that strangely misnamed combination such a message would have signified no more than an emission of hot air from the White House, unless it had been backed by a more effective armed deterrent than the United States was as yet capable of furnishing out of her own unaided resources. However skilfully it might be disguised, no Monroe Doctrine or any other statement of American principle would be worth more than the paper it was written on, unless behind the protecting shield of British sea power. It was the known fact of this being always in reserve that enabled Canning, by a series of masterly moves, virtually to checkmate the Holy Alliance by halting it, as Napoleon had been halted, on its own European beaches, thus putting paid not only to any scheme for an imperial penetration of the American land mass, but also, in effect, to the Holy Alliance itself, which never recovered from the deflation of its prestige by this exposure to the world of its continental limitations. Verona was the last of that series of imperial summits by means of which a conspiracy of Caesars had sought to rivet its yoke, and that of the old order of civilization, on mankind.

To Canning, a belated survivor from the age of reason, and therefore anti-visionary on principle, this supreme diplomatic *tour-de-force* that he, as Britain's representative, had contrived to bring off was no more than a masterpiece of diplomatic wrecking, a substitution of international anarchy for an order imposed by tyranny, in reversion to the traditional British policy of keeping Europe divided in order to keep Britain free. And it was with this end in view that he had, as he declared, called the New World into existence to redress the balance of the Old.

This famous flight of rhetoric was not only true in spirit but, like other coruscations of genius, of a profounder significance than its author, probably, had designed it to convey. For Canning was a practical workaday diplomatist, and an English one at that, with a particular aversion to the broad, abstract generalities, or 'doctrines', in which the American political intelligence is perennially prolific. He was by no means inclined to embrace the Monroe Doctrine to the detriment of any British interest, and even the revolted Spanish-American provinces he would have preferred to see respectably established as constitutional monarchies, instead of their going the whole republican hog. But behind these constantly changing expedients his governing intuitions held him constant to the tradition and order of civilization which he had inherited, and made him ready to back the idea behind the Monroe Doctrine with all the might and resources at Britain's disposal.

'Where that standard is planted', he had said of the British flag,[1] 'foreign dominion shall not come', and what held good for the Union Jack in the Old World might equally be claimed for the Stars and Stripes in the New. For the United States, as the inheritor with Britain of a common order of freedom, might be presumed to be no less interested in keeping the New World free for its unhindered growth to maturity. Compared to the magnitude of that joint trust, their sectional rivalries and jealousies were—and are—as the small dust in the balance. This underlying unity in difference was what no man at the time, not even Canning himself, still less President Monroe, was capable of perceiving, and it would take more than a century to bring it to even the dawn of realization; but even then it was the hidden determinant of the Anglo-American relationship.

For even if the counsels of goodwill could have prevailed, and the formal separation of Britain from her thirteen colonies had never taken place, it is hard to see what greater practical advantage either party

[1] In reference to British military intervention on behalf of the constitutional government of Portugal against the would-be autocratic usurper, Dom Miguel.

could have derived from the association. After all, Britain was performing exactly the same service—no greater and no less—for the
United States as she did for the budding nations that still remained
within the orbit of her sovereignty. Under the protection of her sea
power, they were able to enjoy the same advantages of peaceful
evolution that her own insular status had conferred on her. The empires
of the Old World were held at arm's—or rather ocean's—length
without even the necessity of the self-conversion of the New into their
likeness by arming against them. This applied equally, if not more, to
the United States than to the surviving British colonies. For if European
imperialism had been allowed to reach out its tentacles across the
Atlantic, and the Holy Alliance, with an appetite growing by what it
fed on, had extended its operations to the Spanish American-territories,
the United States, even if not directly attacked, could hardly have
avoided militarizing itself as intensively, all the time, as it did for the
limited purposes and duration of its own civil war, and with incalculable deflection of the free development of its democratic liberties. It
was that danger that the Monroe Doctrine was formulated to avert.
But unless Britain had held the seas, no doctrine would have dissuaded
an aggressor from crossing them.

It was an unacknowledged service that in course of time America
would be in a position to requite nobly, and with interest.

But there was no question, even this early, of her being beholden
to, or dependent on, the good offices of the British Empire, because
such an empire neither did nor could exist.

The incipient commonwealth of nations whose membership, being
of no law but of the spirit, was not subject to political vicissitudes,
could and did engender a unity, in face of mortal challenge, sufficient
at least to safeguard its freedom to develop spontaneously on its own
lines.

5

NEW CROWNS FOR OLD

IN A PROCESS of continuous evolution any epoch-marking date must be one of arbitrary convenience but, with this in mind, we cannot do better than fix on that of 1867 as marking in Britain the culminating point of what we might best describe as the high Victorian era, of which the dominant note is that of a bourgeois Whig-Liberalism, whole-heartedly averse to imperial ambition. It is this year that sees the formation of the first of the self-governing Dominions, that of Canada, an example that no one doubted would be followed in due course, and in their own good time, at least by the other white communities now ranked as colonies.

But this same year saw an event on the home front that was destined to have an influence hardly less decisive in shaping the course of what, thanks to it, would be designated, with a certain specious plausibility, as the course of imperial development. This was the Second Reform Bill, carried by Benjamin Disraeli, which enlarged the franchise to an extent calculated to transfer the balance of electoral power from the upper stratum of the bourgeoisie, that had monopolized it since the First Reform Bill, to a predominantly lower-middle and working class electorate, which, as he foresaw, would be more susceptible to the appeal of the colourful and imaginative Toryism that he had it in mind to sponsor.

To all outward appearance, the result of Disraeli's manœuvre was to dish not his opponents but himself. In the following year, having succeeded to the Premiership, he was driven almost at once to the country, and thence, by an overwhelming majority of his newly enfranchised electorate, into opposition. He had probably expected this and, having possessed his soul in patience for three adverse decades, he could wait for the few more years that it would take for his prescience to ripen. As yet the country was still on the flood tide of a material progress and prosperity that was believed to have been the direct result of its conversion to free trade in the mid forties—an economic panacea of which the Liberal party claimed to hold the patent, and whose efficacy was believed to repose on laws which, like those of mathematics, altered not.

As long as this state of mind persisted, there could be no cult of empire or even any special emphasis on colonies. Little England—or rather Britain—was plainly sufficient to itself, the booming workshop of the world, into whose open ports the riches of all countries could be relied on to flow in ever-increasing quantities in exchange for the ever-multiplying products of its factories. Disraeli's rival, the eloquent and immaculate Gladstone, had only to ride as Premier on the crest of this wave, and to remove all hindrances to the free working of these same beneficent laws, and let matters overseas as far as possible pursue their own course, with the colonies free to separate or not as they pleased provided they did not become a source of expense and military commitment to the mother country.

Nothing could have exceeded the ability with which Gladstone and his colleagues set about the implementation of their principles; and yet, in little more than a half of their allotted term of office, they had so signally forfeited their backing of electoral support as to lend only too obvious a point to Disraeli's comparison of them to a range of exhausted volcanoes, and to create the impression that Liberalism was, for the time at least, a spent force. It was the situation that Disraeli had banked on, though there is no reason to credit him with more than a partial appreciation of the forces that were shaping the new age. But he did perceive that a merely negative policy of sitting back and trusting to the free play of capitalized individualism was less calculated to go down with the new electorate than the positive and constructive policy, including one of social reform, that Toryism, adapted to the spirit of the time by its leader, had to offer.

This was merely the up-to-date application of principles that Disraeli had been advocating from the beginning of his now long parliamentary career, and that he had expounded in a unique trilogy of political novels; for he was in the strictest sense a man of principle, and far more so than Gladstone, whose course was notoriously unpredictable —a zigzag of sonorous inconsistencies. But so far as there was any fresh element in Disraeli's later Toryism, it lay in the imperial setting in which he designed to present it, a by no means inconsistent development, and one shrewdly calculated to strike the imagination of the new democracy. In a famous speech in 1872 at the Crystal Palace he defined the objects of the Tory party as being to maintain the country's institutions, to elevate the condition of the people and to uphold the Empire. This was the programme with which he swept the country two years later, and which, backed by the first secure Tory majority since the fall of Peel, he endeavoured to put into practice. And in so doing he may be said to have put the Empire for the first time on to the political map.

It may be well therefore to take a brief survey both of what Disraeli meant to signify by the Empire, and how far it corresponded to the reality. There were first the colonies, still referred to under that designation, though one of them had already, except in the control of its external relations, achieved what was subsequently to be known as dominion status. And when Disraeli enlarged in his decisive speech on the disintegration of the Empire having been foiled by the sympathy of the colonies for the mother country, what for practical purposes he meant to signify was the four adolescent nations that had already achieved, or were plainly destined to achieve, self-government, and whose relationship to the mother country, if it were to endure, could do so only on a footing of eventually equal partnership. Nor must it be forgotten that, of these four, only two could be designated as more than partially British.

Even when we make the fullest allowance for the notorious English faculty for saying one thing and meaning another, to talk of such jealously self-sufficient peoples as part of an empire would appear to be needlessly asking for trouble. And to show the least disposition to put such an idea into practice would be to play with the same fires that had set the so-called First British Empire in a blaze in the preceding century. What had kept these colonies hitherto loyal to the British connection had been, paradoxically, the neglect or refusal of Britain to make the least positive attempt to bind them to her by compulsion. The freer they had been to walk out, the more determined they were to stop in, even though this freedom might have been mainly due to the calculated indifference of successive Liberal administrations.

Not that Disraeli had, in the past, showed markedly greater concern. It is rather less than fair to tax his memory with an unguarded grouse he had once thrown off in a private letter about the wretched colonies being millstones round our neck, which has become as much, and as preposterously, a millstone round his own neck as Dr Johnson's un-Johnsonian definition of patriotism as the last resort of a scoundrel has been about his. But a more significant pointer is his much later inquiry in 1866 when, as Chancellor of the Exchequer, he was writing to his Premier Derby to deprecate the release of public money in providing for Canadian or any other colonial defence:

An army maintained in a country which does not permit us even to govern it? . . . What is the use of those colonial deadweights that we do not *govern*? [1]

That is in direct line with the traditional Tory view of power being an essential attribute of sovereignty—no government, no empire

[1] Quoted Buckle, *Life of Disraeli*, Vol. IV, p. 476.

And when Disraeli came to formulate his new model of policy, it was only too obvious that the British Empire he envisaged was one that he intended to be so in fact as well as name—at least within certain limits of practicability. He had, it is true, the grace to concede the colonies the right of self-government, but he proceeded to qualify this right in a way that, if translated into action, would have been calculated to wreck such imperial or any other harmony as might subsist between mother and daughter nations.

Self-goverment, he believed, should be conceded only as part of a grand policy of imperial federation, which should have been accompanied by an imperial tariff, a trusteeship by the Crown of all unappropriated lands, a military code apportioning the responsibilities of the colonies for imperial defence, and some sort of imperial representative council sitting in London. In the light of our present knowledge, nothing can be more certain than that the least attempt to impose such a scheme, or any item of it, on the colonies, would have come up against a blank wall of refusal, and if persisted in, would have been accepted as a notice to quit. But the matter was never put to the test. Though there is no reason to question the sincerity of Disraeli's imperial professions, it is doubtful whether such a rough and ready folk as the colonists of his day made a more urgent appeal to his essentially romantic imagination than they had to Palmerston's. When he did get into office he found pressing calls on his attention, and he made not the least attempt to get this ambitious programme started— no doubt fortunately for all concerned.

What made a greater natural appeal to him was the oriental part of this prospective Empire—so called, it must be admitted, with a more specious plausibility than the colonial part. And Disraeli—all the more perhaps because his personal experience did not extend farther east than the Levant—was obsessively fascinated by the idea that 'never was a jewel in the Crown of England so costly as the possession of India'. And though he might be content to defer his colonial schemes to the Greek Calends, he was heart set on converting that Crown, with the minimum of delay, into an imperial diadem.

The growth of the British Raj in India, since Warren Hastings had ensured beyond peradventure that it had come to stay, had followed a logical and what might have been a predictable course. Britain had gone there to trade and not to rule, and up to the middle of the nineteenth century she had clung with desperate tenacity to the more and more palpable fiction of not being there at all in any sovereign or imperial capacity, but merely under the guise of a peaceful trading company. But it can fairly be said that there was no time during the two and a half centuries that elapsed between 'John Company's' first lodgment on the Indian mainland at Surat and its final dissolution

H

after the Mutiny at which it would have been possible to have called a halt to a process of expansion that was bound to go on and on, with a momentum as cumulative as that of an avalanche, until it had embraced the whole of the Indian 'Plains'—to adopt the Anglo-Indian vernacular —up to the limit set by the enclosing 'Hills' of the world's greatest mountain range. To have called a halt short of this would have been to have thrown the whole process catastrophically into reverse, with results fatal to British prestige, or even survival, on Indian soil.

On the other hand, so long as the Company continued to go all out for the highest stakes with the necessary measure of support from the home Government, it could confidently reckon on playing a winning hand, not only for itself but for Britain, and not only for Britain but for an India that was not yet in any sense a country, but one vast collocation of populaces in the last extreme of human misery, exploited to starvation limit and beyond by competing tyrants. For there to be the beginnings of an Indian or even a specifically Hindu patriotism, unity had first to be imposed, and a reign of law, under a King's or suzerain's peace, substituted for the chaos of anarchy. And hence there is nothing surprising in India's acquiescence in the process of her own conquest, financed as it was almost entirely out of her own resources, and effected by armies recruited on her own soil, with a mere stiffening of Europeans.

The Company, then, which had never desired anything better than to let up on the path of glory and get down to the prosaic business of fructifying dividends, found itself forced, as a sort of necessary side-line, to take on its unwilling shoulders a burden of sovereignty such as few of the world's proudest conquerors had dreamed of assuming. And as a necessary result the British Government, in turn, was forced, equally in its own despite, to abandon in practice the pretence that it still maintained in theory, of washing its hands of responsibility for the fate of India, and leaving the Company to run its own business in its own way. The honour of the British name was too plainly involved, and the direction of the Company's affairs was put into tighter and tighter governmental leading-strings until, in the second quarter of the nineteenth century, it had practically ceased to be a trading association at all and had become more like a separately functioning department of His, or Her, Majesty's service.

It would have been a comparatively simple matter if an India, united under British auspices, had been free to consummate the 'manifest destiny' of expanding to her own mountain frontiers, and settling down to a future of peaceful self-development within those permanently fixed limits. She would then have come into line with the white colonies—not excepting the seceded American ones—by dint of the same process of virtual insulation, guaranteed by an inviolable sea power, that served as a common—or commonwealth—shield against imperial aggression. But a new factor had begun to bedevil the Indian situation, with a doubt whether the sealing off of the Peninsula —or rather glorified headland—from the rest of the Eurasian land mass by its Himalayan wall was to be taken for granted as final. For on the other side of that wall loomed up more and more ominously the menace of an expansive empire, the largest in point of size that the world had yet seen, and whose Caesar, or Tsar, had inherited the imperial principle in its most undiluted form from the Eastern Roman emperors whose true successor he was. That Empire, which already embraced the eastern half of Europe and the northern half of Asia, landlocked as it was, was notoriously set on securing, at almost any cost, a warm-water outlet on the Mediterranean, or the Indian, or eventually the Pacific Ocean. In central Asia, Russian expansion was approaching nearer and nearer to those passes, or gateways, that had been forced by Alexander and other invaders of the Plains both before and after his time. And why not again?

It cannot be too clearly realized how profoundly this new factor had begun to affect the world outlook of British statesmanship, and how in particular it tended for the first time to impart to Anglo-Indian policy an imperial bias that had hitherto been conspicuously lacking. Once India began to be thought of as possessing a land frontier vulnerable to invasion by an enormous military empire, all the classic reasons for counter-imperialization were brought into play. To stand up to a Russian there ought to be an Indian Empire, which, in existing circumstances, was as good as to say a British empire of India, under a British Caesar, capable of taking on its Russian counterpart at its own game of imperial power politics.

It is beside the point to question how serious the Russian menace to India actually was. But there is no doubt of its being taken seriously in the highest quarters—Palmerston in particular was obsessed by it— and it was a subject on which public opinion in England tended to be particularly sensitive, no doubt because the Tsarist tyranny and all that it stood for were the exact antithesis of everything that Englishmen held sacred. Only thus can we account for the note of aggressive imperialism imparted for the first time to British policy in India at the end of the eighteen-thirties, when an otherwise colourless Governor-General, without even waiting for India to expand to her natural boundaries, launched out beyond them in an attempt, as unscrupulous as it was feckless, to forestall Russian aggression by the conquest of the ferocious and ungovernable tribes who inhabited the highlands of Afghanistan. That attempt resulted, after a specious appearance of success, in the loss of the entire army of occupation, followed, after a face-saving blow in the air, by the evacuation of the whole country, a lesson which one might have thought would have put an effective brake on the expansion of the Raj; but in the stormy decade that followed its pace was perceptibly quickened, and it was marked by at least one act of naked brigandage in the seizure of the rich province of Scinde from its unoffending rulers, a feat immortalized in the British commander's Latin pun of '*Peccavi*' ('I have Scinde').

For the first time, perhaps, on Anglo-Indian record, one gets the impression that it is no longer a question of a trading company being forced into commitments that it would have preferred to avoid, but of Britain herself, or her representatives, pursuing a deliberately forward policy, and applying, to however incipient a degree, a technique of imperial power politics. And it is surely reasonable to connect this with the fact that, also for the first time, Britain finds herself no longer capable of effectually insulating India, behind her mountain barrier, from the menace of aggressive land power.

It was still in the formal capacity of a trading company that, with the annexation of the Punjab, she succeeded in uniting India for the first time in its history up to the limit of its natural frontiers under her domination, either by direct rule, or indirectly by a kind of feudal overlordship. The process of expansion—within the bounds of sanity —having thus been consummated, there now remained no choice but that of transition from an extroverted past to an introverted future. This united India: what was the uniting Power to make of it? and what was the India thus united to make of itself?

It is not altogether surprising that one of the first effects—or at least accompaniments—of this enforced preoccupation of India with her own domestic evolution should have been a violent explosion of the pent-up forces of reaction and xenophobia that had been gathering for a long time below the surface. This took the form of a mutiny, which fortunately was practically confined to the Bengal army. But for an ineptitude and mismanagement almost unbelievable it would never have been allowed to get a start at all, still less to have been presented with a free gift in the shape of the ancient capital of Delhi, with its enormous magazine and palace fort containing the titular Great Mogul, a highly convenient crowned figurehead for a war of independence.

For a brief moment it seemed as if the whole fabric of British supremacy were doomed to collapse ignominiously. But characteristically of the British record, the seemingly hopeless situation was redeemed by men on the spot capable of retrieving the blunders of those top-ranking personages who had allowed it to materialize. Thanks largely to the fact that the newly conquered Sikhs of the Punjab decided to stand in with their conquerors, it proved possible to contain the first impetus of the revolt and to knock the heart out of it by the siege and storming, against fantastic numerical odds, of Delhi. After that British sea power, backed by unlimited economic resources, came into play, and the war resolved itself into a tedious mopping-up operation. British supremacy in India was confirmed in the eyes of the world, on a more impregnable foundation than ever.

But it had been undermined in a more subtle way by the very process of its vindication. What had now become the palpable fiction of the Company's rule was no longer plausible, and the Crown formally took over the sovereignty of those Indian territories that it had directly administered and, to all practical intent, of the whole of India; though a still Liberal public opinion balked at the assumption of imperial status. But it was not easy to see how, in fact or logic, sovereignty imposed by royal proclamation could be perpetuated on any other footing. And there were psychological overtones, about the transition from a professedly business to an undisguisedly imperial relationship, that it might have been safer to avoid.

But quite apart from these somewhat intangible considerations, it was only too manifest that Anglo-Indian relationships could never be the same after as before the Mutiny. Dreadful things had been perpetrated on both sides, the memory of which stuck and corroded. To every English mind, whether at home or overseas, the first association linked with the word Mutiny was that of the well at Cawnpore, into which the bodies of an unknown number of British women and children had been thrown after they had been hacked to death by five hired bazaar-ruffians; the sepoys having flatly disobeyed orders to perpetrate the outrage.[1] It was only human that the British should almost literally have been driven mad by the spectacle, and gone to un-British extremes of retaliatory frightfulness, which in turn were unforgotten. But it must be remembered that not only was the contest from the first waged without quarter on either side, but that even before the main explosion the British had set the tone by the practice of blowing mutineers from cannon, with the literally hellish intent of destroying— in their belief—their souls as well as their bodies.

It would be worse than futile to stir up old fires by nice apportionment of blame. What concerns us here is that the progressive harmonization of racial relationships was rendered far more difficult by these festering and mutual animosities. And quite apart from these, the revolutionary speeding-up of the means of transport, particularly after

---

[1] It is a tragic reflection that the horror might almost certainly have been avoided by the use of the most elementary common sense—had the old imbecile in command chosen to occupy the fortress magazine he might easily have held out until the arrival of relief. And even after the capitulation the garrison appears to have been allowed to straggle down to the boats without any discipline or precaution whatever.

the opening of the Suez Canal, was bound to have a psychologically disruptive influence. The old type of Company's servant, hard-living and seldom long-living, who made his permanent home in India, not infrequently with a native consort, was superseded by state officials and officers who, like the womenfolk they imported, struck no roots in the country, and tended to regard themselves as a master race of sahibs and memsahibs, carrying on a life jealously segregated from the civilization, more ancient than their own, that spread round their enclosed ark like the waters of a horizon-wide flood, unplumbed and vaguely ominous.

When Disraeli came into office, with a mandate for upholding the hitherto neglected Empire, it was in this direction that his thoughts most naturally turned. He was temperamentally a romantic, whose early career had been shaped in the most flamboyant Byronic tradition, and consequently the Orient exercised a lifelong fascination over him that the colonies never could. And by the Orient, in terms of practical policy, was signified India. It was only in that direction that there could be full scope for the highly romantic conception of empire that had grown up in Disraeli's mind.

For we must be clear in our own minds not only how this conception differed from that of the hitherto dominant Victorian, or Gladstonian, liberalism, but how irreconcilably Disraeli's new way of Tory imperialism diverged from all that we are apt to associate with the spirit of the Victorian age at its mid Victorian heyday.[1] For what gives its distinctive note to that portentous epoch is its overwhelming preoccupation with the ethical aspect of everything. It would be absurd to describe it as an age of faith—it was much more, in its leading spirits, one of an agonizing doubt. But it was, emphatically, one of morals. Even those heroic unbelievers who denied every religious tenet or dogma were careful to demonstrate that they could lead more austerely virtuous lives than the most dedicated of the faithful. The much derided cult of respectability was a necessary consequence of this disposition, since morality is after all life in action, and the maintenance of certain outward standards of conduct, being the minimum requirement of a consciously moral age, need not necessarily be tainted with hypocrisy.

This is what makes Gladstone, both in his strength and his weakness, so pre-eminently the representative public man of his time. He

[1] We can never hope to understand Disraeli unless we discard the Stracheyan fallacy of forcing every biography into the prefabricated framework of some single attribute or humour—which in his case is afforded by the largely irrelevant circumstance of his Jewish origin; though anything less Jewish in the vulgar connotation it would be hard to imagine, than one whose besetting weakness, both in his private and public life, was an incurable tendency to extravagance. What a much more typical Jew Gladstone would have made, if he had only been one!

wore moral earnestness like a cloak. He resonated it from the public platform and across the floor of the House, with the compelling sonority of a major prophet, and in a manner so congenial to the temper of his audiences that it goes a long way towards accounting for the hypnotic sway that he exercised over them—so difficult to recapture from the printed record. It was the sort of emotional uplift they demanded and that they got from him in overflowing measure, and his habitual appeal to the moral consciousness of a Christian-minded people never failed to strike home. But it was the worst of Gladstone that his moral reactions, though passionately sincere, were governed by no deeply thought out political philosophy, such as Disraeli's, but were of an almost unbelievable inconsistency. It would seldom have been possible to predict the line he would be moved to take on any given issue except, perhaps, by an appraisal not on ground of principle but of interest, for it was said of him that he always followed his conscience, as the driver follows the horse. And it was from this direction that the Victorian morality, of which Gladstone was the supreme embodiment, was most vulnerable to the criticism that had been passed originally on the righteousness of the scribes and Pharisees.

Now Disraeli, alone among the eminent Victorians of his generation, made hardly the least pretence of homage to its moral imperatives, unless it was that his private life was quite as exemplary and as con-sistently principled as that of Gladstone himself. But with the moral aspect of politics, or of statesmanship, he was hardly more ostensibly concerned than Machiavelli had been. An expression that he once used, 'selfish as patriotism', sufficiently defines the core of intellectual realism that underlay the surface bloom of Disraeli's romanticism. There was nothing specifically Jewish in a reversion from developing the British ideal of international morality, however imperfectly honoured, to the frank pursuit of power free from any moral inhibitions whatever, which was inherent in the Latin tradition and continental practice, streamlined—if we may borrow a word from our own century—by such master practitioners as Bismarck and Cavour.

The romantic element in Disraeli did at least prevent him from pushing these principles—or absence of principle—to a Machiavellian, or Bismarckian, conclusion. And perhaps he was too much acclimatized to the political atmosphere, and sensitive to the trend of public opinion of his adopted country, not to have acquired something of the British instinct of moderation. A lifetime of political experience had taught him to what lengths it was safe or prudent to go. This alone would have disqualified him for a full-blooded apostle of empire. He was an imperial realist—just as Gladstone was a Liberal moralist—within bounds. Even along the path of empire he was not the man to lead the country further or faster than he felt that the country was prepared to follow him.

But a new spirit was beginning to stir in the country, as signified by its new democratic electorate, and in the early seventies, when Disraeli formulated his new policy, some of the gilt had already begun to wear off the somewhat stodgy gingerbread of Victorian complacency. The workshop of the world was no longer assured of the monopoly it had enjoyed when its potential rivals had been too busy in the achievement of mutual or of self destruction to become its effective challengers. But the overthrow of the French by the new German Empire seemed to give some assurance of respite from major continental wars on both sides of the Atlantic for as long as could be foreseen, and the rival workshops were now free to bring their superior resources into play. And far from any disposition to throw open their ports and subscribe to the Cobdenite evangel of unfettered exchange, these competing Powers showed every disposition to enclose themselves, monster-like, in armoured carapaces of protective tariffs, and to revert to the most unqualified eighteenth-century conception of economic policy as an alternative mode of belligerent action. And from their point of view there was much to be said for their refusal to play into Britain's hands by allowing their developing industries to be exposed to the full blast of competition from her fully developed ones. This proved to be the attitude even of the emancipated colonies as soon as they obtained control of their own domestic affairs. Disraeli might as well have stipulated for the moon as for the right of the mother country to impose her own fiscal notions on her daughters. That was a part of his declared programme that he never made the slightest attempt to put into effect, and probably never would have; for he was too consummate a political artist to set himself against the grain of public opinion at home or overseas.

A detached observer might have foreboded in these phenomena the premonitory symptoms of a new iron age. The enlarged electorate was beginning to lust after a more exciting and appetizing political fare than that which had satisfied the highly respectable upper bourgeoisie that had been installed in power by the first Reform Bill. And this Disraeli, with his subtly combined appeal to their material interests and their patriotic pride, offered to give them. A sufficient majority of them were at any rate prepared to give him a try to deliver goods that were not even advertised by his rival, who could think up no better electoral counter than an offer to get rid of income tax—which, as far as it was taken seriously, was more calculated to go down with the old bourgeoisie than the new proletariat.

There is no reason to doubt that Disraeli himself had every intention, once installed in office with a decisive majority, of being as good as his word. But he was no autocrat or dictator—only an ageing man compelled to do the best he could with a ministerial team far below his own intellectual calibre, and within the limits set by the prejudices of a party which, in spite of all his long efforts to educate it, was still to a large extent dominated by upper-class reactionaries of the type that he himself had frequently pilloried in his novels. And like every other man approaching the allotted span, he had to work within the limits set by his own temperament and disposition, which was as different as can be imagined from that of the typical imperialist of the *fin de siècle*. Jew though he was, he was far more attracted by the glamour than by the profits of overseas dominion.

While therefore it would be true to say that Disraeli, in his historic declaration of policy at the Crystal Palace, had revived the cult of the British Empire, that had been in abeyance for the best part of a century, and had identified it with one of the great parties in the State, he himself was interested, to any vital extent, in only the least British aspect of that alleged entity. He was little more inclined to concern himself, in practice, with Colonial Office matters than Palmerston had been before him, and in fact his own Colonial Secretary, Lord Carnarvon, was a good deal more alive to the interests and sentiments of the daughter nations than his Premier. There was nothing to fire Disraeli's romantic imagination in the proceedings of these necessarily prosaic settlers and pioneers of lands without a history. When he thought of empire it was to the gorgeous and colourful East that his mind's eye instinctively turned, and this in a British context signified, for practical purposes, India.

As is the way of master players in the grand game of international power politics, Disraeli visualized this problem in the simplest terms. This vast, subcontinental dominion of which the British Crown had formally assumed control and which to him constituted its brightest jewel, represented power in its most exalted degree and, in the full Caesarian sense, imperial power. The destiny that Virgil had marked out for Augustus, to rule the peoples with his sway, was equally that which he himself visualized, in regard to these hundreds of millions, for the Sovereign whom his romantic imagination symbolized as the Faery, and whose imagination he in turn had succeeded in kindling with the consciousness of her own high part in the drama. To assert this power in the most spectacular way was to enhance it; Disraeli was sufficiently acquainted with the East to realize that in causing the Queen of England to assume the additional and more impressive title of Empress of India he was scoring an important point in the game. It was an honour that Victoria herself claimed, with womanly pride, as no more than her due, and she could neither understand nor forgive the headshakings of old-fashioned Liberals who saw in the new style something ominously un-British.

*H

6

IMPERIUM VERSUS LIBERTATEM

IMPERIAL POWER, so outstanding and flaunted, was not likely to go unchallenged, and Disraeli was the last person to imagine that it could. An even vaster empire than that of India presented itself as the inevitable first challenger. His intelligence was one that framed its combinations, and divined its opponent's, moves ahead. He was not content for India to stand passively on the frontier and await events. The Russian bear must in no case be allowed to seize the initiative. His threat to the Balkans and the Straits, that had been temporarily frustrated in the Crimea, was now beginning to be renewed, and since the opening of the Suez Canal in 1869 it had become more and more essential to prevent the eruption of Russia into the eastern Mediterranean. That was at least how Disraeli saw it from his imperial standpoint. But he was not minded to blunder bullheaded, if he could possibly help it, into another Crimean war. He trusted to his combined nerve and finesse to go just near enough to the brink of war without crossing it. And, by what appeared to be a miracle of diplomatic legerdemain, he contrived in the long run, without a shot fired, to dish the Russians as neatly as he ever had his opponents in the field of domestic politics, to the immense enhancement, in the sight of all Europe, of his own and his country's prestige.

With the European crisis that began with the revolt from the Turk of his Christian subjects in the Balkans and subsided to an unstable equilibrium with the achievement of 'peace with honour' at the Congress of Berlin, we are concerned only in so far as it brings to a head a conflict of vital principle involving the destiny and soul of British civilization. The handling of Britain's affairs by her Jewish Premier achieved a success that, though perhaps more specious than lasting, was enough to move the admiration of Bismarck, and might equally have earned that of Machiavelli. He had applied the technique of power politics with an artistry to which it would be hard to find a parallel in the records of British statesmanship. But to what ultimate profit, if it involved the sacrifice of that for which no success can compensate? What if Britain in scoring all the points in a game from which morals were eliminated had sacrificed her own soul?

It was on that precise point that Gladstone took issue with Disraeli. If Russia was to be stopped, it was essential, in the latter's calculation, to throw the weight of British support on the side of the tottering and hard-pressed Turkish Empire. Disraeli saw it as a problem of political dynamics into which the rightness or wrongness of the respective causes did not enter. And when the Turk, faced with the revolt of his Christian helots in Bulgaria, sought, after his kind, to forestall it by a campaign of frightfulness and extermination, it was Disraeli's cue to make the best of a bad business by playing it down as much as possible in the way of publicity, and washing Britain's hands of a matter in which her interests were not on the side of intervention. But Gladstone, however inconsistent he might be in applying his principles, was at least consistent in maintaining that morals are as binding on nations as on individuals, and ought in every case, with Christian Powers, to have precedence of interest. He was never more zealous in expounding this theme than when it was in the direct interest of his political cause of the moment to start a crusade for it—all the more effective from the passionate conviction that he never failed to generate in his own bosom before infecting with it those of his nation-wide audiences.

His denunciation by speech and pamphlet of the Bulgarian atrocities did undoubtedly succeed in arousing the moral indignation of the nation in a way calculated not only to shake the power of the Tory Government to its foundations, but also to have a wrecking effect on Disraeli's pilotage of the Ship of State on her intricate and perilous course, most of all when he demanded that the Turk should be thrown bag and baggage out of his Balkan provinces—a request with which Russia, for her own purposes, was only too ready to oblige by complying.

But when the grey armies ponderously lumbered into action, and the Turk, from being the barbaric bully, became the little fellow—and an ex-ally at that—putting up a heroic fight against the biggest bully of all, public opinion underwent a revulsion on which Gladstone had not reckoned. The moral indignation evaporated, and the electorate showed itself capable of working itself up into a greater hysteria of belligerency than had precipitated the Crimean War. The Bulgarian atrocities were forgotten, and mobs of excited patriots were roaring themselves fighting drunk on such sentiments as those of the famous 'Jingo' song, which after all was a mild and temperate performance compared with later music-hall efforts:

We've fought the Bear a thousand times before,
And they *shan't* have Constantinople!

In all this there was as yet no tincture of specifically imperialist sentiment—the British Empire hardly came into the picture—and Constantinople, whatever its imperial significance may have been for Disraeli, was, for excited mobsmen, a mere emotional intoxicant like Diana of the Ephesians. A similar phenomenon had been seen seven years previously in the Paris mobs that had paraded the streets shouting for war with Prussia, and it was ominous of the way in which democratic senitment, in the new age, was capable of being worked up into a fever heat of imperial—or suicidal—lunacy.

Luckily Disraeli was no Napoleon III—he was not even a Palmerston —and he had never had the least intention of being pushed over the brink of what he was level-headed enough to realize would be an unthinkable calamity, however near in the way of bluff it might suit him to go. If he played power politics by a technique of Machiavellian calculation, he did so with the finesse of an artist, who prefers the neat to the violent solution.

With Sphinx-like imperturbability he held his course regardless alike of appalled members of his Cabinet throwing up their posts and his Queen, no longer a Faery but a Fury, threatening to abdicate unless she got her war with Russia delivered on the nail. He made a spectacular deployment of the forces of the Empire, from India to Malta, and, with a cool appraisal of just how far it was safe to go, succeeded in halting the now exhausted Bear in his tracks, and in due course getting the dispute referred to a European Congress at which, thanks largely to the by no means disinterested good offices of Bismarck, Disraeli succeeded in bilking Russia of most of her hard-earned fruits of victory and enriching the British Empire at the expense of its Turkish protégé by appropriating the invaluable island base of Cyprus—all as part of a peace settlement most of whose main items might have qualified (as the event proved) for the as yet uncoined epithet 'phoney'. Not that, from Disraeli's standpoint, it was necessarily the worse for that. He was not concerned with the fate of the Balkan peoples or the preservation of the Turkish Empire, except as these affected his grand strategy of imperial power politics, and had enabled him to compass his limited objective of sealing off one way of indirect approach to India from Muscovite expansion.

It was for this that Europe had been kept on tenterhooks for months and Britain brought to the verge of war, but such as it was Disraeli had brought it off with consummate skill and economy of means. But such a diplomatic skin game is not in the tradition of British statesmanship. The eagle, it has been said, never lost so much time as when he submitted to learn of the crow. And in the hands of less skilful practitioners than Disraeli this technique could be fraught with dangerous and even fatal consequences.

Even under his auspices it soon became apparent that it could be practised once, and more than once, too often. The indirect path to India by way of the Straits might have been barred, for the nonce, but the effect on a baffled and now incurably antagonized imperial auto-cracy would be to set it probing after a more direct way of approach. Russian expansion, pushed on with greater vigour than ever in Central Asia, was now becoming a more and more open threat to India, and was lapping round the northern frontiers of Afghanistan. Since the collapse of the former British attempt to intervene in the affairs of that country, it had been a fixed principle of successive Governors-General and Viceroys to resist every temptation to repeat it; and that, in spite of every provocation, was still the advice of those who, like the veteran Lord Lawrence, had the most profound knowledge of Indian affairs. But a Government whose principle it was to infuse new vigour into British foreign policy, and was openly committed to maintaining the prestige of its Sovereign's newly created Empire of India, was incapable of waiting passively on events while the disgruntled Anglophobe, who was titular Ameer of Afghanistan, was being more and more drawn into collaboration with Russian designs. A British counter-move seemed plainly called for—most plainly of all to the talented Lord Lytton, whom Disraeli, with a fellow feeling for a man of letters and a romantic, had chosen to be viceroy.

So Britain found herself committed by the most specious arguments to another plunge forward into these barren and trouble-infested highlands. It was done with a slickness and efficiency that had been so fatally lacking in the former effort. The Russophile Ameer was duly sent packing, a presumably more amenable successor appointed and a British Resident and his staff installed at Kabul, who were all, as Lawrence had in vain tried to warn an unbelieving Premier, duly set upon and murdered; so that a second war, more bloody and expensive, had to be fought, and the country conquered and evacuated all over again. It was a disillusioning object-lesson in the practical working of the spectacular and dynamic forward policy that had seemed to pay off so well in the achievement of 'peace with honour' at Berlin. It was no isolated instance, for on the top of the two Afghan wars came a Zulu war in South Africa, with its even more humiliating opening episode of the annihilation of an entire British force by the spears of naked savages.

This sort of thing was more than the democratic electorate had bargained for when it had put the Tory Government in office, and even without the stimulus of Gladstone's terrific series of Midlothian speeches, in which his rhetorical afflatus was given vent at its fullest blast of moral indignation, it would have been ripe for a return to the economical and peaceful ways of the former Whig-Liberalism. It had had its bellyful of imperial adventure, even of the limited kind that

Disraeli had been prepared to sponsor. For as a practical proposition, Tory imperialism under his auspices had been concerned almost entirely with India. To the colonial part of the so-called Empire his attachment had never been more than platonic, and he had not made the slightest attempt to realize the pre-election prospects he had held out of binding it together either politically or economically. That he came to be involved in a South African imbroglio was none of his seeking. Indeed there is no reason to believe that he had ever taken any special trouble to inform himself about the differences between white and native, or between rival breeds of whites, in that remote part of the world. His mind had been formed in a different mould, and he was content to leave the unravelling of these problems to the Colonial Office and the men on the spot. And these men let him down, or in for it, in a way that he had never reckoned on—most conspicuously of all in the case of this Zulu war, which, with his hands full in Afghanistan, was the last additional burden he wanted to have on them.

But Sir Bartle Frere, the Governor whom he had chosen for the *siege perilous* of the South African assignment, had so convinced himself of the imminence of a concerted native attempt to drive the white men into the sea that he sought to forestall it by what amounted to a declaration of war off his own bat. It must be remembered that there was not yet telegraphic communication with Britain and that it was a matter of weeks for instructions to be transmitted from Downing Street. The effect of this trigger-happy assumption of responsibility was to saddle the home Government with all the odium and expense of an unpopular and (in its opening stages) bungled war which, coming on the top of the Afghan adventure, not only completely deflated the prestige it had acquired after the Berlin settlement, but created a revulsion of feeling against a line of policy that had become stigmatized by its association with the unfortunate 'Jingo' chorus. The imperial bubble was in fact pricked, and a government that, by general admission, might only two years previously have swept the country, was now swept from office by an overwhelming majority. It was one of the most astonishing reversals of popular favour on British record, but not nearly as astonishing as the sequel, after the prophet of Midlothian had come into office with a clear mandate to implement his own exhortations.

But before coming to that it will be as well to see in due perspective this fall of the newly created Lord Beaconsfield and his Government. No doubt they had come under suspicion, with the electorate, of whoring after strange, or at least un-British gods of imperial domination. But nothing could be more misleading than to brand them with the stigma of imperialism in its *fin de siècle* connotation. Nobody, not even Gladstone, had ever been less infected by the 'Jingo' virus than

this survivor from the epoch of the dandies, who, in the heyday of
Victorian earnestness, retained his Regency pose of ironic detachment
that had itself been inherited from the age of reason.

He had nothing of the itch for expansion, or painting the map red
for its own sake, that was proper to the emotional imperialism of the
nineties. Even for the Indian Empire, save for a strategic and defensive
rectification of the frontier, he harboured no expansionist ambitions.
His acquisition of Cyprus was merely by way of completing this same
linked system of Indian defences by a sort of detached flank guard. But
for the colonial part of what he had glorified as the Empire, he had
showed little disposition in practice to depart from the policy of his
predecessors, of leaving it to run its own affairs with the minimum of
assistance or interference—his unforeseen involvement in the Zulu
War notwithstanding. As for the great no man's land of tropical
Africa, his urge was rather to cut down than to expand the British
coastal settlements; and though Bismarck, anxious to sow dissension
between rival Powers, had already sought to tempt Britain with the
glittering prize of Egypt, 'the old Jew', as he used to call Beaconsfield,
was too wary to rise to the bait.

And yet, though on his actual record, and that of his Government,
Beaconsfield would appear to have been anything but empire-minded,
there is a sense in which he can be described as having set Britain—
and more especially the Tory part that he had done so much to re-
model—in the way of latter-day imperialism. For the spirit of empire
is the spirit of power; the will to empire is the quintessence of the will
to power, and the pursuit of power politics is bound, given suitable
opportunity, to become that of imperial expansion. And Beaconsfield,
in contrast to Gladstone, never made the least pretence of pursuing
anything else, though he did so with an artistry that preferred the
finesse of diplomacy to the crude violence of military action. Blood
and iron formed no part of the Disraelian technique.

And indeed—whether we are to regard it as a weakness or a redeeming virtue—there was always a suspicion of the theatrical about this
spectacular policy, that kept it from being pushed to its grim but
logical consummation. Beaconsfield was no Bismarck. He was in the
highest sense a comedian, with perhaps a touch of the mystery man,
and he wished to play his part on a level, and in a setting, suited to his
genius. Up to a point he carried it off superbly, to the astonished
admiration of Europe. But after that point things began to slip out of
control.

Precisely how and why is not too easy to define. It is tempting to
put it down to sheer hard luck; and that no doubt entered into it to a
remarkable extent. Most responsible of all perhaps was the unprecedented succession of rain-drenched summers at the end of the

seventies, which overwhelmed British agriculture, already unable to
hold its own against importation from virgin lands overseas, with
irretrievable disaster. Indeed there is at least a case for saying that the
decisive factor in bringing about the Government's defeat was its
failure to control, not so much Afghans and Zulus, as the British
weather.

But that, at best, is only part of the truth. Power politics, even when
played with the light touch of a master, is a game that depends on the
co-operation not only of ordinary and unimaginative men, but of
masses of men, whose passions are bound to be stimulated and to get
out of hand. What may be no more than diplomatic bluff in high
quarters may arouse the team spirit of the mob to jingoistic frenzy
against whatever Power may be cast for the villain's part in an international melodrama. And what may be fraught with even more serious
consequences is a tendency to assume that a forward or spirited policy
is now the order of the day, and that servants of the Crown who push
it with all their might, and even on their own responsibility, will be
sure to have the backing of the home Government. Once that impression comes to be firmly enough planted, trouble is bound to follow as
surely as night follows day.

Beaconsfield may have sincerely desired to keep out of these niggling
but costly wars that were sapping the popularity of his administration
and hamstringing that policy of incipient social reform which had been
an essential feature of his new Toryism. But in spite of his otherwise
deeply thought out political philosophy, he had contrived to impale
himself on the horns of a self-created dilemma. For in committing
himself equally to the maintenance of British institutions and the
promotion of a British Empire, or—as he signified in his famous
formula—of *imperium et libertas*, he was really trying to ride two
horses simultaneously in opposite directions. For *libertas* is the direct
negation of *imperium*.

That is why the Disraelian programme of Tory imperialism never
even got started in the colonies or daughter nations, which were
tacitly recognized as the domain of *libertas*,[1] whereas all that mattered
of empire was comprised in those mainly oriental dependencies, and
particularly the Indian Empire, which were assumed to be proper fields
for the application of the imperial principle, since oriental and especially
Indian peoples were supposed to be permanently wedded to the principle of despotic government, and positively to demand to be ruled by
a paternal autocracy, the more spectacular and imperious the better.

And yet there might have been detected an ominous significance
in the fact that Disraeli's own chosen viceroy had found himself

[1] Except for the casual and almost absent-minded annexation of the Transvaal
Republic, for which see next chapter.

constrained to turn aside from his grandiose anti-Russian combinations to safeguard his home front, by a law curbing the freedom of the native press to indulge in openly seditious agitation for the overthrow of the imperial Raj. It was a mild enough measure in itself and soon rescinded, but it showed what fires might be smouldering below the placid surface of Indian life.

Any moderately impartial observer, surveying the political scene in England at the beginning of the eighties, after the overwhelming defeat at the polls that had followed Beaconsfield's confident appeal to the country, might have concluded that Tory imperialism, even to the very limited extent that his Government had been able to put it into practice, was a spent force; that the brief experience the British public had had of the cult of power signified by *imperium* had been judged by its fruits and found wanting, and that in response to Gladstone's eloquent appeal the nation had come down squarely and decisively for *libertas*, and to make all sure, had committed its guardianship into his keeping. And to whom would it have occurred to ask:

Quis custodiet custodem ipsum?

7

FROM MIDLOTHIAN
TO KHARTOUM

GLADSTONE'S second Government, with its overwhelming mandate for renouncing imperialism and all its works, and getting back to the ways of peace and liberalism, found itself confronted with a task whose nature had been defined by Gladstone himself with an explicitness that for once left no loophole for evasion.

Nor, as far as India was concerned, was there the least attempt at it. Nothing could have been more sensible or statesmanlike than the way in which the new Government contrived to pull out of the Afghan entanglement by abandoning the needlessly advanced base of Kandahar, and at the same time retaining the strategic frontier that had been the one profitable result of all the expense of blood and treasure incidental to Lytton's spectacular forward policy. Afghanistan was wisely left to stew in its own juice under an Ameer who was shrewdly determined to keep it as free as possible from all contact with Western progress, and thus ideally suited to keep the irresistible force of Russian from impinging on the immovable obstacle of Anglo-Indian imperialism.

So far, so good; and there could have been no better advertisement for the programme so eloquently put forward in the Midlothian speeches.

That a Government under such leadership and wedded to such principles should not only have proceeded to dishonour them in practice in the most flagrant manner, but should also have drifted into a course of imperialistic aggression that plunged the country into incomparably more ruinous expense and bloodshed than was ever debited to Beaconsfield's Tory account, might have seemed beyond the prospect of belief. And yet it is a matter of simple fact that this is just what did happen, in the two vital fields of South African and Egyptian policy.

In South Africa they had admittedly, as in India, to clear up a mess bequeathed them by their predecessors. It is true that the Zulu War—

which, though it had been forced on Beaconsfield's Government in its own despite, had provided the most damaging count in the electoral indictment against it—had been duly settled by the suppression, as a military force, of that bloodthirsty horde which Gladstone had not scrupled to dramatize as composed of patriots engaged in the rightful defence of their liberties. But there were other patriots, of a less equivocal complexion, in the neighbouring Transvaal, in the shape of the Boer farmers, who were equally concerned with the recovery of the liberties that their fathers had gone to such lengths to win for them, and of which they had recently been deprived by an act of arbitrary annexation by the very Power that had stood to them for the Egypt of their Exodus.

That, at least, was how they dramatized the situation, with slightly more excuse—but not much more—than Gladstone in the case of the Zulus. For in the second generation things had gone from bad to worse with the children of the *trekkers*. Divided among themselves, tyrannous towards the Africans in their midst, many of whom they had reduced to virtual slavery under the transparent fiction of indentured labour, bankrupt financially, and recently worsted in conflict by a Kaffir chief, they seemed to have at least some plausible cause for believing that the only way of saving them from utter collapse was for Britain to step in and take over the task of government that they had proved incapable of exercising for themselves.

It was a tragedy partly of good intentions and partly of sheer absent-minded ignorance. For there were few people in Britain who knew much or cared anything about what went on in this remote hinterland of Cape Colony. Perhaps the only member even of the Tory Cabinet who had been at the trouble to give any serious thought to the matter was the Colonial Secretary, Lord Carnarvon, a charming and cultured *grand seigneur* who had been instrumental, in the previous Tory administration, in sponsoring the federation of Canada, and was confident that he could apply the same panacea to the solution of the Anglo-Dutch problem in South Africa. The analogy, as ought to have been apparent even at the time, was dangerously misleading. For one thing, instead of a minority of French-Canadians, and an insignificant aboriginal population, there was already in the Cape Colony a great majority of Dutch over English, and to bring the two wholly Dutch republics to the north into any federation would be to tilt the balance overwhelmingly against the British element—and then what was to prevent the majority opting for an independent republic under its own flag?

Nothing—it ought to have been clear—but the goodwill of the Dutch settlers to remain, certainly not in a British or any other empire, but in formal allegiance to the British Crown, and in free membership of a British Commonwealth of Nations. And as far as the Dutch of Cape Colony were concerned there seemed a reasonable hope of a friendly co-operation between the two peoples being perpetuated. But to hope thus was to leave out of account the fundamental conflict of principle that was bound to arise between the respective ways of free British civilization and Dutch racial imperialism in dealing with the vast aboriginal majority of South African folk—in other words between notions enshrined respectively in the British Common and Dutch Roman Law.

Whatever chance there might have been of these differences being somehow miraculously transcended was thrown away by the almost incredible series of blunders—not to use a stronger word—perpetrated by almost everyone on the British side charged with handling the situation. And yet there is none of these men but acted in honest good faith, on grounds that were speciously plausible. To Carnarvon, obsessed with his dream of federation, it seemed that for Britain to take over the government of a people that had almost ceased to govern itself was in the plain interest of everyone concerned, and most of all that of the Transvaalers themselves who, with the Zulu power still at its height, were threatened with imminent catastrophe. Nor did it appear that the burghers themselves were disposed to put up any active opposition when the British Commissioner, Sir Theophilus Shepstone, rode to their capital, Pretoria, with an escort of no more than twenty-five mounted police, to proclaim that the Transvaal would be henceforth under the Queen's sovereignty.

It all went through with such an absence of fuss that it seems to have occurred to none of those responsible that for one nation to assert, on any pretext whatever, sovereign authority over another, except by its own explicit consent, is by all British principles an act of arbitrary or—what amounts to the same thing—imperial tyranny. It would have been literally true, for perhaps the first time on nineteenth-century record, to say that a province had been acquired for a British Empire, and one peopled by men who had the tradition of resistance to imperial authority in their blood, not to speak of hatred to Britain— a tradition by no means inconsistent with a determination to tyrannize to the limit over such lesser breeds as the Lord had conveniently reserved for their own domination.

The Boers were as shrewd as they were stubborn, slow to wrath but quick to perceive on which side their bread happened to be buttered at the moment. They were practically unanimous from the start that they had no use for any sovereignty but their own, and lost no opportunity of signifying this in quiet but unmistakable terms. But they were well content to sit quiet and let the British redcoats do the dirty work for them of disposing of King Cetewayo's *impis*. The effect of that removal was similar to that of the British conquest of Canada on the American colonies, in setting them free to assert their own independence of the rescuing Power. But though the British control, with a tactlessness almost beyond belief, was exercised in the most irritating way possible by a military martinet, the Boers with patient self-restraint held their hand, for what appeared to be the excellent reason that their cause had been taken up by one of the great English parties, headed by no less an apostle of liberty than Gladstone, who had denounced the annexation in no uncertain terms and pledged himself to repudiate it, as having been obtained by dishonourable means.[1] And when their champion was swept into office by an overwhelming majority, the unsuspecting burghers felt every reason to congratulate themselves on their patience having been rewarded, and never doubted that their promised independence would be conceded as a matter of course.

Little had they dreamed that the only thing that Gladstone, once installed in power, would be prepared to repudiate was his own pledge, and that in the most direct and unqualified manner, by pompously intimating that the Queen could not be advised to relinquish her sovereignty of the Transvaal. But by way of compensation for one repudiated pledge, another was substituted of the fullest possible measure of self-government consistent with the aforesaid maintenance of British sovereignty. But as month followed month not the faintest attempt was made to concede anything of the sort, but the country was left under a partly military, partly bureaucratic and wholly detested régime, until the final break came in the classical way of an attempt to levy a tax without the shadow of representation, and to seize the wagon of a Boer farmer in default of payment. This was the last straw. The Transvaalers rose as one man, and proceeded to besiege the ridiculously exiguous British garrisons dotted about their country, and to dig themselves in on the Natal frontier passes.

Never had there been a more extraordinary transition than that from the great orator's fulminating indictment of imperialism when out of office, and this flagrant practical surrender to it when in. And yet Gladstone was neither a cynic nor a Machiavelli, but an archetypical product of his age, in whom energy proper to genius was harnessed to a less than averagely profound or penetrating intelligence, as witness his fecundity—only equalled even in his own day by Martin Tupper—in the emission of the most sonorous and impressive platitudes, on every conceivable topic—political, cultural, or religious—that fell within the vast scope of his interest. Add to this what was almost an incapacity, fatal in one in his position, for focusing that interest on

[1] At Peebles, 30th March 1880. See *Cambridge History of the British Empire*, Vol. VIII, p. 423.

more than the one topic at a time about which he had stoked up the requisite head of emotion. It would be putting the matter in a false perspective to talk of his having decided to bilk the Boers of their promised independence. With the problems of Ireland and India on his hands and that of Egypt beginning to loom large, he had been subconsciously determined to unload his mind of the affairs of the Transvaal till a more convenient season, and the will-o'-the-wisp of federation under the British Crown had given him a convenient excuse for putting off any decision whatever till a more convenient day.

It was only after the Boers had shot to pieces the handful of British troops under Sir George Colley that had tried to force the Natal passes, and followed up this by the ignominious rout, with practically no loss to themselves, of a mixed body of troops, that the baffled commander, desperately anxious to retrieve his reputation, had led up Majuba Hill with the idea of manœuvring them out of their position, that Gladstone woke up too late to the urgency of the situation, and allowed his moral instincts to come into play. By all the rules of power politics it was unthinkable to allow the British Empire to be branded with the stigma of this unprecedented humliation. Ample British forces were now available, and their commander had promised in the most explicit terms to redeem honour by making a speedy end of the Boer resistance. But the Boer leaders still professed themselves ready to accept the proferred terms that they had been on the point of conceding before the ill-timed aggression of Majuba. And Gladstone was rightly determined not to incur the 'blood-guiltiness' of exacting bloody vengeance for so nobly unexceptionable a feat of arms, or to risk setting the whole of Dutch South Africa in a blaze of rebellion by the attempt to do so.

So the Transvaalers were granted their independence, which was no more than had been promised them, and that they might have accepted with some measure of gratitude if it had been freely conceded to them in the first instance. But now that they had extorted it, as they were human enough to believe, from a whipped bully, who did his grudging best to save face by reserving the Queen's suzerainty [1]—one of those woolly phrases which might signify anything or nothing on paper, but would infallibly mean a head-on collision if any attempt were made to give it practical effect—their inherited hatred for the British was reinforced by contempt, and this bred an answering British determination to even up the score at the first opportunity. What was even worse was that the spirit of militant nationalism, kindled in the Transvaal, had now begun to infect the Dutch in the two provinces

---

[1] Though what conceivable claim a British Sovereign could have to any sort of suzerainty over these unwilling aliens more valid than that of the highwayman to his victim's purse is not obvious—least of all on Liberal principles.

to the south, and the dream of federation on any other footing than that of unqualified independence was made to seem more a mirage than ever. Never had dragons' teeth been more effectively or wantonly sown.

One might have thought that this almost unbelievable combination of tergiversation and ineptitude would have been sufficient to blast the credit of any Government or statesman professing liberal principles. But the ordinary British voter—though he would never feel quite the same about his now venerable spellbinder after this pricking of the Midlothian bladder—did to a certain extent participate in his inability to make heavy weather of what went on in a land that was still almost as much a blank to him as its tropical hinterland was to the mapmakers. No doubt the knowledge of a little British force having taken a licking from these uncouth farmers was a shock to his complacency, but he could console himself with the reflection that these same farmers had more or less capitulated to a deployment of overwhelming force, and had gone home quietly after accepting the magnanimous terms offered them. It had ended, if not exactly happily, at least comparatively cheaply, and whatever might or might not be the difference, if any, between annexation and suzerainty was not a point of sufficient importance to be seriously pressed against the Government at election time. And it is at least conceivable that the Transvaalers might have settled down to their own primitive devices without giving further trouble, had it not been for the then unforeseeable discovery of the world's richest gold mines on their territory that within a few years was destined to revolutionize the whole situation.

But though this South African episode might conceivably have been lived down, the same Government was about to stage an even more catastrophic reversal of its own declared principles at the other end of the African continent. How many of those who had applauded, or even denounced, Mr Gladstone's terrific series of anti-imperial philippics before coming into office would have dreamed that within little more than two years of doing so he would be launching his country's forces on a path trodden by Esarhaddon, Cambyses, Alexander and so many other imperial conquerors of the ancient land of Egypt—a path that Beaconsfield himself could not be tempted to tread. And yet it proved to be even so. Hard as it is to set down the literal facts of the story in the most impartial outline, without being suspected of colouring them, they speak for themselves.

To render them credible, one must see them in international perspective. The year 1871 had brought to a close an epoch of major conflicts which, like that which had followed the French Revolution, had endured for just twenty-three years. The forty-three years that followed were those of the so-called armed peace, a swaying balance of European Powers, arming themselves to the teeth against each other on a scale hitherto unknown, and with Britain and the United States standing, the one uneasily, and the other complacently aloof behind their respective moats.

What kept this equilibrium from the possibility of stabilizing itself, and prevented the peace from ever being more than an armistice, was one dominating circumstance that must never be lost sight of. The last of the series of wars that had preceded it—that by which the unity of the German Reich had been consummated under the guidance of Bismarck—had been closed by a peace treaty, forced on a prostrate France at the bayonet's point, robbing her of two provinces to whose loss she could never be reconciled. Bismarck himself could hardly have failed to realize, when too late, how irretrievably he had blundered in becoming party to these ill-starred annexations. In any case the whole of his subsequent course, so long as he remained in virtual dictatorship of German policy, was governed by the overmastering need of preventing the balance of military power from being tilted sufficiently in favour of any combination including France, as to give her a reasonable hope of winning back her own by precipitating a European war.

Bismarck was a power politician devoid of moral principle of any sort, but this did not prevent him from devoting all the resources of his genius to the preservation of a peace that he knew to be continually threatened, and that, with the unique faculty he possessed of knowing when and where to stop, he made the limit of his ambition. He regarded Germany as what he himself described a 'saturated Power', and envisaged a *status quo* in which she would remain the central orb of the European constellation. He had therefore no wish to enlarge the frontiers of the Reich, nor to encourage it in projects of colonial expansion. When all was said and done, his volitional horizon was that of the hidebound and landbound Prussian Junker caste from which he had sprung.

It is only against this background, or fitted into this pattern, that the British seizure of the Nile valley, under the auspices of a Government and a Premier pledged to the hilt against every form of imperialist aggression, is seen to admit of at least some sort of humanly intelligible explanation. We have to envisage an international situation in which every other influence was overshadowed by the dominance of one man's personality. Without going so far as to claim that Bismarck set the tune to which all the Powers danced, we might say that it was to his diplomatic initiative that they all, in their several ways, reacted. And the subtle and tortuous combinations that he was continually weaving were governed by the one simple conviction that so long as France remained obsessed by the idea of recovering her lost provinces she must be kept diplomatically isolated, even by dint of encouraging her imperialist ambitions so as to embroil her with otherwise possible allies. He had brought off this gamble with brilliant success, by playing pander to France in the rape of Tunis, under the covetous nose of Italy, the result of which had been to drive that Latin Power into the Teutonic orbit of a Triple Alliance straddling central Europe.

That was at the beginning of the eighties. But already, in the previous decade, Bismarck's eye, ranging along the Mediterranean coast, had perceived an equally promising opportunity of starting off a mortal quarrel between France and her British ally of the Crimea over Egypt, which, since the construction of the Suez Canal under French auspices, had now become an area of maximum sensitivity for both their respective policies. This, at the time of the Near Eastern crisis, had been a bait that Bismarck had been careful to dangle before the eyes of Beaconsfield, hinting that Germany would be benevolently disposed towards the idea of a British occupation; but the 'old Jew' had been too wily to be lured into so entangling a commitment, for all his alleged imperialist leanings. But that he would scarcely have been cold in the grave before Gladstone had swallowed the same bait, hook, line and sinker, was a thing that hardly he, in his most cynical mood, would have dared to anticipate.

The ancient land of the Pharaohs had, since the cutting of the canal, become such a bone of European contention that nobody took thought for the plight of its inhabitants, who were the helpless victims of these rivalries. Egypt was still, in theory, a province of the ramshackle and moribund Turkish Empire; its ruler, the Khedive, was no more than a governor, though an hereditary one, and the ruling clique, both in the administration and the army, consisted of persons who like himself were aliens to the country they ruled, or misruled, at their arbitrary pleasure. But as misfortune would have it, the Khedive who was in office at the time that the canal was constructed was no commonplace oriental despot, but one who dreamed of becoming a latter-day Cheops or Rameses, and signalizing his reign by achievements on as colossal a scale as the Pyramids, or the temples of Karnak. And in his simplicity he imagined he had discovered a formula for doing this, of talismanic infallibility. It consisted in availing himself of the resources that Western financiers were ready and eager to put at his disposal, and thus, by no more than a few strokes of the pen, harnessing to his service unlimited power backed by all the resources of Western science. And for a while the magic actually worked, with djinn-like efficacy. The usurers advanced their capital, fixing their own rates of interest in the authentic spirit of Shylock, and projects, as wasteful as grandiose, were put in hand, to the glory of Khedive Ismail and the benefit (as he flattered himself) of his people. Even if he ever realized how he was plunging deeper and deeper into the abyss of bankruptcy, he both could and did put off the evil day by fresh borrowings—and up to a point the sharks were ready to oblige. But he was incurring these ruinous obligations not, like the Merchant of Venice, on his own behalf, but on that of the helpless people of the valley and delta who had no say in the matter, but whose labour and resources, hardly sufficient as they were to keep body and soul together, their Turkish autocrat was recklessly pledging in fulfilment of the bond.

It would have been natural to imagine that, when the day of reckoning did come, and the spendthrift Khedive, with his borrowing powers exhausted and his mountain of debts pressing on him, frankly went broke, the Egyptians would have reacted as any European Government would have done in like circumstances—and as, in the interval between the two World Wars, most of them did with far less excuse—and proceeded to default on his obligations and leave the usurers to whistle for their bond. And this is just the line that he did in fact take. But the latter-day Shylocks were not to be put off so easily. They were determined, come what might, to have the uttermost farthing nominated in the bond, and to sweat it out of the unfortunate Egyptian populace, who had never had the least responsibility for contracting the debt, and had got negligible if any benefit out of the transaction.

England, from her obvious concern about the canal, and France, whose financiers had been most actively involved in the speculation, were the two most obvious Powers to assume the function of bailiffs. Khedive Ismail, who showed signs of being unco-operative, was easily disposed of by putting pressure on his nominal master, the Sultan, to demote him in favour of a successor who it was believed would be a bondholders' stooge, and an Anglo-French joint control was set up over the finances of his administration for the purpose of effecting the necessary process of economic blood transfusion. Resistance was not expected from the Egyptians, who were accustomed to taking what came to them from their rulers. This admirably simple arrangement was working to plan when Gladstone's administration, pledged to the vindication of liberty and international righteousness, took over.

But then the unexpected happened. The patience of all classes of the native population, even down to the humble *fellahin*, was exhausted at the spectacle of their Turkish Khedive functioning as the obedient agent of usurers who were neither Egyptians nor Moslems, and who were animated by no other purpose than that of filling their own pockets with all that their labour and resources could be forced to yield.

The Egyptian resistance took the only possible form, in the circumstances, of a military revolt. The army, whose officers had been just as shabbily bilked as any other section of the population, found a leader in a certain Arabi Pasha, a colonel of humble origin who, though by no means highly educated, was a man of forceful personality and unimpeachable honesty. The declared purpose of his revolt was to force the Khedive to govern the country on constitutional lines and in its own interests, even if these did not happen to coincide with those of the usurers. But as Gladstone's colleague and biographer, Morley, somewhat naïvely admits, the law defining the claims of the bond-holders on the Egyptian revenue 'at least made the policy of Egypt for the Egyptians unworkable',[1] and also, he might have added, any honouring of the principle of taxation by consent.

But if consistency of principle is to count for anything, surely in Arabi had arisen a man after Gladstone's own heart, every bit as much entitled to the honourable style of patriot as Kossuth or Garibaldi, let alone such recipients of his libertarian sympathies as Jefferson Davis or Cetewayo or the Mahdi. What people could ever, on the face of it, have been better described as rightly struggling to be free than the Egyptians, under their peasant colonel's leadership, from this life-draining bondage to the foreigner? But nowhere in the record is there the least indication that it ever occurred either to the English Premier or his colleagues to view the matter of the debt from any other stand-point but that of Shylock. Come what might, there could be no question of bating a farthing of the sum nominated in the bond. Patriotism might be all very well in its proper place but, business being business, that place did not happen to be Egypt. Consequently there could be no question of regarding this latest ebullition of it in any other light than that of a nuisance to be suppressed—the only question being by whom and by what means.

That was not quite so easy, for though Britain and France were operating the joint control, neither of them was anxious to commit its armed forces to the expense and complications involved in a joint military intervention, and still less did either of them wish to see the other assuming sole occupation. The solution that Gladstone would have preferred would have been to have called in the Sultan, as nominal overlord, to dispatch his own forces to perform the dirty work of suppressing Arabi—in other words, he would, without turning a hair, have let loose those Turkish hordes, whose recent atrocities in Bulgaria he had held up to the horrified execration of all civilized peoples, to repeat the performance on the recalcitrant Egyptians. It was no fault of his, but of the shifty and evasive potentate who was afterwards to be known as Abdul the Damned, that this ingenious solution failed to materialize.

Something, however, had got to be done, if the spirit of Egyptian nationalism, encouraged by the success of Arabi's revolt, were not to

[1] Morley's *Life of Gladstone*, Vol. III, p. 78.

get completely out of hand. The privileged position that the European settlers had managed to secure for themselves by numerous 'capitulations' that constituted them a law, or anarchy, unto themselves in the land, had its natural effect in fomenting anti-foreign feeling, which began in the great cosmopolitan port of Alexandria to assume riotous proportions, and to cause the British and French fleets to demonstrate in the harbour for the ostensible protection of Europeans, though such a gesutre, unsupported by a landing force, was better calculated to act as an irritant than a deterrent to mob violence in the city, and did provoke the Egyptian forces on shore to the counter-demonstration of strengthening the fortifications. The British admiral was determined to carry matters with a high hand, and when it became plain that he intended to knock the forts about their builders' ears, his French colleague, rather than be involved in such proceedings, acting under the orders of his Government, took his fleet out of the harbour, whereupon the British ironclads opened a full-scale bombardment which, at trifling loss to themselves, effected its object of silencing the forts and accounting for many hundreds of their defenders,[1] with what might have been the foreseen effect of inciting the mob to worse anti-foreign outrages than before.

Here was an act so flamingly at variance with all that Gladstone and his Government professed to stand for that it was widely believed that the bombardment would be followed by his resignation of the Premiership. And indeed the most universally respected of his Radical colleagues, the Quaker, John Bright, did resign from the Cabinet in horrified protest. But Gladstone, who blamed all the bloodshed on what he chose to regard as 'the seemingly wanton wickedness of Arabi', merely hardened his heart, and determined to go through with it to the end, even if this were to mean going it alone, without the co-operation of France, who had hitherto taken the lead in putting the financial screw on the Egyptians, but now drew back from trying to subdue them by force of arms.

This refusal was hardly in accordance with the alleged French addiction to logic, and indeed it is hard to discover any thread of consistent purpose underlying the unpredictable changes of administration and policy under the Third Republic. But however erratic these variations, the essential France never shook herself free from the urge for the recovery of her lost territories. Even her politicians had begun to realize how neatly they had been fooled into playing Bismarck's game by swallowing the bait of Tunis, and they realized that by tying up their forces in Egypt they would be allowing him to bring off an even more damaging coup, by involving them in complications that

[1] Though as a matter of fact it was disappointing target practice, with significantly little damage to either forts or guns for a vast expenditure of ammunition.

would inevitably disrupt their precarious *entente* with Britain. Unfortunately the way they took of standing aside and leaving the door open for a British conquest of Egypt was an even more certain way of engendering an irreconcilable quarrel between the two countries. Perhaps they had never realized the un-Gladstonian lengths to which Gladstone was prepared to go.

One can only account for it on the assumption that his resentment against Arabi had become a crusading obsession, blinding him to every other consideration except that of smashing his nationalist revolt at all costs. The full apparatus of military conquest was rushed into action in a way that Disraeli would never have dared to envisage, and the French were invited to co-operate. This their Government of the moment offered to do, with the reasonable stipulation that operations should be limited to the safeguarding of the canal, though even this was so far in advance of the now resolutely pacific policy favoured by the majority of deputies as to precipitate its fall. But it made little difference, since nothing but an offensive *à outrance* would satisfy Gladstone and his colleagues. It was mounted 'all Sir Garnet'—as popular slang characterized the staff-work efficiency of its commander Wolseley. An excellently appointed little army, the last to take the field in the now traditional, and originally Cromwellian, scarlet of the British infantryman, was in an incredibly short time deployed on the shores of the canal, and proceeded to stage a military pageant of the most satisfactory kind. The Egyptian rank and file hardly put up the pretence of a fight, but bolted for their lives at the first assault, and the pursuing cavalry crowned the performance by riding hell for leather across the desert and bluffing the citadel and garrison of Cairo into surrender. Egypt in all her long experience of conquests had never known one more expeditious. No wonder both Sir Garnet and the bombarding admiral received peerages.

It was in fact a model of what was to become the standard pattern of imperialist technique, and Gladstone, if he could have got his way, would have been in advance of his time by proceeding to the liquidation of his prisoner, the unfortunate Arabi, by handing him over to the tender mercies of the puppet Khedive, to be dealt with as a rebel and a traitor. It was only with difficulty that the implacable old gentleman could be diverted from his fell purpose by the remonstrances of men like John Bright and his Home Secretary, Sir William Harcourt. For 'it is a great mistake', as John Morley, in the palmiest style of the Victorian biographer, is moved to comment, 'to suppose that Mr Gladstone was all leniency, or that when he thought ill of men, he stayed either at palliating words or at half measures' [1]—and the fallen

---

[1] Morley's *Life of Gladstone*, Vol. III, p. 86. Gladstone found himself for once in agreement with his Sovereign, who was also out for Arabi's blood.

patriot might have accounted himself lucky to have eventually, in consideration of an arranged plea of guilty, been allowed, as he was, to fade out into civilized internment at Ceylon.

Such are the bare facts of this Egyptian tragedy, and it is hard to account even now for the part played by the leading actor without falling into what would certainly be the error of assigning him a villain's part. But no one who has studied Gladstone's complex personality can possibly doubt his passionate persuasion of his own integrity. It was simply that his mind lacked the detachment and clarity, that it was neither broad enough nor deep enough, to be the master and not the slave of those subconscious urges that the newest psychology designates as the *libido*, but that his own century would have referred to more crudely as the emotions. Add to this an incapacity or unwillingness to be diverted from the pursuit of the one mastering cause to which he might at the moment be emotionally committed, a tendency that grew in him with advancing years, and was especially handicapping to one whose position called for unremitting concentration on a variety of pressing issues.

And in fairness it must be admitted that behind its imposing façade of Liberal unity his own Cabinet was a house divided against itself, and that between its solid *bloc* of reactionary peers from the great Whig houses and the dynamic Joseph Chamberlain with his left-wing Radicalism, the venerable Premier could count on hardly more than one or two loyal supporters of his own kidney.

It would have needed nothing less, and perhaps even more, than the demonic will-power and drive of a Chatham to have driven such a team along all the various lines of a comprehensive anti-imperial policy, however eloquently it might have been proclaimed from the platform, and Gladstone would seem to have been sufficiently conscious or subconscious of his limitations to have made no serious attempt to do so. He was by nature an economist of the mind no less than of the pocket, and more and more, as time went on, he tended to focus his liveliest interest and devote his best energies, with one-pointed concentration, to what had become for him the line of least emotional resistance, or that which most fired his crusading ardour.

No one who has followed Gladstone's later career could be in the slightest doubt what that line was. He had formed the conviction, reasonable enough in itself, that the problem of all others that demanded solution was that presented by the distressful and deteriorating state into which Ireland had fallen and which even from the English standpoint had the effect of a perpetually running ulcer weakening and poisoning the whole system. To find a remedy to this had become with Gladstone a dominating—and threatened to become an all-absorbing—ambition, from the pursuit of which he became more and more unwilling to have his attention diverted to other objectives.

We have seen how this one-way habit of mind had had the effect of allowing dragons' teeth to be sown in South Africa, and one cannot but feel it to have played a similar part in allowing the Egyptian situation to drift out of control through sheer slackness of handling, and lack of any thought-out or one-principled line of policy. It is surely inconceivable that he had planned to stultify all his declared principles by conquering Egypt for the Empire, or that having allowed such a situation to develop as that of a military occupation he had the remotest intention of accepting its implications. Indeed he was even more anxious to pull out than he had been to plunge in, and in this intention he had for once the solid backing of his Cabinet. But it proved no more easy to find a practicable path of return than for the lobster who has crawled his way into the fisherman's pot. The Khedive's Government, with no other support in the country but that of the occupying army, would have collapsed as soon as that army departed, leaving a vacuum of anarchy that some other European Power would no doubt have hastened to fill, thereby acquiring control over the life-line to India. And that was a contingency that even the least imperially minded of British Governments dared not envisage.

Cui bono? Here was Britain sitting tight on her unwished-for conquest because she dared not rise and abandon it, and France, standing by glaring in impotent fury because, after she had at the last moment drawn back and refused to have part or lot with her British partner in the enforcement of their disrupted joint control, Britain had gone in and enforced it alone, thereby turning it into what was in effect a single control. France's sudden access of cold feet had been due to her fear of playing Bismarck's game by allowing herself to be diverted from her quest of her lost provinces into this Egyptian adventure, and yet by her very refusal she had played straight into his hands, and involved herself in a quarrel with her English neighbour, that was to outlast the century and was to bring them to the brink of an actual war that would have redounded to no one's advantage but Germany's, and would have confirmed her till the Greek Calends in the enjoyment of her ill-gotten gains.

Had Gladstone been capable of accepting the consequences of his own action, he might have simplified Britain's self-imposed task of holding her latest conquest, by going the whole imperial hog and causing her to assume at least the protectorate if not the sovereignty of Egypt. This would have so suited Bismarck's book that it would have been fairly safe to count on his diplomatic 'all clear'. But the apostle of freedom and Christian morality, who had not been in the least put out of his stride by the deaths of thousands of Egyptians incidental to his successfully launched invasion, having broken all these eggs in the process of making his imperial omelette, had now no other thought than to unscramble them as soon as practicable. There was no conscious hypocrisy in this attitude. By some thought process not too easy to formulate, he believed that he could still hold fast to his Liberal integrity. The idea of adding another patch of British red to the map of Africa would have genuinely shocked and scandalized him. He seems to have imagined that in some way or another it would be possible to nurse Egypt back into a condition in which it would be safe to leave her to stand on her own feet, under a duly reformed administration, unpropped by British bayonets.

But whatever hope of this there might have been, had been conditional on the assumption that the situation thus stabilized could be prevented from deteriorating still further. But the application of force to the crazy structure of the Egyptian polity had set up repercussions of an unforeseen kind. For Egypt, under her Turkish Khedives, had taken to herself an empire of vast extent, stretching down nearly to the equator, which she sought to govern, or rather exploit, through the agency of pashas who were as incompetent as they were tyrannous, and depended for their authority on the prestige value of Egyptian soldiers who, when put to the test, proved incapable of retaining even the use of their legs, let alone that of their arms. And the effect of the rout and dissolution of the home army on the warlike tribes of this 'Land of Blacks', or Sudan, had been to precipitate a general revolt under the leadership of a Mahdi, or self-proclaimed Messiah, with which the Khedive's forces on the spot were powerless to cope.

This was a situation for which the British Government had been utterly unprepared, and though it had come about as the result of their own action, they tried to wash their hands of all responsibility for it, and instead of giving a firm directive to their puppet Khedive, whom they were prepared to help neither with men nor money, that he had got to draw in his imperial horns and leave the Sudan to work out its own destinies, they allowed him to persist, with oriental fatalism, in the hopeless task of trying to reconquer it. The immediate result was that a so-called army of over ten thousand half-starved and unpaid peasants in uniform, under an English colonel, were sent out from the capital, Khartoum, to look for the Mahdi and to be duly massacred to the last man by the first wild rush of his Allah-drunken spearmen.

It was now evident to everybody concerned that nothing but British intervention would save the Sudan for Egypt, and since no European financial interests were threatened by the Mahdi as they had been by Arabi, Mr Gladstone was free to arrive at the congenial and economical conclusion that here at least was a case of a people rightly struggling to be free. Consequently there was nothing for it but for Egypt to abandon her empire and retire within her own proper frontiers on the Lower Nile.

Yes—but what was to become of the Egyptian garrisons isolated at different points of that vast territory? To abandon them to perish miserably would seem rather too cynical an expedient, and yet to get them out, with the Mahdi sweeping everything before him, was easier said than done. It was at this point that Gladstone bethought him of the expedient of invoking a *deus ex machina*. One was at hand in the person of General Charles Gordon, whom his contemporaries had come to regard, with no sarcastic implications, in the light of a Christian hero. And though his original title to fame had been founded on the not-too-obviously Christian exploit of putting down a popular revolt in China against a corrupt and decaying autocracy, he must be allowed to have earned his reputation by his subsequent work as the Khedive's Viceroy for the Sudan itself, where he had performed prodigies of dedicated valour against the slave trade, a cause that the Victorians enthused over for his own sake, and without any afterthought of imperial interests.

Gordon would not have been Gordon had he hesitated for a moment about accepting the assignment in the spirit that had enabled him to surmount so many apparent impossibilities, but he was too practical a realist not to have it borne in on him, as soon as he got into touch with the actual situation, that the means did not exist for the cheap and bloodless evacuation that he had been sent out to effect. He had not the faintest conception of political expediency, and never doubted that those who had sent him out were actuated by the same simple good faith as he was, and would allow him the necessary latitude to act according to what he conceived to be the spirit of his instructions, where the letter failed.

The one chance that he could use of fulfilling a task that was now fantastically beyond his resources was to stake everything on the admitted gamble of putting up a certain Zobeir Pasha, a powerful slave-trading chieftain whose son Gordon had executed, and who himself was held honourably interned in Egypt, as the one man strong enough to rally the Sudanese against the Mahdi for long enough to allow the departure of the garrisons, after which they could be left, in Gordon's phrase, 'as God placed them'. It was such an expedient as only a realist, and a realist of genius, could have thought up, for saving what could be saved from the wreck of the Egyptian Empire, without involvement of the occupying Power, and it had the backing of the British representative at Cairo, Sir Evelyn Baring. Gladstone himself, if he could have had his way, would have been fain to adopt it, but the proposal was calculated to arouse such pious or interested opposition in the House of Commons and the Cabinet itself, that it had to be

I

dropped as politically inexpedient. The result of this decision had the effect of a death sentence on the doughtiest practical opponent of slavery of his generation. For Gordon, whose sense of military and Christian honour did not permit him to save his own life by abandoning to their fate those whom he had gone out to save, once he had taken up his post at Khartoum as Governor-General of the Sudan, could only stay to be cut off and stand a siege, to which, failing relief by his own countrymen, there could be only one end.

Gladstone thus found his hand forced in Egypt for a second time, which explains why his reaction to Gordon was hardly less bitter than that against Arabi. Indeed his real feelings are sufficiently indicated by his considered opinion, vouchsafed to a colleague years after the event, 'that it is harder to justify our doing so much to rescue him than our not doing more',[1] which would seem to imply that the harassed Premier regarded the elimination of the Christian hero by the Mahdi with hardly more feelings of regret than he would have that of the rebel Arabi by the good offices of the Khedive. And whatever our own reactions may be, it is a point of view that is at least understandable.

The often but never too often told story of the months of bickering and havering that delayed the launching of the ultimately inevitable relief expedition until it had become a forlorn hope, of the heroic and heroically resisted forced march across the desert, and the final dash up the river in 'penny steamers' that brought relief just two days after the town had fallen and Gordon perished, are events of an interest unsurpassed by that of any epic or saga since the dawn of history, but it is just that dramatic interest that confers on them the greater part of their historic value.

For before the personality and fate of Gordon had captured the imagination of the British public, from the Queen downwards, there had been no marked disposition to regard the occupation of Egypt as more than a temporary expedient, and it was generally assumed that evacuation would follow in due course, and the sooner the better. But now the name of Egypt was threatening to become a patriotic reaction stimulus only secondary to that of India. To evacuate it, at any rate before the Mahdi's power had been broken and Gordon avenged, would have been regarded by the man in the street or public house in the light almost of a personal humiliation, and though the official British attitude was still as decided as ever on the resolve to quit Egypt at the first opportunity, to put it into effect had become little short of a psychological impossibility.

And indeed feeling had been worked up to such a pitch by what an overwhelming majority of the nation, led by the Queen—who

[1] Ibid., Vol. III, p. 169.

publicized her opinion of her Prime Minister by a scathing telegram *en clair*—regarded as the betrayal of a great and good man, that it seemed almost impossible for the Government, if it were to survive at all, to call off the expedition it had launched so unwillingly, and whose declared objective was now no longer in existence. To withdraw now would be to drain the cup of humiliation to the dregs. The least that could be expected was that the invincible Wolseley, whom no one thought of blaming for the delay, should be allowed to go on with his belated but glorious campaign until the Mahdi's power had been smashed and Gordon avenged. That this would have involved a full-scale war for the reconquest of a vast and useless territory for the Khedive and his unspeakable pashas was what nobody considered and few realized. It was the common Englishman in his most intractable mood of refusing to give best to his opponent in a fight after receipt of a bloody nose. It is hard to see how Gladstone's, of all Governments, could have done anything so openly un-Gladstonian as to have embarked on such a course, and yet it seemed almost impossible that they could have remained in office on any other terms.

But at this juncture fate intervened, to give them the chance of doing the trick, by diverting patriotic bellicosity into another and more familiar channel. The tension that had been generated in the previous decade by the Near Eastern crisis had left public opinion in Britain acutely sensitive to the menace of a Russian advance towards the Indian frontier, especially as few people in England had more than the vaguest idea of the real geographical factors involved, barring a few impressive-sounding names on maps. One of these was Herat, which had been brought into prominence by an alarming pamphlet entitled *The Russians at the Gates of Herat*, which had created a general impression that this remote city, which had only recently passed into the nominal possession of the rulers of Afghanistan, was in some way the key to that country, and therefore, at second remove, the key to India, and that Muscovite designs on it were to be resisted at all costs. When the creeping advance of Russian expansion had overlapped the Turcoman oasis of Merv, it produced such jitters among a British public that had only the vaguest idea where or what Merv might be, as to lead to the temporary coinage of a word—'mervousness'. And now a place that nobody had ever heard of before, called Pendjeh, which was understood to be somewhere on the vaguely defined northern frontier of Afghanistan, suddenly blazed into the news.

A trigger-happy Russian commander on the spot had ordered the local Afghan forces to retire behind what he claimed to be their proper frontier, and on their refusal had proceeded to drive them out at the bayonet's point. It was an obviously indefensible action, but the sort of border clash that is only too liable to occur when barbarian and semi-barbarian forces are in contact, and the situation was aggravated by the refusal of the Tsar's Government, which was on the worst of terms with England, to make the least concession or withdrawal.

The place was of no strategic importance, and the Ameer, who was at least as much concerned to keep his English backers, as his Muscovite attackers, at arm's length, was not disposed to make heavy weather of the incident; but it detonated a blind fury among the civilian population of Britain, who, on being informed that Pendjeh lay midway between Merv and Herat, thought their worst fears realized.

One might have imagined that Gladstone of all people would have exerted himself to lower this temperature, and to counsel patience, in preference to sabre-rattling, at least until the possibilities of diplomatic action had been exhausted. But to think thus would have been to ignore the repercussions of the domestic situation. The Government had got itself into such a pickle in Egypt—and for that matter with the electorate at home—that it is doubtful whether anything short of a popular war scare could have got them out of it. The card was at any rate played, and it proved a winner. Gladstone came out with a defiance of Russia that would have appalled Disraeli in his most flamboyant mood. He made one of the most impressive orations of his career, in which he worked up to the ominous climax: 'All I say is, we cannot . . . close this book and say "We will look into it no more".' [1]

And lest there should be any doubt as to his meaning, he demanded, and got, from a now enthusiastically united House of Commons, the then substantial war credit of eleven million pounds. Never had there been a more extraordinary political transformation. The politician who had barely been able to retain the support of his own party and who had become the target of an execration more reminiscent of the days of Walpole or Wilkes than anything in Victorian times (his popular epithet of the 'G.O.M.' [2] was inverted into M.O.G.—'Murderer of Gordon') had blossomed out, as if by magic, into the patriot statesman, rallying his country against a gigantic challenger, and quite literally out-jingoing 'Jingo', for it was now no longer 'they shan't have Constantinople', but—to descend from the sublime to the ridiculous—'they shan't have Pendjeh'.

Under this martial smoke-screen, it proved the easiest thing in the world to withdraw the British forces quietly from their campaign against the Mahdi, on the plea that their services were likely to be required against a mightier foe.

It may charitably be assumed that for once the master spellbinder was the master and not the slave of his eloquence. The Tsar, though no doubt out to cause all the trouble he conveniently could to the

[1] Ibid., Vol. III, p. 184.
[2] 'Grand Old Man', it seems hardly necessary to say.

detested British, had no serious thoughts of marching with fire and sword over the Himalayas into India, or even through the gates of Herat. The dispute soon resolved itself into the customary diplomatic haggle. The 'book' was quietly closed, and the Bear did get Pendjeh after all without anybody being very much the wiser, or the worse for it.[1] But the pass behind it, which was all that mattered, remained, and still is, in Afghan hands. The war scare subsided as quickly as it had arisen, but not before its political fruits had been duly harvested and the tottering Government had got another brief lease of life.

But graver issues were involved than those that determine the calculations of party Whips and organizers. At both ends of the African continent forces had been set in motion that were to transform the world situation, not so much by the deliberate policy of this ill-starred administration, and still less by the Liberal principles with which it was formally identified, as by its signal failure to follow any principled line of policy whatever in matters that lay outside the essentially insular, or, at widest, European scope of its own vision or that of its now venerable chieftain. Gladstone, one feels, was concerned to the depths of his soul about the fate of Ireland, and he was even capable of working himself into a frenzy about the Christian peoples in the Balkans, but his now hardening mind had scarcely registered the existence of the Transvaal, and he did not want to be bothered more than he could help by the affairs of Egypt. And consequently he failed to go all out in applying his own declared principles to problems that he was more inwardly concerned to shelve than to solve.

When one turns back to the printed record of the one or two supreme oratorical masterpieces that were the highlights of his Midlothian campaign, one cannot but feel how very little the principles there laid down, of peace, non-aggression, international co-operation and righteous dealing, are in any way accountable for the frustrations and disasters that came not from the attempt, but the failure of him who had constituted himself their evangelist to put them into practice.

It requires no straining of the imagination to figure out how easily these troubles might have been avoided, had the same Gladstonian formula been applied with what now seems obvious consistency, first by the prompt restoration to the Transvaal Boers of their cherished independence, and secondly by a rigid abstention from armed involvement in the affairs of Egypt, except in the highly improbable event of a direct Egyptian threat to the freedom of the international waterway, and then only to the extent deemed necessary to safeguard it. And if this had involved leaving the bond-holders to digest the consequences of their own cupidity, that would have been infinitely preferable, by

[1] On the excellent map in *The Oxford Atlas* it is not even marked on the frontiers of Afghanistan.

every Liberal or Gladstonian reckoning, to combining the roles of bailiff and highwayman by compelling not the original borrower but his unhappy people to stand and deliver the uttermost farthing at pistol-point. It was as simple as all that, and this double divergence from the way of British liberty into that of its imperial antithesis was destined to set on foot a train of consequences that might quite conceivably have proved not only troublesome but fatal.

The virus of empire, we might say, had been injected into her system by the hand, of all others, from which it could least have been predicted, and only when it had run its course could it be sweated out. But in a system long inoculated against it, the attack might be no more than superficial. Even so, the element of mortal danger could not be positively excluded.

BOOK FIVE

1

FIN DE SIÈCLE

IT IS HARD, in this seventh decade of the twentieth century, to recapture the atmosphere of an epoch so fantastically different as that which coined for itself the style of *fin de siècle*, without having actually lived through it—and best of all having done so as a boy—for there was something peculiarly naïve and schoolboyish about its prevailing spirit of rumbustious optimism, as if Britain had in some way contrived to hit, by anticipation, on the talismanic formula of 'every day and every way I get better and better'—which was assumed to amount to the same thing as bigger and bigger.

The establishment and culmination of this spirit can be dated respectively with some approach to precision by Queen Victoria's two Jubilees of 1887 and 1897, which were, in effect, deliberate national acts of self-congratulation. The little old lady in the widow's weeds emerged from her quarter of a century's hibernating seclusion to play the part of a crowned goddess, an imperial mascot, at once grandmotherly and record-breaking, from whose stage personality, largely of her own creation, the traits of an unaccommodatingly masterful individuality had been successfully eliminated. As the leading lady of the nation she had at least come to achieve as unqualified a triumph as the great Elizabeth, though it had taken more than the length of that predecessor's whole reign for her to hit upon her true *métier*.

It was Disraeli who had coached her for the part, and who had dedicated her to it by putting an imperial crown on her head. But her first appearance in it had been too un-British an innovation to command more than a dutifully perfunctory applause, tempered by considerable head-shaking, from an audience not yet capable of being worked up into a fever heat of an empire-consciousness of which only the premonitory symptoms were as yet to be detected. But at the time of the first Jubilee, though we may perhaps suspect a certain heightening of temperature, there was no suggestion as yet of the delirious condition that developed in the closing years of the century, and was at its peak at the time of her second Jubilee.

255

It was but natural that the nation should have united to honour its now venerable Sovereign under whose auspices it had made such miraculous progress, and only human that it should, in the process, have worked itself up into an ecstasy of self-admiration at its achievement in the space of half a century. But the main emphasis was as yet national and even insular. The enlargement of the Queen's dominions was accorded a sober recognition, but no more, in the celebrations, and the popular attitude was sufficiently indicated by Tenniel's double-page cartoon in *Punch*, in which the Queen's triumphal chariot is flanked by four majestic-looking knights in armour, representing England, Scotland, Ireland and Wales, with two dusky Indian magnificos bringing up the rear, and on the side of the cavalcade an uncouth-looking rider, with an enormous beard beneath a slouch hat, holding up the staff of a pennon bearing the legend *Colonies*.

It is true that this Jubilee did play its part in enhancing the Home public's awareness of the existence and potentialities of what were still thought of as rather barbarous and primitive, if commendably virile, offshoots of the native stock. A movement was already on foot, and a powerfully supported League already in being, for uniting them in some sort of federation to which the word 'imperial' was attached without too nice a regard to any other implication than that of bigness. The occasion was deemed convenient for assembling their leading representatives, who had converged on London for the festivities, in what was modestly styled a colonial conference, with the idea of working out some sort of practical scheme of partnership, but except for some insignificant minor adjustments, it soon became apparent that there was nothing doing or to be done beyond the exchange of platitudes. Colonial loyalty did not extend to the least compromise with colonial freedom, nor, when it came to the point, were these already jealously self-conscious young nations ready to tie their hands in any way. This was a feature of the situation that was slow to dawn upon ardent advocates of empire, but like it or not, there it was, and as far at least as three of the four nascent dominions were concerned, their right to stand aside from anything remotely capable of being, in anything but name, a British Empire, was, even at the height of the imperialist fever, tacitly conceded. The freedom of the fourth, where the alternative to a British appeared to be a non-British empire, might be less easily conceded. Even thus early it was becoming apparent that South Africa might be capable of striking as jarring a note in the imperial symphony as was too plainly audible from Ireland, above the blare and flourish of the Jubilee overture.

But it would be premature to speak of the first Jubilee as ushering in an epoch of conscious imperialism. In itself, as I have tried to show, it was not, like its Diamond successor ten years later, primarily an advertisement of 'the Empire on which the sun never set'. It is true that a variety of converging influences had been working to impart an imperial bias to the national psychology, but it would have been premature to speak of their having made a conquest of it—so far.

It was not only that the cult of Empire had found such eloquent evangelists in their respective lines as Dilke, Froude and the Cambridge Professor of Modern History, Seeley, whose lectures on *The Expansion of England*, published in book form in 1883, attained so phenomenal a success as to demonstrate the ripeness of the educated public for such pabulum. These surface phenomena were indicative of a deeper change of thought and feeling, an undermining of moral foundations. What we usually mean when we talk of the Victorian age, which was at its height in the fifties and sixties, had already, in the last two decades of the century, begun to merge into something more aptly hit off by the epithet 'Edwardian', which signified a relaxed abandonment of that intense preoccupation with the moral aspect of everything that had pervaded every department of life from the Court downwards and made every matter, public or individual, a matter of principle.

Now there is one thing we can say with certainty about the application of moral principle to the practice of international politics. It is, by its very nature, anti-imperialistic. The cult of empire is necessarily the sublimation of immorality. Its informing spirit is one of power; might is its right, and power its principle. And as far as it is consistent, it seeks to enlarge the scope of its power in the spirit of uninhibited realism expounded by Machiavelli, and practised by such master technicians as Cavour and Bismarck. But Victorian public opinion had expected British statesmanship to conform to higher standards than those of naked power politics, and—at least before the advent of Disraeli—not in vain.

Even the raffish and bullying Palmerston had stood forth in the eyes of his countrymen as the generous champion of liberty and challenger of tyrants everywhere, and it was in pursuit of such principles, and certainly not of any selfish or imperialistic aims, that the ordinary Englishman had allowed himself to be worked up into the Crimean War fever. And the leaders of the Manchester school, who had opposed that war, and earned all the greater respect in the long run from having done so, were uncompromisingly pacific and found a mighty champion of their principles in Gladstone. Indeed the gospel of free trade, which had become a sort of national orthodoxy, was the direct negation of imperialism and power politics, and had tended to regard a British empire in the light of a liability rather than an asset. It had been seriously believed that the world would be prepared to follow Britain's lead in the peaceful and profitable exchange of goods and services, and

*I

come to realize the advantage of turning swords into ploughshares as a simple business proposition no less than an obvious moral one.

Periods of tension, and particularly of moral tension, are in the normal course of events liable to be followed by those of compensatory relaxation, and it is not altogether surprising that towards the close of the century there should have been a fairly wide tendency, particularly in advanced circles, to discard or debunk the ostentatious rigidity of Victorian moral standards, and even to revolt against any ethical intrusion whatever, not only in the aesthetic but even the political sphere. This, in itself, might have represented a tendency like that of primitive Christianity, to supersede the letter of the law by the freedom of the spirit. But it might also have the effect of removing the last inhibitions from a spirit as positively evil as one of those sealed-up djinns in the Arabian Nights whose escape was fraught with such sinister consequences.

And as far as we can identify as evil, or, in the Miltonic sense, Satanic, the militant pursuit of their own power by individuals or communities as the sole sufficient end of all human endeavour, we can say that such a spirit had been gaining strength on the Continent ever since the collapse of the Liberal idealism that had seemed on the verge of triumphing in the revolutions of 1848, and towards which both policy and public opinion in Britain had been openly, if not always actively, sympathetic. But even in Britain signs had been manifest of an incipient tendency to turn her back on those high and generous traditions of freedom that had come to be regarded as her peculiar heritage, in favour of the hard realism of imperial power politics.

Realism, however, is the last thing one would have been inclined to predicate of the great proto-evangelist of this cult in Britain. Thomas Carlyle had been an inspired man if there ever was one, and with something of the force of a major prophet; but the intensity of a force is no guarantee of its beneficence, and it may be questioned whether it had ever occurred to him to doubt the divine credentials of the spirits to whose afflatus he spread his sails, and that had turned him from one of the most humane and human of social critics into a worshipper of power for its own sake, with a positively sensual delight in the spectacle of armed might triumphing ruthlessly over right or, what signified even more from the English standpoint, over rights of every description. The worst frightfulness that had ever been recorded of, or alleged against, Cromwell became Carlyle's precise reason for applauding him, and the cynical consistency of the godless Frederick of Prussia in making evil his good provided Carlyle with the opportunity of writing up his career into what—if the word had been coined—would have stood for an epic of the superman. And it is no accident that almost the last of his public pronouncements had been an impressive plea for the tearing by the Prussian military clique of two provinces from the body of prostrate France. Thus early had the seeds been sown that were to ripen to the harvest of *fin de siècle* imperialism, and it would be hard to set limits to the influence of this dyspeptic, neurotic and perhaps sexually impotent man of genius, with his Teutonized idiom, in undermining the moral foundations on which the architects of the Victorian age, with all their faults and failures, had sought to build.

As early as 1865 a significant episode had showed how deeply this infection had bitten. The island of Jamaica, the overwhelming majority of whose inhabitants consisted of emancipated slaves, had fallen on lean times from a variety of causes, and the resulting discontents had been exacerbated by the bullying methods of the Governor, Eyre, one of those intensively tough characters whom the conditions of pioneer life in virgin colonies are apt to produce—he had been the most intrepid of the explorers of central Australia. A riot had broken out on a corner of the island in which a score or so of whites had perished, but which prompt military action had put down without difficulty. Eyre, however, with one or two officers of like kidney, determined to stage an exhibition of frightfulness on which Himmler himself could hardly have improved. The only excuse or explanation had been the obsessive horror excited by the Indian Mutiny, and the fixed notion that only a strong man, with the freest hand to strike terror into all and sundry of a native population, could avert a repetition of all the horrors of Cawnpore. In all over six hundred blacks were hanged or otherwise disposed of by way of reprisal, and as many more flogged, including numbers of women.[1]

The report of these proceedings excited the greatest indignation among liberally disposed circles in England, and a committee was formed under the chairmanship of John Stuart Mill, which comprised such eminent members as John Bright, Herbert Spencer, Huxley, Goldwin Smith, Frederic Harrison and Thomas Hughes, with the object of calling Eyre to account. And it was not surprising that Carlyle should have incontinently plunged into the fray on behalf of an exponent of ruthlessness on a heroic scale, who had the supreme merit of operating on what the Sage of Chelsea was in the habit of contemptuously referring to as 'niggers', and as such excluded from the pale of human justice or even mercy. That, of Carlyle, was only to be expected, but a more disquieting pointer to things to come had been that such universally respected figures as those of Tennyson, Ruskin, Kingsley and Dickens should have lined up on the same side.

I have permitted myself this glance back at what, by the time of the

---

[1] See J. H. Eyre, in *The Dictionary of National Biography*, Suppt. II.

Jubilee, was an almost forgotten episode, because it shows how deep-seated were the forces that had been gathering below the surface, and which were to erupt into the open imperialism of the *fin de siècle*. The Eyre affair had ended in the typically common-sense British solution of allowing the delinquent Governor to fade out under a cloud into a not uncomfortable retirement, without either further employment or the dignity of a martyr's crown, and Carlyle had found peace at last in the kirkyard at Ecclefechan; but a fire once started needs little stoking, and the cult of strength for its own sake and success as its own justification, that his influence had done so much to kindle, was encroaching more and more on the freedoms and decencies of Victorian morality.

It had gained added strength from a new influence against which Carlyle himself had revolted, that emanating from the theory of biological evolution sponsored by Darwin in his revolutionary treatise on the origin of species. There was no reason why a working hypothesis, brilliant and fruitful as it might be in the context of one particular science, should ever have been dragged out of that context, and made the basis of an all-embracing faith or code of ethics; and Darwin himself, a biologist pure and simple, had never dreamed of anything so absurd. But by a combination of muddled and passionate thinking masked as scientific, and appropriately finding its most powerful European propagandist in the more than doubtfully sane Nietzsche, the conditional mood of a purely biological hypothesis was transformed [1] into the dogmatic imperative of a new morality purporting to be subversive of all morals, and as such beyond good and evil—which, as far as it means anything, would seem to signify,

> Fair is foul and foul is fair,
> Hover through fog and filthy air!

The Nietzchean superman found his ultimate embodiment in the totalitarian dictators.

We are speaking of tendencies that in their very nature are undefinable and whose influence at any given time we must be careful not to overestimate in the light of later events. Though the rumpus about the Darwinian theory was already, in the eighties, of long standing, it still, in its English setting, mainly took the form of a rearguard action fought by the mostly reverend champions of the Mosaic account of creation against these new subversive theories that were undermining the foundations of faith, and said to be degrading God's image to monkey-house level. But it had hardly yet begun to undermine the foundations of Victorian morality. Not many people in England had

---

[1] Not, however, by Huxley who, with his sturdy nonconformist conscience, came out boldly on the side, if not of the angels, at least that of the moralists.

heard of Nietzsche in the year 1889, which was that of his translation into an asylum—and also that of the birth of his disciple Adolf Hitler. But his influence was growing on the Continent, where its grosser elements of ruthlessness and predatory violence, combined with an exaltation of the Aryan 'blond beast'—easily equated with the Teutonic master man—only too readily fitted in with existing and inherited tendencies. It is worth noting that Nietzsche's last of several compilations of oracular outpourings should have been entitled *The Will to Power*.

That will, which was also the will to empire, was more and more coming to be the sole impelling force in international politics during the last quarter of the nineteenth century. But Britain, which had been, or believed herself to be, actuated by an ideal of peaceful co-operation and developing freedom, had hitherto managed to preserve an attitude detached from the conflicting imperialisms and power politics of her continental neighbours. But it was a question of how much longer she would be able to avoid being herself sucked into the imperialistic maelstrom.

2

AFRICAN SHARE-OUT

SINCE THE achievement of some semblance of European equilibrium by the union of Germany and that of Italy, things had been shaping more and more ominously from the British standpoint. The vision of a free interchange of goods and services binding the nations together in bonds of mutual advantage, which had seemed almost in sight of realization under the inspiration of enthusiasts like Cobden, was proving a mirage. The European Powers were tending more and more to build up their own industries behind high barriers of protective tariffs. This meant that the commercial advantages that Britain had derived from her invasion-proof insularity, and which had accounted for her unexampled prosperity in the third quarter of the century, were no longer to be taken for granted. She was ceasing to be the workshop of the world, and was forced to compete with rival workshops of superior capacity. And with her own agriculture ruined, as it had been by the series of bad harvests in the late seventies, and by competition from virgin lands overseas against which her free trade dogma forbade her to protect herself, she was now more and more coming to depend on what she could persuade foreigners to give her in exchange for the products of her teeming industrial population. In all the paeans of self-congratulation at the Jubilee this element of the situation was discreetly passed over, but already the danger signs might have been sufficiently visible to anyone not blinded by optimism.

And it was no doubt an instinctive apprehension of these accumulating stresses and frustrations that engendered a desire to open out new fields for commercial exploitation in parts of the globe hitherto unappropriated—fields moreover that were liable to be grabbed up by rival Powers who would promptly enclose them and monopolize their products. And the most obvious and almost inevitable field for such exploitation was presented by the interior of the African continent, which up to a very recent date had been indicated on the maps by a blank, relieved only by the presence of what the cartographers impressively styled *The Mountains of the Moon*. And just as under

Disraeli's auspices the mention of Empire was enough to turn the ordinary Englishman's thoughts in the direction of India, so now, in the two last decades of the century, the focus of imperial interest had shifted to what was still styled the Dark Continent.

It would however be a mistake to imagine that even as late as the Jubilee there was any significant British hankering after imperial expansion in Africa. Indeed the Victorians had been more desirous of cutting down than of enlarging their comparatively few African commitments, mainly in the shape of footholds on the seaboard, which they tended to look upon in the light of unprofitable superfluities, and on which they grudged spending a single penny of the taxpayer's money. Indeed there is little doubt that they would have abandoned them altogether had they consulted merely their own economic interests, but their main concern was of a different and more generous kind, and no crusade of the Middle Ages had commanded a more enthusiastic backing of public support than that against the slave trade did in Victorian England. It is true that it was partly motivated by an element of narrow and puritanical fanaticism, summed up in the phrase 'Exeter Hall', which was seldom referred to except by such sneer words as 'boom', 'bellow' and 'bray'; but Exeter Hall, with all its faults, did stand for an ideal of high and disinterested philanthropy that is not common in shaping the policy of nations, and a policy that kept a sizable proportion of the British Navy, year in and year out, engaged in unhealthy and unspectacular patrol work was something more than a mere pious gesture. And it was this that tilted the balance in favour of hanging on to any *pied à terre* on the long African coastline, rather than any calculation of material advantage.

Nor was this spirit necessarily outdated when, thanks to the efforts of a few heroic pioneers—for the third quarter of the century might have been described as the heroic age of African exploration—the interior of the continent at last ceased to be a *terra incognita*, and became a land of limitless opportunity. But we should be doing our Victorian fathers wrong if we were to imagine that their first impulse was to regard it as a mere field of commercial exploitation or imperial expansion. That was far from being the spirit of the greatest explorer of all, David Livingstone, who was possessed by as pure a missionary fervour as Paul of Tarsus, and by an utterly unselfish and fully reciprocated devotion to the welfare (in every sense of the word) of the native tribes among whom he fared, and whom he sought to bring into the Christian fold. But Livingstone was enough of a practical Scot to realize that the European trader, as well as the evangelist, had his part to play in rescuing these primitive folk from the desperate straits into which they had fallen.

For the slave trade was an endemic disease, rotting away the body and soul of a population that had come to be looked on as so much raw material for its markets. And though the Christian share in its guilt had at last, largely owing to the unceasing British efforts, been more or less eliminated—though not till the middle of the sixties—the Mahommedan peoples of the Near East had taken it up with enthusiasm, and pursued it with an organized cruelty that rivalled the palmiest Western records. It cannot be too clearly realized that the effect of this abominable traffic had been to destroy any chance of the free development of native life even on the tribal level, and besides the state of terror and misery that was created over the whole vast area of the operation of the system, it encouraged the rise of ferocious native tyrants who themselves co-operated with the slavers. It would have been no exaggeration to apply the description of the Hebrew prophet to the greater part of Africa:

The whole head is sick, and the whole heart faint. From the sole of the foot even unto the head there is no soundness in it; but wounds, and bruises and putrifying sores: they have not been closed, neither bound up, neither mollified with ointment.—Isaiah i. 5-6.

At least a plausible case could have been made out for saying that things had reached such a pass that only the strong arm of a European conqueror could have stricken enough order out of this chaos to provide the minimum prerequisites of a tolerable native existence. When we talk of the scramble for Africa, it is only fair that we should bear this in mind. The black man was in urgent need of a breathing space, or period of tutelage, before there could be any question of his working out his own salvation. And even when the motives of his white brother in providing him with this were little more disinterested than those of the slave traders themselves, the black man stood to gain on the balance.

But as regards Britain, there can be no question of the disinterested sincerity both of her African policy and of its backing by public opinion—at least in its opening stages. She was not in the least concerned to carve out an empire there, but she was very actively concerned indeed to bring to completion the long campaign she had waged against this foul thing by which, in past generations, her own hands had been stained. She had abolished it in her own dominions, including India, and she had been chiefly responsible for closing its Atlantic outlet; now she was determined to put a stranglehold on this latest development. There were no more universally applauded figures than those of her dedicated heroes, Livingstone and Gordon, and it was by a diplomatic *tour de force* that her representatives secured the closing by the Sultan of Zanzibar of the great slave market at Mombasa and the sealing off of the main outlet of the trade on the east coast. But as long as the interior remained a no man's land there would be no chance of making a clean end of so long established and profitable a business. Even so, it was no part of the British intention to take the lead in a share-out of African territory or to have part or lot in it.

So much, at least, could have been truthfully said up to the time that Gladstone's second Government had come into office at the beginning of the eighties, with its specifically anti-imperialist mandate. And then, as I have tried to show, that same Government had proceeded to take action at both ends of the African continent that had rendered British participation almost a matter of necessity. In South Africa the seeds had been sown of a racial conflict between British and Dutch, with the odds heavily weighted in favour of the latter. And even more serious had been the entanglement resulting from the act of reckless and single-handed aggression that had left Britain with an informally conquered Egypt on her hands, sitting with such comfort as she might on her own bayonets—and the longer she sat the more difficult it became for her to get up and go. However determined her Premier might be to preserve the façade of his Liberal integrity by refusing to accept the logical consequences of his own action, the logic of facts was not to be evaded. Britain was there, and after the spectacular heroism and humiliation of the Gordon tragedy it had become more than ever a point of national honour to stay there. Public opinion, that is not apt to draw nice distinctions of legality, was hardened in the conviction that 'we had *got* Egypt', and that to get out now would be, in the slang of the time, to 'scuttle'. And so for year after year Britain remained immovably in occupation, protesting her intention to evacuate at a date that came more and more, in practice, to suggest the Greek Calends.

The consequences, not only to herself, but to Europe, were of the most insidious and far-reaching nature. It must never be lost sight of that during all this period of the so-called armed peace the determining factor in the international situation had been the malignant tumour that had been planted in the body of Europe by the German rape of the two French provinces. Henceforth, as no one knew better than Bismarck, the peace imposed at Frankfurt was an armistice that would be denounced the moment the balance of military force had shifted sufficiently in favour of France to make her resumption of her territories a practical proposition. To prevent such a situation ever coming about had been his object in spinning a diplomatic web of matchless subtlety and entire absence of scruple. And nothing could have played into his hands more neatly than this ill-starred Egyptian adventure, which put Britain under the necessity of feeding out of Germany's hand, and for the rest of the century ruled any idea of a renewed French challenge out of practical possibility.

It might have been argued that France had only herself to thank for Britain's determination to go it alone in Egypt. But such logical detachment was not to be expected of human, and least of all of French, nature. Egypt had been marked out by France as her special preserve, to which first Napoleon, and latterly the cutting by a French engineer of the Suez Canal, had given her a sort of divine right, and that Britain had snapped it up under her very nose was rendered all the more maddening from the fact that France, in a moment of aberration, had in effect stepped aside and invited her to do so. Even France could not make an open grievance of Britain's entry in these circumstances, but that did not prevent her occupation from becoming a chronic irritant, and producing an attitude of nagging hostility to everything British all along the moving perimeter of French imperial expansion, and in particular an active determination to render Britain's anomalous position in Egypt intolerable. Thus was created a situation in which she, or her representative at Cairo, Sir Evelyn Baring (Lord Cromer), could carry on only by the calculated benevolence of Germany and her satellite Austria. It was the supreme triumph of Bismarck's diplomacy. His artificial creation of a Prussian-dominated Reich could tyrannize in absolute security over its conquered provinces, so long as the attention of their rightful owner was distracted to a perpetual quarrel with the island Power whose eventual alliance against the Caesar or Kaiser of a potential new Western empire it was essential for France to secure.

Best of all would it have been, from the German imperial stand-point, if the rivalry between Britain and France could have been exacerbated to the pitch of actual war. Then indeed the way might have been open for the achievement of an empire far beyond the scope of Bismarck's limited vision; for the old Junker desired nothing more than the peaceful perpetuation of the existing *status quo*. But if these rivals proceeded to commit *felo de se*—and they were to come to the verge of this—there can be little doubt that the event would have been welcome to so inveterate an opportunist, even if it formed no part of his programme. Meanwhile he would be pleased enough for Britain's entanglement in Egypt to keep her revolving in Germany's orbit, and for France's preoccupation with her own imperial ambitions and injured pride to wean her thoughts from troubles nearer home, and in time, perhaps, to put the spire of Strasbourg and the *glacis* of Metz out of her dream picture.

I am not concerned to record the successive stages by which, in the *fin de siècle*, nearly the whole of Africa came to be partitioned out between the various European Powers, but only to call attention to those aspects that directly bear on our main theme. It cannot be too clearly emphasized that, far from there having been the least disposition to take part in an imperialist scramble, the policy of successive British Governments had been to cut down imperial commitments to the barest limits of practicality. Even in respect of the Egyptian adventure, that was to prove the source of 'woes innumerable', no one can imagine that Gladstone would have been anything but horrified at the thought of acquiring that province for the British Empire. In his confused way he was unquestionably sincere in his asseverations of the purely temporary nature of the occupation. And he and his Foreign Secretary, Lord Granville, were notoriously determined to concede every possible point in dispute to rival claimants to territorial expansion.

This was conspicuously the case when Bismarck, in 1884, suddenly decided to reverse his previous policy, by equipping Germany with an overseas empire commensurate with her European importance. His motives have been variously conjectured, but it would seem that he was actuated less by any far-sighted calculations of statesmanship than by his desire to maintain his own precarious ascendancy over the kaleidoscopic mutations of the German political factions. Almost certainly, in his heart of hearts, he was no more a 'colonial man' than he had ever been, and would have preferred to see his new Reich perpetuating a stable equilibrium, with its central weight, of the European balance, without acquiring such dangerous and expensive luxuries; but once, with his unerring intuition of the trend of public opinion, he had sensed that German *amour propre* would be satisfied with nothing less, and consequently with no Chancellor who failed to deliver the goods, he bent all the resources of his diplomatic genius to supplying the belated demand.

He accordingly proceeded to pounce right and left on every area of African territory not formally annexed, with ostentatious disregard for the feelings and claims of Britain, within whose sphere of interest they had all hitherto lain. And to this brutally cavalier treatment Gladstone's Government submitted with hardly a murmur, though in one case at least, that of the far spread though arid acquisition of what became German South-West Africa, the occupation implied a deeply resented threat to a major British colony, that of the Cape. But quite apart from the known anti-imperialistic sentiments of the Liberal Government, nobody realized better than Bismarck that they were too dependent on his support for the crazy fabric of their Egyptian administration to resent any liberties he might choose to take with them in other parts of Africa. And Bismarck, for all his finesse, would not have been a Prussian unless he had been, to the limit of his capacity, a bully. It would have been entirely characteristic of him to argue that by causing Britain to eat dirt he would make her all the more ready to feed out of his hand in future.

It will be seen how far the British Liberal Government was from desiring part or lot in any game of African grab. Nor would there be any significant breach of continuity when Gladstone's heroic attempt to settle the perennial Irish problem by granting self-government to what in practice amounted to the Catholic majority, with the complete subjugation to it of the Protestant minority, split his own party and brought a Conservative administration into office, under which the control of foreign affairs passed from the feeble hands of Granville to the incomparably stronger ones of Salisbury. It would involve an even greater misconception of Salisbury than it would of Bismarck to think of him as an imperialist or, specifically, a 'colonial man'. He belonged to an older school of statesmanship, in the direct line of tradition from his Elizabethan forbears, William Cecil, Lord Burleigh and his son Robert, Earl of Salisbury. He was a supreme master of the technique of foreign policy, and in this his notions, in British translation, resembled those of Bismarck himself, and were static rather than expansionist. But at the same time, no less than Bismarck, he played to the score of the game, and where Britain's colonial interests were at stake he applied all his technical skill to see that she got her reasonable share of profit out of each particular transaction. But he showed hardly more eagerness than Gladstone himself to go in for expansion for its own sake, or to build up an enormous empire. Such ambitions would probably have impressed him as being tinged with a certain vulgarity.

To think of Britain, therefore, even in this epoch of expansion, as one of several competing imperialistic Powers, is to turn the real truth upside down. France, Germany, Russia, and potentially Italy, were in the fullest sense, and to the limit of their capacity, empires determined to enlarge the scope of their dominions by every means short of precipitating a major war—and even this condition might not be guaranteed to hold in perpetuity. Britain, on the other hand, as far as her official policy was concered, was—at least previously to the concluding half-dozen years of the century—more concerned to minimize than to multiply her commitments.

Even so, it may seem not far short of a miracle that, in what had become a game of international armed grab, the vast African interior did manage to get itself partitioned out without some collision precipitating a war whose extent and consequences none could foresee. But the fact is that, during these concluding years of the nineteenth century, none of the Powers concerned regarded that prospect with anything but effectually prohibitive aversion. France may have ostensibly substituted Britain for Germany as her enemy number one, but in the depths of her soul she was resolved never to be diverted from the supreme objective of recovering her own integrity. What was the loss of Suez, after all, compared with that of Strasbourg?

Nor is there any reason to doubt the entire sincerity of Bismarck when he described Germany as 'a saturated power'; and the whole intricate web of his diplomacy was spun in order to preserve the fabric of European peace on the basis of a *status quo* that he himself desired nothing better than to perpetuate; and even though he yielded to the spirit of the time so far as to humour the lust of his new Reich for the luxury of a colonial empire, there is not the least reason to suppose that this was an object for which he would willingly have risked having the weight of Britain thrown into the balance against Germany, by a challenge to a sea power that, unchallenged, held these new colonies as so many hostages for the peaceful behaviour of their occupier.

That safeguard of an invincible sea power was the factor of the situation that the statesmanlike intuition of Salisbury recognized as vital to the preservation of a peace that he knew to be more in Britain's interest to seek and ensue than any dream of empire. It explains why he was ready to go to all lengths, even so that of jettisoning the most brilliant member of his Cabinet (his Chancellor of the Exchequer, Lord Randoph Churchill) rather than abate one jot of necessary expense for the provision of a fleet unchallengeable by any Power or possible combination of Powers. So long as that fleet controlled the seaways, and the surface of the sea provided the only practicable path of transit from shore to shore, so long would it be an obviously unpaying proposition for any one of these Powers to plunge into hostilities about overseas possessions from which it could be cut off without the possibility of retaliation. And in the final decade of the century, thanks to successive increments of those last words in battle-ship construction, the 'Admirals', the 'Royal Sovereigns' and the 'Majestics', such a fleet was actually in being—and known to be.

Perhaps, though in a very unjingoistic sense, it would not have been so wide of the mark after all to have found the formula for world peace in the words of the song:

> We don't want to fight, but by Jingo if we do
> We've got the ships . . .

It is impossible in the nature of things to assign with any exactitude the proportionate weight of any of these various factors in enabling the African problem to straighten itself out to some sort of agreed solution, without any of the numerous occasions for conflict between its European partitioners coming to the point of actual explosion. But at least up to the advent of the third Salisbury Government in the closing years of the century, it can be said that Britain was a consistently unwilling participant in the share-out, and that to imagine her to have been bitten by an urge similar to that of her competitors for founding, or enlarging, a colonial empire, would be to fly in the face of facts. Time and again her governments demonstrated their willingness to go to the extreme limits of concession and conciliation, not always with too nice a regard to the interests of her own colonists, and however plausibly she might have laid herself open to the imputation of 'scuttle', malice itself could not tax her with anything remotely describable as 'grab'.

3

POWER ON A BUSINESS FOOTING

IT IS HARD to realize, in view of the notorious ebullition of imperial sentiment in the closing years of the nineteenth century, how slow the cult of empire had been to make any significant mass penetration of British consciousness, and even slower to acquire any determining influence on British policy. This applies hardly less to Conservative than to Liberal administrations, for Salisbury had none of Disraeli's romantic delight in the pomp and trappings of imperial power, and it is more than doubtful whether, of his own free choice, he would have sought to add another acre to Britain's already amply sufficient overseas estate; but events and people on the spot were forcing the pace of expansion and the hand of the home Government in the authentic British way, and it was not in Salisbury's nature to force his own side either to disgorge a once-harvested gain or retreat from any position once fairly occupied. The same obstinacy of the *fait accompli* that prevented him from making the least concession to the Irish demand for Home Rule kept him from any serious intention of freeing Britain at a date short of the Greek Calends from Gladstone's fatal legacy of the Egyptian occupation, with its consequent involvement in Nilotic imperialism by Khedival proxy.

None the less it would be premature to imagine that, during the six years of Conservative government that followed on the rejection of Gladstone's Home Rule Bill of 1886, imperial expansion had become a theme of more than secondary political interest. Indeed the electorate had markedly less attention to spare for the British Empire than under Disraeli's or even Gladstone's subsequent auspices. The Egyptian and Sudanese wars, with their thrills and tragedies, were in a state of suspended animation, and few knew or cared much about Cromer's long, thankless endeavour, under almost incredible difficulties, to clean up an Augean stable of misgovernment and corruption on the Lower Nile. Even the perennially expansive Bear had evinced no urgent inclination to renew his advances on the Afghan frontier; the gates of Herat remained closed and Indian affairs showed little tendency to come into the news. The complicated business of partitioning Africa, too, was one that the average Briton was content to leave in his Premier's safe hands without bothering too much about who got what of these outlandish regions. Such things probably did not turn a single vote at any by-election, still less get across the footlights of the halls. At no time during the century had political consciousness in Britain been less occupied with matters of wider than insular concern. Not even the flavour of imperial pageantry imparted to the Jubilee could effect more than a momentary diversion from a party contest that was more and more overshadowed by the all-absorbing Irish controversy, with its highlights of the Pigott forgeries and the Parnell divorce.

When Salisbury was at last fain to seek another mandate from the country in 1892, the Empire might not have existed for any difference it made to the result, which was about the most unsatisfactory conceivable. A Liberal Government came into office on a minority British vote, and depended entirely on the support of the Irish Nationalists; which meant that it would have to enact the solemn farce of wasting an entire session in forcing through the Commons a second Home Rule Bill that no one in his senses could ever have imagined would be allowed to pass into law. To this task Gladstone, who had worked himself up into a frenzy of obsessive exaltation passing all previous records, proceeded to apply himself in a *tour de force* of energy and inspiration unique at his age; though the measure itself took no more account than its predecessor of the now plainly signified determination of the Ulster Protestants to go to all lengths in resisting it. In the circumstances, when, after months of envenomed debate, the third reading was at last carried by an exiguous majority, the Upper Chamber could hardly have been expected to take any other course than that of rejecting it—as it did by a majority so overwhelming as to be effectually contemptuous. That it rightly interpreted the sense of the country was shown by the fact that Gladstone was not even able to get his colleagues to support him in appealing to it.

This ignominious refusal of so flaming a challenge, underlined by Gladstone's own resignation of the Premiership, proved fatal to the Government, but it was a victory even more fatal, in its ultimate effects, to the noble victors. For it kindled, in their not too bright intelligences, a spirit of arrogant insolence that led them to abandon their role, so recently defined by Gilbert, of 'doing nothing in particular and doing it very well', for that of militant alliance with one of the parties in the State, and a readiness to use all their hitherto latent powers of veto so as to render government by any other party, if not impossible, at least sterile—a tactic it might be possible to get away with against a discredited and unpopular Liberal administration, but which involved such an affront to every canon of parliamentary democracy as one would have thought that no hereditary body, not afflicted with suicidal mania, would have dared resort to as part of its normal procedure. And yet the amazing thing is that not even men of the intellectual calibre of the Cecils and Balfours should have shrunk from committing a party nominally conservative to this hare-brained gamble.

It scored a specious success, however, against the discredited and distracted administration, in which Gladstone had been replaced as Premier by Lord Rosebery, who had been chosen by the Queen mainly on account of imperialist sympathies that were conspicuously lacking in the most powerful of his colleagues. The peers, who had now dropped all pretence of impartiality, proceeded to apply their new technique of indiscriminate veto in such a way as to reduce his Government to such a state of helplessness that when it was forced to give up its Sisyphean task it was snowed under at the polls, and Salisbury was back in office at the head of the strongest administration of the reign.

It was stronger than ever from the fact that it no more existed by sufferance of the Liberal Unionists, as the Liberals were called who had seceded from the party in 1886 on the issue of Home Rule, without joining the Conservatives, which they now proceeded to do, in what started as a Unionist coalition but tended inevitably to become a reinforced Tory combination with a new infusion of personnel and quickening of spirit. The tendency of a party largely depending on the support of a foxhunting squirearchy was to live up, or down, to its name of 'conservative' in its most pejorative sense of inertia and stagnation. It was from this that Disraeli had striven to wean it to a progressive and creative policy both at home and overseas, and Randolph Churchill had tried to carry his work a stage further in his drive for Tory democracy, which had come to grief owing to Salisbury's stolid refusal to be hustled out of his stride. But now the exigencies of the new amalgamation freed the old marquis to reinforce his cabinet by the even more formidable personality of Joseph Chamberlain, whose left-wing Radicalism had been too much for even Gladstone to stomach and who was bound to impart his unequalled dynamism to any body of which he was a member. And Chamberlain, unlike such grown-up spoilt children as the irrepressible Randolph, had the successful business man's instinct for adjusting himself to partnership with even so temperamentally incongruous a senior as Salisbury, whose advancing years and huge frame rendered him less and less fitted for decisive self-assertion.

To those whose memory does not reach back to that time, it must be difficult to realize the extent to which this man's personality dwarfed, in the public eye, that of every colleague or rival during these concluding five years of the century. Just as nobody in the field of cricket talked of the champion as anything but 'W. G.', so in that of politics the Colonial Secretary was seldom referred to by any other name than that of 'Joe', and it was 'Joe' first and the rest nowhere. Like Henry Irving at the Lyceum, when he was on the stage he played everyone else off it. And before he had even entered the field of national politics he had, in his native city of Birmingham, set a wholly new standard of municipal government, transforming that dingy warren into a model-run city, and making such a name for himself that, after his disablement and even death, it was many years before the loyalty of its proletarian electorate to his dynasty and tradition was in the least degree shaken.

The character in which Chamberlain succeeded in putting himself over the footlights was one ideally adapted to the requirements of the *fin de siècle*. It was in no sense an endearing or sympathetic image that he sought to create of himself. Not for him the quasi-religious cult that invested that of the 'Grand Old Man', nor the pose of jolly John-Bullishness that had been Palmerston's speciality. Everything about 'Joe' was as incisive and clear-cut as the profile that even the most hostile caricaturists agreed in according him, which is that of an immaculate and monocled dandy, as much younger as the calendar showed him to be older than the whiskered demagogue whom his colleagues-to-be had formerly pilloried as Jack Cade. There was one exception to this unanimity. The intractable pencil of that *pictor subtilissimus*, Max Beerbohm, who had the unique faculty of putting his own vision on to paper without any reference to what his public had agreed to see, presented it with a Joseph unknown to that Pharaoh, one who might have passed for the vulgar quintessence of Brummagem plutocracy, with a hand tucked behind under his coat-tails and a smirk of self-satisfied cunning suffusing his features.

The fastidious Max was no doubt temperamentally averse to a character which admirers could join with opponents in designating by the epithet 'pushful', a characteristic word coinage of the time and one that if it had not been already in circulation might have been struck for Chamberlain, so exactly did it hit off the super-powered dynamism with which he had driven forward to one goal after another, equipping himself with a fat fortune as a preliminary, and applying American methods to the mechanization of British politics in the creation of the famous Birmingham caucus, a hitherto undreamed-of instrument for making the wills of the many pliable to the manipulation of the one—though in his hands at least it was directed to public-spirited ends. For it was here that Chamberlain differed most radically from the Trans-atlantic bosses whose technique he imported; he was neither corrupt, nor in the vulgar sense selfish; his will, even if he was prepared to go to unheard-of lengths for its realization, was, according to his lights, a good will. There is no questioning the sincerity of his patriotism.

Such was the man who, at the age of fifty-eight, and after a decade in the political wilderness, at last came at his own request into that same Colonial Office that he had vainly solicited from Gladstone fifteen years previously, and been turned down with an irritated ejaculation of 'Oh, a Secretary of State!'—for Gladstone cherished the same sort of temperamental aversion to this almost Jacobin upstart as his Sovereign harboured towards Gladstone. But these years of waiting are not necessarily to be written off as dead loss. Chamberlain's self-dedicated task had been to effect as revolutionary a development of the Empire as he had of his native city. He was instinctively drawn towards this as giving the widest possible scope for his boundlessly expansive will-power. And there was a sense in which it might have been said that the Empire, or what passed for it, was ripe for his ambition in 1895 as it had not yet become in 1880.

Certainly his advent to this long-coveted office could not have come at a more propitious moment for the party with whose fortunes he was now identified. It was one thing for the Unionist combination to have installed itself in office with a record majority; but he to whom much is given by the electorate, from him will much be required, and the makings of a positive policy were not to be found in a mere refusal to operate on a deep-seated tumour, which was all that Unionist policy really amounted to in its original and Irish significance. And even though an ultimately fatal crisis might be staved off in the sister island by such temporary palliatives as ingenuity might prescribe, signs were already apparent of another of a different (though not less serious) nature looming ahead for Britain herself. She, no less than Ireland, might have been said to consist of two nations, in the sense indicated by Disraeli more than half a century previously as those of the Haves and the Have-nots. Only the latter were now, largely through his agency, in possession of the vote, which, once they had realized its potentialities, might enable them to transfer as much as they chose of the havings of the Haves to their own side of the account. There had been a formidable old gentleman, of German-Jewish extraction, recently laid to rest in Highgate cemetery, who had explained very precisely and at voluminous length just how this transfer could, ought and indeed was bound to be effected. Not that such persuasions, or persuaders, were likely to cut much ice with the British working man, who was too easy-going and too much a creature of habit to be stampeded into revolution, and in normal circumstances preferred to carry on within the bounds of the existing social order, and according to the known rules of the party game.

Signs, however, were not lacking that such complacency might not be guaranteed to continue indefinitely. Ominous of things to come had been the appearance in the 1892 House of Commons of an individual of leonine aspect, defiantly helmeted by the cloth cap of the conventional working man, and armed with a programme of social revolution as red as his beard and his tie, who represented an East End constituency from which he was duly ejected in the Tory landslide three years later. But this Labour party of one had set a precedent that was not forgotten, and might in due course be multiplied by hundreds.

Social reform was no new idea, and in fact Disraeli had done his best to make it a main plank of the Tory political platform, though under Salisbury's auspices it had made heavy going against the too literally conservative instincts of the lords and gentlemen who formed the backbone, if not exactly the brains, of the party. But the advent to office of Chamberlain, who had come fully primed with these Radical notions that he had applied to the reform of his native city, was, even if his new office precluded him from repeating the performance off his own bat on a national scale, fully determined to keep any Cabinet he was in up to a mark not yet attained by Disraeli's or any other government in this task of transforming—and what the next generation would have called *streamlining*—the social system, even to the hitherto undreamed-of extent of providing State pensions for superannuated workers. This, even though it meant inserting the thin end of the socialistic wedge, Chamberlain made no secret of his intention to see carried through under Unionist auspices, nor did either his Premier or his colleagues venture to demur in principle. But it may be conjectured that few of them would be sorry to see their own and the nation's energies diverted to projects less calculated to disturb an order of things that they had so obvious an interest in considering.

And here it was Chamberlain himself who came to the rescue in his capacity of Colonial Secretary, and caused his own projects of domestic reform to be curtailed or shelved, pending the settlement of matters of more spectacular urgency.

It might have been expected that the first use a newly enfranchised proletariat would have wished to make of its vote would have been in the improvement of its own condition. But so far this seemingly obvious idea had failed to obtain priority. No election since Disraeli's Reform Bill had been fought primarily on any social issue, except in so far as in 1885, immediately after Gladstone's extension of the vote to the agricultural labourers, a substantial though ephemeral success had been secured for his party by an electoral stunt started by Chamberlain's Radical following and summarized in the slogan of 'Three Acres and a Cow', which had gone some way towards turning what might have been a Tory landslide into an electoral tie. But when another election followed on a few months later, the acres and the cow were forgotten, and the British electors, rural no less than urban, were far too much worked up about who was to govern Ireland to bother unduly about improving their own condition. And Gladstone, as long as he lasted, was at least able to keep the Home Rule controversy sufficiently on the boil to provide the main theme of excitement in the indecisive contest of 1892, and its smashing sequel three years later.

But now the very completeness of their own success had deprived the Unionists of what had been their most effective rallying cry. Home Rule had ceased to be even a negative reaction stimulus. With Gladstone and Parnell off the stage, even the Liberals, not to speak of the country at large, were more than willing to let Ireland fade out of the picture for the time being and switch over political controversy to topics of a more obviously self-regarding import for the larger community. The party game might then resolve itself into a competition for improving the condition of the British people rather than that of the Irish peasantry—which would be innocuous enough so long as it continued to be played between the existing gentlemanly teams and according to the established rules. But what if the people, in the sense of the larger of Disraeli's two nations, should insist on taking the improvement of its own conditions into its own horny hands, and manipulating the franchise to its own crude advantage?

I am not suggesting that such possibilities were as yet clearly enough envisaged to have had a conscious influence on the shaping of political policies, but it would have been unrealistic to expect men with an obvious stake in the existing social order not to have instinctively preferred the passions of the electorate to have been diverted to issues of a less ominously tendentious bearing on that order's foundations. Least of all could the genteel core of a party wedded to the Conservative tradition have been expected to enthuse for the social projects of the man they had recently known as Jack Cade, and who had made no pretence of recanting his Radical principles on joining them, even though they might be induced to pay them lip homage for the time being. But all the more when Jack Cade himself provided his own antidote by sponsoring a policy with no dangerous social implications, capable of uniting all classes in the acquisition of glory and profit, by means of the greatest empire on all record, did they agree in accepting him in this new capacity as the statesman for their money. And this was what Chamberlain proceeded to do on his advent to the Colonial Office. As if by the waving of a magician's wand, or the switching on of a current, the heterogeneous assortment of peoples and territories that had been lumped together under the designation of British Empire seemed suddenly to have become infused in all its members with an organic and intensely glowing vitality.

Such was the effect of one supremely dynamic personality, a phenomenon wholly at variance with the reigning historical fashion of playing down the human factor, and accounting everything that ever happens as the resultant of impersonal or economic forces. And yet—however little we may like it or them—certain individuals do from time to time arise with a power of influencing events, even on a world-wide scale, that must be judged in the light of the events themselves as a fact too palpable to be gainsaid. And this doubly applies to Chamberlain, since his impact on the Colonial Office and the colonies themselves was fraught with as revolutionary an effect as it had had on the ordering of his native city, and in the setting up in England of a new model of party organization. To adopt a turn of phrase that was current at that time—when Joe was about, things happened.

Such men, as Wordsworth might have put it, are powers—but this was a time undreamed of by Wordsworth, when power had come to be worshipped for its own sake without reference to good or evil. And the cult of empire was merely the cult of power raised from an individual to a mass footing. It was no accident that the man of incomparably the most forceful personality on the English political scene, after the retirement of Gladstone, should have flung himself heart and soul into the boosting of empire.

It would be doing Chamberlain an injustice to write him down (or, as some might maintain, up) as an undiluted power addict or superman. Though with few engaging or sympathetic traits, he had his own rigid standards of bourgeois morality to which, in spite of all insinuations to the contrary, he rigidly adhered in his public no less than his private life. If he sought power for the Empire, with a ruthless and aggressive concentration, he sought it by honourable means, and with a due regard to the strictest standards of commercial rectitude. For Chamberlain's pushfulness, even in its imperial sublimation, never ceased to be that of the self-made business man who had needed to accumulate a private fortune before there could be any question of his launching out on the public career on which most leading politicians of the time had found themselves able to start—as their grandchildren might have expressed it—from the door of the family mansion with batteries fully charged and all accessories provided.

It was not in the course of human nature that habits of mind implanted in these strenuous and formative years should have ever been more than superficially discarded. Chamberlain's conception of his imperial mission is contained in one of those incisive phrases of which he was so prolific, to the effect that he wanted to put the empire on a business footing—as indeed he instinctively wanted to put everything. And in this desire it could have at least have been claimed that he showed himself thoroughly in accord with the spirit of his age.

There was nothing of the mystic, and not much more, beneath the rhetorical surface, of the idealist about Brummagem Joe. He was out for results, 'things that you can touch and see', things that you can account for to board meetings in terms of statistics; and no one had a greater genius for getting them. When, for instance, a colony in the West Indies, or elsewhere, had fallen into a state of economic depression, the Colonial Office, hitherto regarded as distant and unhelpful, was transformed into the likeness of a friend in need, quick to diagnose the source of the trouble, and apply, with a generous hand, the appropriate remedy. Not only was Britain galvanized into empire consciousness, but the Empire had become conscious of itself as it had never been before, as a going concern, expansive and dividend-paying—which is what the Master (as his subordinates in the Colonial Office instinctively named this magnetic promoter) aimed at making of it, with a startling promise of success.

The idea of an empire on a business footing had already been embodied in Carthage, in Venice and in Holland, and it was on some such lines that Chamberlain tended to imperialize for his British model. He was no imperialist in the classic sense of lusting after power as an end in itself; he was a man not of blood but of business, to whom power was only to be sought as a means—and preferred as a peaceful means—to solidly economic ends. If he blundered into war it would be less likely by design than by miscalculation of forces beyond the scope of his habitual reckoning.

This desire to get tangible results and clear-cut arrangements gave a bias to his projects of empire as essentially un-British as empire itself. It would have been contrary to all his instincts to have gone all out for the idea of a commonwealth of free nations, united by no bonds except those invisible ones of spontaneous co-operation which Burke had defined as thinner than gossamer yet stronger than links of iron. It is true that he had too shrewd a sense of reality to dream of Britain trying to assert any sort of imperial authority over her already self-governing colonies, but he had set his heart on persuading them to pool their freedom in a voluntary merger of forces for purposes of common defence and a system of tariff preferences, failing or pending one of complete mutual free trade, that would give practical expression to the unity of this oddly styled empire. But it soon became apparent that these jealously self-conscious budding nations were in no mood to limit their freedom by the bond of a formal alliance, and that even an adjustment of tariffs would be conditional on Britain's consenting to scrap her own sacrosanct dogma of free trade. The most that could be done would be to get the various Prime Ministers to come together at quinquennial intervals in what was called an Imperial Conference, for the exchange of loyal platitudes. But the impetus of his own volition might end in causing the frustrated empire-pusher to drive to his goal of a working business partnership, by making a clean sweep of all political and dogmatic inhibitions and damning all consequences. That too would be in accord with the spirit not only of the man but of the time. But even a Chamberlain might stick at driving the logic of his own imperialism to this as yet unthinkable conclusion until all else had failed, and then only as a last desperate resort. And at present he was riding on the crest of a flowing tide with everything in his favour. He had struck the exact psychological moment when the country was ripe for the imperialistic lead that, ever since the doors of the Colonial Office had been banged in his face fifteen years before, he had been longing to give.

4

SO MUCH TO DO

I T SEEMS extraordinary now how slow the ordinary Englishman was in adjusting his mind to the stupendous changes that were taking place in regions that were still largely beyond the orbit of his mental vision. He was no doubt vaguely aware that a partition of Africa was going on but, since the excitement about Gordon had subsided, he had tended to regard it as a rather boring and unintelligible business with which the appropriate authorities could be trusted to deal, but about which he could not be expected to work up the same sort of interest as he did about Home Rule or the performance of the Australian cricket team. The news that the Germans had collared the Cameroons would have impressed him more vividly had it not tended to precede the realization that these were in Africa and not in Scotland, while as for potentates like the Sultan of Zanzibar, the Kabaka of Buganda and His Matabele Majesty, Lobengula, his reactions to them might have been sufficiently typified by Lear's query of

> Who, or why, or which, or *what*
> Is the Akond of SWAT?

But influences were at work and events happening that were destined to shatter the fabric of this insular complacency. This third decade of the Armed Peace can be seen in the light of after events as a time of subtle and ominous transition from an overriding prudence to a more and more uninhibited recklesness—or perhaps it would be better to say fecklessness—in the high places of Europe. As long as the controls of German military power, backed by ever more formidable industrial resources, remained in the sure hands of Bismarck, so long was it reasonably certain that the forces making for peace would continue to overbalance those that were making for a renewal, on a global scale, of the wars of the mid nineteenth century. It was a peace that could never be more than an armistice, drawn out at the price of unceasing vigilance on the part of Germany, but it was one that Bismarck had shown himself possessed of the means and technique of maintaining during his long tenure of office, and that there was no reason to doubt might be prolonged by the same methods for as long as could humanly be foreseen. But when Bismarck was thrown out of office by a young master impatient of his leading-strings, there was no one found remotely capable of taking his place—least of all the flamboyant psychopath whom the accident of hereditary succession had thrown up into supreme power. Having dropped its pilot, the mighty Reich was plunging forward, at full speed, with only a hopeless succession of mediocrities, charlatans, or worse, to navigate her course.

The first effect of this was to break up the elaborate double system of alliances by which Bismarck had managed to secure the isolation of a France whose implacable hostility even he had failed to divert. The autocratic Tsar, whose good graces he had gone to all lengths to conciliate, was allowed to slide into incongruous partnership with the Third Republic. The forces for a new world conflict were beginning to line up: a dual alliance encircling a triple, though not as yet of a strength to warrant the desperate gamble of a challenge to arms. But with forces thus balanced, it ought to have leapt to the eye of any statesman that it had become a *sine qua non* of German security to keep on the best possible terms with the remaining great Power, that of Britain, with her measureless resources and her control of the seas. Bismarck himself, who had less than no love for her personally, had had the sense to keep in with her and had even put out feelers for an alliance, and Salisbury, who had no illusions about Bismarck or Germany, had been able to maintain a mutually advantageous business relationship while stalling diplomatically the idea of anything more formal. But after the defection of Russia from the triune league which had formerly been the Holy Alliance, it had become a *sine qua non* of German security to keep on the side of Britain, since it was a matter of simple political arithmetic that her addition to the dual combination would at last enable it to challenge the triple with a reasonable prospect of success—especially as it was more than doubtful whether the third member of the *triplice*, Italy, would ever come up to the scratch against British sea power. But as Britain was in a state of chronic and envenomed friction with France, and regarded Russia in the light of a permanent bogey, nothing appeared less on the cards than that her Teutonic kinsmen would positively go out of their way to force her into taking sides against them.

Nor would there have been the least question of it, if security had been the prime consideration with Bismarck's successors that it had been with Bismarck. But they had other notions beginning to form that were more like the excited fantasies of a drug addict, and to which all considerations of prudence had to give way. But there was an almost insane logic underlying them. Germany was an imperial Power, and even Bismarck, much against his natural inclinations, had been forced to humour her growing desire for world-wide expansion, though it was an objective for which he would never have sacrificed the bones of a Pomeranian grenadier. But the megalomaniac Kaiser and his *entourage* were intoxicated with dreams of a world-wide empire proportionate to their conception of Germany's greatness, and with no prudential inhibitions imposed on its pursuit. And an empire whose sole connection with its overseas provinces was by thousands of miles of circuitous seaways, only held them in the last resort on sufferance of the Power controlling those seaways, especially when that Power was planted right across them, as it had been, with such decisive effect, across those of the Dutch empire of the seventeenth century. Obviously, therefore, if Germany were to consummate her imperial ambition, she would have to arm herself with a power capable of wresting the control of the seas from British hands, and therefore of reducing Britain herself to total ruin and subjection. The mere suspicion of such an attempt—as anyone with the least knowledge of British history and mentality might have foreseen—would be taken as a mortal challenge that Britain would go to all lengths, and join herself to any allies, in resisting.

It would be preposterous to imagine that the half-English Emperor, or any of those whom he appointed to be Bismarck's successors in the office of Reich Chancellor, were capable deliberately and in cold blood of committing Germany to the most fearful gamble ever undertaken, and planning to march through world war to world empire. It might come to this some day, but not until a certain infant of obscure parentage in Upper Austria had grown up to middle age. But the last thing the Kaiser wanted to do was to plunge Europe, and himself, into a blood bath. The part for which he had cast himself was that of a stage hero, and it doubled those of a Prince of Peace and an irresistible war lord, who delighted, on manœuvres, in annihilating whole armies with charges more spectacular than those of Murat, but whose glittering armour was a stage property too precious for exposure to the rough and tumble of the vulgar arena.

Nor was this state of things peculiar to Germany. Previous contests of empires in Europe had been motivated by such purposeful or insatiable ambition as that of a King Philip, a *Roi Soleil*, or a Napoleon, but this tragedy of an armed peace culminating in world war was one without a villain, but merely of unprecedented destructive forces being at the disposal of men who, according to the cockney vernacular, were not fit to run a whelk stall. The description would be modest applied to those responsible for the running of the three great dynastic *imperia* of Central and Eastern Europe, while for sordid squalor nothing under their auspices could surpass the state of things in the French Republic, revealed by the corruption of the Panama scandal and the military gangsterdom in high quarters that shocked a not-too-shockable world in the 'framing' of the unhappy Captain Dreyfus.

It is against this background that we have to visualize the brief and hectic episode of the imperial fever that swept Britain in the last five years of the century. It was as if some continental virus to which she was naturally allergic had effected an invasion of a system which would need all the reserve forces of its inherited constitution to throw off. That she was in mortal peril while it lasted is a fact of terrifying obviousness in retrospect.

Even so it can fairly be said of her that she found herself drawn into the imperial vortex more by constraint than by choice; and this largely because her way of expansion was the opposite of that of genuine empires. It was not the will to power of a central person or authority radiating outwards, so much as the result of seeds from the parent stock each taking root and growing up together into the unity of spontaneous combination; the way of a free commonwealth as opposed to that of an imposed empire.

Thus we find it perennially characteristic of the British way of expansion that its pace and method are set by the men on the spot at least as much as the titular Sovereign Power. Thus it is only to have been expected that British expansion in Africa should have been largely through the traditional British agency of chartered companies nominally in governmental leading-strings, but in fact frankly commercial undertakings, whose prime object was neither imperial nor philanthropic, but the yield of the largest possible dividends to their shareholders. And what made these British companies differ from those sponsored by the genuinely imperialistic European Powers was that they lived up to their ostensible designation to a far greater extent than those controlled and subsidized undertakings which were more in the nature of detached State departments than *bona fide* self-functioning enterprises; whereas it was the way of the British companies to take the bit between their own teeth and confront a reluctant Home Government with the accomplished fact of expansionist commitments that it had been hesitant, or unwilling, to undertake on its own behalf. There was the inevitable danger in such circumstances of its finding itself saddled with the responsibility for proceedings that showed too little respect for its own standards of morality. Commercial undertakings in contact with savages, or faced with the cut-throat competition of imperializing rivals, are under hardly less of a temptation to play diamond cut diamond than in the good old Elizabethan days of no peace beyond the line.

The wonder is that, in these circumstances, such a relatively high moral standard was in fact maintained by at least two out of the three British chartered companies that took a hand in the African share-out —the British East African and the Royal Niger, both of them serving as merely temporary expedients, and by the end of the century resigning their functions to, or being bought out by, the British Government, which henceforth assumed direct control over their greatly expanded territories. This is not to imply that their proceedings were invariably those of a Parsifal at a poker party. But it can fairly be claimed for them that they conformed to standards not only as high as, but in many ways definitely higher than any of their rivals in the field. Even by the bitterest critics of British imperialism, no major scandal was ever alleged against them such as made not only Belgian but French methods of sweating for rubber the wretched denizens of the Congo basin stink in the nostrils of humanity, or of the wholesale massacres that in more than one of their new colonies the Germans saw fit to stage, or to the even more ruthless methods of Russian expansion in Asia. Of the representatives of no other Power could it be said that they emerged from their pioneering task with hands so clean both of innocent blood and of ill-gotten lucre.

This may largely be credited to the outstanding personal quality of the men who were in charge of these enterprises—not only the heads of the two companies, Goldie and Mackinnon, but such colleagues and assistants as Sir John Kirk, Sir Harry Johnston, Sir Frederick (afterwards Lord) Lugard and others of hardly inferior calibre—a galaxy of administrative talent and enlightened goodwill in the handling of more backward communities to which it would be hard to find a parallel in that or any other time of civilized expansion.

And it can be said of them that—at any rate in the pre-Chamberlain era—they found the Home Government at least as apt to damp down as to encourage their expansionist zeal. In fact it is the common form of popular accounts of this period, written when 'British Empire' was still a name to conjure with, to animadvert on this lukewarmness of support accorded by the British, in comparison with rival European Governments, to its imperial pioneers.

Nevertheless, in spite of this governmental foot-dragging, the British Empire—in the usual sense of that question-begging term— did continue to expand in a way that rendered it an object of universal envy, and seemed to threaten such a general predatory combination against it as had materialized against Venice in the League of Cambray, early in the sixteenth century, and which had marked the beginning of her decline. How are we to account for this apparent capacity, which was in evidence long before Britain's brief lapse into imperialistic fever, to win the prize in a race in which she was so notoriously reluctant a starter?

If we focus our attention on the African continent that was the main field of European expansion in the *fin de siècle*, we shall see how inexorably it all follows from the Gladstonian legacy, already recorded, of the seizure of Egypt at one end of it and the goading of the Transvaalers into rebellion at the other. But for these, Britain's part in the great share-out might have been much more modest and less contentious. But as long as she continued to sit on her own bayonets in Cairo, she was not only committed to an envenomed quarrel which more than once brought her to the brink of war with her natural ally, France, but she also found herself in the position of a sort of reversionary legatee of the bankrupt Khedival imperialism. The whole basin of the mighty Nile had by some strange but inescapable logic become, if not her property, at least her preserve off which she was in honour bound to warn trespassers. But this was complicated by the fact that the greater part of the preserve had passed into the hands of the Mahdi and his successor the Khalifa. And to warn them off had so far proved too tough a proposition. Britain's policy, since the fall of Khartoum, had been that of Dogberry, to call the rest of the watch together and thank God she and her Khedive were rid of a knave.

This would have served Britain's turn admirably, had it not been open to the French to argue that you cannot abandon your own or your client's preserves and claim respect for your notice boards. The Khalifa's land had become, as far as European Powers were concerned, no man's—or any man's—land. France had her own designs on the Nile valley, and saw no reason to acknowledge any sort of divine British right to it. It followed, by the rules of imperial grab, that unless the occupying Power in Egypt could bestir itself to drive up river from the north, over the Khalifa's body, in double-quick time, it would find the French already ensconced on its shores, and a situation that could be resolved only by an almost unthinkable climb down, or a combat *à outrance*.

And the rigour of this same imperial game complicated the situation still further by making it imperative for Britain to secure, in order to debar rivals from, access to the Nile *via* the back, or south-eastern entrance, by causing the British East Africa Company to thrust up from the coast to its source in Lake Victoria, just in time to forestall the efforts of a shady German empire-pusher called Peters to stake out a claim for his own country. This involved the grabbing up for the 'Empire' of the central African territory known as Uganda, which the company accordingly obliged by taking into its orbit, but which it found its own already overstrained resources unequal to keeping there, so that it became a question of either abandoning it altogether or of the British Government stepping in and annexing it under the guise of a formal protectorate. This Government happened to be the minority Liberal one which was believed to stand for the repudiation of all forms of imperialism, but its Foreign Secretary, Rosebery, who more than ever, as Premier, was able to ride his policy over the heads of his colleagues, was a much more convinced imperializer than Salisbury, and managed to force through the proposal in the teeth of party and Cabinet opposition. So that this picturesque but inhospitable region, which was quite unfitted for white settlement, became, after some efficient cleaning-up work by the indefatigable Colonel Lugard, added to the portion of the map that was coloured red, which, so far as it might be held to include an unannexed but occupied Egypt, and a Sudan marked down for occupation, extended in a continuous broad belt from the Medterranean to the Indian Ocean. All this was the unforeseen but inescapable result of the rape of Egypt under the aegis of Liberalism.

It would have been well if this had been the whole story. But as I have had to point out, with what I hope has not been undue iteration, the Gladstonian legacy of imperialistic expansion in Africa was two-fold and pincer-like. Gladstone's absent-minded double-cross of those Transvaal farmers who were at least as 'rightly struggling to be free' as the bloodthirsty Dervishes, had started in the south a train of consequences as tragic and far-reaching as in the north.

But in fairness it must be acknowledged that the bedevilment here had been gratuitously and unforeseeably aggravated by the discovery within the newly enfranchised territory of the richest of the world's gold deposits. It is at least a moot point whether, at the time of the Transvaal's achievement of independence, this trove might not have merited Horace's characterization of 'gold unfound and better left so' in the interest of everyone concerned. Found however it was, and attracted a rush to exploit it on an even greater scale than had been seen already in California and Australia. In an incredibly short time a brash, pretentious city had sprung up to house a teeming mixed white population, all impelled by the same motive of filling their pockets as quickly as possible, and as different as can be imagined from the austere and Jehovah-fearing burghers dwelling in pastoral simplicity on their lonely farms, whom these newcomers rapidly threatened to surpass in numbers, and by whom they could hardly fail to be regarded as a godless and menacing riff-raff, by no means rendered more tolerable from the fact that a majority of its mixed membership sprang from the already detested British stock. To the Boers, who were as alive to the main chance as any other farmers, it seemed the most natural thing in the world to make their uninvited guests pay through the nose for the privilege of enriching themselves out of the produce of their soil, and at the same time to take good care to prevent them from acquiring political rights that on a democratic count of heads threatened to make them masters of the land. No man was more imbued with this consciousness than the old *voortrekker* President, Paul Kruger, in whom the best as well as the less desirable qualities of his people were sublimated in an amalgam of massive intractability.

He and his burghers found themselves in a position to profit from the gold rush to a greater extent than the adventurers themselves, by helping themselves to what they considered a legitimate rake-off from the exploitation of their land, but which to minds nurtured in the British tradition involved the most intolerable of all grievances—that of taxation without representation. The Government at Pretoria, which after independence had begun to revert to its chronic condition of pre-annexation bankruptcy owing to the extreme difficulty of touching the farmers for any taxes at all, suddenly found money pouring into its hitherto empty coffers up to ten times and more of the former revenue, and itself blossoming into the richest of the South African provinces, with all the power that money can confer, but without the least experience in handling it; so that Kruger was fain to surround himself with a clique of anything but simple-minded assistants from outside the pale of his chosen people. It would have taken a very dull intelligence not to have perceived the new and menacing turn that had been imparted to the South African situation. Not only had this most hostile of all the Dutch communities in South Africa to the imperial connection inflicted a signal humiliation in arms on its nominal suzerain, but instead of retiring into pastoral isolation had blossomed out into a Power in its own right, capable of assuming the leadership of a pan-Dutch nationalist movement embracing the whole of South Africa and, as the master white race, imposing its yoke on the British minority.

And indeed a party called the Afrikander Bond had been formed in the Cape Province itself that showed every sign of ruling the political roost, whose explicit object was to achieve an independent Dutch-ruled South Africa such as within the span of a long lifetime was destined to become the accomplished fact. Such movements, once the ball has been set rolling, seldom fail to gather avalanche-like momentum, particularly in an age prolific of national and racial obsession beyond all previous record. That Britain would be able to perpetuate her sway willy-nilly upon a Dutch South Africa, as George III had tried to do over what at least had been a British North America, was a proposition that might have daunted even the toughest imperialist. Nor had it come to this yet. But to anyone capable of seeing farther than his nose, it ought to have been obvious that one chance of retaining even the Cape Province for the British connection would be by in some way enlisting the goodwill of its Dutch majority. But, with the Afrikander Bond already in being, was there such a chance? There was one man of genius who thought there was, and was ready to go all out to realize it.

Cecil Rhodes, one of several sons of an English clergyman, who had been shipped off to seek his fortune in South Africa on account of his weak lungs, was of all the leading men of that time the most supremely representative of it. For though it does not appear probable that he had ever heard of his slightly older contemporary Nietzsche, he came nearer than any other Englishman did, or could, to embodying that prophet's frenzied conception of the superman. None of his contemporaries succeeded in more ostentatiously discarding the ethical veneer that had been the *sine qua non* of the high Victorian *persona*, and achieving a greatness so entirely motivated by the will to power and unfettered by the trammels of morality. And greatness, none the less authentic for being tinged with a megalomania hardly inferior to, and scarcely less pathological [1] than, that of Nietzsche himself, Rhodes did possess in fullest measure. But it was a greatness divorced from goodness, or—as the Master himself would have preferred to put it—beyond good and evil.

But in Rhodes the will to power assumed a form that to the *soi-disant* scion of the Polish aristocracy would, beyond doubt, have seemed the limit of bourgeois vulgarity, and yet was ideally suited to the role for which fate or his own ambition had cast him. No man of comparable stature had ever more frankly tended to identify power with money power. This was not surprising when we consider that Rhodes himself had started his career by trekking off from an unprofitable farm in Natal to try his luck at the newly discovered Kimberley diamond mines, amid which none too savoury environment, and with his wits pitted against some of the sharpest on Mammon's earth, he contrived in an incredibly short time to amass for himself a fabulous fortune.

This called for no greater measure of luck or cunning than has accounted for the fortune of scores of undistinguished specimens of the millionaire breed; but what distinguished Rhodes was that by him this realization of most men's wish-dream was not valued as an end in itself, but for the power, the essential money power, that it conferred of operating on the most grandiose scale that his imgination was capable of conceiving, for ends that transcended the limits of commonplace egotism. He would become the shaper of world events, a master builder of a record-breaking imperial fabric. It was a weird coincidence

[1] Though uncomplicated, as in the cases of Nietzsche and that other contemporary, though aesthetic, superman, Oscar Wilde, by the taint of syphilis.

* K

—in the fact that his very name was linked with the notion of the colossal. In no way was he more the representative superman of his time than in this megalomaniac magnanimity.

And in Rhodes this instinct was exacerbated by a sense of perpetual urgency. Like so many other self-conscious addicts of strength and bigness, he was far from exemplifying these qualities in his own individual make-up. Having got over the trouble with his lungs, he developed a weakness of the heart to which his huge frame rendered him especially vulnerable, and which in what is normally still the prime of life proved the death of him. And he never ceased to be haunted by the sense of the shortness of the time allotted for the execution of his designs, as expressed in his dying ejaculation of, 'So little done! So much to do!' and impelling him on all occasions to take the unconditionally shortest and swiftest cut to their fulfilment.

Rhodes's imagination had correctly apprised him of the real crux of the British problem in South Africa. From the Limpopo fringing the north of the Transvaal to the southernmost shores of the Cape Province, the Dutch population of settlers decisively outnumbered the British, and if matters were allowed to take their course it would only be a matter of time before a law of racial gravitation, hardly less certain than the physical one formulated by Newton, would ensure that the Dutch supremacy already visualized by the Bond would duly materialize, unless Britain both could and would impose her yoke by force of arms, and remain sitting on her bayonets in perpetuity.

But Rhodes had visioned a way out of this dilemma worthy of his genius. He would transcend the whole issue between the two races in one corner of Africa, by raising it from a provincial to a continental plane, and give them both a common cause in which they could sink their differences and unite as one imperial master race in the fulfilment of a, to him, already manifest destiny. His eye took the whole map of Africa into its purview, and his imagination, casting aside all prudential and moral inhibitions, expanded to the most grandiose of imperial designs as yet conceived, even in that time of expansion unlimited. To him the simple fact of the British occupation of Egypt, under whatever pledge or pretence, was enough to make it count as an integral part of the Empire, and what could be the more obvious procedure, according to his spacious way of thinking, than to link it up with the Anglo-Dutch colony in the south by a continuous belt of imperial territory stretching from end to end of the continent? The vast distances and areas involved in this project of combined expansion acted more as an incentive than a deterrant to an ambition temperamentally boundless.

It is not easy in practice to draw the line between the magnanimity proper to genius and the megalomania which is its excrescence. But the cloven hoof, as one might put it, of megalomania consists in a blindness to obstacles coupled with an absence of moral scruples. The intellectual counterpart of 'beyond good and evil', is 'beyond prudence and realism'. Rhodes's conception of a grand imperial trans-African dominion affords a classical demonstration of the way in which a conception inspired by genius is capable of being inflated to the proportions of an auto-intoxicated wish-dream. And it is characteristic of such dreams that it should have sought to objectify itself in what, under the guise of practicality, was really no more than a symbolic gesture. This was the much-advertised project of an all-British Cape to Cairo railway, as a sort of connecting thread or backbone. That even if this wonderful line had ever been actually laid along the thousands of miles of its route, it would have produced a tithe of the results that its projector seemed to take for granted, may at lest be doubted, in view of the fact that, when the event of the First World War seemed for the first time to have brought the project within the range of practicality, no one should have bothered to take it up.

A mere glance at the map of Africa will show the audacious recklessness of a plan that aimed at splitting the continent lengthways from south to north, on the assumption that all the other competing Powers would stand by in passive acquiescence, when it was, on the face of it, so much of a simpler proposition to bestride it crossways. This was in fact what not only imperial France and Germany each aimed at doing, to the limit of their respective capacities, but even Portugal had the nerve to claim it had the right to do by joining up its two colonial hinterlands, and that, lastly, the newly enriched Transvaal had begun to harbour ambitions of doing. Each of these stood in the way of a Cape–Cairo drive, not to speak of peoples already in possession of the coveted regions, who being only natives were regarded in the light of removable or suppressible obstacles.

The preposterousness, verging on insanity, of the whole scheme will be apparent from the simple fact that this half continental area marked out for imperial exploitation was designed to bridge the vast hiatus between an Egypt in which Britain had no legitimate *locus standi* whatever, and which she was pledged up to the hilt to evacuate, and a province in which her nationals formed a precariously suzerain minority of what was itself a self-imposed governing minority of the whole population.

It is vain to look for any clear-cut racial philosophy in an intelligence so permeated as that of Rhodes with Cromwell's typically English conviction that a man never rises so high as when he does not know where he is going; but though he could be as prolific on occasion of patriotic and all-British sentiments as the jingoest of imperialists, one can see that with his instinctive opportunism he was moving towards a racial ideal in which British and Dutch could unite on a common footing, and from which the specifically British element was tacitly eliminated. And indeed it is no accident that Rhodes should have evinced an unmistakable Teutonic bias, most conspicuously in his hobnobbings with the Kaiser and in the special provision in his will for German scholarships at Oxford. The words 'Nordic' and 'Aryan' had not yet come into fashion, but Rhodes in his intuitive way was groping towards the master-race conception that reached its insane climax under the auspices of Hitler, whose proposal to guarantee the British Empire on his own terms of racial partnership would at least have wakened a more sympathetic chord in Rhodes,[1] if he could have survived, than it did in a less imperially minded generation of Englishmen than his own.

And it must be admitted that only on some such lines could anything fit to be called a British empire in Africa, as distinct from a scattered miscellany of commercially exploited areas, have been got going at all. For that the co-operation of the two white races in occupation of the habitable south was needed; and that of the Dutch, who under the normal workings of democracy were otherwise bound sooner or later to become the ruling majority, was only to be had by their own goodwill on terms acceptable to themselves. And that goodwill so far at least as the largest and most progressive province, that of the Cape, was concerned, he did not believe it too late to secure. For the Bond itself, in spite of its anti-British origins, contained a progressive element under Jan Hofmeyr that was ready to work in harmony with the British connection. And Rhodes himself who, having established his position as a multi-millionaire, was now concerned only to translate opulence into power, had attained it at the beginning of the nineties in overflowing measure by becoming premier of the Cape, with Dutch as well as British support, and chairman of the greatest of all the chartered companies, the South African.

He was now in a position to go forward to the realization of his wish-dream and, with his haunting sense of the shortness of the time allowed him, he was in no mood to let the grass grow under his feet. His mind's eye was fixed on the vast open spaces to the north between the Limpopo and Zambesi rivers, the first stage in the visionary progress to the distant Mediterranean, and the one with which Rhodes's name will always be associated, because these lands, particularly in their southern reaches, offered not only profits but homes to white settlers, though their attraction to Rhodes and his Company was even more that of the rich gold deposits, rivalling those of the Rand, that his sanguine imagination made him speculate on its containing. Here he would have found the way barred by the claim of imperial Portugal

[1] Though Rhodes was too much of a practical Englishman ever to have had the least truck with such lunatic extravagances as anti-Semitism.

to assert her sovereignty and set up her notice boards over a zone stretching clean across the continent, but this nonsense Salisbury was able to take in his heavy stride, without excitement or ostentation, in such a way as to make it clear to 'England's oldest ally' that it was not to be taken seriously.

But there were other obstacles that did not lend themselves so easily to such methods of indirect control. The coveted lands were already under the sovereignty of their own native chiefs, of whom the most formidable of all was the Matabele King, Lobengula, whose land, only recently conquered by his warrior *impis*, formed a veritable Naboth's vineyard from the standpoint of Rhodes's company, who believed it to contain the mythical gold deposits and whose northward advance it barred. Matabeleland, in consequence, as Queen Henriette had said of Hull, 'must be had'.

The first task, in the drive northwards, was to get a viable corridor to those open spaces north of the Limpopo that the Company had marked out as its first field of exploitation. This involved clawing up from the Cape Province round the north-western corner of the Transvaal and heading off the bands of Boer adventurers who, inspired by a similar lust of expansion, were trying to stake out a prior claim of occupation, but were not in sufficient force to defy a notice to quit. The resident natives, the Bechuanas, were not of the fighting stuff that the Matabele were. All went therefore according to plan; the Bechuanas were duly received into the imperial fold, and the railway crept up, following the flag, round the western frontier of the Transvaal, boosting Chartereds in the stock markets, where the profits from the hoped-for Eldorado in the north were already being grabbed up in advance by bullish punters. The great game had now passed almost entirely out of the hands of the Queen's Government into those of Rhodes and his money-powered adventurers.

They were now at the entrance of Naboth's vineyard, and the next item on the programme was inescapably the liquidation of the officiating Naboth. It must be admitted that King Lobengula was implausibly cast for the role of innocent victim. He and his people, an offshoot of the formidable Zulu stock, were themselves there by right of recent conquest and lorded it over the less efficiently warlike former inhabitants by force ruthlessly applied. But Lobengula, though an illiterate savage, was, according to his lights, a gentleman, and the last thing he wanted to do was to annoy or offend these white-skinned intruders whose power he (sharing their philosophy to that extent) both appreciated and respected.

So there was nothing for it but—in the phraseology best suited to the case—to put him on the spot; a job that Rhodes and his henchmen were better qualified to undertake than the agents of constituted

authority, which had other things to think about than what went on
in these remote regions and, provided only it was not called on to
foot the bill, was more than ready to allow the Company to do its
own work in its own way—a way about which the ordinary British
citizen, and perhaps even Cabinet Minister, was (and preferred to be)
uninformed.

The facts, being well known and not open to dispute, need no
detailed recapitulation. Lobengula never stood the least chance. Fraud
was first applied, and force was ready to back it. The master hand was
apparent in the precision with which the whole operation was put
through. The unfortunate dupe, who had a pathetic reliance on the
power of the Great White Queen to see justice done to him, was
bamboozled by a certain Rudd, who was planted for this purpose on
the royal kraal, to put his mark to a document that neither Lobengula
nor any one of his subjects was capable of deciphering a word of,
making over to the Company the exclusive right to exploit all the
mineral resources of his kingdom.

Having thus got the King fairly into the Company's toils, it remained
to proceed by calculated stages to his total liquidation and the appro-
priation of his reputedly fabulous treasure, and of the far-stretching
lands of his people with their no less coveted herds of cattle. For this
purpose the most trusted of all Rhodes's agents was employed; this
was Dr Leander Starr Jameson, who had thrown up what had promised
to be a brilliant professional career in order to follow the star of his
magnetic leader. 'The Doctor', as everyone called him, had a personal
charm that few were able to resist, but it was to a large extent a fascination of iresponsibility; on the moral side it would seem as if he had
remained stuck fast somewhere in his teens; for he was almost inno-
cently unscrupulous both in word and action, though at the same time
capable of being as generous and loyal as the most approved type of
schoolboy hero. The fact that he had exercised his charm on Lobengula
himself, and earned his gratitude by curing him of an attack of gout,
was no bar to his compassing his patient's destruction. It mattered not
at all that the King had obtained assurances from the British High
Commissioner, and from the Great White Queen herself, that no harm
was intended to himself and his people; Rhodes and Jameson had other
views.

The Company had now at its disposal what amounted to a private
army of mounted police, with a good supply of the new, deadly
machine guns, and Jameson proceeded to whip up their martial
enthusiasm by as frank a programme of loot as was ever propounded
by brigand chief or pirate skipper. A farm of six thousand acres was
promised to everyone taking part in the expulsion of the Matabele
from their lands, and their great herds of cattle were to be shared out

on an equitable basis. Once this was known, the only difficulty was to keep the men in hand till the necessary pretext had been created—a feat as easy as it proved subsequently for Hitler. All went according to plan. The spear-armed *impis* were mown down in swaths by the Company's Maxims. A pleasing touch of heroism was added to the adventure by a patrol of horsemen who, having pressed on too rapidly in advance of the pursuit, were ambushed by the royal bodyguard, and sold their lives as dearly as they could—an incident that was subsequently staged for the edification of London audiences. Lobengula, having burnt down his royal kraal and—it is pleasing to record—succeeded in hiding, without trace, his much-coveted treasure, as a last desperate expedient entrusted a large sum of money to a couple of captured troopers to take to Rhodes as earnest of his submission and desire for peace. This the two, who seem thoroughly to have entered into the spirit of the proceedings, proceeded to appropriate,[1] and Lobengula, his last hope gone, perished miersably in the wilderness.

The great tracts of territory north of the Transvaal now lay at the Company's disposal and formed the newest addition to the British Empire, under the appropriate title of Rhodesia. Rhodes himself was childishly delighted in having a whole country called after him. But the very easiness and slickness of this triumph were not without their dangers.

The African Colossus was now at the height of his achievement. It is true that his supreme project of a Cape to Cairo dominion had been barred by the German colony of East Africa having bulged out westward across the route of his dream railway, but the acquisition of those vast spaces of central Africa was surely enough to satisfy even a superman's ambition, especially as it seemed as if he had found the solution for the otherwise intractable problem created by the anti-British nationalism of the Dutch majority in South Africa. By their acceptance of him as Premier of the Cape Province, it seemed as if both white stocks might be prepared to sink their differences and unite as one master race in a common policy of imperialistic expansion. Even the more progressive elements of the Bond seemed not averse to the idea.

There remained only the immovably uncompromising opposition of the Transvaal Boers, under President Kruger, to any sort of Dutch co-operation with the British, and this was now rendered more formidable by the accession of wealth from the Rand gold mines. But even here Rhodes's policy had achieved a notable measure of success. By occupying the land north of the Limpopo he had completed the encirclement of Kruger's republic and cut it off from any possibility

[1] This, however, was thought to be going too far, as on being discovered they were duly jailed. They were after all only troopers—and, as such, expendable.

of further expansion. That was a notable point gained, for it now rendered it practicable, if not to conquer, at least to contain, the extreme form of Afrikaner nationalism embodied in the Kruger régime. It was only necessary to mark time, because time had ceased to be on the President's side. Even in the Transvaal itself Kruger's domination was less and less to be taken for granted; a younger generation was coming up capable of thinking and acting on relatively progressive lines. These influences only needed time to become dominant over the whole of South Africa and make the old Briton-*versus*-Boer antagonism a thing of the past—provided only that nothing was allowed to happen capable of rekindling fires that, if damped down, were still smouldering. Never had a waiting game been more urgently called for. But a waiting game was the one that Rhodes, with his feverish sense of the abbreviation of his own time, was least capable of playing.

5

THICKER THAN WATER

IT MUST never be forgotten that the heyday of British imperialism, the only time in which empire consciousness could be said with the least plausibility to be the dominating factor in the national psychology, covers little more than the last five years of the nineteenth century. Its history is properly speaking a case history, like that recorded on the chart above a hospital bed during the course of a fever. So abnormal a condition, whether it ends in death or convalescence, can be of no long duration.

And since the fever was, in the event, successfully supervened, it is difficult to realize, looking back on it, how easily things might have gone the other way. We are apt to think of that time as one in which Britain stood, as it were, on the top of the world, at a height of power and magnificence difficult to realize nowadays—and no doubt this was the impression she had of herself. But she was skirting the edge of disaster all the time. Without allies, she found herself on the brink of war with one major Power after another, and quite conceivably with a combination of Powers. The success in colouring the map red, that had come to her more in despite than as a result of her official policy, had aroused the furious jealousy of rivals who with no such hesitations had found themselves out-imperialized at their own game.

That Britain escaped these dangers is undoubtedly due, in the first instance, to her invincible and unchallengeable naval supremacy, and in the second to the fact that, so long as the German forces remained entrenched on French soil, the Franco-German conflict, though suspended, was still on, and had priority over any rival antagonism. A European combination against Britain, pushed to the point of belligerency, might in these circumstances be effectually ruled out.

But it was not only from Europe that mortal peril threatened. Hardly had Lord Salisbury's Unionist Government been installed in office than there loomed up the ostensibly imminent threat of what would have amounted to a civil war between the two great constituent branches of Anglo-Saxon civilization—a conflict more suicidal in its implications for humanity than any between Powers of the Old

World could possibly have been. The occasion seemed almost too trivial for belief. An obscure boundary dispute, about which hardly anyone in England knew or cared, between the Republic of Venezuela and the British colony of Guiana, had suddenly detonated a violent *démarche* from a hitherto singularly unimpressive American President who was nearing the conclusion of his second term of office, and who actually threatened war unless Britain would submit the whole matter unconditionally to American arbitration.

So far as this was taken seriously, it came as a stunning shock to English public opinion, which was rooted in the belief formulated in the phrase, 'Blood is thicker than water', and had regarded such fratricidal hostilities as fantastically beyond the bounds of possibility. But it seemed to confirm the worst apprehensions when this presidential war whoop was followed by an ebullition of Anglophobiac ballyhoo that, taken at its face value, would have signified that a war with England would have been the most wildly popular step with the American democracy that could have been taken.

The whole affair was rather like the bursting of an abscess. It was difficult for the ordinary Englishman to realize how differently the American mind reacted to a world situation from which it had been successfully isolated, up to date, by British sea power backing its own Monroe Doctrine, and how crudely provincial and unrealistic an attitude this had engendered. The myth picture of stainless republicans confronting bad King George and his tyranny had become a sanctified obsession that nobody had ever troubled to debunk or bring up to date; and consequently it had proved the easiest thing in the world for President Grover Cleveland, with an eye on the forthcoming election, to step forth in the cocked hat and frock coat of a second George Washington, thundering defiance at the tyrant's granddaughter. And undoubtedly there were non-British elements in the seething imbroglio of an imperfectly assimilated multi-national populace whose own blood was also thicker than water, and this applied most of all to the descendants of the Irish emigrants of the Black Famine, whose inextinguishable hatred for England acted as a chronic irritant of anti-British sentiment.

It was providential that, at this superficially alarming juncture, the control of British foreign policy should have been in the hands of the man of all others who was most eminently qualified to deal with it. Lord Salisbury, who was not to be put out of his stride by this or any other cause, continued to handle the matter of the disputed boundary with an unimpressed reasonableness that caused the agitation to die down for sheer lack of fuel to sustain it, and the dispute to be eventually adjusted on friendly and business like lines in the ordinary course of diplomatic routine.

The abscess had burst, and there would never be any serious danger of its re-gathering. Once the vapourings and heroics had exhausted themselves, the sober and responsible elements that underlay the surface of American life had time to assert themselves. Though the first effect of the war scare had been to precipitate a slump on Wall Street, the traditional shrewdness embodied in the symbolic figure of Uncle Sam was not long in apprising the ordinary American citizen how little he stood to gain, and how much to lose, from any conflict with England other than one of words. Even as a political stunt, Cleveland's gesture resulted in a flop, if not a boomerang, for in the ensuing autumn his own Democratic party was snowed under in the presidential election.

It is, at any rate, unquestionable that from this time forth the idea of an Anglo-American war was never again broached as a serious possibility in any responsible quarter on either side of the Atlantic.

And indeed the essential unity of a common civilization was shortly to be reaffirmed, when the United States found herself in almost as bad an international odour as Britain, and, ironically enough, from a similar cause. The virus that was raging in the Old World had, to a lesser though perceptible extent, infected her system, and she herself emerged for the first time from her jealously cherished isolation to embark on a spurt of imperialist expansion overseas that was marked, as G. K. Chesterton somewhat unkindly put it, by the very careless choice of a strong line and the very careful choice of a weak enemy in the shape of the Spanish monarchy, whose once vast empire of America and the Indies had been reduced to a few island outposts that it was plainly incapable of defending, and the largest of which, Cuba, was in a state of chronic rebellion.

The eviction by overwhelming force of the Dons from these coveted possessions was an operation hardly fit to be dignified with the name of war, but it aroused a frenzy of patriotic enthusiasm in the United States, whose imperial *début*, on however modest a scale, was the object of scandalized reprobation among the out-and-out imperial-izing Powers of Europe, and most of all Germany, whose Emperor did not hesitate to put out feelers to Britain for a share-out of the American spoils in the Philippine Islands. But not only did Britain turn the coldest of shoulders on such burglarious overtures, but both her statesmanship and public opinion rallied wholeheartedly to the support of her American kinsmen, without too nice a regard to the merits of this particular case. Never was gesture more welcome or more reciprocated. There still lay ahead many misunderstandings and much friction, but henceforth these would partake more and more of the nature of family differences; never again would there by any serious question of Americans and Englishmen regarding each other in the light even of potential enemies. Such crude challenges as that of Grover Cleveland's message to Congress would be inconceivable on the lips of any American President of the twentieth century. The ghost of a mythical George III was at long last laid.

This was no more than a beginning of a process on whose timely consummation the whole future and (not impossibly) survival of humanity might be thought to depend, a process of de-isolation on one side and de-imperialization on the other, that should combine these inheritors of a common tradition in a higher unity than one of monarchy or nationhood—that of a world order of free civilization.

6

UPSET APPLE CART

WHILE THESE momentous developments were transforming the situation in the New World, Britain, in the Old, under the quickening auspices of her new Colonial Secretary, was launched on the tide of as full-blooded an imperialism as her nature was capable of. But it must be borne in mind that, in the most vital field of all, that of South Africa, the shaping of events had largely got out of the control of the Government, and had passed into that of men who were capable at a pinch of dispensing with scruples and even decencies that were a second nature to gentlemen in office at Whitehall, not excepting Chamberlain himself, who, though he never failed to play the political skin game with its utmost rigour, was incapable of deliberately cheating, and had his own rigid standards of nonconformist morality, that found expression in his crushing snub to Rhodes at their first meeting: 'You are reported to have said that every man has his price. That is not true and I do not like the man who says it.'

Like him or not, in Rhodes Chamberlain had come in contact with an imperialistic drive not inferior to his own, and it was inevitable that the two should work together for the realization of a common ideal. At first all went well, and the new spirit that the Colonial Secretary had imparted to Britain's dealings with every one of her colonies and budding dominions was felt most of all in combination with that which the South African Colossus, in his diverse capacities, had already communicated to the drive northward from the Cape into what had now become the chief field of imperial expansion.

With the Chartered Company in the van and Anglo-Dutch sentiment in the Cape Province mobilized by its Premier Controller in its support, all would have been plain sailing, but for the chronic and intractable opposition of Kruger's Transvaal Republic, now reinforced out of measure by the accession of wealth from the Rand, and exacerbated into an open challenge by the President's evident determination to have it both ways with the settlers, or Uitlanders, on the Rand, whom he was determined to sweat for the last extractable farthing of their profits, while denying them the elementary rights of citizenship.

Here the plain dictate of statesmanship was for patience and delicacy of handling, since it ought to have been obvious that, whatever the rights and wrongs of the dispute, once it was allowed to explode into open hostilities all the latent force of Dutch nationalism would inevitably be enlisted on the anti-British side from one end of South Africa to the other. Rhodes's call for a bi-racial imperialism, however vividly it might appeal to the imagination, needed time to penetrate the stubborn subconsciousness of the Dutch nature, permeated as it was with a pride of tradition that had its roots in a struggle for independence against an empire older than the British. The supreme danger to be guarded against from the British standpoint was that of allowing Kruger to dramatize himself as a grotesque reincarnation of William the Silent, which would be the foreseeable effect of his second appearance as the embattled champion of his people's threatened independence against a horde of greedy adventurers, backed by the overweening might of British military power.

And there is no doubt that the Bible-steeped but otherwise illiterate patriarch did take himself with monolithic seriousness in this capacity. And indeed the experience of a visit he had paid to Johannesburg in his presidential capacity, when the Uitlanders had repulsed his advances with organized insult and hooliganism, might have petrified a less prejudiced mind in the conviction that these Gentiles were out to swamp his own chosen people by sheer weight of numbers, and that given an inch in the way of concession they would take an ell. Not that Oom Paul's sincerity in this conviction prevented his bringing to the contention all his innate *voortrekker* toughness and peasant cunning, together with a more than average share of proverbial Dutch addiction to giving too little and asking too much in any sort of negotiation.

In Kruger Rhodes's irresistible force of personality had come up against its immovable opposite. In their first interview he had tried out the persuasive technique that had never failed him with the toughest financial sharks and political bosses, and had baited his hook with a cool proposal that they should combine to realize the long desired and frustrated Boer dream of an outlet to the sea, by seizing it from its Portuguese owners at Delagoa Bay; and he had met with a snub from the genuinely shocked old moralist even more crushing than that which he had received at his first encounter with Chamberlain:

'I can't', Kruger had said, 'take away other people's property. . . . Ill-gotten goods are cursed.'[1]

In such circumstances, unless Rhodes was prepared to wreck the whole delicate balance of political forces he had been at such pains to create, there was no way but the way of patience—but that way was not the way of empire or of a superman, least of all one conscious that

[1] *Cecil Rhodes*, by Basil Williams, p. 155.

his days were numbered. Time, that might otherwise have worked in his favour, was not his to command, nor, if it had been, was it in his nature to trust to its working. His way was not round but through, and—morality being barred—he must needs choose the shortest cut of all: that of criminal conspiracy.

The genuine grievances of the Uitlanders,[1] instead of being ventilated by the tedious process of negotiation, had accordingly to be stoked up by every device of money-backed propaganda into a revolutionary agitation, aimed at realizing the President's worst fears, and overthrowing his régime, by just such a combined technique of force and fraud as had done the business for Lobengula. That the force and fraud were by no means wholly on one side hardly detracts from the immorality of the scheme, and not at all from the wishful blindness to reality of imagining it to be remotely practicable. That men of the calibre of Rhodes and even Chamberlain could have based their calculations on the chances of a civilian mob, even supposing it could have been brought up to the scratch, making the slightest impression on the mounted infantry that had so signally accounted for Sir George Colley and his British regulars, is symptomatic of the abnormal state of mind that had been worked up in these closing years of the century.

Here it is necessary to distinguish between the parts played by the leading actors in the drama. Rhodes, with his immense wealth and the power he exercised in his double capacity of Premier and Company controller, undoubtedly imparted the chief force to the largely phoney agitation [2] in Johannesburg, which was run by a committee on the spot, including his own brother, and was sustained more by the subscriptions of millionaire bosses than by the efforts of the white workers in the mines. The idea was to overturn the existing régime in Johannesburg —if not in Pretoria itself—by a sudden *coup d'état*. Once (but not before) this had thrown the whole situation into the melting pot, a force of the same rough-riders who had conquered the Matebele and who had been unobtrusively concentrated on the western border under the leadership of Jameson, would ride in for the ostensible purpose of restoring order and protecting the lives of British civilians. Even Rhodes was not reckless enough to imagine that it would be practicable, with these few hundred horsemen, to launch, on his own responsibility, the full-scale invasion of a nominally friendly nation. But Jameson, whose mentality was on the schoolboy, and whose morals were on the buccaneering, level, was capable of imagining anything

---

[1] It is by no means certain that the rank and file of the white mining community, who were more interested in coining quick money than in political agitation, were disposed to make unduly heavy weather of them.

[2] It is to be noted that Barney Barnato, the illiterate but not unlikable cockney Jew-boy turned millionaire, refused to have the least truck with it.

and of acting on the wildest impulse, without regard to the consequences either to his own band of jolly adventurers or to the world at large.

Chamberlain, on the other hand, was utterly incapable of having part or lot in such featherbrained gangsterdom. But his personal reactions towards Kruger and his régime were, if anything, more uncompromising than those of Rhodes himself, who had at least knocked about in South Africa enough to appreciate the Boer mentality better than the dapper townsman with his clean-cut forcefulness and the Puritanical integrity of soul from which he never deviated. To a mind so constituted, the peasant blend of cunning and obstinacy that overlay Kruger's equal integrity was, in the original sense of the word, disgusting. It is not without its significance that Chamberlain privately should have been known to apply the adjective 'dirty' to Kruger. It is probably the key to his deepest feeling on that subject.

He was too much of a practical business man to allow his feelings to dictate his policy. But they did perhaps bias his judgment in a more subtle way, for they combined with his lack of the relevant experience to cause him persistently to underestimate the magnitude and toughness of the forces at Kruger's disposal. And indeed the result of their first encounter was calculated to fortify him in this delusion. For on his first assumption of office he had found Rhodes's policy of bi-racial imperialism at the peak of its success, and Kruger's hedgehog-like isolationalism as unpopular with the Dutch as with the British community at the Cape, especially when he proceeded to put the seal on what was practically a trade embargo on the south by closing the drifts over the frontier river Vaal. This was a situation to which Chamberlain's methods of Brummagem pushfulness were ideally suited. He at once approached Rhodes's Government with a clean-cut offer to take up the quarrel if need be with the full force of the imperial Government, provided only that the Cape Province would undertake to accept its full share of any military sanctions that might be entailed. This proposal was cordially agreed to, an ultimatum launched, and Kruger, who desired nothing less than a war with his own Dutch kinsmen, backed down promptly and unconditionally. It was only too easy to deduce that he was a man of straw who would always, in the last resort, be amenable to firm handling.

Chamberlain then was in that dangerous state of mind incidental to men of highly volitional temperament who, like Don Quixote, react with masterful decision to a picture more clear than factual that they have formed of a situation. The advices that he received led him to believe that his oppressed countrymen on the Rand, in whose cause his imperialist sympathies were wholly engaged, were both capable and on the point of taking their destinies into their own hands in the best George Washington style, and though nothing would have induced him to take any action, open or secret, at variance with the strict obligations of neutrality, nothing would have delighted him more than to see what he regarded as a corrupt and reactionary tyranny toppled over by such traditionally commendable means. Thus, though he cannot have realized the lengths to which Rhodes and his fellow conspirators were prepared to go, he was in no mood to inquire too closely, or take any positive steps to curb their machinations.

Not that Rhodes himself, though he was neck-deep in the plot to engineer a rebellion on the Rand, was mad enough to contemplate taking the initiative in any openly aggressive action. Jameson and his band had been planted in readiness to restore order in the anticipated event of a revolutionary *fait accompli*. But it soon began to be apparent that the whole strenuously prepared agitation was likely to fizzle out in talk, and that however much of their superfluous cash its millionaire organizers might be emboldened to part with, few of its prospective rank and file were prepared to risk their skins in the venture.[1] An unexpected light was thrown on its imperial aspect when it transpired that a substantial proportion of the Uitlanders were not prepared to embark on it in any case if it meant substituting the Union Jack for the Boer *vierkleur*. The date of the rising had accordingly to be postponed, and with each postponment it appeared less and less on the cards that there was going to be any rising at all.

This anticlimax was too much for Jameson, whose tough following had had enough of idling and tippling in their unprepossessing quarters to be primed for any desperate adventure. There were among them one or two regular officers, one of them with a handle to his name, seconded from good regiments, who were more than willing to take the lead in what promised to be the sporting opportunity of a lifetime. The valiant doctor, having somehow managed to procure a Life of Clive[2] to solace his enforced leisure, worked himself up into such a state of ecstasy that he is said to have exclaimed, 'Clive would have done it!' and so lightheartedly gave the signal for an action fraught with more terrible consequences than any of modern times, except the shot that killed an Austrian Archduke in 1914.

It was in keeping with the spirit of the enterprise that he should have been careful to provide himself with a piteous S O S, concocted by one of the shadiest of Rhodes's satellites, purporting to come from the women and children of Johannesburg—*with the date left to be filled in* to suit the convenience of the addressee.

---

[1] The mere idea that a rising might be attempted was enough to start a panic exodus from the city, with many of the most notorious trouble-makers in the van.

[2] Said to be Macaulay's—but was Macaulay's *Clive* ever published as a separate volume? Personally I am inclined to suspect Henty's *Clive in India*, as being more likely to appeal to a mind on Jameson's schoolboy level.

But the folly of the whole affair surpassed, if possible, its knavery. Rhodes who, whatever else he was, was no fool, and had never expected his too-Fidus Achates to take the bit between his teeth in this insane way, saw at once that 'Jameson', as Rhodes himself put it, had 'upset my apple cart', and wired frantically to stop him—but the wire had been cut. Chamberlain, who was properly furious, did succeed in overtaking the raiders with a peremptory command in the Queen's name to desist, which Jameson flatly and treasonably disobeyed.

Unfortunately the wire to Pretoria, that it was even more essential to cut than that to the Cape, was left intact because, as was alleged and believed at the time, the two troopers detailed for this service were so far gone in the preliminary celebrations as to satisfy themselves with cutting a length of wire fencing.

Kruger, therefore, who was in no way perturbed, having received timely warning, called out his commandos, who easily rounded up the now starving and exhausted filibusters—their transport arrangements having been bungled like everything else—within a short distance of a peaceful and unresponsive Johannesburg. Here they acted sensibly for the first time by meekly laying down their arms without any last-ditch heroics, and with a minimum of casualties.

This sordid and ignominious escapade might have been fraught with less disastrous consequences if it could have been sealed off, so to speak, by its prompt and unconditional repudiation not only by the Queen's Government, but by public opinion in the Home Country. But the imperialist fever had now effected such a penetration of the mass consciousness that any disillusioning experience that threatened to prick the imperialist bladder had to be denied or explained away at all costs, and somehow woven into the texture of a heroic saga. But even so, that the organs of the new mass propaganda, now beginning to develop their full mechanized power, could have got away with such a barefaced travesty of known fact, might have seemed to put too great a strain even on their newly developed technique of mass conditioning, especially as old Kruger, whether in accordance with his rough-hewn godliness, or through innate shrewdness, was careful not to oblige by conferring a martyr's crown on Jameson and his fellow ringleaders, by stringing them up out of hand—as he had every right to do—but instead delivered them humanely or contemptuously over to the almost farcical lenity of British justice.[1]

---

[1] Jameson himself got off with a beggarly fifteen months' stretch, not as a common convict, but in the comparative comfort and luxury of a first-class misdemeanant. Even so he was let out after serving only a fraction of it, on compassionate grounds. Contrast this treatment meted out to the author of 'woes unnumbered' with that accorded to poor Oscar Wilde, who had harmed nobody but himself.

But at this juncture a new factor was violently imparted to the situation that had the effect of accomplishing the apparently impossible feat of informal canonization. The news of Jameson's outrageous act was naturally received with a world-wide indignation that was particularly vocal in a Germany that even at that date was prepared to stick at nothing in pursuit of its own imperial ambitions. No sooner was the result of the Raid known than the Kaiser butted in with an extraordinary telegram of sympathy to Kruger that, though couched in formally unexceptionable terms, contained a suggestion that the President might have appealed to the help of friendly Powers. This, in the hectic atmosphere of the time, was construed as the personal act of the Emperor and a deliberate affront to Britain, all the more bitterly resented because Germany had always been accepted by the British man-in-the-street as his country's natural and cousinly friend, a state of things symbolized every summer by the presence of His Imperial Majesty's squat, two-funnelled yacht *Hohenzollern* at the Cowes regatta.

And no doubt it was a personal matter to the extent that the news had thrown the neurotic Emperor into one of his periodic brain-storms, in which he was capable of almost any mad folly. But the telegram, as we now know, was an act of deliberate ministerial policy—in so far as any act of post-Bismarckian German policy can be said to have been deliberate, since those of the mediocrities and charlatans who were officially in control of it were as often as not frustrated by the machinations of such unacknowledged powers behind the throne as that of the cunning though questionably sane Baron Holstein. No less a state of anarchy in high places could have accounted for such a monumental blunder as this notorious pronouncement, which seems to have been at least partly motivated by some notion of driving Britain into the orbit of a full-fledged German alliance. Its effect was precisely, and from the German standpoint disastrously, the reverse.

Here was a situation to which Salisbury's diplomatic technique was eminently adapted. He knew—no one better—that thanks to his maintenance of an invincible sea power Britain held the winning cards in her hands, and that it would be suicidal lunacy for Germany to plunge into a war with her. But for that very reason, all that was necessary was to sit quietly and imperturbably tight, as Salisbury had done in every other crisis up to date, and as he did up to a point in playing down this one—in which he had the powerful support of Queen Victoria who, disregarding the advice of her eldest son to 'give William a good snub', wrote him a letter that was such a masterpiece of grandmotherly tact as to extract from him the nearest approach to an apology of which he was capable. But Salisbury was an old and tired man, whose grip on the controls of state was beginning to slacken, and was less and less capable of opposing his calculated inertia to the dynamic pushfulness of his Colonial Secretary. And Chamberlain had the full force of public opinion behind him in demanding a reply in kind to the Kaiser's unprovoked provocation.

Accordingly, to the delight of press and public, a flying squadron was ostentatiously fitted out, more than capable of sending to the bottom all that then existed of the Germany navy, whose weakness had been thus exposed to the world, and most of all to the Germans themselves. The result was to play straight into the hands of the powerful faction, headed by the Kaiser himself, that was agitating for a German navy capable of challenging the British to what was bound in its very nature to prove a duel to the death.

But the short-term combined effect of the Kaiser's *démarche* and Salisbury's *riposte* was that of rehabilitating, in British eyes at least, the tarnished prestige of British imperialism. Foreign patronage of Kruger and denunciation of Jameson had made it a matter of national pride to take a spectacularly opposite stance, and to put any objective appreciation of the relevant events out of the question. The pattern of the appropriate myth was dictated in advance. The Raid had got to be presented as a heroic episode on a par with the charge of the Light Brigade and Gordon's self-immolation at Khartoum; as indeed it was by no less a spellbinder than Tennyson's successor in the laureateship, a worthy but slightly absurd little man called Alfred Austin, whom Salisbury, with a massive indifference to aesthetic considerations, had recently jobbed into the post on political grounds, and who justified the choice of obliging with a ballad entitled 'Jameson's Ride', which, though it has become the fashion to refer to it in terms of indiscriminate denigration, was a reasonably competent specimen of its kind, efficiently adapted to its purpose of stirring up public opinion to regard a filibustering fiasco in the light of a crusade:

> When men of our own blood pray us
> To ride to their kinsfolk's aid,
> Not Heaven itself shall stay us
> From the rescue they call a raid!

and so on in a mounting crescendo, until the whole sorry business appeared to be as much of a feather in the national cap as the greatest of victories.

All was therefore for the best in the most glorious of all possible empires, and 'Doctor Jim', as he was thenceforth affectionately styled, received, in his not uncomfortable durance, all that the megaphones of press and music-hall were capable of conferring of canonization and apotheosis as the embodiment of all those qualities that were supposed to be the peculiar perquisite of the imperial breed. Moreover, since every hero of popular melodrama postulates something corresponding in the line of villainy, it is not surprising that Kruger's top hat and the Kaiser's upturned moustache became not only national hate but even contempt symbols, and their comical but at the same time sinister owners the recognized scapegoats for any blame that might otherwise have been imputed to the agents in foreign parts of honest John Bull.

An attitude of sober realism is not to be expected from a patient in delirium, or even from an audience of the old Surrey side type of melodrama. Little was the man in the English street capable of realizing the significance of an event that had made nonsense of Rhodes's dream of sublimating Anglo-Dutch antagonism in a common achievement of bi-racial supremacy. Whether this dream ever could, or ought to, have been realized is at best doubtful. What is beyond dispute is that its dissolution created a situation in which all the forces were set for a head-on British-Boer collision in the near future which, whatever the immediate outcome, would in the long run render it almost a certainty that a united South Africa would gravitate not into but out of the Empire or Commonwealth orbit.

7

BLIND TONGUES

THE JUST over three and a half years that elapsed between the Jameson fiasco and the South African War that was to result in the pricking of the imperial bubble, are a time whose spirit and setting are hardly conceivable to those whose memories are confined within the limits of the present century.

It was, to judge from outward appearances, as if the collective consciousness had become infected with a Gadarene frenzy that was driving the nation headlong into the abandonment of every hitherto distinctively British principle along a course of aggressive acquisitiveness that was to prove, in both the inward and outward sense, one of suicide—the shameful conquest of herself that alone could make her rue.

What would strike any average person of our own day most forcibly, if he could by some magic be transported back to that time, would be its glorification of war. Such a person's most fervent prayer—if he prays at all—will certainly be for peace in his own time. War stands for him as the supreme and unqualified evil. But to judge by the noisiest and most flamboyant expressions of public opinion in the late nineties, one would have imagined war to be the jolliest and most uplifting kind of activity imaginable, especially in that form which, according to all living experience, it was guaranteed to take, with the civilian spectators ensconced as safe as those at a bullfight, applauding the performance of the hired professionals in the ring.

The typical patriotic songs that were chorused in those days, and whose tunes were whistled by every errand boy, would probably be calculated to turn the stomachs of a present-day audience at Broadmoor. 'Another little patch of Red', 'A little British Army goes a long, long way', 'Oh, I'd love to face the foe'—to take the first samples that come to mind—culminating, just before the South African War, in the now almost incredible 'Soldiers of the Queen', that made the Jingo song seem positively pacifist by comparison, for that had at least postulated that 'we don't want to fight', whereas this roared out that we had buckled on our swords, had done with diplomatic lingo, and would do deeds to follow on our words to show the unspecified enemy 'something more than Jingo', but always with the infinitive splitting, but skin-saving proviso

> Old England's laws do not her sons compel
> To military duties do.

For indeed the British wars of the nineteenth century had been of a purely spectacular concern for the Home-dwelling population. Even such grim affairs as the Crimea and the Mutiny had no more directly threatened the man who stayed at home than if they had taken place on another planet. The work and play had gone on just as usual, except for a somewhat higher proportion than usual of bereavements. And even this element had been reduced to almost negligible proportions in the sort of war that had become a chronic feature of imperial development in the latter part of the century, in which, against uncivilized opponents classifiable as 'niggers', victory, after the spicing of an occasional setback, was the more or less guaranteed conclusion; so that

> When we say we've always won,
> And when they ask us how it's done,
> We'll proudly point to every one
> Of England's soldiers of the Queen.

Such an answer involved a complete turning upside down of the real explanation, which consisted in Britain's possession of a sea power that not only enabled her to maintain an immunity from invasion of more than eight centuries' standing, but also (in conjunction with the world's greatest mountain barrier sealing off India) to deny the access of the vast armies of the continental Powers to regions of imperial contention in distant parts of the world. And her power to do this had received spectacular confirmation in the all too public advertisement of German impotence in the matter of the Kaiser's telegram and the flying squadron. The insulation of Britain was a fact which the continental Powers had come to take more or less for granted, but the insulation of everything that Britain chose to include within the compass of a hugely expanding empire was presented as an intolerable grievance by rivals who, unlike her, having the imperial instinct rooted in their nature and tradition, were minded to stick at nothing in the acquisition of as much as possible of the earth's surface for empires of their own.

Looking back on it now, what strikes one as the strangest feature of this access of excited abnormality by which the normally phlegmatic British mentality had become infected, is its extraordinary underlying

complacency. Never in the whole of her history had Britain stood in a
position of greater apparent danger, without a friend or ally of any
significance anywhere, confronted with military Powers in comparison
to whose armies her own might be counted as a drop in the bucket,
and whose peoples were worked up by propaganda into a frenzied
state of hostility towards her, not untinged with envy, and who were
capable, if at any time they could agree to suspend their own differences,
of bringing to bear on her their united forces from the Atlantic to the
Pacific.

And yet the unquestioning assumption common to all the diverse
manifestations of British public opinion, imperialistic or otherwise, was
that the country stood as by right on a pinnacle of power and greatness
unprecedented in her own and perhaps in any history, which happy
state of things was sure to last, and go on improving, as far into the
future as was likely to matter to anybody. Wider still and wider should
her imperial bounds be set, and under the Almighty patronage that
was confidently claimed for her, how could she fail to go on waxing
mightier and mightier? Such claims, even by those who were accustomed to laugh at the Kaiser and his 'good old German God', were
accounted the merest commonplaces in that now hardly imaginable
epoch. It is surely putting it mildly to say that the nation was passing
through a phase, on the plane of mass psychology, that had its individual counterpart in the state of a patient in high fever. Or perhaps we
might put it on a more homely level by saying that a surfeit of the new
wine of empire had made the man-in-the-street fighting and shouting
drunk.

It culminated in the orgy of self-congratulation that was unloosed
on the occasion of the Queen's second or Diamond Jubilee, which
differed from the first in being devoted almost wholly to the assertion
of the armed might of empire, and in taking the form of a vast military
pageant, or triumph, with the most conspicuous emphasis on slouch-
hatted colonials and turbaned sowars,[1] to be followed by an even more
spectacular advertisement of naval supremacy in the form of line upon
line of warships in the Solent, contrasting significantly with the much
more modest effort on the same lines of ten years previously. The
festivities were graced by the assembly in imperial conclave of the
Premiers of the now fully formed daughter nations, under the auspices
of the Colonial Secretary, whose hopes of getting the Empire federated
on a business or any other footing were nevertheless doomed to
evaporate in platitude. The last thing that these young nations wanted

---

[1] These, it may be noted, with the exception of the four identical figures of
1887 representing the members of the United Kingdom, are allowed to monopolize Tenniel's Diamond Jubilee cartoon to the exclusion even of 'The Little
British Army'.

was to be included in any sort of empire on any footing whatever. But that did not prevent the growth of a different sort of free association to any of which so economically oriented an intelligence as that of Chamberlain was capable of envisaging as a practical proposition.

The most enduring memorial of the Diamond Jubilee is the poem written for the occasion by the universally acclaimed laureate of empire. And indeed it would be hardly possible to overestimate the part that Rudyard Kipling, now at the peak of his reputation, played as the inspired propagandist of the imperial idea. Books like those of Seeley on the *Expansion of England* or Dilke's *Greater Britain* had no doubt contributed to the necessary task of putting the Empire, so to speak, on the map, but it was the magic of Kipling that captured the moderately educated and literate classes, and percolated by various channels to a wider and lower circle than that of his actual readers.

Such indiscriminate adulation, followed by a more prolonged and equally tendentious fashion of denigration, has caused even more critical hot air to be emitted, one way or the other, on the subject of Kipling, than on that of any other key personality of modern times. His cult of empire was poles apart from the popular jingoism of the music-halls, and even his conception of empire was in some respects sublimated out of all resemblance to the pedestrian reality. The empire of the sharepushers and bondholders, and of the company promoters and millionaire bosses, did not figure in even his most realistic prose, let alone verse. He might indeed have been described as the last of the Victorian romantics. It was his ability to conjure up a glamorized vision of empire, and to put it across to his nation-wide audience, that ranks him with those poets of whom it can indisputably be asserted, as of Byron and Tennyson, that they were living forces—spellbinders of mass consciousness, palpably modifying the trend of historic developments.

It was the secret of Kipling's magic that he was uniquely qualified to supply the most deep-seated demand of the majority of stay-at-home Britons for an antidote to the drabness and overstrain of a life speeded up and mechanized to an ever-increasing extent. The human machine part, the little man of villa and block, of office and factory, found his horizon widened and himself transported in imagination to a world of brave adventure, of colour and romance, in which the likes of his own minimal self could find uninhibited scope for their repressed impulses, and lord it like kings over inferior and picturesque peoples.

The combined result of his native genius, and his Anglo-Indian environment, was the application of this technique by way of a start to the most extreme case of all, that of the down-and-outs and bottom dogs who formed the bulk of the rank and file of the British regular

L

forces garrisoning India.[1] He wisely (or instinctively) eschewed the Victorian convention of bowdlerizing and idealizing these wearers of the Queen's uniform into 'thin red 'eroes', and portrayed them with as wholehearted a gusto as Burns had his jolly beggars, or Shakespeare the companions of Falstaff, in all their ruffianly humours, but with a seasoning of exuberant brutality that was characteristic of one side of Kipling, and added not a little to his popularity with the public, whose taste he catered for and, in turn, helped to form. And surely nothing subsequently laid to the charge of the toughest Storm Troopers or Gestapo men could have beaten, in its own line, the cynical claim put into the mouth of a presumably typical Soldier of the Queen, that 'if you treat a nigger [a Burmese subject, to judge from the context, of the same Queen Empress] to a dose o' cleanin' rod, 'e's like to show you everything 'e owns'—and this in a lilting catch to cornet accompaniment that is plainly supposed and intended to be uproariously funny. It seems to have occurred to no one at the time to regard such allegations in the light of a horrifying indictment.

But it is impossible to appreciate Kipling without facing up squarely to this pervading duality of his genius which does, for once, warrant the application of what has succeeded the Oedipus complex as the reigning psychological *cliché* of schizophrenia, or split personality. For the two elements in his composition are sharply distinct, and his noblest work seldom fails to be marred by the incongruous intrusion of an element of blatant vulgarity, or worse, by which the whole is all too frequently judged and damned. Thus the magnificent 'English Flag', which develops the theme of

What do they know of England who only England know?

is consigned to a decent oblivion on the strength of one line of hardly intelligible balderdash about 'an Irish liar's bandage and an English coward's shirt' that has no apparent connection with the rest of the poem; even the Jubilee 'Recessional' is marred to all eternity by its spatchcocked reference to 'lesser breeds without the law', so excruciatingly at variance with its solemn refrain of 'Lest we forget!'

The 'Recessional' was indeed less in the nature of a laureate ode than of a writing on the wall at the Jubilee feast. The prophet of empire was its Jeremiah, crying, 'Spare us yet', and, 'Thy mercy on Thy people Lord', as if haunted by the prevision of impending catastrophe. Hi

---

[1] I cannot help recalling the pained surprise of the mostly respectable youn men of a Territorial regiment in 1914, who, on being hospitably entertained o arrival at an Indian cantonment, were bombarded with pamphlets on the eviden assumption that they were of the same tough stuff of which their Regular pre decessors had been composed.

public of jubilating islanders, 'drunk with sight of power' and carried off its feet by the added intoxication of his rhythms, little realized the contempt that he himself entertained for this 'poor little street-bred people who vapour and fume and brag', this *bander log* or race of chattering monkeys, who formed the *hoi polloi* of British democracy.

It was perhaps a pity that this product of an alien environment could not have reframed his famous query so as to read:

What can they know of England who only Empire know?

For Kipling's imperialism was compounded of the twin notions of the Blood and the Law. By the Blood was signified that cult of a Master Race, imposing its supremacy on lesser breeds; and by the Law, not only the disciplined pattern of thought and action that these master races impose on their subject peoples, but still more that to which they themselves are subjected by divine or dictatorial fiat, and by which their individual wills are fused into the unity, not only of an army predictably responsive to the will of a divinely commissioned *imperator*, but even—to take one of Kipling's own most striking images—of the harmonious controllability of machine parts in a ship's engine-room.

The Law of the Blood is essentially an imposed law, a law not of freedom but—as Kipling himself loses no opportunity of emphasizing —of unqualified servitude; the imperial law, of which he himself writes:

Keep ye the law, be swift in all obedience.

Such was the voice of Rome; and it is significant of Kipling that he was never more happily inspired than in his fictional revivification of the Roman overlords of Britain. But it was the direct negation of all that Britain herself had, and that the British Commonwealth of nations would, come to stand for.

Kipling's vision of a British empire was indeed that which sprang naturally from the circumstances of his Anglo-Indian upbringing, an exiguous and alien minority imposing its allegedly beneficent yoke upon a vast recalcitrant majority of 'sullen, silent peoples', in the spirit of the command laid on imperial Rome to rule the peoples with her sway. And at the acme of the imperial intoxication he was even capable of being carried far enough out of himself to present the English to themselves in the wishfully inappropriate guise of 'men of the blood', stark, stern and silent, 'slower to bless than to ban', as dedicated and disagreeable and un-English an *élite* of master bullies as the ancient Spartans.

Naturally such a view of empire ruled out absolutely any possibility of sympathy or partnership between rulers and ruled, even when these latter happened to be the inheritors of far older civilizations than the British. The idea, sponsored by the pre-Mutiny generation of Victorian Liberals, of a trusteeship for liberty, to be realized at the earliest possible date and to the fullest possible extent, was utterly beyond the scope of this latter day purview. Not liberty, even in the remotest future, was now the goal, but

Law, Orrder, Duty an' Restraint, Obedience, Discipline

imposed and maintained by compulsion and, on due occasion, enforced

By a stick (which is really half the trick),

as when the ubiquitous 'Sergeant What's-his-name' was given a free hand to apply such methods of persuasion to the rank and file of the Egyptian armed forces.

But the most revealing defect of Kipling's genius lay in its failure to comprehend the very civilization in whose shadow it had matured. Kipling's knowledge of India was no doubt unsurpassed on the ground level of observation. He could describe the life of bazaar and village with the microscopic realism and eye for significant detail that constituted his unique gift as a story-teller, and he could outdo all competitors in enlarging on the humours of such stock figures of white man's fun as that of the 'jabberacious babu'.[1] But against the intellectual and spiritual life of India, with its ancient and profound philosophic tradition, and above all with its already perceptible gropings towards national or supernational self-determination, his mind was as obstinately closed as that of the most purple-faced *Qua Hi*, laying down the law in his club bar. It is not without its significance that when, in what was obviously his supreme attempt to hold up a comprehensive mirror to the life of India, he felt the need to display at least one figure of religious or other-worldly significance, he must needs import a Thibetan and Buddhist lama, a dear and delightful old primitive, but one incapable of arousing any hostile reaction. But inquire how Kipling may have reacted to a Tagore, a Gandhi, or even a Nehru, and it would be approximately true to answer that he did not, and did not want to. He had his world, and these were not of it. Happily, he did not survive to see that world burst to pieces. It would have distressed him too terribly to bear thinking of.

But Kipling was too much of a seer, in the most literal sense, to be an effective propagandist, even of that gospel of empire of which he

[1] The Hurry Chunder Mookerjee of 'Kim' is the Baboo Jabberjee of the contemporary *Punch* in one of his many aliases.

was the accredited evangelist. The idea of an aristocracy of supermen ruling the lesser breeds with its sway failed to correspond to the facts *as he saw them* and as his Muse moved him to record them. No nationalist or hostile propagandist could have thought up so convincing an exposure.

Not that the picture that Kipling draws of the imperial Raj in India is one of which the most patriotic Englishman need feel anything but proud—within limits. If we are denied the spectacle of a superb and supermanly ruling caste, we are treated to that of hard-working Government servants performing with efficiency and integrity, in their several posts, the routine of a task indispensably necessary to any shaping of a united India, and often in conditions of appalling climatic discomfort and high occupational mortality. But we are also given a devastating insight into the social life of this governing caste in its clubs and cantonments, completely cut off from that of the country, and killing the time of its exile from home in a round of brainless and tasteless futility, seasoned by sexual titillation which, whatever other epithet it may or may not have merited, unquestionably qualifies for that of the Dantesque *vile* or *basso*, which are more accurately expressive than the plain English stigma of vulgarity.

This portrait of the British sahib class forms a worthy companion piece to that which Kipling draws of the British private soldier in India, and in either case, such is the magic that he imparts to it, that through laughter we find ourselves coaxed almost into affection towards its subjects. But as advertisement of Empire its value is something less than negative. It might even be argued, with a certain plausibility, that Kipling's real significance in the unfolding drama of Indian history was to have taught India, by exposing the spiritual bankruptcy of an alien domination, to seek her salvation in the revival of her own soul. In that sense he may even be regarded as having been driven forth in his own despite, and in the spirit (as he might no doubt have phrased it) of the Lord, to make straight the path before the feet of Mahatma Gandhi.

It may at least be conceded that, even at the height of the imperialist boom, Kipling's genius and fundamental integrity kept him on a level incomparably superior to that of the hundred-per-cent empire boosters who were making a good thing out of its promotion and exploitation by manipulating the new techniques of mass persuasion. These included politicians, financiers, entertainers, and above all the organizers of the new type of popular journalism that aimed at cashing in on the need of a literate rather than educated public for combining the maximum of mental stimulus with the minimum of mental effort.

At first, in the eighties, this was both catered for, and intensified, by a new and immensely successful type of popular magazine that battened on nothing more tendentious than the time-killing futility of snippets and titbits of highly spiced information of a kind which, if spoken, would be said to go in at one ear and come out at the other, and was harmful only in its long-term effect of softening the mind and breaking down its powers of resistance to mass conditioning by financially or otherwise interested operators.

But a more serious twist was given to the screw when the Harmsworth brothers, who had been among the most successful purveyors of this new sort of journalistic dope, turned their combined talents to revolutionizing the newspaper in addition to the magazine press. Their decisive irruption into this field of exploitation was timed to coincide with the culmination of the imperialist boom by the launching of their new model popular journal, the *Daily Mail*, on 4th May 1896. This most efficiently conducted venture owed its phenomenal and expanding success to its all-out application of a technique that subordinated every other consideration to the achievement, under stress of the keenest competition, of the maximum volume of sales. This is often expressed in the formula of giving the public what it wants; but that, as it stands, misses the essential point that the wants of the public have not to be followed, but *created*. No journalist of the new school was simple enough to imagine that this was to be achieved by any other means than that of stimulating the passions and keeping them perpetually on the boil. And of all passions the most rewarding—certainly at that time—from the selling point of view, were those of a combative-acquisitive order, stemming from the lust to power. It was at any rate the principle on which the Yellow Press, as it came to be called, consistently acted in the shaping of its highly lucrative policy.

The nineteenth century was going out with a bang, or rather a series of bangs as thrilling and as harmless to the spectators as the best of Brock's Jubilee firework displays. There were a sufficiency of assorted wars, imperial and foreign, to provide the necessary headline material for recurrent sensations, and a whole series of crises and tensions that always seemed to resolve themselves, after redounding to the greater glory of the imperial breed. Nobody, least of all the 'Yellow' publicity bosses, dreamed of bothering about their bard's warning of 'lest we forget'. That was no doubt a poet's way of putting things, and they knew how to make allowance for it; neither the Harmsworths themselves nor any of their rivals and successors were, or could be, in the remotest degree highbrows, and neither to them nor to the public they catered for was there the least difference in point of sentiment between the 'Recessional' and 'Soldiers of the Queen'. To apply the necessary stimulus of 'frantic boast and foolish word' to getting Sons of the Blood 'drunk with sight of power', was after all what they were out to do, since a drunken crowd is notoriously more disposed to be free with its halfpennies than a sober one. That they themselves were so intoxicated with their own dope as to render them, after their own garish lights, sincere patriots, need not be disputed; but that they or the country stood to be any the better for that, perhaps may.

It would be labouring the obvious to pile up evidence of the abnormal state of the public mind during this brief but hectic interlude. It is sufficiently summed up in an essay penned by the aged philosopher, Herbert Spencer, at the beginning of the new century, on the theme of re-barbarization. As a pacifist and Liberal of the most uncompromising though now out-dated Victorian school, Spencer was well qualified to appreciate the catastrophic extent of the relapse into the exaltation of brute force, and the replacement of 'the ideas and feelings and institutions appropriate to civilized life . . . by those appropriate to fighting life'. He shows how 'this diffusion of military ideas, military sentiments, military organization, military discipline' has been pervading every department of national activity—religion, literature, education, journalism, art and, last but not least, sport; '. . . it has long', he says, 'been remarked that a noted athlete is more honoured than a student who has come out highest from the examinations'. And he does not stop short of characterizing a society of this kind as a fit habitation for hooligans.

There is no disputing the factual accuracy of an account that is amply confirmed by the experience of those who can still remember that time. But it may be questioned how far it gives the whole picture or, more specifically, how it applies to the depths as well as the surface of national life. Bouts of fever, when not mortal, seldom permanently affect the patient's constitution. Whatever may be the fate of a British Empire, or the cult of it, there will always (as the wartime song puts it) be an England.

8

IMPERIAL MIRAGE

LOOKING BACK on the closing years of the nineteenth century, one cannot but be impressed, in the light of fulfilled developments, with the tragic futility of the national and imperial ambitions, few if any of which have proved capable of realization even by the victors in the two world wars that they eventually precipitated. What now signify the Franco-German rivalry for the control of Morocco, or the Anglo-French conflict of ambitions on the Nile, or who should have what in a European share-out of Africa or even China? These, and the like issues about which the dynasts and statesmen were arming their countries to the teeth and pushing their claims to the brink of universal catastrophe, have now come to seem too utterly devoid of rational content to be—or to have been—worth quarrelling, let alone fighting, about.

It is hard to find any thread of statesmanlike consistency running through the policies (or what passed for such) of the leading continental Powers. The day of the Bismarcks and Cavours was past; the little men were in the saddle, and the reins were slipping out of their grasp.

British foreign policy at least shows a firmness and consistency out of all comparison with these others, under the Salisbury régime and that of his two successors, Lansdowne and Grey. But Salisbury was an old and tired man and, with his policy of calculated restraint, was less and less capable of applying the brake to the hustling pushfulness and forcefulness of his Colonial Secretary, who had made imperial affairs his almost undisputed province, and was conceded a practically free rein in the handling of the crucial South African problem. This informal division of functions, which amounted to little less than dual control of government policy, did in fact work with an almost complete absence of friction or jealousy between these magnanimous archetypes of aristocratic Toryism and bourgeois Radicalism. But the proverb that 'two heads are better than one' does not apply to State policy, and the danger involved needs no emphasizing.

In Salisbury's own department of specifically foreign policy, the master touch continued to be applied with undiminished sureness, and never had there been greater need for it. The bullying and blundering aggressiveness of the competing imperialisms had produced an international situation of continual tension and recurrent crises, to the accompaniment of wars and threats of war from one end of the world to the other. The main focus of contention had now shifted to the Far East, where the recently modernized and militarized Japanese, by demolishing the (hardly fit to be called) armed forces of the Manchu Empire in China, had started the European Powers swooping down like vultures on what appeared to be the helpless body of that ancient civilization, and starting what bade fair to be another partition on the lines of that of Africa.

In this Britain had no desire to take a hand except in so far as to preserve an open door for her own trade on an equal footing with that of rival nations, though she allowed herself to be drawn into the scramble to the extent of seizing—under the conventional form of leasing—the port and harbour of Wei-hei-wei for no other conceivable reason than the enhancement of her imperial prestige. But apart from this sacrifice to the fetish of the hour, Britain, under Salisbury's guidance, pursued an extremely skilful course governed by the principle of refusing to be drawn into trouble even under the direst provocation, and at the same time building up what, on a short-term view, might be an invaluable friendship with the rising Power of Japan, which had been mortally incensed by the cynical affront inflicted on her by the three chief European empires, in forcing her to disgorge the most coveted item of her Chinese loot in the shape of the naval base of Port Arthur, in order shortly to include this among their other pickings of the same capacious pocket.

But if Britain succeeded in keeping out of trouble in this Asiatic field of imperial expansion, there was ripening for her, in the African continent, a bitter and double harvest of her own sowing, or more specifically, that of her greatest professed opponent of the imperial principle. For we must never lose sight of that inescapable double commitment, under Gladstone's auspices, of the invasion of Egypt and the refusal of independence to the Transvaal. Now, with an openly imperialist Government installed in office, Gladstone's chickens were coming home to roost.

It must be borne in mind that in the informal division of functions (to which I have already referred) between the Premier and the Colonial Secretary, the problem of Egypt came within the sphere of Salisbury's responsibility, and that of South Africa, at the other end of Cecil Rhodes's proposed Cape–Cairo axis, or railway line, within that of Chamberlain.

* L

As regards Egypt, all Salisbury's instincts were in favour of sitting tight and letting sleeping dogs lie as quietly as they could be persuaded to. However deeply Britain might have pledged herself in the first instance to end her occupation at the earliest opportunity, to do so now or in any foreseeable future would not have struck Salisbury in the light of practical policy, if only because he would have had his own party solidly united against what would certainly have been regarded as 'scuttle'; besides which the supremely competent British representative on the spot, now Lord Cromer, was wrestling, in the virtual capacity though without the formal status or legal powers of an imperial proconsul, with the more than Herculean labour of cleaning up the Augean mess of Egyptian administration and finance, and there could be no question of removing him with the task half done, and throwing everything back into chaos. So Britain continued sitting, for want of any practicable alternative, on her own bayonets, and maintaining an administration which, whatever practical benefits it may have conferred on the Egyptians, earned her neither their loyalty nor their gratitude, and imposed a chronic liability on British foreign policy.

Inevitably in the process, Egypt came to be taken more and more for granted by an imperially obsessed public opinion at home, as constituting as much part of the British Empire as India; and in the conception of Egypt was included the whole basin of the White Nile up to its sources—that is to say all the vast, non-Egyptian territory of the Sudan which had lapsed by conquest into what, for nearly a dozen years, had been the unchallenged sovereignty of a tyrant who, whatever else he was, was at least a native of the country.

Nothing would have suited British policy better, on a realistic calculation of imperial interests, than to have left the Sudan to stew in its own juice indefinitely, and to treat it as a derelict and abandoned property to be reoccupied and reclaimed when, if ever, it suited the owner's, or the owner's master's, convenience. Certainly Salisbury would have been the last man to be tempted by ethical or idealistic considerations to disturb so convenient a *status quo*, provided it could only be guaranteed to last. But could it?

Salisbury's sources of intelligence had warned him that, prohibition or no prohibition, France had it in mind to carve for herself in the Nile Valley; and indeed, in her Congo Province, an expedition was already being fitted out, under the intrepid Major Marchand, to force its way through the Mahdi's territory to the prohibited river, with the ultimate object of staking out a claim, in the recognized imperial style, to a continuous belt of territory, joining up the French possessions on the Atlantic to those on the Indian Ocean [1]—the horizontal tit-for-tat

[1] A projected expedition from the East to join up with Marchand failed to get started.

to Rhodes's Cape to Cairo project, and one more nearly within the range of practical possibility.

Salisbury reacted to this situation in his deliberate, unostentatious way. He saw that the time had come to resume the advance up the Nile that had been broken off after the elimination of Gordon. Among the other achievements of the British occupation had been the formation, with the aid of 'Sergeant What's-his-name' and his stick, of an Egyptian army of at least superior calibre and equipment to that formerly commanded by the unfortunate Arabi. The command of this had been entrusted to a Royal Engineers officer with a knowledge of Arabic and a genius for organization—Herbert Kitchener. This grim pioneer of the new spirit of imperialism, who put himself across the footlights as a frozen incarnation of supermanly ruthlessness (though like Bismarck he had a pronounced neurotic streak in his actual composition), was allowed, in 1896, to try out his new model in an upriver push as far as the Dervish advanced base at Dongola. This he accomplished with mechanical precision exactly according to plan and with no perceptible effect on the pocket of the British taxpayer. Henceforth it was obvious that the advance to Khartoum and beyond had become a task not of strategy but of logistic calculation, the pace of the army's advance being determined by that of laying down the accompanying railway, a merely incidental part of the process being the occasional blasting of human obstacles out of the path by instruments that, when brought to bear on hordes of primitive tribesmen, turned battles into mechanized holocausts, but which did not prevent them from being boosted by the organs of imperial publicity into victories fit to rank with the most heroic achievements of the past.

It took Kitchener another two years—years it must be remembered when the imperial fever at home was at its height—to move forward, at this pace that he had set himself, from Dongola to Khartoum; and to clinch the concluding stage of the advance, the Government was induced to go to the modest expense, to the British taxpayer, of sending out a division of Regulars, who imparted that touch of patriotic colour that might otherwise have been lacking to a pageant of Empire as popular and carefully staged as the Diamond Jubilee of the year before. The managing star performer played up to the part expected of him to the point, as some old-fashioned critic might have thought, of over-playing it. For to celebrate a successful dawn attack, in the course of which, after a little over half an hour's fighting, the fortified camp of the last of the Khalifa's field armies had been stormed and given to plunder, Kitchener arranged a parade march, to impress the inhabitants of the neighbouring town of Berber, that outdid the worst features of a Roman triumph—the gallant young enemy commander, hobbled and loaded with chains, being literally thrashed along, pelted by the crowd, in the wake of the conqueror.[1] It was explained and believed at the time that Kitchener's unrivalled knowledge of the oriental mind apprised him not only of the necessity but even the popularity of such exhibitions of imperial power. The event would show.

The eagerly expected climax of the drama was reached when, in the late summer of 1898, the ponderous advance had rolled up to within striking distance of its goal, and the Khalifa's devoted horde, some of them in armour that had done service against the Crusaders, proceeded to attempt just such a wild rush as that of the clansmen at Culloden, and were scientifically wiped out in a glorified *battue* that made thrilling reading when written up for the delectation of imperially minded civilians at home, by what Kitchener characterized, to their faces, as the 'drunken swabs' of the press. Hundreds, literally, of Sudanese warriors were slaughtered for every one of the less than fifty [2] of the victors who became a fatal casualty, and many of the wounded on the losing side, when not dispatched out of hand, were perforce or otherwise abandoned to the vultures where they lay. It was the sort of ruthlessness that had come to be expected of Kitchener, and rather enhanced than detracted from his reputation with a public who, as any reader of contemporary magazines or adventure fiction will realize, demanded a hardening overlay of this quality in its hero supermen.

But even this public found it hard to stomach the ghoulish violation of all previously accepted standards of Christian decency involved in its hero's treatment not only of the domed mausoleum which he had levelled with the ground, but even with what was left of the carcase of Gordon's enemy, the Mahdi—though this, to be sure, was no worse than that meted out to Gordon's own body by the Mahdi and his followers. But from even so uncompromising an imperialist as the old Queen, such skull-for-a-skull logic of barbarism elicited, to her honour, a shocked remonstrance which even Kitchener had to heed. But there is no reason to doubt the genuineness of his emotion when, having settled these various matters to his satisfaction, he broke down and wept on the singing of Gordon's favourite hymn at a parade service held as near as possible to the site of his death. 'K's' was perhaps a simpler and more human soul than he, or his fans, would have preferred to admit.

But the wheel of fate continued to turn. Kitchener's statue in due

---

[1] See *Kitchener*, by Philip Magnus, p. 125. Kitchener, as this biographer does not fail to point out, took care to reserve the pick of the loot for himself.

[2] And a good proportion of these in a ridiculous cavalry charge, staged by the colonel of a crack regiment, apparently with the sporting object of giving the enemy his one chance to engage man to man on equal terms. The most important outcome was the survival of Lieutenant Winston Churchill.

course became as symbolic a monument at the junction of the two Niles as the Mahdi's tomb had been; and when a Sudanese college was founded there under Kitchener's auspices, Rudyard Kipling celebrated the event in a poem exhorting the students to attend it carrying their shoes in their hands and bowing their heads on their breasts in awe of this terrible teacher. But the time would come when a Sudanese règime would again be installed at Khartoum, and the conqueror's effigy be cast out in its turn with at least more decency and respect than the prophet's bones had been.

Kitchener had not arrived a moment too soon—if indeed he had arrived soon enough. For it turned out that a more formidable claimant to the lordship of the Sudan than the fugitive and shortly-to-be-destroyed Khalifa had arrived on the scene, and that Marchand's devoted band had actually succeeded in establishing a precarious lodgment on a pestilential site higher up the river, where only Kitchener's victory had saved it from destruction at the hands of the Dervish hordes. But according to the strange rules of the game of imperial grab, its mere presence was enough to establish the sovereignty of the French Empire over a vast undefined portion of the Nile basin already claimed by Egypt, and through Egypt, Britain.

A situation had thus arisen involving these two neighbouring Powers, so recently allies in arms, in a head-on confrontation that there was no face-saving means of resolving short of a full-scale war, on account of this valueless parcel of desert ground of whose very existence no inhabitant of either of them had previously been aware, and which was no more, on any intelligible reckoning, the property of either than one of the craters of the moon. Such might have been deemed the *reductio ad absurdum* of the imperialist logic. But in the mood of delirious exultation into which Britain, and of inflamed *amour propre* into which France, had been worked up, there seemed no escape from its being pushed to its insane conclusion of a conflict in arms from which neither Power stood to derive any conceivable advantage, and in which both had everything to lose, since it would have opened up the almost certain prospect of European, and perhaps ultimately world, domination to the already overweening military power of the German Reich, which would have had the choice of throwing in its decisive weight, at its chosen moment, on the side of whichever combatant might best accord with its own interested calculations.

One can see now that the fate not only of Britain but of civilization itself trembled in the balance during these weeks of autumn crisis, which the British press, with a recklessness that is hardly credible, spared no pains to exacerbate by a coat-trailing arrogance that recalled its most flamboyant excesses of the Palmerstonian heyday.

Providentially the supreme control on both sides was exercised by men with enough saving sense to avoid the suicidal plunge into belligerency. Not only was Salisbury, with his massive imperturbability, the statesman of all others fitted to handle a crisis of this sort, but even the grim Kitchener turned out to have at command a diplomatic genius vouchsafed to few soldiers, and utterly at variance with the reputation he had built up for himself of intransigent ruthlessness. He had, as an unfledged subaltern, contrived to serve a brief apprenticeship with the French forces in the latter stages of the Franco-German War, and this stood him in good stead in soothing the sensitive pride of the gallant Marchand, whom he was able to approach on the easy footing of a comrade in arms—a comradeship one day to be renewed on the field of battle.[1] And the control of French foreign policy was in the hands of one of those clear-sighted and utterly unsentimental realists who are France's peculiar speciality. M. Delcassé never for a moment allowed his attention to be diverted from his country's prime need of settling accounts with the invader actually encamped on her soil, to a quarrel with the very Power that it would be the clinching master stroke of his diplomacy to enlist as an ally, and with whom its command of the sea would render it unprofitable ineptitude to embark on a necessarily amphibious conflict.

France, therefore, having manœuvred herself into this impossible position, acted according to form, through the agency of this highly representative Frenchman, by putting her imperial pride into her pocket and, as it were, with a contemptuous shrug, conceding the point at issue and allowing Marchand and his band to fade out of their uncomfortable predicament under cover of a terrific press barrage. Relations between the two countries could hardly have been worse, as the flaming scandal of the Dreyfus frame-up, then at its height, had outraged every English instinct of justice and decency, and insults were enthusiastically bandied to and fro across the Channel. But the patient realist at the Quai d'Orsay continued to bide his time, caring for none of these things, and with his mind's eye fixed not on the valley of the Upper Nile but on that of the Upper Rhine, over which the wrong sort of tricolour continued to wave.

No further opposition was now to be apprehended to the restoration of the pre-Mahdist *status quo* in the Sudan, under the auspices of the Khedive's Sirdar, or Commander-in-Chief, which was Kitchener's official designation. The Khalifa and his faithful band of surviving emirs were duly rounded up, and met their fate with dignity, but there were few regrets over the disappearance of a régime that had revived

---

[1] Rudyard Kipling, as I had the fortune to hear from his own lips, was a witness, somewhere on the Western Front, of this historic reunion, against a Rabelaisian background to which only he would have been capable of doing justice.

the worst features of the native tyrannies that had ruled the roost in darkest Africa before the coming of the white man, and under which the population of the Sudan had shrunk to an extent about which estimates differ, but which was certainly devastating. But with all its evils, it had at least been a genuine Sudanese creation, for which tens of thousands of Sudanese had been ready to lay down their lives with a devotion never surpassed by any patriot host on historic record.

Thus alien domination had been restored with one highly significant difference. The country was no longer called the Egyptian, but the Anglo-Egyptian, Sudan. It was as if the Khedive's property had been restored after the restorer had appropriated fifty per cent of it as the price of his services. But there was a further implication. Such a joint régime would be plainly unworkable if Britain were to honour her own repeated undertaking of evacuating Egypt. The new arrangement tacitly assumed the occupation to be permanent. And it is easy to see how in fact, if not in form, this might result in the extension of the British Empire to cover the whole Nile Basin from source to delta.

How the Egyptians themselves, or the Sudanese, might react to this disposition of themselves and their lands was a question that nobody, in those days of the white man's burden and imperial grab, troubled to ask. But an answer might in due season be—as it in fact has been— forthcoming.

9

THE WAR THAT ONE MAN WANTED

WHEN WE SPEAK of the concluding lustrum of the nineteenth century, dating from the commencement of the third Salisbury administration, as marking the culmination of British imperialism, we shall be well advised to apply to even so superficially unchallengeable a description the tests of 'How much?' and 'How deep?'

Admittedly, to judge by the noisiest and most obvious phenomena of the press, the music-halls, and other recognized stimulants and outlets of mob emotion (not excepting that of organized state pageantry), it might have been concluded that the new-born lust for conquest and empire had rendered England's shameful conquest of herself, and everything that England had ever stood for, an already accomplished fact.

But there are some things that are too bad to be true, and this is one of them. Rocks and narrows may cause froth to accumulate on the surface which adverse winds may blow back, but beneath, the flow continues as pure and powerful as ever, until it broadens out, foamless and unruffled, on its passage to the sea.

It is as well to realize how factitious and worked up an excitement all this about a British Empire actually was. Even the Conservative Liberal-Unionist combination, which more or less assumed sponsorship for the cult of it, had not been swept into power—as is too often assumed—on the crest of an imperialist wave. Indeed the Empire had hardly been an issue of the 1895 election, if only because the Liberal Premier, Rosebery, had tended to be at least as much as, if not more ostensibly of an empire booster, than the unenthusiastic Salisbury, whom the electorate had preferred largely because, in the absence of any positively urgent issue, it saw a greater chance of its being godly and quietly governed by an impressive team of elder statesmen than by the distracted factions that were too busy fighting among themselves for the control of the Liberal party to find any agreed platform to stand on.

But a party with nothing more substantial to offer than a time-marking stability has no chance of stabilizing its own hold on a democratic electorate, that is insatiable in its demands for some positive return for its suffrages, whether in the way of practical benefits or psychological stimulus—the up-to-date equivalents of bread and circuses. The demand for the bread of social reform might be allowed to stand over for so long as the imperial circus, under the direction of the incomparable Joe, could be kept booming from one sensational turn to another. But the most thrilling of entertainments cannot be prolonged indefinitely, and for even the most hypnotized of audiences the spell will eventually be broken, and the prosaic business of life resumed.

Even when the imperialist fever was at its height, its hold on the community was, at most, partial both in extent and depth. Large and important sections were actively against it, and this included the core of the Liberal party, which had lost no time after the election in shedding its imperialist leader, and which, in spite of a small but intellectually distinguished imperialist splinter group, was under the official leadership of such Gladstonian survivals as Harcourt, Campbell-Bannerman and Morley, who, whatever their differences between themselves, were at least united in their uncompromising rejection of imperialism. There was a left-wing section, including the wealthy and cynical Labouchere, that carried their hatred of empire to fanatical lengths by backing every enemy of their own country blind, on every conceivable issue, regardless of merit; and the most distinguished of all the intellectuals, Herbert Spencer, once actually went so far as to welcome the prospect of a foreign invasion. In self-consciously advanced circles indeed it was apt to be regarded as more of a *cachet* than a stigma to take sides not only against the British Empire but against Britain herself, on every conceivable issue, and the names of Chamberlain, Rhodes and Kipling, of the Randlords and press bosses, were pejorative cockshies—symbols of outsiderdom.

Undoubtedly the Unionist Government found the continual stoking up of imperialist sentiment its strongest—almost its only—political asset, but even while the bubble continued to expand unpricked, the electoral pendulum was beginning to gather its customary momentum, and the erosion of by-elections was gradually but significantly taking its toll of the still enormous majority. On the basis of past experience it might have been predicted with some confidence that if this Parliament were allowed to run its course, without the irruption of any new and sensational electoral issue, the best of the Unionists could expect would be a repetition of their experience of the 1892 election, in which their opponents had been put in office by Irish support. For the penalty of their own success in defeating Home Rule had been that, short of an odd hundred British majority over its Liberal opponents, no Unionist Government could ever hope to govern at all; while without a similar majority over the Unionists even the Liberals could not themselves form a Government except by yielding to the minimum Nationalist demand for a Home Rule for the Catholic that would include the enslavement of the Protestant Irish community, setting the stage for civil war in the lesser island, and constitutional deadlock in the greater.

In these circumstances the obvious lead for a Unionist administration was to play up the empire stunt for all it was worth; but even if the necessary frenzy could have been maintained at fever heat by a perpetual series of fresh stimulants in the way of wars, crises and paintings of the map red—which was too much to hope for—it did not seem as if the remorseless swing could be more than slowed down. Even so there was no alternative, in the circumstances, to going all out and giving Chamberlain the freest possible hand, even if some of his colleagues in the ministry did so more of necessity than of choice— for the imperialism of perhaps a majority of these old political hands was, to say the least of it, lukewarm.

Still, there it was, and it was indisputable that 'Joe', with his orchid and eyeglass (as effective strength-symbols as the moustache of Kitchener or the pipe and dressing-gown of Sherlock Holmes), was the personality that dwarfed all others, both as the most applauded and best hated figure in the public eye. His multifarious activity in developing the resources and promoting the interests of the Crown Colonies, and even his abortive efforts to federate Britain with her self-governing dominions on a militant or business footing, did undoubtedly have the effect of creating an empire consciousness such as had never before, even under Disraeli's auspices, struck such roots in the mind of the common Englishman.

But immense as this achievement was on any reckoning, Chamberlain had played a secondary part in the imperial drama during the three years that had elapsed since the Jameson fiasco. The main interest had shifted to the Egyptian field, which was out of his province. But after Kitchener's triumph, and the trumpetings and junketings with which it had been celebrated, Egyptian affairs had faded out of the headlines, and the Khalifa's existence was forgotten even before it was snuffed out. A new and even more sensational turn had to be put on, if the already overstrained excitability of the audience was to be maintained at the boiling-point so urgently required in the interests of the financial, journalistic, political and other promoters of the imperial boom.

Luckily for them, if for no one else, the turn was already billed, and in fact overdue. The South African crisis might be in abeyance, but it was in no way resolved. Jameson's reckless act had indeed failed, thanks to a degree of restraint on both sides most uncharacteristic of South African controversy, to detonate an immediate explosion, but a situation had been created that only a continuance of such restraint, and a spirit of mutual accommodation that had hitherto been far to seek, could prevent from precipitating a catastrophe that would be all the worse when it came the longer it was delayed.

The elements of the problem were so simple that it might seem almost incredible that they should have been so little appreciated even by those in the highest authority, let alone by a tragically uninformed, or rather misinformed, public opinion. But in an atmosphere of artificially worked up excitement, and with the urge to sensationalize and melodramatize every day-to-day item of news, it would be as sensible to look for considered judgment to emerge in the course of a drinking bout. Even statesmen, with a very few outstanding exceptions, are, like stockbrokers, notoriously disinclined to lay their plans further ahead than next settling day. And if Salisbury was to be counted among the exceptions, Chamberlain most emphatically was not. His instinct was all for the *ad hoc* solution of each problem immediately confronting him, and getting on to the next with all possible speed and energy. And here was a problem that required patience more than drive for its solution, and patience was a quality in which Chamberlain, like Rhodes, was conspicuously lacking.

It must never be forgotten that the basic nature of the South African problem was not two- but threefold. The British there constituted a minority of the white population, committed to maintain British sovereignty over a predominantly Dutch majority; and British and Dutch combined constituted a white minority seeking to impose its sway upon a black majority of the total population. And to complicate things still further, the inherited principles that governed British and Dutch in their dealings both with the native majority and each other were fundamentally opposed. The Dutchman, or Boer, was an imperialist in the Roman and a racialist in the Hebrew tradition. Like the Hebrew, he believed himself to be the member of a chosen people, with a divine mandate to turn the Canaanites of his promised land into hewers of wood and drawers of water; and like the Roman, he believed in ruling other peoples, as opportunity served, with his sway. He stood for liberty with invincible determination, provided it was the liberty of himself and his people to be slaves to no man and, on due occasion, slavemasters of other men.

The British, on the other hand, were in process of evolving an order of civilization that was based not on some abstract conception of liberty but on the concrete rights and liberties of each and every individual member of it, without distinction or exception, as its multiple and unalienable foundation. This idea of honouring one's neighbour's liberties as one's own implies the direct negation of both racial and imperial principles. Unfortunately it would be more accurate to say that Britain was moving towards this goal than that she had already attained it. At this very moment strong influences were at work to prevent her from resting true to herself, and standing fast by her own inherited tradition.

These considerations must be borne in mind if we are to understand what was at stake in the tragic conflict of principle that, after the abortive attempt to solve it by Jameson and his troopers, was working up more and more ominously towards a major conflict in arms. For the moment his easy and plainly justified suppression of that act of banditry had put Kruger in a morally unchallengeable position that he had proceeded to exploit with studied restraint and moderation. But the old patriot could hardly be blamed for believing his worst suspicions of the English, both within and without his gates, to be confirmed by this barefaced invasion of his country in time of peace, in conjunction with a well financed plot to overthrow its government by armed revolution; nor yet for employing the toll he exacted from the Uitlander immigrants for their use of the Rand mines in buying weapons from abroad to strengthen his country's defences.

And it was at least understandable that he should have become more hardened than ever in his determination to keep the government of that country in the hands of the God-fearing people who had won it with such difficulty, and not, by conceding the franchise to those unassimilable denizens of what he regarded as a sink of iniquity, to allow its control to pass into their hands by sheer weight of numbers.

But there was another side to this question, and indeed to the President's own character. Sincere as he undoubtedly was in this simple faith in the righteousness of his own and his people's cause, he was far from being a simpleton in other ways, but combined a Calvinist hardness with the acquisitive shrewdness of a peasant farmer, and a Dutch farmer at that. The régime that he set up on the Rand was based on a frank determination to sweat the aliens for all that they could be made to yield, without regard to the British taboo—which Kruger as a Dutchman saw no particular reason for honouring—on taxation without representation. On that principle the British Government, and Chamberlain in particular, had what from the British point of view was a watertight case for the strongest diplomatic pressure, if nothing else.

But there was another element that entered into the dispute of a more questionable order, in the shape of the claim to sovereignty or suzerainty that, as we have already seen, Britain was determined to assert over the Transvaal. This, which apart from its being based on a highly questionable interpretation of treaty wording, was as flatly in violation of every British principle as Kruger's own claim to impose an arbitrary sway upon the Uitlanders, reposed on no other ground than that of imperialism naked and unashamed—the right, that is to say, of the stronger Power to lord it over the weaker to the limit of its capacity. The Transvaalers, who had gone out into the wilderness for the precise object of being their own masters in their own country, saw even less reason for entering into allegiance to a British Empire than their ancestors of the United Provinces had for continuing in that of Spain. Kruger was therefore merely vindicating British principles against Britain herself, in standing out as unconditionally—though not yet as belligerently—for the independence of his people, as William the Silent or, for that matter, George Washington, had in the past.

But it was just on this issue, on which it might have been supposed that Britain would have been ready to go to the greatest lengths to meet him, that he came up against a blank wall of negation. The imperial fever in Britain was mounting towards its own crisis, and the Unionist Government was playing up the Empire for all it was worth as its only way of staving off its own political bankruptcy. For Chamberlain, the great imperial architect and showman, to have allowed Kruger, of all people, to get away with what the imperialist press would have construed as the insolent repudiation of his lawful allegiance, thereby diminishing the Empire to the extent of an entire province, would have been construed as an unthinkably humiliating surrender; and to allow this precious suzerainty to be made the subject of a bargain would have been deemed a concession to blackmail. Chamberlain himself would certainly have viewed it in that light.

For indeed he must have realized that, except in the alleged capacity of suzerain Power, Britain would have been without a leg to stand on in asserting her right to intervene in so strictly domestic a concern as the franchise laws of the Transvaal Republic, however hardly these might have borne on the Uitlander or any other section of that community. One can imagine what her own reaction would have been to the attempt of some foreign government to have had a voice in the framing of one of her own Reform Bills. And yet the grievances of this dubiously reputable but certainly overtaxed and under-represented populace of gold-hunters were being stunted and inflated so intensively that their formal redress had come to be regarded as a test case of imperial prestige, particularly since the promotion of the imprisoned Jameson to the status of a national hero had made it no less a call of honour to avenge him than to avenge Majuba. And it was being asked how long 'Joe', of all people, was going to stand for this sort of thing. His own prestige as the strong man, the potent spellbinder of empire, was also at stake. And it was not Chamberlain's way to shrink from the challenge.

And yet, on a long-term view of the South African situation, there can never have been a more overwhelming case for the exercise of restraint and conciliation to the extreme limit of practicability. For its inescapably governing factor consisted in the decisive numerical preponderance of the total Dutch over the total British white population. One of the most outrageous of the South African War choruses posed the question

> Is Boer or Briton going to rule?
> That's what we want to know.

Just so. But if Boer were to make up his unanimous mind that *he* was going to rule, what was Briton going to do about it? Or indeed what *could* he do about it? He could, if he chose, flatly repudiate his own British principles and take the imperial strong line of asserting his right to rule by dint of superior force, trusting to his practically unlimited reserves of wealth and manpower to beat or wear down any direct challenge in arms to his supremacy. But supposing him to have accomplished this feat—what then? Short of exterminating or expelling the entire Dutch population, he would be committed to holding it down in perpetual armed subjection, a thing that even if it had been physically possible—let alone profitable—would have so plainly have involved Britain's sacrifice of her own soul as to amount to a psychological impossibility. War therefore—even a successful war—would be no solution, but rather an aggravation of the problem.

All this might have been foreseen from the first by anyone capable of seeing beyond the fleeting issues and contentions of headline interest. It ought to have been as plain as a pikestaff that the sole British alternative to clearing out of, or knuckling under in, South Africa lay in winning the spontaneous co-operation of at least a sufficient portion of the Dutch settlers to form the substance of a united nation within the unity of a free commonwealth. The way of force and empire led nowhere, or worse than nowhere. The way of conciliation, however hard or humiliating it might be to tread, was the only one that offered the least hope of arriving anywhere.

That hope had been woefully compromised by recent events. The spirit of racial partnership that had been fostered by Rhodes, on however questionable a footing, had been blown to the winds by his own and his too zealous henchman's criminal folly. All over South Africa the fires of Boer nationalism, that in the Cape Province at least had seemed to have been effectively banked, were kindled into a blaze. Kruger, whose tenure even of his presidency had been far from secure, now came to be elevated to the status of a patriot hero, and at the next presidential election his majority, from being precarious, became overwhelming. The neighbouring Orange Free State, which had hitherto kept strictly to itself in peaceful isolation, and had

harboured no ill feeling against the British, was now so far bitten by
the infection as to allow itself to be drawn into what became the
equivalent of an offensive and defensive alliance with the Transvaal.
And at the Cape, the Bond, that had now reverted to the anti-British
principles that under Rhodes's influence it seemed to have shed, was
in political control.

This was a calamitous worsening of the situation, but given time
and patience it need not have been irremediable. Even in the Transvaal
Kruger could not in the natural course of things have been expected to
last much longer, and with that immovable obstacle out of the way,
time and patience might yet have opened a path to a reasonable
accommodation with Britain, even in the matter of the Uitlanders.
Never had there been a case in which every consideration of sense and
sanity had more plainly indicated the need for a policy of temporization,
though such a line was not the one best suited to the pushful genius of
the Colonial Secretary.

None the less Chamberlain was no reckless thruster or man of
blood, and was fully alive to the calamitous consequences that would
be bound to result from a war with the Transvaal. And for the time
being he had enough on his hands with the scandal and recrimination
that had been unloosed by the Jameson episode, in the guilty foreknowledge of which it was implausibly sought in some hostile
political quarters to implicate him. But in the spring of 1897 he took
a step of apparently the most unexceptionable nature. The post of
High Commissioner at the Cape had fallen vacant, and Chamberlain
managed to secure the appointment to it of Alfred Milner, a man whose
parts and record were admitted on all hands to render him ideally fitted
for it. And indeed, during his long career of public service, there was
no one ever found to question either the brilliance of his intellect or
his personal integrity. But Milner, who, besides having German blood
in his veins, had been born and partly educated in Germany, had
acquired a mentality far more Teutonic than British, in its cold and
dedicated intransigence of authoritarianism, that, once it had fixed on
its goal, drove forward to its realization without ruth or compromise,
regardless of every other consideration. Milner was in fact—what no
genuine Englishman has it in him to be—an imperialist pure and
simple to an extent bordering on the totalitarian, and all the more
effectively from his entire personal disinterestedness.

He addressed himself to his task with characteristically Teutonic
thoroughness, and spent the first nine months of his commissionership
in a comprehensive survey of the whole situation, even going so far as
to learn the local Dutch patois or *taal*, before deciding on his line of
policy. But his conclusion, when he did finally arrive at it, was communicated with a clear-cut incisiveness in a letter to Chamberlain to the

effect that there was no way out of the present troubles in South Africa but that of reform in the Transvaal or war, and that the chances of reform were worse than ever.[1] This was a declaration such as might have come from Hitler himself—and such as actually did fall from the lips of Ribbentrop in one unguarded moment [2]—to the effect that the way of war was now irrevocably decided on, and it was certainly the line that Milner henceforth pursued with unswerving consistency.

This is not the place to chronicle the negotiations that pursued their course with gradually accelerating tempo to the conclusion coldly envisaged by Milner, and light-heartedly sought by the most vocal section of the civilian public at home and its mentors of the Yellow Press. But it is essential to note the tragic failure on either side to realize what a desperate undertaking a war, if it were once allowed to break out on the scale now threatened, would be for whichever party decided to take the plunge. But Boer and Briton, if they differed on all other points, resembled each other in the sort of intoxicated self-confidence that has been dubbed by the unintentionally significant epithet of Dutch courage.

Certainly the Boers themselves possessed this in full measure, and their easy triumphs over Colley and Jameson had convinced them of their ability to deal in like manner with any amount of the despised *Rooineks* (or Rednecks), as they called the English Tommies, particularly as they were now in process of arming themselves to the teeth with weapons made in Europe and purchased with the Rand gold. And this confidence had been still further inflated by the false hopes of German intervention on their behalf that had been raised—perhaps intentionally—by the Kaiser's sinister performance on the telegraph wires. How far Kruger himself was swayed by these calculations it is impossible to say; but it is at least in character that with him it was not a matter of calculation, but of simple faith in a divine Ally whose choice of him and his people could be taken for granted.

Such a blind confidence might have been excused in an illiterate old Dopper evangelist, but it seems strange that hard-bitten men of the world like the protagonists of British imperialism—and this applies equally to Rhodes, Chamberlain and Milner—should have been at least as obsessively puffed up by it, and as seemingly incapable of a realistic adjustment of political ends to the military means at their disposal. They all, not even excepting the unconditionally bellicose

---

[1] Quoted in the article on Milner in the *Dictionary of National Biography*.

[2] See *Ciano's Diary*, trans. M. Muggeridge, p. 558. In W. Blunt's Diaries it is stated, on the authority of Sir W. Harcourt, that Milner had said to Lady Cowper: before leaving for the Cape, 'If I come back without having made war I shall consider my mission has failed' (p. 334).

Milner, seem to have convinced themselves, in the abstract, of the necessity of a firm line with Kruger, without the least serious attempt to work out in the concrete what such firmness would postulate in the way of wealth and manpower. Their forces on the spot were negligible to start with, and as their policy waxed stronger and stronger their visible power to back it, relatively to that being built up by their prospective enemy, waned feebler and feebler.

No doubt they were civilians, who were not trained to reckon in military terms, but it was not as if they were without warning from those who were. It so happened that when after eighteen months of unremitting work, that had overstrained not only his nerves but his eyesight, Milner, who had already, by a deliberately inflammatory speech, clearly indicated the uncompromising line he meant to take, returned to England for a couple of months' leave, his functions as High Commissioner devolved automatically on the new military commander, Sir William Butler, whose arrival at the Cape had more or less coincided with the High Commissioner's own departure. This remarkable Irishman, in addition to a brilliant military record, was a man of outstanding culture and an independence of judgment unusual in his profession. His previous knowledge of South Africa convinced him that the Uitlander agitation that was being worked up into a *casus belli* was a ramp engineered in their own interests by intriguing financiers, and he took it upon him to turn down a petition that had been got up on the Rand with the purpose of invoking British aid for the redress of Uitlander grievances—a refusal calculated to infuriate his civilian superiors.

This was not Butler's only deviation from the prescribed line. As the commander of whatever British forces might be available for the implementation of a war policy, it was his duty to take stock of the military situation, and he arrived in the course of this survey at some highly disquieting conclusions. Not only was the skeleton force at his disposal incapable of executing more than a delaying withdrawal to the coast before that which the Boers were capable of putting into the field against it, but the minimum manpower that would need to be mobilized, equipped and transported to South Africa in order to turn the tables would be far in excess of the light-hearted estimates of the civilian authorities—Butler did not hesitate to put it at the then incredible figure of eighty thousand. This, far from being excessive, proved in the event to work out at less than a half, and not much more than a third, of the number that would be in fact required. But Milner and Chamberlain, in their wishful optimism, did not want to have this sort of home truth thrust under their noses. Quite obviously this amiable eccentric, in addition to being a Home Ruler, was also, on his own showing, a Pro-Boer—which would account for anything. They had never wanted to have him sent out by the War Office in the first place, and they now proceeded to lever him out of harm's way as unostentatiously as possible, by getting him transferred to the Western Command at home.

The stage was now set for the concluding act. Milner knew exactly what he wanted and drove ahead with remarkable consistency, dragging the reluctant Chamberlain, who to the last clung to the hope of a peaceful solution, in his wake. But public opinion at home was being aroused to frenzy on behalf of the Uitlanders by such provocative dramatization of their case as the High Commissioner's description of them as 'helots', which, unless he were to be publicly repudiated, made it an accepted point of national and governmental honour to take up the cudgels on their behalf.

While he was still in England an incident had occurred that played straight into Milner's hands. An English miner called Edgar, of a disposition well adapted to that tough environment, got involved in a drunken Johannesburg street brawl, and laid out a much smaller man unconscious in the gutter. Being followed to his nearby domicile by a Boer policeman, bearing the incongruous name of Jones, who endeavoured to force an entry, the enraged Edgar proceeded to set about him with a stick weighted with a metal knob. The man who, like all his colleagues, was armed with a revolver, regrettably, but understandably, loosed it off point-blank, with the inevitable result. Jones was duly brought before a court which, again understandably, refused to convict him in circumstances of such extreme provocation. But the bearer of the fine old Saxon name of Edgar was exalted to the status of a national martyr, and the whole rather sordid incident dramatized as the culminating proof of a diabolical police tyranny. A second petition that was duly got up to take advantage of its excitement obtained a much greater number of signatures than the one turned down by Butler.

In this atmosphere of gathering crisis it was sought to obtain a reasonable settlement of the Uitlander problem in a personal conference between the Transvaal President and the British High Commissioner, in the Free State capital of Bloemfontein, and hopes naturally ran high of a peaceful solution of the whole dispute. 'Oom Paul' had come, as anyone who had known him or indeed any other farmer, might have anticipated, prepared to sit down to the threshing out of a hard and long-drawn-out bargain, no doubt in the traditional Dutch spirit of giving as little and asking as much as possible, and for as long as possible. But Milner made it clear from the start that he had not come to strike or even consider any bargain at all. He was there not to discuss but to dictate. He had his minimum terms for a settlement laid down in advance, and Kruger might take them as they stood or leave them and take the consequences.

If Milner had had any experience in dealing with farmers, he would have realized that such tactics would get him nowhere except deadlock. Kruger was plainly incapable of adjusting his mind to this way of doing business. He kept on producing arguments and objections that Milner brushed impatiently aside. He kept harping on his fear of allowing the independence of his own people to be submerged, but Milner intimated with some brusqueness that he had heard enough of this. Finally, Kruger came out with what he had no doubt intended for his trump card, a Reform Bill all cut and dried of his own drafting, in reply to Milner's proposals, no doubt in the expectation that some kind of compromise might eventually be hammered out between the two. But Milner had not come to compromise, and made it brutally clear that there was nothing doing along any lines but his own. Finally the poor old man bowed his head and burst into tears, crying, with obviously genuine emotion: 'It is our country you want!' The only effect on Milner, who perhaps realized that there was more truth in this than he would have cared to admit, was to make him break off the conference altogether, with an abruptness that shocked even Chamberlain, and that Milner himself had the grace to admit had been wrong, and due to his extreme fatigue. But the mischief was done, and the golden opportunity had passed. The stage was now plainly set for war.

Even so it need not have come. Chamberlain certainly did not want it, and it is to the last degree improbable that Kruger did. It is a possibility that cannot be absolutely ruled out that he had all along been merely playing for time, and that he was only waiting for the ideally favourable moment when the grass had started growing on the veldt to unloose the forces that he had armed so lavishly and that had been building up along the frontier in a supreme attempt to crush the hated British. But Kruger was no fool, and such a theory would argue him the most inept of conspirators, in the light of the actual event. It seems far more probable that even Milner's abrupt *démarche* had failed to put him out of the bargaining habit of mind that was ingrained in him, and that he continued to plod on at his ox-like gait towards the eventual settlement that he meant to secure on the best terms that could be got. He had been enough impressed by Milner's insistence on the Uitlander franchise to see that, distasteful as it was to him, he would eventually have to stomach most at any rate of that bitter draught, but he thought something might be obtained in the way of compensation if he could only get some relaxation of that irritating if undefined claim to British suzerainty.

Accordingly therefore, through the agency and probably the initiative of a rising young lawyer politician of whom more was to be heard later, Jan Smuts, he came forward in the middle of August 1899, more than two months after the Bloemfontein episode, with an offer to grant everything, and more than everything, that Milner had demanded on behalf of the Uitlanders, on condition that Britain should refrain from interfering henceforth in the internal affairs of the Transvaal, and that no more should be heard about suzerainty. What this amounted to but a frank proposal to apply British principles of liberty and self-government all round it is hard to see. But the cult of empire, which had nothing to do with British or any other liberty, had become a ruling obsession with Chamberlain, and the least suggestion of yielding a jot or tittle of any claim to imperial sovereignty was enough to arouse him to positive fury. The Transvaal 'belonged' to the Empire; Britain was the paramount Power and meant to remain so. And so this eleventh-hour attempt to bring about a solution of the crisis in what would have been the commonwealth way was turned down without even an attempt to explore whether, with patience, a bargain might not after all have been arrived at along these lines. Had it been, it is probable that there might have been no South African War, and at least conceivable that there would have been no eventual secession of South Africa from the Commonwealth.

10

CRISIS AND CONVALESCENCE

MATTERS HAD now got too far out of hand for the drift to war to be averted. British public opinion had been worked up to such frenzy on behalf of the 'helots' and against Kruger, that the Government was practically forced into grasping the nettle; and it is doubtful whether Kruger, for his part, would have been able much longer to hold back the burghers who were mustering on the frontier, primed up for a final settlement of accounts with an enemy whose reserves of strength they, in their peasant simplicity, were incapable of appreciating.

Chamberlain, who at last seems to have got some inkling of the hopelessly weak hand he had to bluff from, had woken up to the urgency of having force to back his demands, though, like everyone else in England except the unfortunate Butler, he grossly underestimated the amount of force that would be required. But on 22nd September, and with the full backing of the Cabinet, he signified in terms of now open menace that the British Government absolutely repudiated the claim of the Republic to be an independent sovereign power, and that they intended to present their terms for a final settlement at a later date. This amounted to a cool proposal that the Boer forces should keep themselves in suspended animation on the frontier for the few weeks it would take to mobilize and transport a British army capable of crushing them. They naturally accepted this as a plain intimation that, short of surrendering unconditionally, their only choice was to anticipate the British ultimatum with one of their own.

Even as it was, they were too late off the mark, for while they still hung back the British authorities had time to transport a division of white troops, hurriedly combed out from the garrison of India, to the vital and almost undefended Natal salient. The number might have been trebled, and Natal rendered practically invasion-proof, had Britain decided to avail herself, as she was to do in later and greater wars, of the full Sepoy resources of her Indian army; but it was a unique feature of this war that though the two white races confronted each other in a state of mortal enmity, they were by tacit but inviolable agreement, if not in offensive, at least in defensive, alliance against the third party in the land, its indigenous black majority. The British were equally ready to throw away their chance of enlisting what would no doubt have been the willing support of the warlike Bantu peoples against the detested Boers. The war therefore never, like later and greater ones, threatened to become total.

Voluminous and exhaustive accounts, now almost wholly unread, have been written of its every phase, but all that is essential to know about it can be briefly set down.

Most essential of all is it to realize that it was won in effect, before it started, by the British Navy. That played the decisive, the army only a secondary, part. So long as Britain, through her command of the seaways, could be sure of bringing her vast superiority in wealth and manpower to bear, so long could she be sure of wearing down her enemy's resistance in the long—even if it were to prove very long —run.

Then again, so far as it can be said that the issue was ever in doubt, the decisive event was one that failed—and just because it failed—to materialize. The one chance of victory the Boers had to bank on was that of a knock-out in the opening round, and that they never made the least attempt to exploit it is the best reason for believing that the war was no result of a planned conspiracy on Kruger's part, but that he, no less than the equally reluctant Chamberlain, though not the trigger-happy Milner, had been sucked into its maelstrom by forces they had allowed to get beyond their control. Seldom has fate presented any combatant at the outset of a war with a more dazzling opportunity. The Boers, the finest mounted infantry ever seen, every man a crack shot and an experienced horseman, were capable of making rings round the foot-slogging and mostly town-bred mercenaries who formed the bulk of their opponents, and they had an additional advantage in the fact that none of the military experts of that time had the remotest appreciation (though it had been set forth with prophetic exactitude by a disregarded Polish theorist called Ivan Bloch) of the murderous defensive potentiality of the magazine rifle with its flat trajectory, which rendered the old type of infantry offensive suicidal.

The Boers therefore, with their overwhelming initial qualitative and quantitative superiority, had only to ride straight ahead, brushing aside or containing the few British forces that stood in their path, and swelling their numbers snowball-like with their Dutch kinsmen who could have been counted on with certainty to join them, to confront the British reinforcements, when they did finally land up at whatever ports might still be holding out, with a Dutch South Africa united in arms from the Limpopo to the sea, and needing to be conquered all over again—a truly colossal undertaking for even the greatest of empires.

But however inept the British strategy might have been, that of the Boers was to all intents and purposes non-existent. Their army was hardly fit to be called one at all in the modern significance, but was a self-functioning organism of that primitive type whose constituent parts have not even come under the control of a directing brain. The undisciplined commandos, whose members were a law unto themselves, went forward into action more by instinct than by plan, and against the most obvious objectives. Consequently they played into the British hands, as accurately as if their movements had been directed from Whitehall. During those critical weeks of grace when the game was in their hands and every hour counted, they sat quietly down as if they had unlimited time before them to the leisurely sieges, or block-ades (a form of warfare that cancelled out all their advantages of superior mobility), of the three British frontier bases of Ladysmith, Mafeking and lastly Kimberley, where Rhodes, now drawing near his end, made the characteristic and most effective gesture of presenting himself in person as an irresistibly attractive bait,[1] though with his undisciplined megalomania he became almost as sore a trial to the unhappy British commandant as to the besiegers. And so the tardily mobilized British army corps, when it at length landed up, found, contrary to all rational expectation, that except for a few marginal advances on the frontiers, the threatened invasion had not even got off from the starting point, and that Kruger had, as a later statesman might have put it, missed his bus—and for him, the last bus.

What followed was, in spite of its sensational overtones, extremely and almost predictably simple. The much boosted army corps, which, like a later steam-roller, was supposed to be capable of crushing down all opposition, was, as Sir William Butler had plainly foreseen, utterly inadequate to the task assigned to it. Its much advertised commander, Sir Redvers Buller, who turned out to be an esurient numskull of more than Crimean incompetence,[2] had no other choice than to split it up on arrival and rush its several portions up to the securing of the frontier and the attempted relief of the besieged garrisons, where their efforts to pierce the Boer lines were shot to bits by the deadly 'Mausers' of invisible marksmen.

This was the famous Black Week, the defeats of which, being just

[1] It is said that the Boers intended to exhibit him in an iron cage—and how thoroughly he would have enjoyed that colossal advertisement!

[2] Buller, to do him justice, not only believed in doing himself well but his men too, which partly accounts for the extreme slowness of his movements as his army crawled forward on its much-too-well-lined belly, while the Boers, with their rapid movements, made rings round it. But Tommy, with his tent to sleep in and his full rations, continued to swear by his old 'Sitting Bull'.

as much grist to the mills of the sensational press as any victories, were stunted as imperial disasters of unprecedented dimensions, though it is doubtful whether the civilian public, which saw no prospect of its being put to danger or serious inconvenience in its own proper persons, was altogether disagreeably thrilled at this super-sensational turn of events. As a matter of fact the army corps had done all that could reasonably have been expected of it by pinning the Boers down to their siege lines, so that when the further reinforcements that were now seen to be required, and that the wealth and sea power of Britain were capable at a pinch of supplying, were rushed out to the scene, they would find the enemy immobilized exactly where they wanted him.

The Government, at last aroused to the reality of the situation, rose to it with tardy vigour, and by almost denuding the home country of troops succeeded in swelling their forces in the field to a size reasonably proportioned to the task in hand. They sent out the two acknowledged leading soldiers of the Empire, Lords Roberts and Kitchener, to take over the supreme command from the sluggish Buller, which they did with such workmanlike efficiency as to transform the military situation at one blow, by enveloping and capturing the entire Boer army that had been besieging Kimberley, and sweeping on thence to capture the Free State capital, while even Buller, by dint of much prodding from behind, succeeded at long last in somehow butting and blundering his way through the demoralized and depleted resistance on his own front, to relieve the besieged garrison, now at its last gasp, of Ladysmith. Henceforth it was plain to the world that the Boers had no army capable of standing up to the British in the field, and it was a matter of simple logistics to push on to the formal conquest and occupation of both Republics. With the completion of this process, and the flight of Kruger himself overseas, it was assumed, not only by the Government and public at home, but by Roberts himself, that the war was as good as over, except perhaps for the cleaning up of one or two local pockets of resistance.

At this culminating point, in the summer of 1900, it was still just possible to fit the story into the pattern of the reigning melodrama, and to believe that in spite of Black Week, and the debunking of the all-conquering Buller, and the discovery that it required three 'Tommy, Tommy Atkinses' (as it would have required a greater number of his French or German counterpart) to get the best of one Piet on his home ground, all had come right in the end, and that the Queen's horses and Queen's men had really, under the auspices of

dear old Bobs
The little tradesman who does all the thickest jobs,

patched the imperial Humpty Dumpty together again.

Rudyard Kipling was under no such illusion, and fulminated an apocalyptic denunciation of a degenerate and shortly-to-be-enslaved England, in which an American cartoonist depicted him as swinging the lion by the tail and banging the poor animal's head against a wall. But these were not the strains by which the lion was in a mood to be charmed, even by his chosen laureate of empire. Granted there had been one or two setbacks, all had come right in the end; every one of the British objectives had been attained, and when the last of the three garrisons was duly relieved, as a side-show of Roberts's main advance, the event was celebrated by an orgy of mob hysteria that enriched the pejorative resources of the language with the participle 'Mafficking'. For the last time it was possible for the organs of imperial propaganda to get away with the screaming assurance that all was for the best in the most glorious of all possible empires. But was it?

The Government was at least shrewdly advised, politically, to cash in on this mood while it lasted, by going straight to the electorate for a fresh mandate. The dynamic superman, 'Joe', still continued to dominate the scene, and was able to win more than half the battle in advance by proclaiming—not without a certain veneer of plausibility—that every vote given to the opposition was a vote given to the Boers. Even so the Unionists were returned to office by a majority substantially less than that of the previous election, though marginally increased over that which they had had at the time of the dissolution. That even with the laurels of the alleged victory fresh on its brow, this specious appeal to the imperial team spirit should have barely enabled it so precariously to arrest its own decline, was ominous of the extent to which the tide of popular favour was threatening to turn against the Government and the imperialist cause with which its fortunes were identified.

Had Chamberlain and his colleagues been actuated by a spirit of more far-sighted statesmanship than normally resides in the breasts of politicians, they might have exploited even the appearance of victory to a better effect than that of momentarily dishing the other side in the party game. Honour having been satisfied and the Majuban slate wiped clean, now would have been the time for a gesture of magnanimity whose motive could not have been mistaken for weakness. A disillusioned and at least temporarily demoralized enemy might have been presumed to be in a malleable mood. Even Kruger, along with his fellow President of the Free State, had, as soon as the tide had unmistakably begun to turn in the British favour, put out feelers for peace, though the indomitable old patriot had qualified them by stipulating for that independence of his country which it was not in his nature to forgo even in the hour of defeat. But it seems at least on the cards that even Kruger might have conceded terms that would have realized

M

and safeguarded every legitimate aim, on British principles, of the national war effort. The chance at least might have been worth trying. But what had been an obsessive complex even before the war had now hardened into an imperial imperative beyond argument or reason. More than ever since the launching of the Boer ultimatum it had become a British *sine qua non* that, willy-nilly, the Boer had got to eat humble pie and come quiet and loyal into the Empire before there could be any question of coming to terms with him. The popular mood had been accurately depicted, as it so often was in those days, by the cartoonist of *Punch*. The bull-witted and ox-bellied old buffer who then figured as the national archetype was displayed on the opening of hostilities as bearing down with bulging eyes and rolled-up sleeves on a villainous but wiry-looking Boer (who in real life would have doubled him up out of hand with a punch in the stomach), and bumbling: 'This time it's a fight to a finish.'

It was the foretaste of the 'unconditional surrender' slogan of a later war, and it had the effect of cutting off the user of it from his own freedom for pacific manœuvre. Kruger's overture was therefore turned down with a contemptuous snub, and none came from the British side.

And so the opportunity to make it a finish of the deeper Anglo-Boer contention that had been festering above and below the surface at least since the time of the Great Trek, was, like so many previous ones, allowed to slip, and it all too soon became apparent that the end of the actual conflict, so far from being attained, was not even in sight. The collapse of their attempt to wage war of the conventional European type had caused the Boers to discover the form, peculiarly suited to their genius and circumstances, of a mobile guerrilla in which every commando and, at a pinch, every burgher, was capable of functioning independently, and which the vast spaces of their native veldt presented them with every prospect of keeping up until their ponderous adversary, exhausted by his own continual blows in the air and bled white by the pinpricks of innumerable unreturned blows out of the blue, decided that the game was no longer worth the candle.

Nothing could be imagined more deflating to imperial pride and self-esteem than this long-drawn-out anticlimax to the melodrama on which the curtain had been thought to have descended to the strains of 'God save the Queen', but which was destined to go on dragging on its weary length for little short of two mortal years, with all the honours resting with those irrepressible and elusive bands of patriots, and all the heroic highlights concentrated on their leaders, particularly the almost legendary De Wet, whose never-failing succession of audacities and escapes appealed irresistibly to the sporting instincts of the British public, and rendered his a more popular star part than that of Kitchener, to whom Roberts had left the uncongenial work of clearing up the mess in his own wake, and who went about it with the same steam-roller-like deliberation that had characterized his operations in Egypt, seeking to crush the Boer resistance by sheer weight of numbers and material, in a sure but unspectacular process of attrition.

Unhappily more was involved in this process than a salutary sweating of the imperial virus out of the British system. It would have amounted to giving the game irrevocably into the hands of the commandos to allow the innumerable farms dotted about the veldt to be used in the light of arms dumps and recruiting depots. But to have combed out the supply of arms and ammunition that is part of the equipment of every Boer farm would have been to abandon its inhabitants to the tender mercies of their native staffs, and this would have been to have violated the unwritten provisions of the white man's defensive alliance against the native. So even if it had been practicable to leave the farms themselves standing, it would have been none the less of a humane imperative to remove their inmates to a place of safety. This was well understood by the burghers in the field, who were not sorry to be set free from the responsibility. But the task of organizing the huge camps in which these primitive farming folk, whose habits were grossly unsuited for the requirements of a gregarious existence, were crowded together, proved beyond the capacities of the already overstrained military authorities, who made, in more senses than one, a hopeless mess of it, with the result that disease swept through the camps and took a ghastly toll of their inmates.

It was done with no sinister intent, and when news of the mortality penetrated to England, it caused such a wave of genuine horror that no trouble or expense was spared towards remedying the situation which, once it had been taken out of the hands of the military, was rapidly brought under control, the death rate falling as steeply as it had risen. But it would be taking an unrealistic view of human nature to have expected husbands and fathers, fighting a lone battle for their freedom, to take a detached view of this holocaust. Least of all when people in such high authority in Britain as the leader of the Liberal Opposition denounced such methods as those of barbarism. The goodwill which, on any sane or civilized reckoning, it was so much more essential for Britain to win from the enemy than his formal allegiance, was being recklessly sacrificed, and a legacy of mutual antagonism bequeathed to future generations of British and Dutch in South Africa, which was destined to survive any British Empire or question of one.

Had her rulers been wise in their generation they would have perceived that it would have been incomparably more in Britain's ultimate interest to avert these consequences, by agreeing with her adversary quickly on almost any not openly dishonourable terms, than to insist on making it a fight to a finish. To win the war for the Empire would, as we can now see, be a fool's bargain, if it would involve the ultimate certainty of losing the peace for the Commonwealth.

In the early spring (by British reckoning) of 1901, at what proved to be approximately half-time in the actual war, and while the guerrilla phase was only in its opening stages, there had seemed to be a chance of cutting short the whole lamentable contention before—as an Italian proverb says—it had lengthened into a serpent. The initiative came from Kitchener, who realized better than any civilian what a long and unrewarding task lay before him in the wearing down, to the bitter end, of the Boer resistance; and the intractable Kruger having now removed himself from the scene, the control of the Transvaal resistance had passed into the capable and statesmanlike hands of General Louis Botha. Him therefore Kitchener, as the mandatory of the British Government, decided to approach as the sort of man with whom one could do business, and the two got to discussing the draft of a peace settlement that would have included the British *sine qua non* of formal sovereignty. But the two commanders, in their difficult and delicate task of mutual accommodation, had reckoned without the wrecking interference of the fatal Milner, who was almost insanely determined to allow nothing short of unconditional surrender, and would rather that the war should be prolonged indefinitely, with all its bloodshed and misery, than include in the general amnesty the handful of Cape Dutch who, by joining their kinsmen from over the frontier, had put themselves in the legal position of rebels. This was a point of comradely honour on which Botha did not feel he could give way, and so on what appeared to be the verge of agreement the negotiation had to be broken off. It is not certain whether, even if agreement had been arrived at, Botha would have had enough authority with his own burghers, or with the far more uncompromising De Wet and his Free Staters, to get it accepted; but Kitchener at least believed that with a free hand he could have got peace.

But when after fifteen more months of this hate-breeding and—from the British standpoint—inglorious degradation of warfare, terms of peace were at length arrived at, they differed in no substantial respect from those that might have been had on this earlier occasion. Even so Milner, if he could have got his way, would have wrecked the whole proceedings by his all-or-nothing intransigence, but this time Kitchener, who was fed to the teeth with the whole wretched business, and wanted to get on to the more congenial task of reforming the army in India, was determined to stand for no more of this nonsense, and in this he had the now practically unanimous backing of public opinion at home, which had ceased to be interested in a fight to a finish, and only wanted a finish to the fighting.

And so peace was concluded, and the Boers, who in the eyes of the whole world had reaped all the ostensible honours of an epic struggle against odds, many of them with the seeds of inextinguishable hatred planted in their hearts, were allowed to acknowledge themselves—for whatever that might be worth—subjects of a stout gentleman thousands of miles away, of whom they knew nothing, and who had no intention, for his own part, of becoming more closely acquainted with them. Having, in their stolid fashion, done what was needed on the dotted line of the official form, they were allowed to go back to their mostly destroyed farms, with the proceeds of a liberal indemnity, conceded contrary to the usual custom, to the vanquished by the victors, to provide for the restoration of their rather flimsy structures, and with the indispensable rifles, which were all that was needed for their reappearance on commando, allowed them on registration. But they had had a sufficient bellyful of belligerency to digest, until such time as the next convenient opportunity presented itself, when they were to find that the petrol engine had put their tactics of equestrian mobility as much out of date as the British infantry ones of the last war had been.

A feature of this settlement, hardly regarded at the time, was an innocent-looking stipulation that until a representative constitution had been granted, no franchise should be conceded to the natives. This might have served as a reminder of the existence of the third, and numerically the largest, party involved in the South African conflict of races. It will be remembered that the original source of cleavage between British and Dutch, which had led directly to the Great Trek, had been that the British had at least made some attempt to apply their own inherited principles of free civilization in dealing with the natives, whereas the Boers had no other way than that of the naked imperialism and tyranny of a master race, enforced, if and when necessary, by the *sjambok*. During the war British propaganda had made full, and perhaps too full, play with the alleged brutalities of the Boers to their natives, whose friends and protectors the British made themselves out to be. But both in what the peace terms stipulated and what they failed to stipulate, there was at least a suggestion that a *modus vivendi* might be patched up between the two white sides of the South African triangle at the expense of the black third, that the British South African might be induced to turn a Nelson eye on the Boer's determination to wallop his own niggers in his own way; and that having consented to waive his own principles to that extent, he might even in time come to abandon them altogether and with them his native birthright of civilization, to end up as an imperialist in good earnest, but no longer of an empire calling itself British.

But this lay in an as yet distant future. What concerns our present purpose is to note that the futility and boredom of this ignoble entanglement, if they had done nothing else, had not only finally sweated the imperial virus out of the British system, but had effectively immunized it against any recurrence of the infection. That is not to say that there was any formal and open repudiation of the cult of empire. To judge by the language of the press and platform, it continued to flourish as luxuriantly as ever. But the substance had gone out of it. The word was no longer charged with the same emotional significance as in the hectic days of the *fin de siècle*. More and more it was tending to shed its specifically imperial connotation, and to become a mere convenient device for lumping together under one designation the whole miscellaneous assortment of peoples and territories that came within the orbit of the British connection.

The psychological atmosphere at the end of the war had undergone a revolutionary transformation from what it had been at the beginning. The braggadocio and mafficking of the opening phases had gone out of fashion and almost out of credibility. Those rabble-intoxicating choruses about adding patches of red to the map, about buckling on swords (by proxy), and taking off the lion's muzzle and letting him have a go, were remembered, if at all, as the ravings of delirium are in a state of convalescence. Britain, with her imperial pride thus rudely deflated, had emerged none the worse for the experience, free to recover her true self again and get back to the line of her own proper development—and not a moment too soon, for a far sterner ordeal lay ahead of her than that through which she had just passed.

Here, in the dawn of a new century, opens an as yet unfinished chapter of the story that does not fall within the scope of the present volume. We do not even know as yet whether or not it is destined to rank as the culminating or even the final chapter. However much it may go against the grain to break off at what must in its very nature be an arbitrarily chosen point, the temptation must be resisted to anticipate the course of its development.

One thing only let me beg leave to say before laying down my pen. If it has been necessary to write dead and damned to an empire that it would be a contradiction in terms to describe as British, it is only in anticipation of a world commonwealth whose greatness that originating epithet may yet prove too narrow to comprehend.

INDEX